The Friars and the Jews

The Friars and the Jews

THE EVOLUTION OF
MEDIEVAL ANTI-JUDAISM

JEREMY COHEN

CORNELL UNIVERSITY PRESS

Ithaca and London

Cornell University Press gratefully acknowledges a grant
from the Andrew W. Mellon Foundation that aided
in bringing this book to publication.

First published 1982 by Cornell University Press.
Published in the United Kingdom by Cornell University Press Ltd., London.

Second printing, 1983

International Standard Book Number 0-8014-1406-7

Library of Congress Catalog Card Number 81-15210
Printed in the United States of America
*Librarians: Library of Congress cataloging information
appears on the last page of the book.*

*The paper in this book is acid-free and meets the guidelines for permanence and
durability of the Committee on Production Guidelines for Book Longevity of
the Council on Library Resources.*

Contents

Preface

This book seeks to bridge two scholarly disciplines, which despite their mutual concerns have long been separated by a definite,
albeit at times subtle, line: the history of the medieval Church
and the history of the Jews in medieval Europe. To be sure, the
interactions of Jews and Christians in medieval society have commanded the attention of Church historians as well as Jewish historians. The former have often come to realize how the position
of the Jews in Christendom, that of a minority of infidels whose
religion had given birth to Christianity, constituted a complex
theological issue with immediate political and socioeconomic ramifications; and the latter have grown increasingly sensitive to the
influence exerted by Christian authorities and ideas on all aspects
of medieval Jewish life and culture. Nevertheless, much of the
extant source material, not to mention the modern historiography,
of value in one field has remained largely unexamined or else
unappreciated in the other. This tendency has regrettably impeded
a joining of scholarly forces and the convergence of perspectives
necessary to focus on those issues at the intersection of the two
disciplines.

The medieval Christian perception of the Jew is a case in point.
Grounded in the intricacies of Christian doctrine and conditioned
by the historical reality of medieval Europe, it derived on the one
hand from much that has normally eluded the consideration of
authorities on medieval Jewry. On the other hand, the theological
status of the Jew naturally entered into the elaborate web of
Christian-Jewish relations and thereby was influenced by them. At
the same time that Christian theology affected the Jew, then, the
particular character of the Jewish community—especially its reactions to the ideas and institutions of Christendom—reflected and
even contributed to important developments in Christian society

at large. Fruitful study of this issue accordingly demands a blend of traditionally distinct scholarly interests, and such a venture can be a perilous one, fraught with practical and conceptual obstacles along the way and capable of eliciting hostile reaction at the end. Conventions revered among students of both fields must at times be overlooked; customary valuations must be challenged; diverse species of primary sources must be used and cited selectively. In spite of these difficulties, I hope that the ensuing treatment of the friars and the Jews will succeed not only in arguing its revisionist thesis but also in establishing the worth of such an interdisciplinary approach.

This undertaking would have been inconceivable without the instruction and assistance afforded me in recent years by teachers, institutions, and friends too numerous to list, all of whom I take great pleasure in thanking. Inasmuch as the idea for this book originated during my graduate studies at Cornell University, I am most indebted to Brian Tierney, who guided me through several arduous years of conceptual struggling. Professor Tierney is a master of historical synthesis, with a knack for showing his students how the smallest of details figures significantly in the overall formulation of an idea or picture of a period; in his quiet, reserved way, he also became for me a model of how history can bring meaning and value into one's personal life. Benzion Netanyahu introduced me to the study of medieval religious polemic and reviewed this work meticulously at various stages of its development. Alvin Bernstein has been for me at Cornell a teacher, a colleague, and a friend; his suggestions with regard to this book, as well as his assistance and support in all dimensions of my academic career, have been invaluable. My appreciation extends to Gerd Korman and David Powers of Cornell and David Biale of the State University of New York at Binghamton for their advice during the final stages of writing and revision. I also thank the Graduate School of Cornell University, the Danforth Foundation, the National Endowment for the Humanities, and the Cornell Humanities Faculty Research Grants Committee for the generous fellowships and stipends that enabled me to pursue and complete my research.

Finally, on a different plane, I must express my gratitude to my parents, Gerson and Naomi Cohen. Both historians in their own right, they have read portions of this work and provided me with useful criticisms; much more important, they have offered me constant encouragement, transmitting their love for their work and their respect for the past. My wife, Deborah, has also read several drafts of the book with a helpfully critical eye, and my son Raphael has not; yet together they have given me the emotional wherewithal to write about the thirteenth century without letting me forget that we live in the twentieth.

JEREMY COHEN

Ithaca, New York

Abbreviations

AFP	*Archivum Fratrum Praedicatorum.*
AHR	*American Historical Review.*
CCSL	Corpus Christianorum, Series Latina.
Chavel	Moses ben Naḥman. *Kitvei ha-Ramban.* Ed. Charles B. Chavel. 2 vols. Jerusalem, 1963.
CSEL	Corpus Scriptorum Ecclesiasticorum Latinorum.
HJ	*Historia Judaica.*
HLF	*Histoire littéraire de la France.*
HTR	*Harvard Theological Review.*
HUCA	*Hebrew Union College Annual.*
JIM	Paul Wilpert, ed. *Judentum im Mittelalter. Beiträge zum christlich-jüdischen Gespräch.* Miscellanea mediaevalia 4. Berlin, 1966.
JJL	*Juifs et Judaïsme de Languedoc. Cahiers de Fanjeaux 12.* Toulouse, 1977.
JJS	*Journal of Jewish Studies.*
JQR	*Jewish Quarterly Review.*
KS	*Kirjath Sepher.*
MGH	Monumenta Germaniae Historica.
MGWJ	*Monatsschrift für die Geschichte und Wissenschaft des Judentums.*
MT	*Mishneh Torah* (Code of Jewish Law).
PAAJR	*Proceedings of the American Academy for Jewish Research.*
PL	Patrologia Latina.
Pugio	Raymond Martini. *Pugio fidei adversus Mauros et Judaeos.* 1687; repr., Farnborough, Eng., 1967.
REJ	*Revue des études juives.*
RLT	*Rassegna di letteratura tomistica.*
SRH	Salo Wittmayer Baron. *A Social and Religious History of the Jews,* 2d ed. 17 vols. New York, 1952–80.
ST	*Summa theologiae.*
TB	Babylonian Talmud.
Wikkuaḥ	Yehiel ben Joseph of Paris. *Wikkuaḥ.* Ed. Samuel Grünbaum. Thorn, 1873.
X	*Decretales*

Introduction

Commenting on Deuteronomy 32:21, a verse in which Moses foretells the future punishment of the Jews at the hands of "a no people," a Jewish writer of the late thirteenth century explained: "He means at the hands of the Franciscans and Dominicans; for they are everywhere oppressing Israel, and they are called 'a no people' because they are more wretched than all mankind."[1] That the friars of the orders of Saint Francis and Saint Dominic were perceived by medieval European Jews as mortal enemies should not surprise students of the period. From the establishment of these first and most important mendicant orders in the Roman Church early in the thirteenth century, until the end of the medieval period and even beyond, Dominican and Franciscan friars directed and oversaw virtually all the anti-Jewish activities of the Christian clergy in the West. As inquisitors, missionaries, disputants, polemicists, scholars, and itinerant preachers, mendicants engaged in a concerted effort to undermine the religious freedom and physical security of the medieval Jewish community. It was they who developed and manned the papal Inquisition, who intervened in the Maimonidean controversy, who directed the burnings of the Talmud, who compelled the Jews to listen and respond to their inflammatory sermons, and who actively promoted anti-Jewish hatred among the laity of Western Christendom.

In view of the extent and the implications of the friars' concern for the Jews, the absence of any sustained, analytical account of the confrontation between the two groups is striking. Historians have frequently pointed to the need for such a work, but no one has undertaken it—perhaps because the study of the friars and that

1. *Sefer Da'at Zeqeinim*, ed. Isaac Joseph Nunez-Vaez (Leghorn, 1783), p. 88a. Cf. also Israel Lévi, "Manuscrits du Hadar Zekènim: Recueil de commentaires exégétiques de rabbins de la France septentrionale," *REJ* 49 (1904), 33–38.

of the Jews in the Middle Ages both comprise vast subjects unto themselves, and those immersed in one area of research have felt the other to be beyond their purview. The present work derives from such considerations, and it will attempt to place the known encounters between the mendicants and the Jews from the Fourth Lateran Council (1215) until the Black Death (1347–1350)—that is, during the first generations of the orders' existence—in a single, comprehensive framework. Yet the prime concern of this book is with the hitherto unappreciated substance of the friars' attack upon the Jews, the basic ideas and theological considerations that under-lay their anti-Jewish activities and polemics. I shall argue that the Dominicans and Franciscans developed, refined, and sought to implement a new Christian ideology with regard to the Jews, one that allotted the Jews no legitimate right to exist in European society.

Prior to the thirteenth century, Catholic theology had demanded that the Jew be tolerated in Christendom. Augustine of Hippo (354–430), whose teachings provided the foundation for medieval Christian thought in the West, instructed that God had ordained the survival of the Jews, in order that their presence and continued observance of Mosaic Law might aid the Church in its mission to the Gentiles, and so they might convert at the end of days. By the early fourteenth century, however, friars openly advocated that Latin Christendom rid itself of its Jewish population, whether through missionizing, forced expulsions, or physical harassment that would induce conversion or flight. This new theological pos-ture jibed well with contemporary political events, inasmuch as King Edward I of England ordered the first permanent expulsion of Jews from a medieval European kingdom in 1290, an example followed in France, Spain, Sicily, Portugal, the Kingdom of Naples, and much of Germany during the next 250 years. Historians both Jewish and Christian have disputed for more than a century about the underlying causes of the dramatic decline of medieval European Jewry, and they have also disagreed as to its particulars: when it began, and which events and ideas of the period best illustrate its processes at work. Many have looked to the anti-Jewish vio-lence that accompanied the Crusades of the eleventh and twelfth centuries as the watershed of medieval Jewish history, evidencing a new anti-Jewish animus among European Christians which caused irreparable damage to the toleration and physical security of Jews, who had previously maintained congenial relations with their Christian neighbors. Some have associated the challenge to the Jews during the crusading period with the simultaneous emergence of Europe from a basically feudal economy into one oriented more toward money and profit. The rise of a Christian middle class made the Jews, who had long figured prominently in European commerce, objects of considerable resentment, and they became increasingly dependent on the protection of kings and princes. These rulers, in turn, emptied the coffers of the Jews as the price of physical protection and used Jews as their financial agents— which only further aggravated the growing tensions. At the point when the rulers came to believe that maintaining and safeguarding the Jews was no longer worth the alienation of a potentially useful Christian bourgeoisie, expulsion became a logical and practical option. Other historians stress the increased legal discrimination against the Jews during the late twelfth and thirteenth centuries as the best index of their decline. In particular, the notion of Jewish servitude or serfdom, as it was expressed in the papal and imperial legislation of the period, did much to degrade Jews socially, to deprive them of basic civil rights, and to make them the objects of popular disdain and hostility. Finally, various writers have sought to postpone the beginning of the demise of medieval European Jewry until the fourteenth century, noting that the prosperity of the Jewish community, in economic, demographic, and cultural terms, peaked not long before that. The long-term expulsions of the Jews from European kingdoms, according to this view, derived from incipient medieval nationalism and had little, if anything, to do with developments in Christian theology.

All these interpretations make it reasonably clear that those rulers who ordered the banishment of the Jews responded more directly to political and socioeconomic considerations than theoretical religious ones. But given the influence and involvement of the Church in all avenues of medieval life, one still wonders if the expulsion of the Jews from most of Western Europe could have proceeded as smoothly as it did, without interference or voiced opposition from the clergy, had Christian thought of the later Middle Ages remained steadfastly committed to Augustinian teaching.

How did such a radical departure from patristic theology develop and gain acceptance? After briefly considering Christian attitudes toward the Jews in the early medieval period and the rise of the mendicants in the thirteenth century, Part One of this book will show how the friars' inquisitorial efforts to police the intellectual and literary activity of Europe first led them to condemn rabbinic literature, because it allegedly distorted the true biblical Judaism whose observance theoretically entitled the Jews to remain in Christendom. Other friars subsequently concluded that if rabbinic Judaism had no legitimate place in a properly ordered Christian society, neither did the Jews who subscribed to its teachings, and they employed every available means of harassment to undermine the security of Jewish existence. Part Two will describe how mendicant missionaries and scholars refined this initial attack into an elaborate polemical ideology that justified in theological terms the attempt to purge Christian Europe of its Jewish population. And Part Three will consider the efforts of the friars to implement and disseminate their new ideology, with grandiose schemes for the systematic conversion or expulsion of all European Jews, and by infusing their attitudes into the general world view of the Christian laity, either in works of popular literature or simply by preaching.

Finally, this book will endeavor to account for the anti-Jewish ideology of the friars—whence it arose, and what expedited its rapid acceptance and diffusion. I shall seek the ideational roots of mendicant anti-Judaism in various currents and transformations within the evolving self-consciousness of high medieval Christendom. Ultimately, these trends had little to do with medieval Jewry, and they thus have usually failed to interest historians of the Jews. But they do manifest the outlook of a society which one prominent historian of the Church has characterized as totalitarian.[2] That this sort of society facilitated the original vision of a Europe *judenrein* should prove instructive to Jewish and ecclesiastical historians alike; and the confrontation between the friars and the Jews will, I hope, be recognized as an important development in the evolution of anti-Semitism.

2. Walter Ullman, *A History of Political Thought: The Middle Ages*, rev. ed. (Baltimore, 1970), p. 105.

PART ONE

The Emergence of Mendicant Anti-Judaism

1

The Early
Medieval Background

During the early Middle Ages, the Roman Church's attitude toward the Jews emanated from what may be termed an Augustinian theology of Judaism. In preaching against the Jews, Augustine naturally echoed the arguments of previous patristic writers that Jesus had fulfilled the messianic prophecies of the Old Testament, that his new covenant of grace had abrogated Mosaic Law, and that his Church had replaced the Synagogue as the community of God's chosen.[1] But the exigencies of Augustine's particular situation moved him to add an important element to the early Christian theological stance. On the one hand, he witnessed the still frequently successful cases of Jewish proselytization among Christians; he felt bound to emphasize the notion that the Jews, in their dispersion throughout the world, have been punished for rejecting and killing Jesus and are hardly to be emulated or esteemed. On the other hand, Augustine could not, in defense of the Church, completely repudiate Jewish traditions, for he also had to confront the threats of pagans and heretics who questioned the historical

1. On anti-Jewish polemic before Augustine, see S. Krauss, "The Jews in the Works of the Church Fathers," *JQR*, o.s. 5 (1892), 122–57, 6 (1894), 82–99, 225–61; James Parkes, *The Conflict of the Church and the Synagogue: A Study in the Origins of Antisemitism* (London, 1934), pp. 27–195; A. Lukyn Williams, *Adversus Judaeos: A Bird's-Eye View of Christian Apologiae until the Renaissance* (Cambridge, Eng., 1935), pp. 3–104, 117–40; Bernhard Blumenkranz, *Die Judenpredigt Augustins: Ein Beitrag zur Geschichte der jüdisch-christlichen Beziehungen in den ersten Jahrhunderten* (1946; repr., Paris, 1973), pp. 9–58; Marcel Simon, *Verus Israel: Etude sur les relations entre Chrétiens et Juifs dans l'empire romain, 135–425* (Paris, 1948), pp. 166–213; Rosemary R. Ruether, *Faith and Fratricide: The Theological Roots of Anti-Semitism* (New York, 1974), pp. 64–183; and N. R. M. de Lange, *Origen and the Jews: Studies in Jewish-Christian Relations in Third-Century Palestine* (Cambridge, Eng., 1976), pp. 75–102.

and theological consonance of Christianity with the teachings of the Old Testament.

Augustine made an innovative response to these interrelated challenges. In answer to the charges of the pagans and the heretics, he affirmed the perfect concordance of Old and New Testaments; the significance of the former in the divine plan for human salvation was primarily prefigurative, and many of its precepts therefore lost their validity after Jesus' crucifixion. As for the Jews, who retained this invalid law, who bore the guilt for Jesus' death, and who continued to prey upon the Christian community, did they now deserve to survive in Christian society? On their own merits they did not, but Augustine argued that God preserved them for the sake of the Church, so that in adhering to the Old Testament they might witness the truth of and historical basis for christological prophecy, and so that they might ultimately accept the implications of this prophecy by converting to Christianity at the end of days. Although they now remain blind to this truth, their biblical tradition offers cogent proof of Christian doctrine, enabling the Church to respond effectively to its enemies. "We see and know that it is in order to bear this witness—which they [the Jews] involuntarily supply on our behalf by possessing and preserving these same books—that they themselves are scattered among all peoples, in whatever direction the Church of Christ expands." The dispersion and degradation of the Jews, if insured by the regnant Church, would both alleviate the problem of the Jewish encroachments upon Christianity and enhance the value of their survival—by emphasizing the deplorable wretchedness of their error.[2]

The elements of this Augustinian approach toward the Jews and Judaism determined the basic stance of virtually all early medieval Christian polemics against the Jews. First and foremost, Augustine

2. Augustine, *De civitate Dei* 18.46, ed. and trans. George E. McCracken et al., 7 vols. (London, 1957–72), 6:50–51. See also ibid., 20.29, pp. 432–33; as well as his *Tractatus adversus Judeos*, PL 42:51–67; *Sermo* 200.2, PL 38:1030; *Enarrationes in Psalmos* 58.1.21–22, CCSL 39:744; and *De fide rerum invisibilum* 6.9, CCSL 46:15–16.

Augustine's conception of the Jewish mission has been most extensively analyzed by Bernhard Blumenkranz; see both his more recent "Augustin et les Juifs; Augustin et le Judaisme," *Recherches augustiniennes* 1 (1958), 225–41, and his more thorough *Die Judenpredigt*. Cf. also the rather apologetic presentation of Augustine's views in Jesús Alvarez, *Teología del pueblo judío* (Madrid, 1970). And on Augustine's scheme of salvific history in general, see G. L. Keyes, *Christian Faith and the Interpretation of History* (Lincoln, Neb., 1966), esp. pp. 147ff.; R. A. Markus, *Saeculum: History and Society in the Theology of St. Augustine* (Cambridge, Eng., 1970); and Auguste Luneau, *L'histoire du salut chez les pères de l'Eglise* (Paris, 1964), pt. 4.

saw a definite need and place for the Jews within Christian society. God had preserved them to play a specific role, and they consequently could not be killed or otherwise purged from Christendom. To be sure, the rights of the Jews in the society were carefully delimited and restricted: the Church endeavored to prohibit fraternization between Christians and Jews; Jews could not legally own Christian slaves, nor were they supposed to hold positions of authority over Christians; and Christian princes were exhorted not to favor Jews over Christians in any way whatsoever. But the initial assumption that Jews belonged in Christendom underlay all such decrees, and this maxim provided the theoretical bedrock of Jewish survival in medieval Christian Europe, as long as it was pursued as official Church policy. For centuries after Augustine, Jews managed to live relatively peacefully among their Christian neighbors; Christians rarely called for their extermination or expulsion from the community, and when they did, Jews often had recourse to intervention from higher ecclesiastical authority.[3] Second, the anti-Jewish polemic of Augustine and his early medieval successors was generally limited to an attack upon the Jews' obstinate and incorrect interpretation of the Old Testament, which led to a denial of the divinity and messianic nature of Jesus. Because the Jewish community served a positive purpose for the Church, Augustine and those who followed him had no reason to challenge the legitimacy of its existence in Christendom. The substance of their polemics was accordingly, as Amos Funkenstein has written, "a stereotyped enumeration of proofs taken from the Bible for the truth of Christianity, and the detection of prophecies and prefigurations that were enriched with arguments taken from the present status of the Jews in 'servitude' and dispersion."[4] Third, Augustine and

3. On official Church policy toward the Jews, see Solomon Grayzel, "The Papal Bull *Sicut Judaeis*," in *Studies and Essays in Honor of Abraham A. Neuman*, ed. Meir Ben-Horin et al. (Leiden, 1962), pp. 246 ff.; and Kenneth R. Stow, "Sin'at Yisra'el 'o 'Ahavat Yisra'el: Gishat ha-'Appifyorim la-Yehudim," in *Anti-Semitism Through the Ages* [Hebrew], ed. Shmuel Almog (Jerusalem, 1980), 91–107. Bernhard Blumenkranz, *Juifs et Chrétiens dans le monde occidental, 430–1096* (Paris, 1960), pp. 3–64, provides the best description of the resulting good atmosphere in which the Jews lived, but he points out that this must be understood within a medieval perspective; later medieval writers did not all consider Augustine's stance in regard to the Jews a particularly kind one. See Blumenkranz, "Une survie médiévale de la polémique antijuive de Saint Augustin," *Revue du Moyen Age latin* 5 (1949), 193–96.

4. Amos Funkenstein, "Basic Types of Christian Anti-Jewish Polemics in the Later Middle Ages," *Viator* 2 (1971), 374. For brief summaries of most of the extant polemics of this period, see Williams, *Adversus Judaeos*, pp. 207–27, 295–374; and Bernhard Blumenkranz, *Les auteurs chrétiens latins du Moyen Age sur les Juifs et le*

his successors polemicized against Judaism in defense of Christianity—that is, to prevent judaizing among Christians or simply to boost Christian morale. Converting the Jews was always an objective held in great esteem, but because the Synagogue had a rightful place in Christendom, the mainstream of early polemic spoke to Christians rather than Jews. And because the judaizing tendencies of Christians derived in part from the vitality of contemporary Judaism, the Christian polemicists found it expedient to approach the Jewish religion as a theological artifact, a faith that had long become obsolete, and not as a living and dynamic tradition. To the extent that the early polemics did not directly attack the Jews of their own day, they betray a highly literary and theoretical character; dialogues between Christians and Jews and *sermones contra Iudeos* usually represent adherence to literary genres in vogue and not records of actual exchanges with Jews.[5] Finally, just as Augustine had made minimal use of rabbinic literature in his writings—and none at all in his anti-Jewish treatises—so the writings of post-biblical Judaism did not really enter into much of the early medieval polemic, and the Talmud and writings of medieval rabbis remained generally unknown to Christians for centuries after Augustine. Even pronounced enemies of the Jews such as Isidor of Seville (ca. 570–636), Julian of Toledo (642–690), and Agobard of Lyons (769–840), although they lived in large and flourishing Jewish communities, acquired their knowledge of Judaism from biblical, classical, and patristic sources.[6]

Judaisme (Paris, 1963). A more topical breakdown and summary appear in Blumenkranz, *Juifs et Chrétiens*, pp. 216–89; and "Die jüdischen Beweisgründe im Religionsgespräch mit den Christen in den christlich-lateinischen Sonderschriften des 5. bis 11. Jahrhunderts," *Theologische Zeitschrift* 4 (1948), 119–47.

5. Blumenkranz, "Augustin," pp. 230–31; *SRH*, 5:108–17. On the greater number of Christians who converted to Judaism before the Crusades than Jews to Christianity, see Blumenkranz, "Jüdische und christliche Konvertiten im jüdisch-christlichen Religionsgespräch des Mittelalters," in *JIM*, pp. 264–65. And with regard to the abstract nature of this polemic, in addition to the works cited in the previous note see Amos Funkenstein, "Changes in the Patterns of Christian Anti-Jewish Polemics in the 12th Century [Hebrew]," *Zion*, n.s. 33 (1968), 126–29; and Arthur Cushman McGiffert, ed., *Dialogue between a Christian and a Jew* (New York, 1889), pp. 1–10. Blumenkranz, *Juifs et Chrétiens*, pp. 67–158, posits a much greater strength, relevance, and immediacy in early medieval Christian missionary efforts among the Jews. But as will be suggested later in this chapter, he has probably gone too far in arguing for the historical reality of some of the extant written polemics.

6. Blumenkranz, *Die Judenpredigt*, pp. 65–66, 72–73; Ch. Merchavya, *The Church versus Talmudic and Midrashic Literature, 500–1248* [Hebrew] (Jerusalem, 1970), pp. 3–92. Specifically with regard to Agobard and his successor Amulo, who was actu-

A prime example of this breed of religious polemic is the *Altercatio Aecclesie contra Synagogam et Synagoge contra Aecclesiam* of the tenth century. Modeling his work on the fifth-century pseudo-Augustinian tract of the same name, the anonymous polemicist has here adhered well to the Augustinian polemical approach just outlined. One can find little aggressiveness throughout the entire dialogue; both disputants are apparently women of a similar stature and level of articulateness.[7] The Bible—and mostly the Old Testament—supplies the substance of the debate, which extends over seventy printed pages. *Aecclesia* begins the dialogue, asserting that by divine grace the Church has replaced the sinful Synagogue as God's chosen. Having commented on the question of how the Jews after Jesus stand in God's eyes, the debate then passes to the nature and birth of the messiah and to the time of the fulfillment—past or future—of Old Testament messianic prophecy. This dialogue, conforming to a literary genre popular among Christian writers since ancient times, undoubtedly exemplifies an abstract or fictitious sort of polemic.[8] The text, despite its great length, affords no particulars as to the setting of any real disputation which may have transpired, and the conversation itself is weighty and stilted. The participants do not so much discuss and analyze their opposing scriptural "proofs" as they stockpile them, in great numbers; some of the speeches fill over seven manuscript folios. And the dialogue concerns itself not at all with the Judaism or the Jewish literature of its own day; as Bernhard Blumenkranz has shown in his indices to the work, few of the arguments departed from those of earlier polemics. Clearly intended for a Christian rather than a Jewish audience, this dialogue presents the life of the Synagogue

---

ally reproached by a contemporary for disputing with Jews despite his ignorance of Hebrew, cf. Matthias Thiel, *Grundlagen und Gestalt der Hebräischkentnisse des früheren Mittelalters* (Spoleto, 1973), pp. 183–85. Manfred Kniewasser, "Bischof Agobard von Lyon und der Platz der Juden in einer sakral verfassten Einheitsgesellschaft," *Kairos*, n.s. 19 (1977), 218, 224, who argues that the two bishops did know Hebrew, has simply failed to recognize that in every case, they drew their references and allusions to Hebrew words directly from Jerome or Bede.

7. With later developments in medieval religious polemic, this equality was not preserved; see Wolfgang S. Seiferth, *Synagogue and Church in the Middle Ages: Two Symbols in Art and Literature*, trans. Lee Chadeayne and Paul Gottwald (New York, 1970), pp. 77ff., passim.

8. On the dialogue as a Christian literary genre in late antiquity and the Middle Ages, see, for example, Bernd Reiner Voss, *Der Dialog in der frühchristlichen Literatur* (Munich, 1970); Charles Homer Haskins, *The Renaissance of the Twelfth Century* (1927; repr., Cleveland, 1957), pp. 188–89; and Peter Dronke, *Poetic Individuality in the Middle Ages: New Departures in Poetry, 1000–1150* (Oxford, 1970), pp. 84–86.

as something stagnant, not as a dynamic reality. As a result, it did not threaten the security of medieval European Jewry.[9]

Few historians would reject this characterization of early Christian polemic against the Jews, or disagree that by the end of the Middle Ages, the tone of such polemic had become markedly more violent, more aggressive, and less abstract. Nevertheless, because historians have generally overlooked the importance of the role of theology in the worsening plight of the medieval Jewish community, they have expended relatively little energy on pinpointing the time, nature, and causes of this development. The most penetrating recent attempt to deal with the problem was made by Amos Funkenstein, who discerns the decisive change in anti-Jewish polemic as occurring in the twelfth century and acknowledges its broad significance. A new immediacy and a newly hostile mood came to pervade the polemics, deriving from a growing alienation of the Jews from the Christian community and linked also to increased Christian understanding of contemporary Judaism. The first stage in this transition, maintains Funkenstein, grew out of the rationalism of Anselm of Canterbury (ca. 1033–1109), who infused his theological investigations with a tolerant spirit of free intellectual inquiry; although Anselm himself did not write anti-Jewish polemic, his students and followers did, trying to prove the truth of Christianity not merely with quotations from Scripture but with rational arguments. Peter Alfonsi (1062–ca. 1140), for example, endeavored to explain the philosophical necessity of Christianity, at the same time contrasting it with a Judaism placed outside the realm of philosophy by the numerous unscientific and overly imaginative homilies of the Talmud. Another portent of change in the development of the new polemic came in the generation after Alfonsi with the writings of Peter the Venerable (ca. 1092–1156). The great abbot of Cluny departed from Alfonsi's rationalist approach to conclude that if any man is naturally endowed with the mental faculties to recognize the truth of Christianity and the Jews have not acknowledged that truth, then the Jews must not be human. Peter supported his conclusion by citing the irrational absurdities he claimed to have found in the Talmud, and this argument against the Jews based on their own rabbinic literature stamped his polemic with an important novelty. Still greater famil-

---

9. *Altercatio Aecclesiae contra Synagogam: Texte inédit du Xe siècle*, ed. Bernhard Blumenkranz (Strasbourg, 1954; also in *Revue du Moyen Age latin* 10 [1954], 5–159).

iarity with contemporary Jewish literature produced yet a third step in the worsening of anti-Jewish polemic. By the end of the twelfth century, one finds Alanus ab Insulis trying to use rabbinic literature as evidence in his proof of Christianity, a trend that Funkenstein sees as thenceforth predominant in polemics until the end of the Christian Middle Ages.[10]

Funkenstein's thesis merits careful attention. Most helpful are his observations linking the worsening of anti-Jewish polemic with the turning point in the plight of medieval Jewry and with the efforts among Christian polemicists to increase their knowledge and argue on the basis of contemporary Jewish beliefs and practices. The particular writers whom he discusses did indeed open the door to Christian exploration of rabbinic Judaism, and one therefore ought not to underestimate their importance. One finds some discrepancies, however, in the correlation of Funkenstein's conclusions with the reasonable expectation that a move away from the Augustinian brand of anti-Jewish polemic would involve departure from its basic defining characteristics.

If Anselm of Canterbury gave rise to the first, rationalist stage in the evolution of the new polemic, one would think that the anti-Jewish tracts of various heirs to his teaching—Odo of Cambray, William of Champeaux, or even Peter Abelard—might have embodied some of the novelty. Yet despite the scholastic nuances in motivation and methodology, these polemics also tend to preserve the traditional reliance on the Old Testament for evidence, the literary and unreal nature of Christian-Jewish dialogue, and the lack of relevance to contemporary Judaism.[11]

More surprising in its lack of innovation is the polemic upon which Anselm's influence is most probable, the famous dialogue between Gilbert Crispin and a Jew, a tract written by that abbot of Westminster in the final years of the eleventh century and dedicated to the archbishop of Canterbury himself. This text is of considerable importance, both because of its popularity among Christians

10. Funkenstein, "Changes," pp. 133–44; parts of Funkenstein's argument have been summarized in English in "Basic Types." Cf. also Manfred Kniewasser, "Die antijüdische Polemik des Petrus Alphonsi (getauft 1106) und des Abtes Petrus Venerabilis († 1156)," *Kairos*, n.s. 22 (1980), 34–76.

11. The three dialogues appear in PL 160:1103–12, 163:1045–72, and 173:1611–82, respectively. Cf. Margaret Schlauch, "The Allegory of the Church and the Synagogue," *Speculum* 14 (1939), 456–64; Hans Liebeschütz, "The Significance of Judaism in Peter Abelard's Dialogus," *JJS* 12 (1961), 1–18; and Liebeschütz, "Relations between Jews and Christians in the Middle Ages," *JJS* 16 (1965), 44–45.

in the twelfth century and because of the responses it ultimately elicited from Jewish writers.[12] The modern editor of the dialogue, Bernhard Blumenkranz, vehemently insists that a debate between Crispin and his Jewish friend from Mainz really did take place just as the abbot describes it, and several scholars have praised Crispin for the enlightened, scholastic, and friendly tone of the disputation. Others, however, have posed serious challenge to Blumenkranz's claims, asserting that the extant text does not manifest the reality of any interchange between the two disputants.[13] And whether or not the debate actually did transpire, the old-fashioned character of the polemic evinces itself clearly. As much as Anselm may have fashioned Crispin's forensic reasoning, the argumentation during the debate consists almost entirely of proof-texts from the Old Testament. Like the tenth-century *Altercatio*, Crispin's dialogue first deals with the obsolescence of the Old Testament's law and the Jews' error in observing it, next examines the incarnation of Christ and the Trinity, and then turns to the messianic salvation of humanity by the Church. The literary artifice in Crispin's account of the dialogue—if one really did occur—is unmistakable: the Jew begins the discussion and speaks again, usually briefly, six times, posing a total of seven questions to be answered by Crispin in seven rather lengthy monologues. What Jew well trained in debate and accustomed to exchanging ideas with his friend the abbot—the way in which Crispin describes him—would have willingly submitted himself to such an exhausting harangue?[14] And

12. Richard W. Southern has argued rather convincingly that Anselm had a marked influence on Gilbert Crispin, both in the latter's basic theological approach and in his polemical strategy. Southern even goes so far as to argue that Crispin collaborated with Anselm while preparing his anti-Jewish arguments. See Southern's "St. Anselm and Gilbert Crispin, Abbot of Westminster," *Medieval and Renaissance Studies* 3 (1954), 78–115, and *Saint Anselm and His Biographer: A Study of Monastic Life and Thought, 1059–c.1130* (Cambridge, Eng., 1963), pp. 89–95. For the dedicatory prologue, see Gilbert Crispin, *Disputatio Iudei et Christiani*, ed. Bernhard Blumenkranz (Utrecht, 1956), pp. 27–28. On the importance of this polemic, see Blumenkranz's introduction, pp. 13–16; and David Berger, "Gilbert Crispin, Alan of Lille, and Jacob ben Reuben: A Study in the Transmission of Medieval Polemic," *Speculum* 49 (1974), 37–47.

13. Blumenkranz's introduction to Crispin, *Disputatio*, pp. 7–11; cf. Williams, *Adversus Judaeos*, pp. 375–80; and R. W. Hunt, "The Disputation of Peter of Cornwall against Symon the Jew," in *Studies in Medieval History Presented to Frederick Maurice Powicke*, ed. Hunt et al. (Oxford, 1948), pp. 146, 151. The opposing view appears in R. J. Z. Werblowsky, "Crispin's Disputation," *JJS* 11 (1960), 65–77; and Liebeschütz, "Relations," p. 44.

14. Crispin, *Disputatio*, p. 27. Crispin writes to Anselm in his prologue that he is "pagine commendans que Iudeus quidam olim mecum disputans contra fidem

Crispin himself relates that he has recorded the debate at the request of his Christian audience in case others in the future might find it useful.[15] Finally, Judaism in this debate still appears to be treated as a stagnant theological artifact. Crispin deals neither with postbiblical (rabbinic) Jewish practice nor with the Jews of his own day; he makes no mention of his opponent's name, nor does he know his birthplace.

If the anti-Jewish polemicist most directly under the influence of Anselm departed but little from the patterns of his predecessors, what change can one discern in the writings of Peter Alfonsi, whom Funkenstein selects to represent the new rationalist polemic? Alfonsi was born Jewish and given the name Moses in 1062 in the Aragonese city of Huesca; a court physician schooled in both philosophy and science, he converted to Christianity in 1106 in the firm belief that he had found the most intellectually progressive religion. In the years following, Alfonsi composed his *Dialogus Petri et Moysi Iudaei* to justify his own conversion by establishing the rational superiority of Christianity. As well as in the rationalist emphasis of his arguments, Alfonsi was innovative in attacking Judaism on a doctrinal level; the first three of his work's twelve chapters dwell heavily on the homiletical interpretations of Scripture, *midrashim* of the rabbis of the Talmud, which struck Alfonsi as utterly irrational and absurd. Particularly with regard to anthropomorphic tales concerning God in the talmudic midrashim or their description of the afterlife in terms of corporeal return to Palestine, Alfonsi asserted that the rabbis betrayed the obstinate foolishness of their beliefs—that obdurate irrationality which also led them to reject Jesus.[16]

Since Alfonsi did attack Judaism on the basis of its postbiblical literature, his polemical approach evidenced a significant change

---

nostram de lege sua proferebat et que ego ad obiecta illius pro fide nostra respondebam. Nescio unde ortus, sed, apud Maguntiam litteris educatus, legis et litterarum etiam nostrarum bene sciens erat, et exercitatum in scripturis atque disputationibus contra nos habebat ingenium. Plurimum mihi familiaris sepe ad me veniebat, tum negotii sui causa, tum me videndi gratia, quoniam in aliquibus illi multum necessarius eram; et quociens conveniebamus, mox de scripturis ac de fide nostra sermonem amico animo habebamus."

15. Ibid.

16. The *Dialogus* appears in PL 157:535–672; cols. 541–93 contain Alfonsi's discussion of talmudic *aggadot*. On Alfonsi's life and work see Merchavya, *The Church*, pp. 93–127; and Williams, *Adversus Judaeos*, pp. 233–40. For the suggestion that Alfonsi migrated to England after his conversion, where he may well have come under the influence of Anselm, see Hunt, "The Disputation," p. 147.

from that of his predecessors; but the remaining nine chapters of his treatise revert almost entirely to older methods. He first argues that the Jews in their exegetical blindness fail to observe most of the Mosaic Law—that is, those commandments dependent on inhabiting the land of Palestine—anyway and should acknowledge its invalidity. Then, after devoting one chapter to a refutation of Islam, he tries to establish, primarily with recourse to the Old Testament, the major tenets of Christianity: the Trinity, the virgin birth and incarnation of Christ, Jesus' fulfillment of biblical messianic prophecy, his willingness to be crucified, and his resurrection and ascension to heaven. Furthermore, Alfonsi makes no attempt to hide the fact that no conversation between a Jewish Moses and a Christian Peter ever occurred; the author has simply used his names before and after his conversion to contrast in a popular literary style the differences between the two faiths.[17] And although he does attack aspects of the Judaism current in his own day, he refrains from the step taken by some polemicists after him— namely, the declaration that rabbinic Judaism did not warrant preservation in Christian society. He notably attacked only the talmudic homilies (*aggadah*) but never the legal traditions which determined contemporary Jewish practice (*halakhah*). Alfonsi in fact may never even have read or used the Talmud but perhaps only had a compendium of quotations in front of him.[18] Neither he nor Gilbert Crispin appears to have departed radically from the Augustinian type of anti-Jewish polemic.

Written several decades after Alfonsi's death, Peter the Venerable's *Tractatus adversus Iudaeorum inveteram duritiem* represents the second stage in Funkenstein's scheme, that of polemic against the Talmud. In contrast to Alfonsi's calm and measured dialogue, the abbot of Cluny's work was a bitter invective against the irrationality of the Jews, especially that manifested in the midrashim of the Talmud, which he mentions by name. For Peter, the Jews' refusal to submit to incontrovertible proofs and accept Christianity has placed them outside the realm of human reason, in the category of beasts. And the ridiculous and absurd tales and homilies of the Talmud exemplify their inherently blasphemous beliefs and rejection of true biblical revelation. The Jews even deceived Muhammad

17. PL 157: 538: "In tutandis etiam Christianorum rationibus, nomen quod modo Christianus habeo, posui: in rationibus vero adversarii confutandis, nomen quod ante baptismum habueram, id est Moysen."
18. Merchavya, *The Church*, p. 94.

with their Talmud, dissuading him from converting to Christianity, and they have not yet ceased opposing the books of God with their own diabolic and bestial ones. Therein lies the singular nuance of Peter's polemic: the idea that the Jews, in preferring absurd talmudic interpretations of the Old Testament to the "rational" Christian ones, blasphemed and were sacrilegious as far as genuine divine teaching was concerned. From what he learned of rabbinic literature, Peter may almost have arrived at the conclusion that for medieval Jewry the Talmud had supplanted the Bible as the basis of religious life and teaching—as did those who officially condemned and burned the Talmud in the thirteenth century.[19] But Peter apparently stopped short; he did not attempt to implement such ideas to the extent that subsequent generations of churchmen did, and in large measure his polemical stance remained in line with the predominant Christian theological attitude toward the Jew of the previous 750 years. Like Peter Alfonsi's *Dialogus*, the Cluniac *Tractatus* concentrated mainly on the traditional proofs of Christianity from the Old Testament; the attack on the Talmud comprised only the last of five chapters. Here again was a polemical treatise probably not intended for missionizing among the Jews since its blatant hostility in style and contents would have evoked little empathy from a Jewish audience. Instead, Peter directed his ideas to Christians. (In 1147 he wrote a letter to King Louis VII of France, upbraiding him for embarking on a crusade against the Muslims in Palestine when the blasphemous Jews exploited his Christian subjects at home.[20]) Even so, he never called for the elimination of an observant Jewish community from Christian society. Rather, he followed Augustine in recognizing the valuable service performed by the Jews who preserve the books of their Bible and continue to live by its laws. In attacking the Talmud, Peter never treats rabbinic traditions as anything other than the real substance of Judaism, however abominable they might have been in his eyes. In other words,

19. Peter's *Tractatus* appears in PL 189:507–650; the invective against talmudic *aggadot* spans cols. 602–50, but on Jewish irrationality and inhumanity, see also cols. 550–51, and on Jewish responsibility for the perfidy of Muhammad, see Peter's *Summa totius haeresis Saracenorum*, ed. by James Kritzeck in his *Peter the Venerable and Islam* (Princeton, 1964), p. 206 (trans., p. 131).

20. See Peter the Venerable, *Letters*, ed. Giles Constable, 2 vols. (Cambridge, Mass., 1967), 1:327–30. On Peter's preference for Muslims over Jews, see Kritzeck, *Peter the Venerable*, pp. 21–22 and n. 63. For a recent analysis of Peter's letter to King Louis, see Yvonne Friedman, "An Anatomy of Anti-Semitism: Peter the Venerable's Letter to Louis VII, King of France (1146)," in *Bar-Ilan Studies in History*, ed. Pinhas Artzi (Ramat Gan, 1978), pp. 87–102.

talmudic Jews are not heretics; in fact, Peter explicitly links the midrashim he attacks with the Jews' obstinate, literal understanding of Scripture. Since the time when Jewish prophets stopped appearing in Israel—that is, long before the coming of Jesus—all that the Jews did or wrote was "blasphemous, sacrilegious, ridiculous, and false"; the rabbis of the Talmud did little to alter the nature of Judaism.[21] Furthermore, although Peter frequently mentions the Talmud and even claims that his knowledge thereof was revealed directly to him by Jesus,[22] he really had less access to rabbinic literature than did Alfonsi. The assertion of James Kritzeck that Peter approached his talmudic investigations with dispassionate and scholarly meticulousness notwithstanding, careful textual research has revealed the opposite: Peter, totally ignorant of Hebrew, took most of his talmudic quotations directly and almost verbatim from Alfonsi and the remainder from a French rendition of the strange medieval Jewish anthology entitled the *Alphabet of Ben Sira*.[23]

Just as Peter the Venerable's *Tractatus* did not depart radically from the basic characteristics of Augustinian anti-Jewish polemic, so one ought to be wary of exaggerating the importance of Alanus ab Insulis, whose use of a rabbinic source constituted the third and final phase in Funkenstein's schema. Trying in his *De fide catholica contra haereticos* to convince the Jews of the advent of the messiah, Alanus adduced a well-known talmudic statement of the tannaitic "School of Elijah."

21. Peter praises the Jews for preserving the biblical tradition in his *Adversus nefandam haeresim sive sectam Saracenorum* 1.20, ed. Kritzeck, *Peter the Venerable*, pp. 252–53 (partial trans., pp. 178–79); he recognizes the continuity between biblical tradition—and the Jews' literal interpretation of it—and the talmudic teachings under attack in the *Tractatus*, PL 189:622–23, 626–28, 648–49. On Peter's treatment of the Talmud as embodying true Jewish belief, and his resulting use of it simply to illustrate the Jews' failure to interpret scriptural testimonies correctly, see Merchavya, *The Church*, p. 134; and Kniewasser, "Die antijüdische Polemik," p. 70.
22. PL 189:602.
23. Kritzeck, *Peter the Venerable*, pp. 26–27; Saul Lieberman, *Shkiin: A Few Words on Some Jewish Legends, Customs, and Literary Sources Found in Karaite and Christian Works* [Hebrew], 2d ed. (Jerusalem, 1970), pp. 27–42. Ironically, Kritzeck has cited Lieberman's work as vouching for the interest of rabbinic textual scholars in Peter's *Tractatus*, assuming to have found sympathy for his view that "one who made it a point to verify his quotations and obtain the exact literal sense of the Hebrew texts he was quoting . . . who, in sum, developed in himself a profound knowledge of the Jewish mind, was already well beyond the bounds which could (even optimistically) be set down for a Christian prelate." Lieberman, however, has demonstrated (p. 33) why "this book full of recklessness and foolishness—especially in its [textual] additions and explanations—has never been considered authoritative" in its rendition of rabbinic sources.

In its greatest part the Law has been abolished; it seems therefore that the Law should have no validity. Indeed in *Sehale* Elias says that the world will endure six thousand years—two thousand shall have been of vanity, which refers to the time before Mosaic Law, two thousand under Mosaic Law, and the following two thousand of the messianic age. But it is obvious that more than four thousand have passed; thus it is apparent that the Law has passed and the messiah has come.[24]

What corruption or confusion that led Alanus to label his source with the meaningless word *Sehale* is not of present concern, but the error brings Funkenstein to conclude convincingly that Alanus must have learned of the passage by word of mouth; he himself evidenced no real knowledge of rabbinic literature.[25] Moreover, the remainder of his anti-Jewish polemic adhered rather strictly to the style of most such early medieval compositions, harping on Old Testament testimonies with perhaps some greater use of rational argumentation, but dealing not at all with contemporary Judaism. And in itself, the reference to Jewish homily or exegesis by a Christian scholar constituted nothing new. The value of such allusions had long been recognized by Christian exegetes, even if ignorance of Hebrew limited knowledge of the sources to that conveyed in patristic writings.[26] The same Peter Alfonsi who had maligned the Talmud for its foolishness also used several talmudic legends to explicate the validity of Christian ideas. He referred, for example, to the story of Elijah telling Rabbi Joshua ben Levi that the messiah would come immediately, if only the Jews heeded his words, to establish that one only need accept Jesus in order to be saved. He also described the world to come in rabbinic terminology and quoted the talmudic statement that God had not heeded Jewish prayers since the destruction of the Temple.[27] Alanus' only innovation appears to have been his citing the mysterious *Sehale* as the source of his rabbinic evidence.

To be sure, the methodological nuances of writers like Peter Alfonsi, Peter of Cluny, and the English Alanus in their anti-Jewish

24. *De fide catholica contra haereticos* 3.10, PL 210:410. Cf. TB Sanhedrin 97a.
25. On *Sehale*—discussed by Funkenstein, "Changes," p. 142, n. 62, and Merchavya, *The Church*, p. 216, n. 15—as well as on the lack of real contact between Alanus (and several other Christian polemicists of the turn of the twelfth and thirteenth centuries) and Jews, resulting in the traditional abstract, theoretical nature of their polemics, see Marie-Humbert Vicaire, "'Contra Judaeos' meridionaux au début du XIIIᵉ siècle: Alain de Lille, Evrard de Bethune, Guillaume de Bourges," in *JJL*, pp. 269–93.
26. Merchavya, *The Church*, pp. 5, 27ff., 41ff.
27. PL 157:581, 588–89, 596. Cf. TB Sanhedrin 98a, Berakhot 32b.

polemics were noteworthy. Their direct allusion to or citation of the Talmud clearly represented a novel element in the Christian attack on Judaism and set the stage for more important developments to follow. Yet the basic characteristics of twelfth-century polemic differed little from those of the polemic that had preceded it, and the polemicists considered thus far did not alter the theological status of the Jews and their religion in the eyes of many influential churchmen of their day.[28] The continued literary nature and, as far as the Jews were concerned, remoteness of Christian polemic during the twelfth century is evidenced also by the paucity of extant anti-Christian tracts written by Jews in this period.[29] Jewish feelings of insecurity admittedly did increase—and for good reason—with the onset of the Crusades and did induce the growth of anti-Christian hostility on the part of Jews, expressed in biblical commentaries as well as the few extant polemics.[30] The major changes in anti-Jewish polemic, however, came only in the thirteenth century with the inquisitorial and missionary efforts of Dominican and Franciscan friars.

28. See, for example, the rather traditional anti-Jewish attitudes discussed by David Berger, "The Attitude of St. Bernard of Clairveaux toward the Jews," *PAAJR* 40 (1972), 89–108; and Solomon Grayzel, "Pope Alexander III and the Jews," in *Salo Wittmayer Baron Jubilee Volume*, ed. Saul Lieberman and Arthur Hyman, 3 vols. (Jerusalem, 1974), 2:570–72.

29. Judah M. Rosenthal, "Anti-Christian Polemic from Its Beginnings to the End of the 18th Century [Hebrew]," *Aresheth* 2 (1960), 138–39; D. Berger, in "Gilbert Crispin," p. 35, has termed the late twelfth-century *Milḥamot ha-Shem* of Jacob ben Reuben the earliest anti-Christian polemical treatise composed by a medieval Jew.

30. In addition to the works cited in the previous note, see Yitzhak Baer, "Rashi and the Historical Reality of His Times [Hebrew]," *Tarbiz* 20 (1949), 320–32; Erwin I. J. Rosenthal, "Anti-Christian Polemics in Medieval Bible Commentaries," *JJS* 11 (1960), 115–36; and Judah M. Rosenthal, "The Anti-Christian Dispute [Hebrew]," in *Rashi: His Teachings and Personality*, ed. Simon Federbush (New York, 1958), pp. 45–59. Cf. also the warning of the twelfth-century rabbi Judah ben Samuel the Pious against debating with Christians in his *Das Buch der Frommen* [Hebrew] § 811, ed. Jehuda Wistinetzki, 2d ed. (1924; repr., Jerusalem, 1969), p. 204.

2

The Mendicant Orders

The confrontations between the friars and the Jews ought not to be viewed out of context. The particulars and the significance of mendicant anti-Judaism had much to do with the character of the Dominican and Franciscan orders, the factors that contributed to their establishment, and the general nature of European religious life in the thirteenth century.

The State of Christian Society

The friars first made their appearance in European society during a period significant for the development of the medieval Church; a curious combination of trends, individuals, and institutions rendered the beginning of the thirteenth century a crucial time in ecclesiastical history. Having weathered the storm of the investiture controversy at least partly successfully, having spearheaded the whole movement of the Crusades, and having emerged from the first major round of conflict with the imperial House of Hohenstaufen, the medieval papacy stood at the height of its power. The pontificate of Innocent III (1198–1216) was notable for achieving internal Church reform as well as earning respect for the curia in virtually every sphere of temporal affairs. Innocent's was a reign of creativity and enthusiasm within the Church, factors that had far-reaching effects on all facets of European society.[1]

1. For such a perspective on this period within the broader context of the history of the medieval Church, see, for example, Hans-Georg Beck et al., *From the High Middle Ages to the Eve of the Reformation*, Handbook of Church History 4, ed. Herbert Jedin and John Dolan, trans. Anselm Biggs (New York, 1970), pp. 136–37; Walter Ullmann, *A Short History of the Papacy in the Middle Ages* (London, 1972), pp. 215ff.; and Brian Tierney, *The Crisis of Church and State, 1050–1300* (Englewood Cliffs, N.J., 1964), pp. 127–31.

Yet these advances were achieved in the face of crisis. Saracens still ruled the Holy Land and large portions of Spain; Holy Roman Emperors and popes still disputed over the division of spiritual and temporal dominion as well as over respective spheres of influence in Italy. Perhaps most significant, the Crusades had fostered growth and diversity not only in the Church, but also in the European community at large. Just as the *ecclesia* became more worldly, so did the industrious layman; the rise of towns and cities in the twelfth century spawned a new, more civilized class of burghers who led more cosmopolitan lives. Novelty and growth bred skepticism in addition to a desire for sophistication, and these attitudes in turn nourished the quest for all kinds of knowledge and learning. Moreover, the orientation of the urban economy and society toward monetary gain and profit clashed with Christianity's traditional view of commercial activity as sinful. The expanding Christian middle class required new forms of spirituality that would respond effectively to socioeconomic change, enabling burghers to rid themselves of the guilt they experienced in the pursuit of profit and to continue the worldly society they had begun to develop. Such aspirations inevitably led to the growth of heterodox movements. The relatively undereducated secular clergy of the average diocese could offer the Christian layman little guidance in his quest; and the existing forms of Benedictine and Cistercian monasticism, expressions of religious piety that had originally answered to the needs of a feudal society by preaching withdrawal from it and had then often resulted in the accumulation of tremendous wealth by monastic houses, did not respond to the urban situation either. Heterodoxy soon gave way to heresy, and by the time Innocent III ascended the papal throne in 1198, the Cathari and Waldensians in Languedoc and Lombardy posed a serious threat to the Church's internal security. Many of those disenchanted with the ways and means of the established clerical hierarchy, among them Joachim of Flora, were becoming ever more hopeful of a speedy if turbulent apocalyptic redemption.[2]

The diverse responses of Innocent III and the Church matched the challenges confronting them, in spirit as well as substance. In

2. On the link between early medieval monasticism and the feudal ethos, and on the resulting inability of traditional monasticism to meet the spiritual needs of later medieval society, see Barbara H. Rosenwein and Lester K. Little, "Social Meaning in the Monastic and Mendicant Spiritualities," *Past and Present* 63 (1974), 4–19; and Lester K. Little, *Religious Poverty and the Profit Economy in Medieval Europe* (Ithaca, 1978), pp. 3–41, 61–96.

encouraging the papally supervised growth of the University of Paris, for example, Innocent hoped to keep pace with the trends of progressive intellectual inquiry and the scholastic thirst for knowledge.[3] At the same time, however, the Church waged campaigns against its various enemies, endeavors that evinced and promoted great feelings of hostility toward all who might be considered threatening to Christendom. Diplomatic maneuvers continued against the anti-papal factions in the Empire. The call for a crusade to recapture Jerusalem from the Saracens constituted one of the *raisons d'être* for the Fourth Lateran Council of 1215, and contemporary Christian polemic against Islam simultaneously assumed a much more vehement, hostile, and often irrational character.[4] Innocent launched a crusade against the intransigent Cathari too, in addition to increasing missionary, polemical, and proto-inquisitorial efforts against them.[5] Apocalyptic and evangelical movements in general incurred suspicion, and the Fourth Lateran Council forbade the establishment of new rules for religious orders.[6] Such an aggressive reaction against all except the truly orthodox and faithful could not but have struck at the Jews, who became the subjects of a flurry of ecclesiastical legislation, most notably at the council of 1215. The Jews' appreciation of the importance of these events and signs of hostility was evidenced in their reactions to them. Rabbinical synods convened before both the Third and Fourth Lateran Councils to agree on strategy for interceding with the Church and preventing overly aggressive legislation. And the Jews' now rather regular appeals for the protection of the decreasingly effective papal constitution *Sicut Iudeis* witnessed the reality of the danger to which they had become subject.[7]

3. Hastings Rashdall, *The Universities of Europe in the Middle Ages*, 2d ed., ed. F. M. Powicke and A. B. Emden, 3 vols. (Oxford, 1936), 1:299–338; Gordon Leff, *Paris and Oxford Universities in the Thirteenth and Fourteenth Centuries: An Institutional and Intellectual History* (New York, 1968), pp. 24ff., 191ff.

4. On the origins, legislation, and the effects of the Fourth Lateran Council, see Raymonde Foreville, *Latran I, II, III et Latran IV*, Histoire des conciles oecuméniques 6 (Paris, 1965), pp. 228–44, 286, 320. On anti-Muslim polemic see Norman Daniel, *Islam and the West: The Making of an Image* (Edinburgh, 1960), pp. 229, 234, 241.

5. Walter L. Wakefield, *Heresy, Crusade, and Inquisition in Southern France, 1100–1250* (Berkeley, 1974), pp. 82–113.

6. Joseph Alberigo et al., eds., *Conciliorum oecumenicorum decreta*, alt. ed. (Basel, 1962), p. 213.

7. Solomon Grayzel, *The Church and the Jews in the XIIIth Century*, rev. ed. (New York, 1966), pp. 86–141, 296–313; such anti-Jewish legislation generally remained unenforced in some countries but not in all. See also Grayzel, "Jews and the Ecumenical Councils," in *The Seventy-Fifth Anniversary Volume of the Jewish Quarterly Re-*

Yet perhaps the most important and lasting reaction of the Church to the problems at hand came in the establishment of the two major mendicant orders, the Dominicans and the Franciscans. To deal with the spread of heresy and the decadence of the secular clergy, Innocent III had first appealed to the order of Cîteaux, whose more capable and noted members often undertook special legatine missions. But such employment of the Cistercians constituted the direction of monastic energies toward more worldly pursuits than those for which the order was originally intended and thus had to be restricted to individual and exceptional cases. "The only remedy for the situation," writes one of Dominic's biographers, "lay in the formation of an apostolic clergy, zealous, virtuous, and poor";[8] and because the feudal-manorial social unit was giving way to a larger and more fluid one, the Church required a body of religious no longer confined to houses but possessing the self-consciousness of citizens of a universal Christian society, one that included the marketplace as well as the cloister.

Saint Dominic and Saint Francis

In 1204, Innocent III dispatched Diego de Acebes, the bishop of Osma, to preach among the Cathari in Languedoc and reinforce the efforts of the Cistercian legates already there; accompanying and assisting Diego was Dominic of Caleruega, the subprior of his cathedral. Recognizing that the heretics would acknowledge as preachers of the Gospel only those who accepted their own evangelical customs, Diego and Dominic adopted a mendicant way of life as they taught and disputed, a tactic officially countenanced and encouraged by the pope as early as 1206. Diego died in 1207, but Dominic remained in Languedoc throughout the first stages of the Albigensian Crusade, working behind the scenes out of his convent at Prouille, constantly disputing with the Cathari and preaching in defense of the faith. So impressive were his efforts that in 1215 Archbishop Foulques of Toulouse recognized Dominic and his compatriots as a community of mendicant preachers and made them responsible for preaching the Gospel in his diocese; later that

---

view, ed. Abraham A. Neuman and Solomon Zeitlin (Philadelphia, 1967), pp. 295–96; and "The Papal Bull," pp. 250, 275–80.

8. Pierre Mandonnet, *St. Dominic and His Work*, trans. Mary Benedicta Larkin (St. Louis, 1944), p. 8.

year, the Fourth Lateran Council ordered such measures undertaken by the bishop in every diocese.

Thus began the Order of Preachers, which by the time of Dominic's death in 1221 had adopted a modified version of the Augustinian Rule, had spread throughout Christendom and even beyond, and had started to accumulate a corpus of legislation that would help to insure its survival and organizational flexibility over the years to come. Having begun their endeavors in the thick of the Albigensian heresy, the Dominicans were from the outset an order devoted to the teaching of the faith and the eradication of heterodoxy. For centuries they were to excel as educators, missionaries, and inquisitors, all functions that Dominic himself—in founding a whole hierarchy of *studia* (houses of study) for his order, perhaps in traveling to missionize among the Saracens, and in fighting heretical dualism in Languedoc and Lombardy—had filled.[9] Quite appropriately, Honorius III's confirmation of the order in 1216 stated that the Dominican friars were "about to become the pugilists of the faith and the true luminaries of the world," and in 1217 the pope wrote to the Dominicans:

> While the flame of charity glows within you, outwardly you exude a fragrance of good repute, that both delights the senses and heals infirm minds—with which attributes you further show yourselves to be zealous physicians, and you fertilize those minds with the seed of the word of God by means of your salutary eloquence, lest they remain sterile, spiritual mandrakes. Indeed, as if you were faithful servants investing the money entrusted to you that you might carry it back doubled to your master, like invincible athletes of Christ, armed with the shield of the faith and the helmet of salvation and not fearing those who can slay the body, you magnanimously exert against the enemies of the faith the word of God, which is more penetrating than any two-edged sword; thus you despise your lives in this world, so that you might preserve them in the eternal life. Moreover, since the goal and not the contest itself bestows victory, and when all the virtues are racing on the track perseverance alone takes the allotted reward, we beseech your charity and urge emphatically, ordering you with Apostolic writ and enjoining you in the remission of your sins, that having been ever more strengthened in God, you be zealous in

9. On the founding and early history of the Dominican Order, see ibid., pp. 21–26; Marie-Humbert Vicaire, *Saint Dominic and His Times*, trans. Kathleen Pond (London, 1964); and R. F. Bennett, *The Early Dominicans* (Cambridge, Eng., 1937), pp. 21ff. On Dominic's possible mission to the Muslims, see Berthold Altaner, *Die Dominikanermissionen des 13. Jahrhunderts* (Schleswig [Habelschwerdt], 1924), p. 3.

evangelizing the word of God, persisting under opportune and inopportune circumstances and laudably completing the task of the evangelist.[10]

Although the Order of Preachers originated entirely within the clerical establishment, the Order of Friars Minor certainly did not. Unlike his contemporary Dominic, Francis of Assisi at first struggled hard to prevent any official enfranchisement of his small group of followers by the Church. Having undergone his famous conversion from the frivolity and profligacy of his youth, Francis wished simply to exemplify an evangelically perfect way of life as he wandered around in complete poverty, a virtue extolled by many of the contemporary heretical groups. Yet despite a distaste for organizational formalities and structure, the growth of his order moved Francis to solicit ecclesiastical recognition, and in 1209 he presented himself before Innocent III, seeking approval for the original rule of the order. Although Innocent may have been somewhat taken aback by Francis's boldness and apparent naivete, the curia soon came to appreciate the value of the Franciscans and their endeavors; freshness and change were needed in much of Christendom, in view of the state of the secular clergy and the dissidence of the heretics, and the Franciscans seemed to proffer a way to true reform. Ugolino, the cardinal-bishop of Ostia, in particular recognized the potential of the Friars Minor; owing much to his efforts, the order soon became part of the established clergy. Francis returned to Rome in 1215, where Innocent III decreed to the Fourth Lateran Council that his prior encouragement of the Franciscan undertaking justified their exclusion from the synod's ban on new religious rules. Honorius III formally recognized the order the following year, and in 1223 the pope accepted a new, much more detailed version of the Franciscan rule. When Francis died in 1226, his order was already a permanent institution of the Church and, like the Dominicans, an elite clerical force in the service of Rome.[11]

By the middle of the thirteenth century, few differences in func-

10. Thomas Ripoll, ed., *Bullarium Ordinis Fratrum Praedicatorum*, 8 vols. (Rome, 1729–40), 1:4.
11. On the novelty of the Franciscan world view, cf. David Knowles, *The Religious Orders in England*, 3 vols. (Cambridge, Eng., 1948–59), 1:121–22. For accounts of Francis's life and work, see John Moorman, *A History of the Franciscan Order from Its Origins to the Year 1517* (Oxford, 1968), pp. 3–80; and Omar Englebert, *Saint Francis of Assisi*, trans. Eve Marie Cooper, 2d ed. (Chicago, 1966), both of which include extensive bibliographies.

tion and life-style remained between the Dominicans and the Franciscans; both orders had among their ranks university professors, inquisitors, preachers, and missionaries. At its inception, however, the Franciscan order was neither a teaching order nor one devoted to the defense of Catholicism against heresy. Francis had even forbidden the ownership and excessive reading of books by his followers and certainly did not create an educational system for his friars as Dominic had done. Regarding true simplicity, Thomas of Celano wrote that Francis "thought it easier to be gotten as a habit [than through knowledge and wisdom] and more ready to be used by those who are poor as regards learning."[12] Nevertheless, inherent in Francis's thought too was a basic and important concept of mission which proved to be a valuable weapon in the Church's fight against its enemies. Contrasting this ideology with other approaches to missionizing, a modern scholar notes that "whereas philosophical debate called for a rational approach to Christianity and Joachitism posited miraculous wholesale conversion, the Franciscans sought personal spiritual perfection that they might teach men by example how to prepare themselves for the final judgment."[13] Renouncing the way of the world, converting to the life of the kingdom of heaven, and being willing to undergo martyrdom were what the friars saw as the most effective tactics against the dangers confronting Christendom; mission meant nothing more than true service to the Franciscan ideal under the direction of the papacy.[14]

Such ideas received noteworthy attention in the advice Francis gave to his followers. The draft of the rule he wrote in 1221 places restrictions on preaching but still lists it as an important activity of the friars. The rule accords particular praise to missionaries among the infidels and instructs the friars that they may propagate the faith not only by disputing with the infidel but also by simply

12. Thomas of Celano, *Vita secunda S. Francisci* § 189, in *Analecta franciscana* 10 (1926–41), 238; trans. in Marion A. Habig, ed., *St. Francis of Assisi: Writings and Early Biographies* (Chicago, 1973), p. 513. Cf. § 62, pp. 194–95; and the *Legenda perugiensis*, § 66. On the original differences between the two orders, see Bonaventure, *Collationes in hexameron* 22.21, *Opera omnia*, 11 vols. (Florence [Quaracchi], 1882–1902), 5:440: "Hi sunt Praedicatores et Minores. Alii principaliter intendunt speculationi, a quo etiam nomen acceperunt, et postea *unctioni.*—Alii principaliter *unctioni* et postea *speculationi.* Et utinam iste amor vel unctio non recedat a Cherubim." See also Altaner, *Die Dominakermissionen*, p. 225.

13. E. Randolph Daniel, *The Franciscan Concept of Mission in the High Middle Ages* (Lexington, Ky., 1975), p. 22.

14. Ibid., pp. xii–xiv, 36.

exemplifying a life of true piety. Franciscan ministers are in turn directed to allow all qualified friars desirous of engaging in missionary work to do so.[15] And insuring the value of the Franciscan life for the Church, the rule emphasizes that it must adhere to the tenets of orthodoxy and thereby serve the interests of the ecclesiastical hierarchy.

> All the friars are bound to be Catholics, and live and speak as such. Anyone who abandons the Catholic faith or practice by word or deed must be absolutely excluded from the Order, unless he repents. We must regard all other clerics and religious as our superiors in all that concerns the salvation of the soul and is not contrary to the interests of our religious life. We must respect their position and office, together with their ministry.[16]

Francis himself accepted the exhortations of the rule and several times resolved to missionize among the Saracens, actually hoping to die a martyr. Inclement weather and illness thwarted his first two attempts, but in 1219 he joined the fighters of the Fifth Crusade in Egypt and even attempted to convert the Turkish sultan there in a personal audience with him.[17]

Fundamental in the foundation of both mendicant orders, therefore, were obedience to Rome and an eagerness to propagate orthodoxy, either by exemplifying or by teaching it. In view of the risks that founding new orders posed to the Church in a time of crisis, approving of the friars evidenced considerable determination on the curia's part to respond to the dangers at hand. Soon, although not without opposition, the two orders came to dominate the faculty of theology at the University of Paris, thereby directing the potentially dangerous course of philosophical investigations. The friars led the Church's fight against heresy, both in preaching against it and in its prosecution by the Inquisition. With the decreasing popularity of armed crusades, Dominicans and Franciscans filled the ranks of most thirteenth-century missions to the infidels; they sharpened Christian intellectual inquiry and developed a new combative spirit of dialogue. Despite any wishes of their founders to the contrary, the mendicant orders quickly gained prominent representation in the ecclesiastical hierarchy, and sim-

15. Regula prima §§ 16–17.
16. Regula prima § 19, in *Opuscula Sancti patris Francisci assisiensis*, 3d ed. (Florence [Quaracchi], 1949), p. 49; trans. in Habig, *St. Francis*, p. 46.
17. Thomas of Celano, *Vita prima S. Francisci* §§ 55–57.

ply through their preaching and their accessibility the friars freshened the religious experience of Europe's lay population. Friars served the papacy and individual popes in numerous capacities, and by means of their affinities with temporal rulers often managed to exert increased ecclesiastical influence over the formulation of royal policy.

Drawn in large numbers from the rising middle classes, the orders came to represent a new brand of religious piety, one that did not demand withdrawal from the hubbub of worldly society. Rather, the mendicants remained in society and sought to involve the layman in their program of moral theology. The friars thereby accorded legitimacy to the commercial and profit economy of cities and towns; although they repudiated financial gain with their vows of poverty, they involved themselves in numerous aspects of urban life. As one pair of writers recently concluded, "the spirituality developed by the friars belongs unmistakably to the work they rejected." They participated in the cultural and intellectual life of the towns, took an active role in urban politics, and in their religious vocabulary and pedagogic method exhibited a strong tie to the mores of the marketplace. It was not sheer accident that an early Franciscan work bore the title *Sacrum commercium*, that a Dominican writer named his book *Regula mercatorum*, or that Francis of Assisi, himself the son of a wealthy businessman, was often hailed as the patron saint of urban merchants. Nor ought one to overlook the leading role taken by mendicant theologians such as Albertus Magnus and Thomas Aquinas in explicitly recognizing the value and the rightful place of private property, trade, and commercial speculation in a properly ordered Christian society. The friars responded to both the social and the spiritual needs of high medieval Christendom. They comprised the single most decisive element in molding the character of religious and cultural life in thirteenth-century Europe.[18]

18. Quotation from Rosenwein and Little, "Social Meaning," p. 23. On the growth, functions, and influences of the two orders, see Moorman, *A History*, pp. 226–304; Badin Gratien, *Histoire de la fondation et de l'evolution de l'Ordre des Frères Mineurs au XIIIᵉ siècle* (Paris, 1928), pp. 513–676; William A. Hinnebusch, *A History of the Dominican Order*, 2 vols. (New York, 1966–73), 2: passim; and Robert I. Burns, "Christian-Islamic Confrontation in the West: The Thirteenth-Century Dream of Conversion," *AHR* 76 (1971), 1386–1434. With specific regard to the socioeconomic background and functions of the mendicants, see Jacques le Goff, "Apostolat mendiant et fait urbain dans la France médiévale: L'implantation des ordres mendiants," *Annales* 23 (1968), 335–52, and "Ordres mendiants et urbanisation dans la France médiévale," ibid., 25 (1970), 924–46; John B. Freed, *The Friars and German Society in the Thirteenth*

Members of the two new mendicant orders had much contact with European Jewry from the earliest years of the orders' existence. So much do the Dominicans and Franciscans dominate the relations between the Church and the Jews during this period, that many different aspects of the contacts between them have been singled out for attention. Some thirty years ago, Yitzhak Baer tried to prove parallel and causal interconnections between the development of the Franciscan order and that of the German pietist *Ḥasidim*, although more recent scholarship has cast serious doubts on the far-reaching nature of Baer's conclusions.[19] Perhaps somewhat more convincingly, Baer also attempted to demonstrate links between the radical Joachimite Spirituals among the Spanish Franciscans and the various strains of Jewish mysticism in thirteenth-century Spain.[20] Dominican historians like Pierre Mandonnet call attention to Dominic's reported love for the Jews, about which the saint's act of canonization reports that Friar Iohannes Hispanis attested: "He [Dominic] used to show himself as loving to all, the rich, the poor, the Jews, and Gentiles—of whom there were many in Spain—and he was loved by all excepting heretics and enemies of the Church, whom in his disputations and sermons he reproached and defeated."[21] More dispassionate and credible are contemporary reports about friars who protected Jews from persecution, as did members of both orders in the wake of the ritual murder charges leveled at the Jews of Lincoln in 1255, even at the cost of alienating much of the local population who in turn withheld alms

Century (Cambridge, Mass., 1977); and L. K. Little, *Religious Poverty*, pp. 146–219. And on the role of mendicant scholars in changing Christian attitudes toward money and profit, see, for example, Richard Schlatter, *Private Property: The History of an Idea* (London, 1951), pp. 33–55; John F. McGovern, "The Rise of the New Economic Attitudes—Economic Humanism, Economic Nationalism—during the Later Middle Ages and the Renaissance, A.D. 1200–1500," *Traditio* 26 (1970), 225–31; and Raymond de Roover, "The Concept of the Just Price: Theory and Economic Policy," *Journal of Economic History* 18 (1958), 418–34.

19. Yitzhak Baer, "The Religious-Social Tendency of 'Sefer Ḥassidim [Hebrew],'" *Zion*, n.s. 3 (1937), 1–50. In response to Baer, see the rejoinder of Ephraim E. Urbach in his edition of Abraham ben Azriel, *Sefer 'Arugat ha-Bosem* [Hebrew], 4 vols. (Jerusalem, 1936–63), 1:xii, n. 1 [first printing only]; and above all Ivan G. Marcus, "Penitential Theory and Practice among the Pious of Germany: 1150–1250," Ph.D. diss., Jewish Theological Seminary of America, 1974, ch. 7.

20. Yitzhak Baer, "The Historical Background of the 'Raya Mehemna' (A Chapter in the History of Religious-Social Movements in Castile during the Thirteenth Century) [Hebrew]," *Zion*, n.s. 5 (1939), 1–44; and *A History of the Jews in Christian Spain*, trans. Louis Schoffman et al., 2 vols. (Philadelphia, 1961–66), 1:270–77.

21. Angelus Waltz, ed., *Acta canonizationis S. Dominici*, Monumenta Ordinis Fratrum Praedicatorum historica 16 (Rome, 1935), p. 127; cf. Mandonnet, *St. Dominic*, p. 61.

from the mendicants. Several years later, Robert Kilwardby, the Dominican archbishop of Canterbury, and the Franciscan Adam Marsh tried to intervene with the king on behalf of a particular Jew.[22]

Nevertheless, the most predominant attitude of the friars toward the Jews was marked by an aggressive missionary spirit and often violent animosity. Since the friars represented the Christian middle classes both in their personal origins and in their religious program, their hostility toward the Jews may have derived in part from anti-Jewish sentiments typically harbored by European merchants. By the thirteenth century, the Jews of Europe were engaged almost exclusively in commercial activities, especially the lending of money; their success and influence in the marketplace set them among the chief competitors of the new Christian bourgeoisie. This situation added a dimension of immediacy to the age-old conflict between the Church and the Synagogue, and appropriately the mendicant orders assumed the leading role in that conflict shortly after they were established. As soon as the Dominicans entered England, they opened a priory in the heart of the Jewish quarter in Oxford; several documents remain concerning one Robert Bacon, O.P., who appears to have been responsible for the education of new converts from Judaism and the rehabilitation of relapsed ones. The Franciscan Henry of Wadstone in 1271 played an instrumental role in securing a decree forbidding Jewish ownership of freeholds in England, and the register of the Grey Friars of London notes that owing to his efforts all Jews were finally expelled from England.[23] In 1247, two Franciscans managed the inquest following the death of a young girl in the French town of Valréas; the resulting blood libel (the accusation that Jews killed Christians in order to make ritual use of their blood), based entirely upon confessions exacted under torture, cost many Jews their lives and others their property and even elicited several protests from Pope Innocent IV.[24] Dominicans and Franciscans together engineered the

22. William A. Hinnebusch, *The Early English Friars Preachers* (Rome, 1951), pp. 29, 32; E. R. Daniel, *The Franciscan Concept of Mission,* p. 59; Ellen M. F. Sommer-Seckendorf, *Studies in the Life of Robert Kilwardby, O.P.* (Rome, 1937), pp. 29, 32.

23. Cecil Roth, *The Jews of Medieval Oxford* (Oxford, 1951), p. 19; Hinnebusch, *The Early English Friars Preachers,* p. 11, n. 36; A. G. Little, "Friar Henry of Wadstone and the Jews," in *Collectanea franciscana II,* ed. C. L. Kingsford et al., British Society of Franciscan Studies 10 (Manchester, 1922), pp. 150–57.

24. August Molinier, "Enquête sur un meurtre imputé aux Juifs de Valréas (1247)," *Cabinet historique* 29 (1883), 121–33; Auguste Prudhomme, "Notes et documents sur les Juifs du Dauphiné," *REJ* 9 (1884), 231–39; Moritz Stern, *Urkundliche Beiträge über die Stellung der Päpste zu den Juden,* 2 vols. (1893–95; repr., Farnborough, Eng., 1970),

massacre of Troyes's Jewry in 1288 after a similar blood accusation. In 1305 in Aragon, a Dominican of Huesca tried to entrap the rich Jew Isaac ben Solomon on charges of blasphemy, while in 1328 a Franciscan in Navarre, Peter Olligoyen, was temporarily jailed for his Jew-baiting.[25]

These are only examples of numerous sporadic incidents which occurred throughout Europe during this period and which evinced a determined attitude of hostility that the Jews—witness the quotation that opens the introduction to this book—clearly recognized. Yet the brunt of the friars' attack upon the Jews came not in these isolated occurrences but in concerted efforts usually undertaken with some degree of official sanction: in inquisitorial and missionary campaigns that expressed a basically new Christian polemical attitude toward medieval Jews and Judaism.

The Mendicant Inquisition

One of the most important and controversial institutions in all of Church history, the Inquisition provided the initial context for the friars' attacks upon the Jews. Its origins and character therefore warrant attention in any attempt to appreciate the nature and significance of those activities. Although the Inquisition emerged as a highly effective weapon against the threat of heresy confronting the Church in the late twelfth and thirteenth centuries, it lacked any formal founding or inauguration as such. Rather, it evolved out of various developments in the Catholic counteroffensive against heresy, and one can perhaps even view the Inquisition as the sum total of all such activity which took place during any particular period. In 1184, Pope Lucius III issued his famous decretal *Ab abolendam*, which called for a vigorous campaign against heresy by local diocesan authorities—the traditional and established means for combatting heresy—with the aid of the temporal powers.[26] Fifteen years later Innocent III labeled heresy the worst sin possible, a crime which corrupted all of society and an offense no

---

2:46–58; and Grayzel, *The Church and the Jews*, pp. 262–65. Specifically on the importance of the Franciscans in engineering this blood libel, see Gavin I. Langmuir, "L'absence d'accusation de meurtre rituel à l'ouest du Rhone," in *JJL*, pp. 243–44.

25. Arsène Darmesteter, "L'autodafé de Troyes (24 avril 1288)," *REJ* 2 (1881), 216–17, 231; Y. Baer, *A History*, 2:7–8; *SRH*, 10:152–53.

26. X.5.7.9.

less grave than treason, or *lèse-majesté*, which justified depriving perpetrators of basic civil rights.

> For since, according to legitimate sanctions, in crimes of *lèse-majesté* after the guilty have been executed, their property is confiscated and the lives of their children are spared only out of mercy, how much more do those who offend the son of the Lord God, Jesus Christ, by deviating in their faith deserve to be cut off from our head, which is Christ, by ecclesiastical sentence and to be deprived of temporal goods. For it is far more serious to attack the eternal majesty than the temporal [majesty].[27]

Innocent also augmented the episcopal prosecution of heresy with special legatine missions, conducted most notably in Languedoc by Cistercians and distinguished prelates. Most Church historians agree, however, that the Inquisition commenced with the establishment of permanent judicial machinery to fight against heresy outside the diocesan hierarchy. Such a step may perhaps be seen in the employment of Dominicans in such a capacity by Gregory IX as early as 1227; some scholars discern it by 1231.[28] But certainly Gregory's letters to the Dominicans in April of 1233 calling for their large-scale prosecution of heresy in southern France and granting them complete judicial powers to deal with heretics heralded the institutional permanence of the Inquisition.[29]

Conscious of the inadequacies of the anti-heretical efforts of the local secular clergy, the papacy insured the mendicant character of the Inquisition from its inception. Zealously committed to orthodoxy, directly and exclusively obedient to the papal curia, and ideologically not bound to a life of monastic seclusion, the Dominicans and Franciscans provided the ideal inquisitors, and they dominated the Inquisition for centuries. Although the Dominicans were the order founded specifically for the extirpation of heresy and thus the first of the inquisitors,[30] the Franciscans soon rallied in

27. X.5.7.10, in *Corpus iuris canonici*, ed. Aemilius Friedberg, 2 vols. (1879; repr., Graz, 1959), 2:782–83.

28. See, for example, Albert C. Shannon, *The Popes and Heresy in the Thirteenth Century* (Villanova, 1949), pp. 49–51; and Fernand Hayward, *The Inquisition*, trans. Malachy Carrol (New York, 1966), p. 39.

29. A. S. Turberville, *Medieval Heresy and the Inquisition* (London, 1920), p. 147; Jean Guiraud, *Histoire de l'Inquisition au Moyen Age*, 2 vols. (Paris, 1935–38), 2:34–36; and Wakefield, *Heresy*, p. 140. Gregory's bulls *Licet ad capiendas* and *Ille humani generis* may be found in Ripoll, *Bullarium*, 1:47–48.

30. See, for instance, the remark of Honorius III to Dominic in 1221 in the bull *Quoniam habundavit* in Ripoll, *Bullarium*, 1:11: "Ecce Ordinem dilectorum filiorum

their eagerness to participate. An abundance of enthusiastic zeal produced a sometimes unhealthy rivalry between inquisitors of the two orders or between mendicants and secular clergy engaged in combatting heresy.[31]

Numerous interpretations have been advanced as to reasons for the founding of the Inquisition. Looking beyond its ostensive goal of eradicating heresy, Celestin Douais explained the birth of the Inquisition as a papal response to the threats of Frederick II.[32] A. L. Maycock linked it instead to the revival of Roman law and the appearance of sixty laws against heresy in the *Corpus iuris civilis;* Frederick II therefore could follow the lead of Innocent III in declaring heresy treason and a capital offense not out of allegiance to the Church but because heresy constituted a crime against the state and medieval society at large.[33] Yet whatever the immediate cause of the Inquisition, many historians have correctly viewed its institution as a defense of, and even an expression of, the fundamental world view of medieval Christendom. Explaining the legislation of Innocent and Frederick, Henri Maisonneuve aptly comments: "In a

---

Fratrum Predicatorum Dominus suscitavit, qui non que sua, sed que sunt Christi querentes, tam contra profligandas hereses, quam contra pestes alias mortiferas extirpandas se dedicarunt evangelizationi Verbi Dei in abjectione voluntarie paupertatis." In this regard, see Bennett, *The Early Dominicans,* pp. 129–30, who has attempted to downplay the initial ideological inclination of the Dominicans to take charge of the Inquisition; and Yves Dossat, "Inquisiteurs ou enqueteurs? A propos d'un texte d'Humbert de Romans," *Bulletin philologique et historique (jusqu'à 1715) du Comité des travaux historiques et scientifiques,* 1957, pp. 105–7, who effectively responds to Bennett's contention. Nevertheless, the medieval traditions that Dominic himself was the first inquisitor are also erroneous; see Celestin Douais, *L'Inquisition: Ses origines—sa procédure* (Paris, 1906), pp. 22–26; and M.-H. Vicaire, "Saint Dominique et les inquisiteurs," *Annales du Midi* 79 (1967), 173–94.

31. A. G. Little, "The Mendicant Orders," in *Cambridge Medieval History,* 8 vols. (Cambridge, Eng., 1911–36), 6:752; F. Darwin Swift, *The Life and Times of James the First* (Oxford, 1894), p. 242; and Henry C. Lea, *A History of the Inquisition of the Middle Ages,* 3 vols. (New York, 1888), 1:300,302. The need for papal attention to conflicts between bishops and mendicant inquisitors was evidenced in the decree of *Multorum querela,* issued by Clement V at the Council of Vienne; see *Clementinae* 5.3.1.

32. Douais, *L'Inquisition,* pp. 123–44.

33. A. L. Maycock, *The Inquisition from Its Establishment to the Great Schism: An Introductory Study* (London, 1926), pp. 86–92. See Frederick's constitution of November 22, 1220, in MGH, LL 4,2: 108: "Chataros, Patarenos, Leonistas, Speronistas, Arnaldistas, Circumcisos et omnes hereticos utriusque sexus, quocumque nomine censeantur, perpetua dampnamus infamia, diffidamus atque bannimus, censentes ut bona talium confiscentur nec ad eos ulterius revertantur, ita quod filii ad successionem eorum pervenire non possint, cum longe sit gravius eternam quam temporalem offendere maiestatem." For the law of March 1224 prescribing death by fire for heretics, see pp. 126–27.

world where one cannot conceive of the State without religion or where the religion of the State is imposed on all its citizens, every serious and public offense against the religion is a crime of treason."[34] As the Church in the thirteenth century came closest to a corporate realization of the Gregorian notion of a universal Christian society, heresy became at least as much an ecclesiological problem as a theological one. Upsetting the Church's hierarchy, it attacked the whole fabric of society, not only its dogmas. The Inquisition was a response not only to the dualists in Languedoc and Lombardy but also to the growing need that Christendom felt for regulation and order in its midst. During this period when legalism above all else characterized the Roman curia, institutionalized judicial means were sought to safeguard the collective rights of the Catholic community against encroachment by the deviant individual.[35]

The Inquisition's dealings with the Jews must be appreciated in just such a perspective. From a strict legal point of view, the Inquisition had no jurisdiction over the Jews per se, because officially Judaism was tolerated within Christian society. But Christendom was growing ever less amenable to the existence of any religious minorities, and the Inquisition did not hesitate to attack the Jews under whatever pretext it could find, rationalizing such action with the currently accepted policy for treatment of infidels. Thomas Aquinas expressed the policy thus:

Among unbelievers there are some who have never received the faith, such as heathens and Jews. These are by no means to be compelled, for belief is voluntary. Nevertheless the faithful, if they are able, should compel them not to hinder the faith whether by their blasphemies or evil persuasions or even open persecutions. It is for this reason that Christ's faithful often wage war on infidels, not indeed for the pur-

---

34. Henri Maisonneuve, *Etude sur les origines de l'Inquisition*, 2d ed. (Paris, 1960), p. 367. For a detailed description of the development of the notion of heresy as treason, particularly as a factor in the founding of the Inquisition, see Maurice Bévenot, "The Inquisition and Its Antecedents," *Heythrop Journal* 7 (1966), 384–93, 8 (1967), 52–69. Cf. also Walter Ullmann, "The Significance of Innocent III's Decretal 'Vergentis,'" and Henri Maisonneuve, "Le droit romain et la doctrine inquisitoriale," both in *Etudes d'histoire du droit canonique dédiées à Gabriel le Bras*, 2 vols. (Paris, 1965), 1:729–41, 2:931–42 (respectively).

35. R. Morghen, "Problèmes sur l'origine de l'hérésie au Moyen Age," *Revue historique* 236 (1966), 5; Beck, *From the High Middle Ages to the Eve of the Reformation*, p. 210; and especially Walter Ullmann's historical introduction to Henry C. Lea, *The Inquisition of the Middle Ages: Its Organization and Procedure* (London, 1963), pp. 31–46.

pose of forcing them to believe, because even were they to conquer them and take them captive, they should still leave them free to believe or not, but for the purpose of stopping them from obstructing the faith of Christ.[36]

This outlook facilitated attacks upon Jews on several grounds. First, Jews were often accused of promoting heretical ideas and giving aid to heretics. Although such ties may indeed have existed in Languedoc and Lombardy, the charges of the Inquisition were undoubtedly much exaggerated; even the anti-Jewish Cathari were accused of using Judaism as a cover for spreading their own ideas.[37] Second, both Christian converts to Judaism and Jewish converts to Christianity who "relapsed" into their former religion came under the jurisdiction of the Inquisition, as did by extension those Jews who consorted with the converts and *relapsi* in their practice of Judaism. As I shall demonstrate in a subsequent chapter, such an extension of inquisitorial jurisdiction to any who aided heretics could easily be exploited by friars to harass entire Jewish communities. Clement IV thus issued the following impassioned appeal to all Dominican and Franciscan inquisitors in 1267:

> With our heart in turmoil [*Turbato corde*] we have heard, and we now recount, that exceedingly numerous reprobate Christians, denying the truth of the Catholic faith, have gone over, in a way worthy of damnation, to the rite of the Jews. This is realized to be the more reprobate in that thus the most holy name of Christ is the more heedlessly blasphemed by a kind of enmity within the family! . . . We command your

36. Thomas Aquinas, *ST* 2–2.10.8, 60 vols. (Cambridge, Eng., 1964–76), 32:62–63.
37. On the associations between heretics and Jews, see Richard W. Emery, *Heresy and Inquisition in Narbonne* (1941; repr., New York, 1967), p. 136; Shulamit Shahar, "Catharism and the Beginnings of the Kabbalah in Languedoc [Hebrew]," *Tarbiz* 40 (1971), 483–507; Shahar, "Ecrits cathares et commentaire d'Abraham Abulafia sur le 'Livre de la création': Images et idées communes," in *JJL*, pp. 345–62; Wakefield, *Heresy*, p. 61; Judah M. Rosenthal's commentary to his edition of Jacob ben Reuben, *Milḥamot ha-Shem* (Jerusalem, 1963), p. 134; and on the limited truth to the Inquisition's accusations see *SRH*, 9:57–58; Lena Dasberg, *Untersuchungen über die Entwertung des Judenstatus im 11. Jahrhundert* (Paris, 1965), pp. 173–80; Louis Israel Newman, *Jewish Influence on Christian Reform Movements* (1925; repr., New York, 1966), pp. 134–43; Frank Ephraim Talmage, "An Hebrew Polemical Treatise, Anti-Cathar and Anti-Orthodox," *HTR* 60 (1967), 323–48, passim; and David Berger, "Christian Heresy and Jewish Polemic in the Twelfth and Thirteenth Centuries," *HTR* 68 (1975), 287–303. See also Yosef Hayim Yerushalmi, "The Inquisition and the Jews of France at the Time of Bernard Gui," *HTR* 63 (1970), 341–42, which argues that Bernard Gui's silence on this question of Jewish-Cathari connections shows that there must not have been any.

organization, *universitas*, that, to the limit of the terms designated for you by the authority of the Apostolic See with respect to holding inquiry against heretics, concerning the aforesaid, whether done by Christians, or even by Jews, having diligently and faithfully sought out the truth of the matter, you are to proceed against Christians whom you shall have discovered to have committed such things in the same way as against heretics; Jews, however, whom you shall have discovered inducing Christians of either sex into their execrable rite, before this, or in the future, these you are to punish with due penalty.[38]

The papacy must have viewed this as a very important function of the Inquisition, since Clement's *Turbato corde* was reissued by Gregory X in 1274 and again by Nicholas IV in 1288 and in 1290; in the next century, the Dominican inquisitor Nicholas Eymeric cited *Turbato corde* as the justification for inquisitorial proceedings against Jews who associated with such relapsed converts.[39] A bull which included provision for inquisitorial jurisdiction over the children of the *relapsi*, *Sicut nobis significare curastis*, was issued to mendicant inquisitors by Nicholas III in 1277 and confirmed by Nicholas IV in 1288. The latter reiterated his appeal for zealousness on the part of the friars in *Ad augmentum catholicae fidei* only two years later. And a similar decree by Boniface VIII became a lasting provision of canon law by virtue of its inclusion in the *Liber sextus*.[40] Finally, the Inquisition naturally took pains to shield Christians from heterodox ideas. Just as it attempted to enforce decrees ban-

---

38. Ripoll, *Bullarium*, 1:489; trans. in Edward A. Synan, *The Popes and the Jews in the Middle Ages* (New York, 1965), p. 118.

39. Ripoll, *Bullarium*, 1:517, 2:22; Joannes Sbaralea et al., eds., *Bullarium franciscanum romanorum pontificum*, 7 vols. (Rome, 1759–1904), 4:173. See Nicholas Eymeric, *Directorium inquisitorum* 2.44.3–4 (Rome, 1578), p. 242, for the citation of *Turbato corde*; 2.46, pp. 244–51, contains extensive justification for inquisitorial jurisdiction over the Jews. An interesting account of a trial of Jews of Manosque on the basis of *Turbato corde* has been published by Joseph Shatzmiller, "L'Inquisition et les Juifs de Provence au XIIIᵉ siècle," *Provence historique* 93–94 (1973), 327–38. And on the overall significance of the bull in the deteriorating relationship between medieval Christians and Jews, see Solomon Grayzel, "Popes, Jews, and the Inquisition from 'Sicut' to 'Turbato,'" in *Essays on the Occasion of the Seventieth Anniversary of Dropsie University*, ed. Abraham I. Katsh and Leon Nemoy (Philadelphia, 1979), p. 173–88.

40. Ulysse Robert, "Catalogue des actes relatifs aux Juifs (1183–1300)," *REJ* 3 (1881), pp. 217, 219; Sbaralea, *Bullarium*, 4:136; *Sexti decretales* 5.2.13, in Friedberg, *Corpus*, 2:1075: "Contra Christianos, qui ad ritum transierint vel redierint Iudaeorum, etiamsi huiusmodi redeuntes, dum erant infantes, aut mortis metu, non tamen absolute aut praecise coacti, baptizati fuerint, erit tanquam contra haereticos, si fuerint de hoc confessi, aut per Christianos seu Iudaeos convicti, et, sicut contra fautores, receptatores et defensores haereticorum, sic contra fautores, receptatores et defensores talium est procedendum."

ning Christian lay ownership of Bibles and preaching of theology, so it naturally endeavored to apply regulations prohibiting Jews from debating religious questions with lay Christians.[41]

The exaggeration of Jewish support for Christian heretics and the extension of inquisitorial authority over Jews who consorted at all with judaizing Christians betray an anti-Jewish aggressiveness on the part of the Inquisition greater than that strictly necessary to defend the Church against the Jewish community, narrowing still further the already constrained niche permitted it in Christian Europe. Although the inquisitors were often limited in their access to the Jews themselves, the Dominicans and Franciscans found ways to strike at basic pillars of contemporary Judaism, thereby hindering the practice of daily Jewish life.

41. On the ownership of Bibles, see the decree of the Council of Toulouse in 1229 in J. D. Mansi et al., eds., *Sacrorum conciliorum nova et amplissima collectio*, 53 vols. (Florence and Rome, 1757–1927), 23:197; on the preaching of theology see the bulls of Innocent III, X.5.7.12 (1199), and of Alexander IV, *Sexti decretales* 5.2.2 (1254–61); and, on debate between Jews and Christians, see the decree of Gregory X in 1233 to the prelates of Germany, *Sufficere debuerat*, in Grayzel, *The Church and the Jews*, pp. 198–201, the regional legislation cited by Grayzel, p. 27, n. 24, and Peter Browe, *Die Judenmission im Mittelalter und die Päpste* (Rome, 1942), pp. 88–90.

3

The Attack on
Rabbinic Literature

The Augustinian policy of tolerating a Jewish presence in Christendom placed strict limitations on the rights and freedoms of European Jews. Ever since Christianity became the official religion of the Roman Empire late in the fourth century, the Church had endeavored to insure that Jews would by no means gain superiority over Christians or in any way enjoy greater privileges than they. Rather, the opposite—the degradation of the Jews—was necessary in order for them properly to fulfill their divinely ordained mission in the Diaspora. The Church expressed this concern in numerous synodal decrees and papal letters, which generally aimed either to prevent Christians from interacting with Jews or to restrict the political and economic rights of the Jewish community. During the early Middle Ages, additional factors combined with such legal means of discrimination to impinge upon Jewish security still further. Popular anti-Jewish sentiment occasionally erupted into violence, most notably in the eleventh century with the massacres of Jews that accompanied the First Crusade. The dangers of pogroms grew during the twelfth century, as the Crusades continued, as the Jews were driven more and more into the hated role of moneylender, and as the ritual murder charge first appeared in medieval Europe. The threat of physical violence made the Jews increasingly dependent upon the protection of Europe's kings and princes, who exploited Jewish weakness for their own financial gain, levying enormous tallages upon the Jews whenever their royal coffers grew bare.

Even so, despite the legal discrimination and the illegal harassment, the medieval European Jewish community continued to grow and to flourish, both economically and culturally. Perhaps this achievement resulted in part from the measure of religious and civil autonomy enjoyed by European Jews before the thirteenth century, the hardships that they suffered notwithstanding. Their theoretical right to live in Christendom as Jews—to regulate their own religious affairs, to solve their own doctrinal and philosophical disputes, and to determine their own cultural priorities—had not been questioned. Before the advent of the Dominicans and Franciscans, the Christian establishment protected this fundamental privilege. But with the appearance of the new orders and the Inquisition, the situation changed drastically. Within a generation after the deaths of Dominic and Francis, the friars spearheaded a major ecclesiastical attack on the religious life of medieval Jews, a campaign that first intervened in their community's internal religious politics and then proceeded to condemn rabbinic Judaism *in toto*.

The Maimonidean Controversy

When the scientific and metaphysical works of Aristotle began to reach Western Europe in the thirteenth century, the Church quite naturally reacted defensively. Preserved and nurtured by the rationalists among Muslim philosophers, Aristotelian ideas entered Christendom embellished by and understood in terms of obviously heretical speculative traditions—most notably those leading back to Averroës. The skepticism bred by the new philosophy posed an added threat to a Church already in the thick of combat against French and Italian dualists, and accordingly evoked a quick reaction. In 1210 a clerical council banned all study of Aristotle's works on natural philosophy at the University of Paris for three years, burned all the philosophical works of one David of Dinant, condemned various other heretics to the stake, sentenced still more to perpetual imprisonment, and even ordered the body of a deceased theological doctor named Amauri de Bène exhumed and reburied in unconsecrated ground in the disgrace of posthumous excommunication. The statutes of Robert de Courcon, Innocent III's legate in Paris in 1215, extended the previous ban to include Aristotelian metaphysics and enforced on all students in the faculty of arts an oath not to read heretical works. Gregory IX himself renewed the prohibition of the study of Aristotle in 1231 until such time as a censorship commission could expurgate all heterodoxy from his works. This ecclesiastical fear of philosophical skepticism provides the immediate background to the first clash between the mendicant Inquisition and the Jews.[1]

The incident occurred far away from the University of Paris but in the thick of inquisitorial activity, in the Provençal capital of Montpellier. Internal strife had plagued the southern French Jewish community since the death of Moses Maimonides in 1204, because of conflicting views as to the orthodoxy of Maimonidean philosophy. Just as Church authorities condemned Aristotle's works (and even ideas of Thomas Aquinas later in the century), so various elements in the rabbinate denounced the *Guide of the Perplexed* and philosophical portions of the *Mishneh Torah* (Maimonides' code of Jewish law) as guilty of rationalist, heresy-inducing skepticism. One of the most active anti-Maimunists of the period was Rabbi Solomon ben Abraham of Montpellier, who expended considerable energy in trying to have the study of Maimonidean works prohibited. Along with his disciples Rabbi David ben Saul and Rabbi Jonah ben Abraham Gerundi, Solomon turned for support to the Ashkenazic rabbis of northern France and managed to elicit various anti-Maimonidean decrees from them. He was less successful in Provence and Spain, however, and several rabbis there waged violent propaganda campaigns against him, which in turn led to the legislation of counterbans against the anti-Maimunists, as well as the repeal of the French edicts. Frustrated and angry, Solomon returned in 1232 to Montpellier, where the strange event involving the Inquisition took place.[2]

1. Rashdall, *The Universities*, 1:354ff.; Leff, *Paris and Oxford*, pp. 191ff. On the infiltration of Greek and Arabic philosophy into the West, see Etienne Gilson, *History of Christian Philosophy in the Middle Ages* (New York, 1955), pp. 179–224, and on the further condemnations of Aristotelian and Averroistic doctrines in the thirteenth century, pp. 385–427.

2. Owing to the paucity of sources, historiography of the Maimonidean controversy remains dreadfully inadequate. The best existing summaries of what transpired are probably Y. Baer, *A History*, 1:96–110; and Daniel J. Silver, *Maimonidean Criticism and the Maimonidean Controversy, 1180–1240* (Leiden, 1965), esp. pp. 148–98. On the date of the incident at Montpellier, 1232 or 1233, see Silver, p. 148, n. 1. On the participation of the Ashkenazic rabbis in the conflict, see Ephraim E. Urbach, "The Participation of German and French Scholars in the Controversy about Maimonides and His Works [Hebrew]," *Zion*, n.s. 12 (1947), 149–50; Joseph Shatzmiller, "Towards a Picture of the First Maimonidean Controversy [Hebrew]," *Zion*, n.s. 34 (1969), 126–38; Shatzmiller, "A Letter from Rabbi Asher ben Gershom to the Rabbis of France at the Time of the Controversy about the Works of Maimonides [Hebrew]," in *Studies in the History of the Jewish People and the Land of Israel in Memory of Zvi Avneri*, ed. A. Gilboa et al. (Haifa, 1970), pp. 129–40; and Azriel Shohat, "Concerning the First Controversy on the Writings of Maimonides [Hebrew]," *Zion*, n.s. 36 (1971), 27–45.

The handful of documents that describe what occurred at Montpellier in 1232 or 1233 unfortunately derive almost entirely from pro-Maimunist sources, and some have therefore questioned their credibility. Nonetheless, there must have been some kernel of truth to the story to arouse all the bitter reactions. First, in a recently discovered circular letter directed to the Jewish communities in Spain, warning them not to accept the anti-Maimonidean decrees of northern France, the rabbis of Lunel and Narbonne thus described the actions of Solomon and his followers:

> Who has heard of such a scandal concerning men of good repute, in which children of the faith have gone to serve a foreign faith, to disgrace an oath and violate a covenant—the covenant which the Israelites struck with the Lord to be his people? And they have made it [the covenant] the object of curse and execration—the heretical evildoers of Montpellier who collaborate with the Baal of Peor [a derisive allusion to the God of Christianity; cf. Numbers 25:5], and who follow the advice of Balaam ben Beor [Rabbi Solomon?] to break down the defenses of the faith in many ways and to lead our people over all the earth into utter destruction. For they turned to men of power and deceit; they went to the deceived and deceiving Minorites, the squeaking and gibbering Preachers. Scoffing, with no understanding, they revealed to them hidden secrets of the Torah, and they turned over the holy books for burning at the hands of the Christian authorities. And they called that painful day a day of relief, making it a day of rejoicing . . . feasting at the time of ruin.[3]

Soon thereafter, Rabbi David Qimḥi of Narbonne, who had journeyed to Spain on behalf of the Maimunist cause, wrote of Solomon to the influential Spanish Jewish physician, Rabbi Judah Alfakhar:

> When he saw that the rabbis of France turned their backs upon him, regarding him a fool and recognizing him to be a bearer of false testimony, he turned to the idolators and appealed to them, and they hearkened to him to help in his actions against the Jews. He applied first to all the barefoot Minorites and said to them, "Behold, most of our people are unbelievers and heretics, for they were led astray by the words of Rabbi Moses of Egypt, who wrote heretical books. Now, while you are exterminating the heretics among you, exterminate our heresies as well and order the burning of those books, namely, *The Book of Knowledge* [the philosophical introductory volume of the *Mish-*

3. Shatzmiller, "Towards a Picture," p. 141; on the interpretation of this passage, see Shoḥat, "Concerning the First Controversy," p. 46.

neh Torah] and the *Guide*." And his uncircumcised heart did not rest until he applied also to the preachers (Predicatores) and to the priests, making the same request, until the matter reached the cardinal, putting the Jews of Montpellier and its satellite communities in great danger, and exposing them to the mockery and ridicule of the Gentiles. The wicked report spread from city to city, and they—the Christian clergy—said: "Behold the Torah of the Jews is in ruin; for they have split into two sects over it. And there is no true faith except ours."[4]

At virtually the same time, Judah and Abraham ibn Ḥasdai, leaders of Barcelona Jewry, issued a pro-Maimonidean decree which they sent to all the communities of Castile and Aragon.

When their hope had vanished and their counsel was not upheld by the French sages . . . , they banded together . . . , and they handed the *Book of Knowledge* and the *Guide* over to the priests and the prelates and the Minorites, and they said to them: "Why do you weary yourselves and traverse the distant seas to the end of the world in pursuit of heretics, in order to eliminate the evil from your midst? We too have heretical works, called the *Book of Knowledge* and the *Guide*, guilty of terrible crimes. On you is the obligation to guard us from error in the exact same way as yourselves. Arise, set upon them, expose them as empty vessels; if you hurry, you will catch them; light a fire in their midst. Do not return until you have exposed them." For they showered them with gifts . . . and gave them all clothing. . . . Nevertheless, nothing materialized . . . , and again they plotted designs of evil and guile. . . . They beseeched them [the Christians] before their judges and officials. . . . They repeated their folly and like dogs returned to their vomit. They came begging and pleading to the Franciscans, the high clergy, and the Dominicans . . . , asking them to wreak judgment upon the surviving holy books. At their command a huge bonfire was built, and they took the "bar of gold and fine mantle" [see Joshua 7:21], the two exalted tablets of the covenant [metaphors for the two works of Maimonides], and they broke them for the second time by burning them.[5]

4. This translation and the three that follow have borrowed from those in Y. Baer, *A History*, 1:400–401, n. 60. For the original of Qimḥi's letter, see Moses ben Maimon, *Qoveṣ Teshuvot*, ed. Abraham Lichtenberg (Leipzig, 1859; pts. 2–3 repr., Jerusalem, 1970), 3:4b. On Qimḥi's role in the controversy, cf. Frank Ephraim Talmage, *David Kimhi: The Man and the Commentaries*, Harvard Judaic Monographs 1 (Cambridge, Mass., 1975), pp. 27–39.

5. Moritz Steinschneider et al., eds., "Milḥemet ha-Dat: Qevuṣat Mikhtavim be-ʿInyenei ha-Maḥloqet ʿal Sefer ha-Moreh weha-Madaʿ ʿim Heʾarot," *Jeschurun* 8 (1871), 49–50.

The event shook the entire Jewish population of Europe and even that of the Near East. Rabbi Joseph ben Todros ha-Levi Abulafia of Toledo, who once had voiced anti-Maimonidean sentiments, after the incident at Montpellier decried what had happened:

> It is not right to turn Israel over to the uncircumcised Gentiles and to let our enemies be our judges, they whose word and deed seek to sully our honor and mar our glory, to subject our Torah to false interpretation, and to bundle and hurl us about like a ball. . . . And certainly [it is not right] when they [Jews] carry their controversy for judgment to our lord the bishop . . . , in whose hand the beauty of the Torah decomposes, the savor of the Torah becomes putrid, and the Torah itself is consigned to the flames. This is what led to the burning of this book by the clergy, and the vilifying, blaspheming enemy feasted and grew fat upon seeing God's word burnt, going up in smoke.[6]

Rabbi Samuel ben Abraham Saporta similarly reproached the rabbis of northern France for having issued their anti-Maimonidean decrees: "the Divine Name was profaned publicly, and the cause of idolatry was advanced before the eyes of the Gentiles as our faith was desecrated, when the principles of these books were revealed in their midst, and even more so when they were judged by them in their courts."[7] News of the event even reached the Jewish community of Egypt, where Maimonides' son Abraham lamented it in his *Sefer Milḥamot ha-Shem* (Book of the wars of the Lord).[8]

These accounts, which rocked the stability of Jewish life in the thirteenth century, have also penetrated much of modern Jewish historiography, giving credence to the popular tale that Maimonides' books were burned in the streets. Some writers have simply echoed the basic message of the sources: that Dominican and Franciscan friars burned Maimonides' writings at the instigation of Rabbi Solomon ben Abraham and his followers.[9] Other scholars have al-

6. Ibid., p. 43.
7. Ibid., p. 154.
8. Abraham ben Moses Maimonides, *Milḥamot ha-Shem*, ed. Reuben Margalioth (Jerusalem, 1958), pp. 54–56.
9. See Heinrich Graetz, *Geschichte der Juden*, 3d (used for vols. 6–7 quoted herein) and 4th eds., 11 vols. (Leipzig, 1873–1911), 7:53–56; Moritz Güdemann, *Geschichte des Erziehungswesens und der Cultur der abendländischen Juden während des Mittelalters und der neueren Zeit*, 3 vols. (1880–88; repr., Amsterdam, 1966), 1:59; Newman, *Jewish Influence*, pp. 317–18; Abraham A. Neuman, *The Jews in Spain: Their Social, Political and Cultural Life*, 2 vols. (Philadelphia, 1942), 2:122; *SRH*, 9:63; Judah M. Rosenthal, "Ha-Wikkuaḥ ha-'anti-Maimuni ba-'Aspeqlariah shel ha-Dorot," in his

lowed a propensity for myth to invade their accounts of all the attacks of the Inquisition on Jewish books, virtually abandoning any grip on factual historicity. Joseph Sarachek, for instance, concluded as follows: "In 1210, the Physics and Metaphysics of Aristotle had been ordered burnt by the Dominicans. The Talmud and other Hebrew books had been burnt by the Church. The *Guide* was only another book found objectionable for spreading Aristotelian ideas."[10] The Dominican order did not yet exist in 1210, nor were Aristotle's works then burned, nor had the Talmud been burned or even attacked by the Church at that time. The only truth in Sarachek's account is that the Inquisition may have found Maimonides objectionable because of his reliance on Aristotle. Other authorities, however, doubt the accuracy of the Maimunist accounts on several grounds. First, although evidence exists that those who actually informed to the Inquisition were punished by having their tongues cut out, never were Solomon ben Abraham and Jonah Gerundi mentioned in this regard; on the contrary, subsequent reports reveal that they were held in great esteem by Jews of France and Spain.[11] Second, except for David Qimḥi's letter, none of the documents directly accuses Solomon of informing to the Christian clergy. Because both Qimḥi and the brothers Ibn Ḥasdai seem to have learned of the story from the same source—witness the strange detail common to both their accounts that at least two betrayals to the friars were necessary it remains quite possible that Qimḥi merely embellished his own version to incriminate his enemy Solomon.[12] And third, especially when stripped of their biblical imagery and obvious bias, some of the documents—the letter from Lunel and Narbonne, and even that of Qimḥi—do not establish that the great bonfire ever took place, only that it was plotted. Such discrepancies have led to a number of interesting alternative conclusions. Ephraim Urbach has suggested that pro-

Studies and Texts in Jewish History, Literature and Religion [Hebrew], 2 vols. (Jerusalem, 1967), 1:135; Moshe Carmilly-Weinberger, *Censorship and Freedom of Expression in Jewish History* (New York, 1977), p. 36; and Charles Touati, "Les deux conflits autour de Maimonide et des études philosophiques," in *JJL*, p. 176. Martin A. Cohen, "Reflections on the Text and Context of the Disputation of Barcelona," *HUCA* 35 (1964), 170, has apparently accepted the doubtful report of Hillel of Verona (see below, n. 16) that Maimonides' books were burned in the squares of Paris.

10. Joseph Sarachek, *Faith and Reason: The Conflict over the Rationalism of Maimonides*, 1 (Williamsport, Pa., 1935), 87.

11. See above, n. 8, and Silver, *Maimonidean Criticism*, pp. 153–56.

12. Silver, *Maimonidean Criticism*, p. 153; Shatzmiller, "Towards a Picture," pp. 133–34; Shoḥat, "Concerning the First Controversy," p. 45.

Maimunist propagandists may have fabricated the whole story. Yet most acceptable are the more moderate interpretations of Yitzhak Baer, Daniel Silver, and A. Shoḥat, who suggest, with only slight differences, that the *Guide* and *Book of Knowledge* were handed over to the Christian clergy and that parts may even have been burned, but that the noted anti-Maimunist rabbis were themselves probably not responsible for the betrayal.[13]

Until scholars unearth more evidence, one cannot be sure about the extent of the actual burning and the role of Solomon ben Abraham. For purposes of this book, however, the well-known documents quoted have considerable importance. All the sources corroborate the interest in the orthodoxy of Jewish writings taken by the Dominican and Franciscan inquisitors at Montpellier, then working under the direction of the papal legate Cardinal Romanus, the "cardinal" or "bishop" mentioned by Qimḥi and Joseph ben Todros Abulafia;[14] on this particular point, no ulterior motive could have led them to depart from a straightforward account of what occurred. The letter from Lunel and Narbonne expresses no amazement at the fact that the friars would have willingly consigned a Jewish heretical work to the flames. Qimḥi notes that the involvement of the Cardinal-inquisitor in the affair boded ill for all of the surrounding Jewish communities; was the Inquisition perhaps actively looking for an excuse to strike out at the Jews? In the epistle of the ibn Ḥasdai brothers, the informers admonish the friars, "On you is the obligation to guard us from error." It is doubtful that the zealous inquisitors had to take instruction in the extent of their duties from dissident Jews; rather, here was the Inquisition's own rationale for involvement in the dispute, which this pro-Maimunist source spitefully placed in the mouths of its opponents. Whether the informers did actually bribe the friars, as the ibn Ḥasdai brothers relate, or this detail too just added to the epistle's defamation of the anti-Maimunists, the satisfaction of the clerics at having condemned these books, as described by Joseph ben Todros, appears extremely plausible. Indeed, Samuel Saporta's account confirms that a formal judicial proceeding did occur "in their courts ['arka-'ot]"; for this to have happened, the Inquisition must have had a clear and vested interest in what transpired.[15]

13. Urbach, "The Participation," pp. 156ff.; Y. Baer, *A History*, 1:105–10; Silver, *Maimonidean Criticism*, p. 156; Shoḥat, "Concerning the First Controversy," p. 50.

14. Silver, *Maimonidean Criticism*, p. 153; Lea, *A History*, 1:202,316.

15. Cf. the suggestion of J. L. Teicher, "Christian Theology and the Jewish Opposition to Maimonides," *Journal of Theological Studies*, o.s. 43 (1942), 68–76, that be-

Any pro-Maimunist bias notwithstanding, these Jewish writers recognized the grave dangers involved in the Inquisition's unprecedented intrusion into internal Jewish affairs. The ecclesiastical institution established to defend Christian orthodoxy now appeared willing and eager to try and equate Jews with heretics. Previously, Jews had usually enjoyed complete doctrinal autonomy; even the Christian polemics had not attacked them or their religious practice so much as an inaccurate, strictly biblical conception of what Judaism once was. Now the friars, perhaps spurred on by the fear of Aristotelian ideas and certainly in a new mood of anti-Jewish zeal which far exceeded the legal prerogative of even the most conscientious inquisitors, undertook to pass judgment on what constituted heresy for Jews as regarded their own Judaism. Judaizing among Christians could naturally fall under inquisitorial jurisdiction as heresy. But never before had the Church presumed to interfere with current rabbinic theology, enforcing one doctrinal opinion as opposed to another on the Jews of its own day.

The Church's interest in contemporary Jewish life that began with the Maimonidean controversy boded ill for the Jews, a fact of which one Jewish writer of the late thirteenth century, Rabbi Hillel of Verona, was well aware.

Burning [Maimonides' works] alone did not suffice for them [the anti-Maimunists]; they transferred the fire with which they burned them from the large candle that was lit in the great convent of Paris before the altar; the priests lit the fire and set it to the books which were burned in the streets of Paris before all the people. . . . The Lord looked down from heaven and was jealous for the honor of our holy teacher [Maimonides] and his books, and he sent his wrath upon the community of France and did not even spare his Torah. . . . And therefore, my brother, do not be amazed if the Lord punished the Torah study of the rabbis of France for the sake of Rabbi Moses and did not spare their copies of the Talmud. And he looked down upon them in a pillar of cloud and fire until he aroused the entire [Christian] clergy against them. The great persecutions were then renewed: the communities were butchered, more than three thousand souls; all their copies of the Talmud were consigned to the flames; and then was enacted the decree against public study of the Talmud, in force to this very day. And if you ask, how does one know that those burnings were on account of the burning of the *Guide* and the *Book of Knowledge*,

cause of the Aristotelian ideas in Maimonides' works, the Inquisition would have proceeded against them entirely of its own accord; the rabbis Solomon and Jonah were thus only witnesses at an inquisitorial tribunal.

I answer with the following proof: forty days did not pass from the burning of our teacher's works until that of the Talmud; all the orders and commentaries [of the Talmud] found in Paris were burned in the very same place; and the ashes of the Talmud were mixed with those of the *Guide* and the *Book of Knowledge*, since there was still ash at the site.[16]

Writing at least half a century after the incident at Montpellier in 1232, Hillel has obviously confused it with the great burning of the Talmud at Paris early in the next decade, and his account can hardly be considered factual. Nonetheless, the thrust of his argument reveals the perspective of contemporary Jews. The anti-Maimunists may well have introduced the fire of the Inquisition into their attack on Jewish books. And hardly had the first storm subsided than a new one arose in its place. "The great persecutions were then renewed. . . ."

The Condemnation of the Talmud

"The sentence, *habent sua fata libelli* [books have their own destiny], applies to no monument of literature better than to the Talmud."[17] Heinrich Graetz did not exaggerate. For centuries the mainstay of Jewish civilization, the Talmud suddenly became a prime target of Christian anti-Judaism.

In 1236, Nicholas Donin of La Rochelle, a Jewish convert to Christianity and possibly a Franciscan as well, approached Pope Gregory IX with a list of charges against rabbinic Judaism—the postbiblical, "oral" tradition to which the Jews of his day adhered. Donin leveled most of his accusations against the Talmud, but he also used Jewish liturgy, rabbinic commentaries on the Bible and Talmud, and various collections of midrashim to substantiate his charges.[18] Historians have disagreed as to Donin's motivations. Some

16. Eliezer Ashkenazi, ed., *Ṭaʿam Zeqeinim* [Hebrew] (Frankfurt, 1854), p. 71. Hillel's account is the only source that relates the burning of the Talmud to the slaughter of Jews in France. Perhaps he refers to the attacks on French Jewish communities during the Shepherds' Crusade of 1251; see Abraham David, "Pogroms against French Jewry during the Shepherds' Crusade of 1251 [Hebrew]," *Tarbiz* 46 (1977), 251–57.

17. H. Graetz, "Die Schicksale des Talmud im Verlaufe der Geschichte," *MGWJ* 34 (1885), 529.

18. See the prologue to Donin's *Articuli litterarum pape*, in Isidore Loeb, "La controverse de 1240 sur le Talmud," *REJ* 2 (1881), 252: "Anno enim ab incarnacione

have seen in his plaints the anti-rabbinic leanings of the Karaites and suppose that he actually had access to various Karaitic manuscripts. Others view Donin as one who had come under the influence of rationalist philosophy—perhaps that of Maimonides—to the extreme point of growing disenchanted with much of the Talmud and rabbinic tradition. If Maimonides' works were ever burned as a result of rabbinic opposition to them, such an event may have given Donin the impetus to leave Judaism altogether and accept baptism. Whatever motivated him, his outspoken opinions had led his Jewish teachers to anathematize him some eleven years prior to his audience with the pope.[19]

Domini MCCXXXVI circiter, pater misericordiarum Iudeum quemdam nomine Nicholaum Donin de Rupella vocavit ad fidem in hebreo plurimum eruditum eciam secundum testimonium Iudeorum, ita ut in natura et gramatica sermonis ebraici vix sibi similem inveniret. Hic accessit ad sedem apostolicam et bone memorie Gregorii pape, pontificatus eius anno XII, predictorum librorum nephandam detexit maliciam et qousdam specialiter expressit articulos super quibus ad reges Francie, Anglie, et Hyspanie litteras apostolicas impetravit, ut si in prefatis libris contingeret talia reperiri, igni faccrent eos tradi."

19. On the history of Donin's life, see Alexander Kisch, "Die Anklageartikel gegen den Talmud und ihre Vertheidigung durch Rabbi Jechiel ben Joseph vor Ludwig dem Heiligen in Paris," *MGWJ* 23 (1874), 124–26; Grayzel, *The Church and the Jews*, pp. 339–40; and Merchavya, *The Church*, pp. 229–40. The view that Donin was of Karaitic leanings is espoused by Grayzel; Yitzhak Baer, "The Disputations of R. Yechiel of Paris and of Nachmanides [Hebrew]," *Tarbiz* 2 (1931), 173, and *A History*, 1:151; *SRH*, 9:64; Blumenkranz, "Jüdische und christliche Konvertiten," p. 279; and especially Judah M. Rosenthal, "The Talmud on Trial," *JQR*, n.s. 47 (1956), 64–69, 145–69 with nn., passim. This opinion finds some documentary support in the account by the thirteenth-century Dominican Thomas of Cantimpré, of the attacks on the Talmud, *Bonum universale de apibus* 1.3.6, ed. Georgius Colvenerius (Douay, 1627), p. 18: "Nota autem lector, quod omnes Orientales Iudaei, haereticos et excommunicatos reputant hos Iudaeos, qui contra legem Moysi et Prophetas, hunc librum, qui Thalmud dicitur, recipiunt et conscribunt." Kisch; A. Lewin, "Die Religionsdisputation des R. Jechiel von Paris 1240 am Hofe Ludwigs des Heiligen, ihre Veranlassung und ihre Folge," *MGWJ* 18 (1869), 100–101; and Merchavya, *The Church*, p. 233, on the other hand, prefer to see Donin as a rationalist skeptic greatly incensed by the Maimonidean controversy. Furthermore, Karaism's indictment of rabbinism spread rapidly to Muslim and Christian polemicists, and Donin need not have been personally involved with Karaites in order to acquire his anti-rabbinic outlook; see Abraham ibn Daud, *Sefer ha-Qabbalah*, ed. Gerson D. Cohen (Philadelphia, 1967), pp. xliv–v and nn. Whichever of the two interpretations is correct, Donin's Jewish opponent at the disputation over the Talmud in 1240, Rabbi Yehiel ben Joseph, referred to him as "this sinner, who already apostasized with regard to rabbinic doctrine fifteen years ago, believing only in the written text of the Bible— without any oral interpretation"; see *Wikkuah*, p. 2. Lewin further maintains that it was Yehiel himself who had excommunicated Donin in 1225. Kisch; Merchavya, p. 237; and Charles Singer, "Hebrew Scholarship in the Middle Ages among Latin Christians," in *The Legacy of Israel*, ed. Edwyn R. Bevan and Charles Singer (Oxford, 1928), p. 295, all argue that Donin became a Franciscan after his conversion.

On June 9, 1239, Pope Gregory finally responded to Donin's petitions by dispatching him with a letter to William of Auvergne, bishop of Paris, to which he appended Donin's compilation of accusations (the *Articuli litterarum pape*) and instructions for William in turn to transmit to the archbishops and kings of France, England, and all of Spain and Portugal. The papal directive commanded that all the books of the Jews be confiscated on the first Sabbath of Lent in the following year—March 3, 1240—while the Jews would be at their synagogue services, and then be transferred to the Dominicans and Franciscans for safekeeping. On June 20, Gregory instructed William and the priors of the two mendicant orders in Paris that any of the books found to contain doctrinal error should be burned at the stake.[20] From the point of view of inquisitorial procedure, such a decree sufficed to burn the Talmud if only the secular authorities would lend their assistance. But even Louis IX of France, the only monarch who complied at all with the papal decree, demanded that the Jews first be given a chance to defend themselves and their books publicly, however predetermined the outcome of such a debate really may have been.[21] According to the Latin manuscript describing the whole judgment against the Tal-

20. Grayzel, *The Church and the Jews*, pp. 238–41. Salo Wittmayer Baron argues that the delay of three years between Donin's appeal to the pope and Gregory's response as well as the omission of the Empire in the list of addresses of the papal letters helps to demonstrate that the Talmud was used by the papacy as a ploy in its battle for power with Frederick II; see "'Plentitude of Apostolic Power' and Medieval 'Jewish Serfdom,'" in his *Ancient and Medieval Jewish History: Essays*, ed. Leon A. Feldman (New Brunswick, N.J., 1972), pp. 292–94, 527–28, 531. Shoḥat, "Concerning the First Controversy," p. 50, has made the intriguing suggestion that William too may have been influenced in his ideas by news of the Inquisition's attack on the works of Maimonides. As had Peter the Venerable, William in his *De universo* 1.3.31, a work completed in the early 1230s, wrote that the Jews had been led astray from their faith by the absurd fables of their rabbinic tradition, except for a few philosophers living among the Saracens who retained their rationalism. Several years later, however, in *De legibus*, ch. 1, William held that Aristotelian philosophy had led the Jews to heresy. Cf. Jacob Guttmann, *Die Scholastik des dreizehnten Jahrhunderts in ihren Beziehungen zum Judenthum* (1902; repr., Hildesheim, 1970), pp. 24–25, n. 2. On William's attitudes toward the Jews in general, see Guttmann, pp. 13–31; and Noel Valois, *Guillaume d'Auvergne, évêque de Paris (1228–1249): Sa vie et ses ouvrages* (Paris, 1880), pp. 118ff.

21. Merchavya, *The Church*, p. 227; Willehad Paul Eckert, "Hoch- und Spätmittelalter—katholischer Humanismus," in *Kirche und Synagoge: Handbuch zur Geschichte von Christen und Juden*, ed. Karl Heinrich Rengstorf and Siegfried von Kortzfleisch, 2 vols. (Stuttgart, 1968–70), 1:228. Kisch, "Die Anklageartikel," pp. 73–75, suggests that the king may have demanded a debate simply for his own pleasure, as well as that of his mother. On Louis IX's interest in religious disputation, see Jean de Joinville, *Histoire de Saint Louis* §§ 50–53, ed. M. Natalis de Wailly, 2d ed. (Paris, 1874), pp. 28–31.

mud, two types of proceedings took place. The first probably comprised the famous disputation between Nicholas Donin and Rabbi Yeḥiel ben Joseph of Paris, held under royal auspices and presided over by the queen mother, Blanche of Castile. The second kind of proceeding may have consisted of more formal inquisitorial interrogations conducted before a panel of distinguished judges, headed by Eudes de Chateauroux, chancellor of the University of Paris. Yeḥiel and three other noted French rabbis, Judah ben David of Melun, Samuel ben Solomon of Château-Thierry, and Moses ben Jacob of Coucy, were ordered to appear before this inquest; but when the first two offered similar testimony under separate interrogation—Yeḥiel on June 25–26, 1240, and Judah on June 27—the other two were left unquestioned.[22] The clerical court found the Talmud guilty as charged and condemned it to the stake. The Jews managed to forestall execution of the sentence by bribing one of the bishops on the tribunal to intercede with the king. But the prelate soon died, Louis IX regarded the death as ominous, and perhaps after further official inquiry twenty or twenty-four wagonloads of manuscripts—probably ten to twelve thousand volumes—were burned in Paris in the Place de Grève over the course of one and one half days in 1242.[23]

22. Loeb, "La controverse," REJ 3 (1882), 55; see also Merchavya, *The Church*, p. 242. The occurrence of two separate inquiries would solve the discrepancy found by Y. Baer between the free-flowing, personal encounter between Donin and Yeḥiel as reported by the latter and the normally impersonal, terse, and direct questioning of defendants by anonymous judges which characterized inquisitorial proceedings; see "The Disputations," pp. 172–74. (Cf. Yerushalmi, "The Inquisition," pp. 350–51, n. 78, who agrees with Baer that the disputation over the Talmud in 1240 "was in reality an inquisition of the work.") Nevertheless, other sources do imply the identity of the supposedly distinct encounters. Rabbi Joseph ben Nathan Official, the student of Rabbi Yeḥiel who edited the latter's rendition of the debate with Donin, writes of that debate as equivalent to the separate interrogations of Yeḥiel and Rabbi Judah ben David by the clerical court; see Joseph's *Sepher Joseph ha-Mekane* [Hebrew], ed. Judah M. Rosenthal (Jerusalem, 1970), p. 141. Eudes de Chateauroux, when recounting to Innocent IV in 1247 the events of 1240, spoke only of one official inquiry, that over which he had presided; see Grayzel, *The Church and the Jews*, p. 276. Moreover, except for the letters of Gregory IX, no Latin source at all mentions Nicholas Donin, not to speak of his debate with Yeḥiel; only the *confessiones* of the latter and his colleague Judah to the tribunal of Eudes have been recorded: Loeb, "La controverse," REJ 3 (1882), 55–57. For other reconstructions of the proceedings of 1240, see Graetz, *Geschichte*, 7:94–98; Lewin, "Die Religionsdisputation," pp. 97–110, 145–56, 193–210; A. Kisch, "Die Anklageartikel," pp. 10–18, 62–75, 123–30, 155–63, 204–12; *SRH*, 9:64–67; J. M. Rosenthal, "The Talmud," pp. 58–76, 145–69; and Robert Chazan, *Medieval Jewry in Northern France: A Political and Social History* (Baltimore, 1973), pp. 124–33.

23. The story of the bribe and the subsequent death of its recipient appears in Thomas of Cantimpré, *Bonum universale* 1.3.6., pp. 17–18. For different identifications

In 1244, Innocent IV asked Louis IX to burn any copies of the Talmud which could be found to have survived the first auto-da-fé. This time, however, the Jews appealed the sentence directly to Rome, and complaining that they could not practice their religion without the Talmud, they persuaded Innocent to reopen the inquiry. The pope commissioned a legatine tribunal, again headed by Eudes de Chateauroux (now cardinal-bishop of Tusculum). The new court reviewed the evidence and findings of earlier proceedings only to renew the guilty verdict, this time with a list of over forty illustrious signatories from the academic and clerical communities of Paris.[24]

---

of the bishop bribed by the Jews, see Graetz, *Geschichte*, 7:404–5; Arié Serper, "Le debat entre Synagogue et Eglise au XIIIᵉ siècle," *REJ* 123 (1964), 312; and *SRH*, 9:271, n. 14, proposing Archbishop Walter of Sens; and Valois, *Guillaume d'Auvergne*, pp. 132–33, who insists on Archbishop Eudes Clement of Rouen. Baron, *SRH*, 9:277, n. 28, suggests that the bribe may have been negotiated by Joseph Official. Likewise, the documentary evidence is not entirely clear as to the number of talmudic volumes actually burned or the date of the auto-da-fé. Rabbi Hillel of Verona, in the same letter quoted in n. 16, reported that 1200 books perished, although *SRH*, 9:270, n. 10, corrects this figure to 12,000 (twenty-four wagonloads). The preface to Donin's *Articuli*, in Loeb, "La controverse," *REJ* 2 (1881), 252, mentions twenty wagonloads, while both the thirteenth-century Hebrew writer Zedekiah ben Abraham ʿAnaw, *Sefer Shibbolei ha Leqet ha-Shalem*, ed. Solomon Buber (Vilna, 1886), p. 252, and the fourteenth-century *Annales erphordenses*, MGH SS 16:37, speak of twenty-four. Whatever the exact number, it was enormous enough to stimulate the composition of elaborate, if bitter, poetic laments among medieval Jewish poets; see, for instance, that of Rabbi Meir of Rothenburg in A. M. Haberman, ed., *Sefer Gezeirot ʾAshkenaz we-Ṣarefat* (Jerusalem, 1945), pp. 183–85. Zedekiah wrote that the burning took place in 1244, while the *Annales erphordenses* gives the date of 1242. Scholars have long debated the question, arriving at still other conclusions, but the most plausible date still seems to be that of Graetz, *Geschichte*, 7:404–5, who adhered to 1242. Cf. Loeb, "La controverse," *REJ* 1 (1880), 248; Newman, *Jewish Influence*, p. 319; Ephraim E. Urbach, *The Tosaphists: Their History, Writing and Methods* [Hebrew], 4th ed., 2 vols. (Jerusalem, 1980), 1:453–54; *SRH*, 9:271, n. 14; S. Ch. Kook, "The Date of the Burning of the Talmud in France [Hebrew]," *KS* 29 (1953), 281; and D. Tamar, "More on the Date of the Burning of the Talmud in France [Hebrew]," ibid., pp. 430–31. For the location of the auto-da-fé—i.e., the particular spot in Paris—see Blumenkranz, "Jüdische und christliche Konvertiten," p. 281.

24. Grayzel, *The Church and the Jews*, pp. 250–53, 275–80, with nn. On August 12, 1247, Innocent wrote to Louis IX to explain the reopening of the proceedings: "Sane magistris Judeorum regni tui nuper proponentibus coram nobis et fratribus nostris quod sine illo libro qui hebraice Talmut dicitur, bibliam et alia statuta sue legis secundum fidem ipsorum intelligere nequeunt, nos qui juxta mandatum divinum in eadem lege ipsos tolerare tenemur, dignum eis duximus respondendum quod sicut eos ipsa lege sic perconsequens suis libris nolumus injuste privare." On Eudes's life and career, see Merchavya, *The Church*, p. 354, n. 24. The official verdict of the legatine court is in Heinrich Denifle, ed., *Chartularium universitatis parisiensis*, 4 vols. (Paris, 1889–97), 1:209–11.

Three sources of information help to illuminate our picture of these events. First, the extant papal correspondence on the subject, as well as that of the legate Eudes, reveals the underlying goals and motivations of the Church in attacking the Talmud. Second, and most important, Eudes directed the compilation—probably in large part by converts from Judaism—of a long volume attacking the Talmud, still extant in the Bibliothèque Nationale in Paris. In addition to prefaces, indices, and supplementary notes, the manuscript contains a collection of objectionable excerpts from the Talmud and Jewish liturgy arranged according to topic, over one hundred folios listing the passages in the order of their appearance in the Talmud (*Extractiones de Talmut*), a listing of noxious passages from the Jewish prayerbook, the thirty-five *Articuli litterarum pape* or specific accusations compiled by Nicholas Donin and issued by Gregory IX with his letters of June 1239, and the "confessions" of Rabbis Yeḥiel (Vivo de Meaux in the Latin) and Judah allegedly made during the interrogations in 1240. Except for their occasionally too literal rendition of talmudic idiom, the Latin translators did not depart from the meaning of the original, and their work is therefore of value even to modern rabbinic scholars wishing to ascertain the original reading of obviously bowdlerized or otherwise unclear passages in the Talmud.[25] Third, Rabbi Yeḥiel's Hebrew account of his disputation with Donin, edited some years later by his student Rabbi Joseph ben Nathan Official, helps to balance our impression by revealing the essence of the attack as viewed by the Jews. Despite its difference in literary genre from the Latin manuscript and its naturally opposing polemical bias, the Hebrew pro-

25. For a description of the Paris B.N. MS Lat. 16558 and its contents, see Loeb, "La controverse," *REJ* 1 (1880), 247–61, 2 (1881), 248–52; Merchavya, *The Church*, pp. 249–348; and J. M. Rosenthal, "The Talmud," pp. 74–76. Loeb, "La controverse," *REJ* 2 (1881), 252–70, 3 (1882), 39–57, has published the *confessiones* of the rabbis and, together with an annotated French translation, the Latin *Articuli* and their supporting talmudic quotations. Rosenthal, pp. 145–66, gives an English translation of the *Articuli* and quotes the excerpts from the Talmud in their original; and Merchavya, pp. 363–418, provides an index of all the quotations from Jewish sources found in the manuscript. Because the anti-talmudic polemic played a great role in the anti-Jewish arguments of Christians for centuries to come, Eudes's compilation enjoyed considerable use by others, and manuscript copies of at least parts of the *Extractiones de Talmut* have been found in libraries all over Europe. See Merchavya, p. 292 and n. 1; Joseph Klapper, "Ein florilegium talmudicum des 13. Jahrhunderts," *Literaturwissenschaftliches Jahrbuch der Görres-Gesellschaft* 1 (1926), 3–23; Erich Klibansky, "Beziehungen des christlichen Mittelalters zum Judentum," *MGWJ* 77 (1933), 456–63; and J. M. Millás Vallicrosa, "Extractos del Talmud y alusiones polemicas en un manuscrito de la Biblioteca Catedral de Gerona," *Sefarad* 20 (1960), 17–49.

tocol corroborates the impression gained from the Latin of what actually happened. Donin's arguments for the most part jibe with those of the *Articuli litterarum pape*, and the substance of Yehiel's responses can without too much difficulty be discerned in his confession.[26] Moreover, even though some modern writers have labeled the Hebrew protocol a prime example of literary polemic, using well-known forensic motifs to reinforce popular Jewish belief rather than actually reporting what occurred, no one denies the possibility of extracting from it a valid impression of the arguments.[27]

What were the Church's underlying theological interests in pursuing this campaign against the Talmud? Prefacing his instructions to the prelates and monarchs of Europe to confiscate the Talmud, Gregory IX made the following complaint:

> If what is said about the Jews of France and of the other lands is true, no punishment would be sufficiently great or sufficiently worthy of their crime. For they, so we have heard, are not content with the Old Law which God gave to Moses in writing: they even ignore it completely, and affirm that God gave another Law which is called "Talmud," that is "Teaching," handed down to Moses orally. Falsely they allege that it was implanted within their minds and, unwritten, was there preserved until certain men came, whom they call "Sages" and "Scribes," men who, fearing that this Law may be lost from the minds of men through forgetfulness, reduced it to writing, and the volume of this by far exceeds the text of the Bible. In this is contained matter so abusive and so unspeakable that it arouses shame in those who mention it and horror in those who hear it. Wherefore . . . this is said to be the chief cause that holds the Jews obstinate in their perfidy.[28]

Gregory seems to have launched the campaign against the Talmud because he believed the Jews' reliance on their "oral" rabbinic legal tradition to constitute a shameful heresy. According to the pope, talmudic Judaism denoted a rejection of biblical religion, and without the Talmud, the Jews would be more likely to accede to the truth of Scripture and accept Christianity. In his letter of May 1244

26. The edition of the *Wikkuah* used herein, prepared by Samuel Grünbaum in 1873, was subsequently reprinted by Reuben Margalioth (Lemberg, n.d.) and, with many errors, by J. D. Eisenstein, *Ozar Wikuhim: A Collection of Polemics and Disputations* [Hebrew] (New York, 1928), pp. 81–86. A highly unreliable translation, made from Wagenseil's text, appears in Morris Braude, *Conscience on Trial* (New York, 1952), pp. 33–68. On Rabbi Joseph Official's role as the original editor of the pamphlet, see his *Sepher Joseph ha-Mekane*, pp. xviii, xxiii.

27. Y. Baer, "The Disputations," pp. 174–76; Urbach, *The Tosaphists*, 1:449.

28. Grayzel, *The Church and the Jews*, pp. 240–41.

to Louis IX, Innocent IV echoed and added to Gregory's accusations:

> The wicked perfidy of the Jews—from whose hearts our Redeemer, because of the enormity of their crime, has not removed the veil but has so far permitted it to remain in Israel in [Israel's] partial blindness—does not properly heed the fact that Christian piety received them and patiently allows them to live in Christendom through pity only. Instead, it [the perfidy] commits such grave sins as are stupefying to those who hear of them and horrible to those who tell of them. For, ungrateful to the Lord Jesus Christ, who, in the abundance of His kindliness, patiently expects their conversion, they [the Jews], displaying no shame for their guilt nor reverence for the honor of the Christian Faith, throw away and despise the Law of Moses and the prophets, and follow some tradition of their elders. On account of these same traditions the Lord reproves them in the Gospel saying: "Wherefore do you transgress the law of God, and render it void because of your traditions, teaching doctrines and commands of men?" In traditions of this sort they rear and nurture their children, which traditions are called "Talmud" in Hebrew. It is a big book among them, exceeding in size the text of the Bible. In it are found blasphemies against God and His Christ, and obviously entangled fables about the Blessed Virgin, and abusive errors, and unheard-of follies. But the laws and doctrines of the prophets they make their sons altogether ignorant. They fear that if the forbidden truth, which is found in the Law and the Prophets, be understood, and the testimony concerning the only-begotten Son of God, that he appeared in the flesh, be furnished, these [children] would be converted to the Faith and humbly return to their Redeemer.[29]

Again the pope reprimands the Jews for discarding their belief in the Old Testament in exchange for allegiance to the Talmud, also comparing the great size of the latter with the brevity of the Bible.[30] Two new elements, however, apear in Innocent's plaint. First, while Gregory contrasted the heretical aspects and absurdities of the Talmud with a true belief in Judaism, Innocent also stressed the talmudic blasphemy against Christianity. Second, Innocent spoke of the permissiveness of Christ—whose vicar and agent on earth was

29. Ibid., pp. 250–53, with several changes in Grayzel's translation.
30. As Synan, *The Popes and the Jews*, p. 112, has pointed out, the judgment of a book of law as heretical because its size exceeded that of the Bible is most surprising in the case of Innocent IV, a seasoned canonist and the author of a long gloss on the *Decretales* of Gregory IX.

Pope Innocent—with regard to the beliefs of the Jews "thus far" (*adhuc*); in other words, the pope intimated that the attack on the Talmud heralded a change in the Church's basic attitude toward Judaism. Three years later, the report of Bishop Eudes's legatine commission manifested an additional ecclesiastical concern.

> Whereas we found that these books were full of innumerable errors, abuses, blasphemies, and wickedness such as arouse shame in those that speak of them and horrify the hearer, to such an extent that these books cannot be tolerated in the name of God without injury to the Christian Faith, therefore, with the advice of those pious men whom we caused to be gathered especially for that purpose, we pronounced that the said books are unworthy of tolerance, and that they are not to be restored to the Jewish masters, and we decisively condemn them.[31]

Not only was the Talmud heretical with respect to biblical Judaism, and blasphemous against Christianity, but the presence of talmudic Judaism in Christian society threatened "injury to the Christian Faith." The Church had to assume the responsibility to obliterate it.

Such were the charges that the Latin anthology of Paris was compiled to substantiate. Their most thorough elaboration appears in Donin's list of thirty-five specific accusations, the *Articuli litterarum pape*, which divide well around the three basic indictments contained in the papal correspondence. The list begins with various particulars of the heresy inherent in the Jews' devotion to the Talmud. The Jews claim, according to Donin, that the Talmud comprises a law given to them by God, which they transmitted orally from one generation to the next. Longer than the Bible, the Talmud asserts that its rabbis are superior to the biblical prophets, that they must be obeyed by the Jews even to the absurd point of abrogating Mosaic Law, and that anyone who disregards their teaching deserves the death penalty. As a result, the Jews prevent their children from studying the Bible, placing the Talmud at the center of their educational curriculum. (At least fifteen of Donin's thirty-five accusations provide illustrations of the absurdity and heresy contained in rabbinic literature—mostly stories imputing human characteristics and weaknesses to God.) From the charge of doctrinal heresy Donin's list moves on to the hostility of the Talmud toward Christians. The rabbis allegedly instructed the Jews to kill Christians and ruled that Jews may blamelessly cheat and deceive Chris-

---

31. Grayzel, *The Church and the Jews*, pp. 278–79, n. 3.

tians in any way possible. Donin found the talmudic laws pertaining to the annulment of vows particularly infuriating, since he understood them as dealing specifically with transactions between Jews and Christians. Finally Donin's *Articuli* accuse the Talmud of anti-Christian blasphemy. The rabbis, he charged, called Jesus' mother an adulteress; they speak obscenely of Jesus, the pope, the Church, and Christianity; and they curse the Church daily in their prayers, believing that Christians are condemned to perpetual damnation, while sinful Jews suffer a maximum of only one year in hell or in purgatory.[32] Different historians may ascribe greater weight in the Christian indictment to the charges of Jewish heresy—that is, belief in the primacy of the Talmud as opposed to Scripture—or to the charges of anti-Christian blasphemy and hostility. But one can perhaps best evaluate the accusations by considering the impression they made on the Jewish disputants of 1240, the responses they elicited from them, and the way the Jewish editor recorded them in his dramatic rendition of the debate.[33]

Yehiel's report of his disputation with Donin as we have it corroborates our impression of the major elements of the Christian argument and their progression. The discussion begins with Donin's announcement that he intends to question Yehiel about the Talmud, which he states is only four hundred years old. In response, the rabbi exclaims that the rabbinic tradition under attack did not at all constitute such heretical innovation. All of world Jewry accepted its authority, which had already endured for 1500 years; even Jerome had written of the Jews' allegiance to the Talmud, a loyalty that had never come under Christian attack before Donin. On the contrary, Donin, in his opposition to talmudic Judaism, was the real heretic, justifiably excommunicated by the Jewish community fifteen years before the debate.

And you [the audience] know that every biblical statement needs an interpretation, and therefore [because of his rejection of the Talmud] we have excommunicated him and anathematized him. From then

---

32. The *Articuli* appear in Loeb, "La controverse," *REJ* 2 (1881), 253–69, 3 (1882), 39–54; they are translated by J. M. Rosenthal, "The Talmud," pp. 145–64.

33. Funkenstein, "Changes," pp. 137–41, emphasizes the charge of heresy; while Simon Dubnow, *Weltgeschichte des jüdischen Volkes*, 10 vols. (Berlin, 1925–30), 5:37f.; and Benzion Dinur, *Israel in the Diaspora* [Hebrew], 2d ed., 10 pts. (Tel Aviv, 1958–72), 2,2:507, stress the blasphemy. However much weight the charges of hostility to Christians carried, they certainly refute the contention of Ruth M. Ames, "The Source and Significance of 'The Jew and the Pagan,'" *Medieval Studies* 19 (1957), 42, that such accusations never entered medieval Christian anti-Jewish polemics.

until now he has plotted against us to destroy [us] completely. Yet in vain has he striven, because for it [the Torah—including its rabbinic interpretation] we shall die, and one who [even] touches it is like one who touches the pupil of our eye. And if you punish *us*, we [Jews] and this our law are dispersed throughout the whole world [punishing French Jewry for the Talmud will be of no avail]; in Babylonia, Persia, Greece, the lands of Islam, and the seventy nations beyond the rivers of Ethiopia—there this law of ours will still be found.[34]

Donin, who is constantly labeled an apostate in the protocol, then proceeds to ask his opponent if he believes in the Talmud, and Yeḥiel explains that the Jew must accept the Talmud's legal interpretation of Scripture, while belief in its legends, fables, and homilies remains optional.[35] As for the allegations of the Talmud's anthropomorphic heresies concerning God and its other absurdities, Yeḥiel responds by pointing to similar statements in the Bible—for example, that God at times regrets his past actions, as in his creation of sinful man or his selection of Saul as king; that God cries when upset; and the obviously symbolic tales that Lot's wife turned into salt and that Balaam's ass spoke.[36] The Talmud is indispensable in the reconciliation of ostensive contradictions in the Bible; without it, the Jew would not know how to behave. Although the Talmud, as a part of God's revelation to the Jews, is thus faithful to Scripture, Donin, in rejecting rabbinic tradition, is not.[37]

The debate soon turned to the charges of talmudic blasphemy against Christianity, substantiated by Donin with passages making very disparaging remarks about Jesus, his disciples, Mary, Joseph, and the Church. To the insinuation that the Talmud had led the Jews perversely to reject Jesus, Yeḥiel responded that the Talmud and the oral tradition of the rabbis could not thus be blamed, for two reasons. First, he maintained that the insults in question referred not to the Christian Jesus but to someone else. "Not every Louis born in France is the king of France. Has it not happened that two men were born in the same city, had the same name, and

34. *Wikkuaḥ*, p. 2.
35. Ibid., pp. 2–3. The contrast of Donin, the apostate (*min*) with Yehiel the believer (*ma'amin, Wikkuah*, p. 2) is a typical motif of medieval Jewish religious polemic; on the usage of the term *min* for an apostate, see Benzion Netanyahu, *The Marranos of Spain*, 2d ed. (Millwood, N.Y., 1973), p. 89, n. 15.
36. Gen. 19:26, Num. 22:28, *Wikkuaḥ*, p. 2; Gen. 6:6, 1 Sam. 15:11, *Wikkuaḥ*, pp. 6–7; Jer. 25:30, *Wikkuaḥ*, p. 14.
37. *Wikkuaḥ*, pp. 2–3.

died in the same manner? There are many such cases."[38] Second, if
rabbinic literature did not disparage the Christian Jesus, Yeḥiel also
had to affirm the Jewish refusal to accept him nonetheless, to prove
that Christianity ran counter to the very essence of Judaism, not
just to the Talmud. In other words, not the Talmud alone but
considerations much more basic were responsible for keeping the
Jews from converting to Christianity. The Jesus of the Talmud, who
is mentioned as condemned to wallow eternally in boiling excrement, had aroused the wrath of the rabbis for rejecting their Phar-
isaic tradition; the Christian Jesus "did not do this alone, but he
deceived and beguiled Israel, purported to be God, and denied the
essence of the faith." When forced to admit that one talmudic
passage mentioning the crimes of Jesus and his execution did indeed apply to the Christian Jesus, Yeḥiel still emphasized that the
Talmud was not responsible for maintaining this opinion among
Jews. "For they [the ancient rabbis] did not speak of him again,
and he was not mentioned in the whole Talmud except there, at
the time of the act [of his execution], and then only briefly, since in
their divine inspiration they saw that you would in the future
interrogate and investigate us in this matter." Just as in his response to Donin's charges of heresy in the Talmud, Yeḥiel began
his defense against the accusations of blasphemy with an attack on
his opponent. "From the day that you left our community fifteen
years ago, you have looked for a pretense to impugn us with
malicious slander."[39] The Jesus condemned to boiling excrement had
"mocked the words of the sages, not believing their teachings
but only the written Torah"; was Donin, previously described by
Yeḥiel in almost exactly the same terms, here receiving a warning?[40]

Yeḥiel relates that Donin, like the papal correspondence considered above, moved from the charges that the Talmud blasphemed
against God, thereby perverting the natural order in the universe,
to its alleged license of grossly unethical and unnatural behavior on
the part of Jews toward Gentiles (*goyim*). The Talmud, claimed
Donin, licensed murder, theft, and religious intolerance, and it
included strictures against trusting Gentiles, honoring them, or
even returning a lost piece of property to them. The worst outrage

38. Ibid., p. 6. On the motif of two Jesuses in the historiography of medieval
Jews, see Isidore Loeb, "Josef Haccohen et les chroniqueurs juifs," *REJ* 17 (1888),
254ff.
39. *Wikkuaḥ*, p. 4.
40. Ibid., pp. 24; see above, n. 19.

for Donin was the prayer in the Jews' daily liturgy uttered against Christians and apostates, which, along with other talmudic excerpts in question, he understood—in some cases correctly—as a direct attack on the Church.[41] The rabbinic treatment of the Gentiles, which for Donin must have constituted a gross violation of natural law, he thus projected onto the medieval Jew's relations with Christians. In a burst of anger he exclaimed: "As you have conspired against us, so it is just to do to you. Who will rescue you as you speak thus, and how will you be able to escape?"[42] Like Innocent IV, Donin revealed that the Church's attack on the Talmud bore a new sort of hostility toward contemporary Jews and Judaism. Arguing here on surer ground, Yeḥiel retorted that current rabbinic practice proved that the medieval Jew was bound to pursue cordial and honest relations with his Christian neighbors; these talmudic passages referred only to the seven Canaanite nations of the Bible and other select individuals guilty of offending God with their abominations.[43] Here again, Yeḥiel took pains to show his Christian audience that it was not the Talmud upsetting the traditional equilibrium of Christian-Jewish relations, only the apostasy of Nicholas Donin. In response to a query of the clerical judges at the close of this section of the debate as to whether they as Christians could achieve salvation, Yeḥiel explained that from a Jewish point of view they need only observe the seven Noachide commandments. "But this heretic [Donin], who was commanded to observe 613 commandments, even if he performed 612 and neglected only one, he would be damned for that one because he entered our covenant, and there is one Gehenna for mortal sinners, whether Gentiles or Jews."[44]

Donin had attacked rabbinic Judaism by stressing both its blasphemy and its hostility to Christianity, the practical effects of Jew-

41. Ibid., pp. 8–11; for the original reading of this benediction appearing thrice in the daily Jewish liturgy, which with the advent of printing was changed to attack informers against Jews rather than Christians, see Solomon Schechter, "Genizah Specimens: Liturgy," *JQR*, o.s. 10 (1898), 657. Cf. also Seligman Baer, ed., *Seder 'Avodat Yisra'el*, rev. ed. (Berlin, 1936), p. 93n.

42. *Wikkuah*, p. 9.

43. Ibid., pp. 9–11. Here is a prime example of how polemical (and social) pressures placed upon Jews in a particular environment could induce a change of direction in the evolution of Jewish law and belief; see Jacob Katz, *Exclusiveness and Tolerance: Studies in Jewish-Gentile Relations in Medieval and Modern Times* (1961; repr., New York, 1962), pp. 108, 111–13.

44. *Wikkuah*, p. 12. On the "seven commandments of the descendants of Noah," see Steven S. Schwarzchild and Saul Berman, "Noachide Laws," in *Encyclopedia Judaica*, ed. Cecil Roth et al., 16 vols. (Jerusalem, 1972), 12:1189–91.

ish belief in the Talmud which later convinced Bishop Eudes's legatine court that "these books cannot be tolerated . . . without injury to the Christian Faith," as well as the issue of its heresy, the sole charge of Gregory IX's bull initiating the action against the Talmud. Yet the fact that Yeḥiel could defend the Talmud against each of these charges with the same response—that he the talmudist was orthodox and his opponent Donin the real heretic—suggests the causal link that he saw among the accusations: in all its forms, the Jews' increasing aversion to Christianity and Christians derived from the doctrinal innovations in Jewish theology. As a consequence, the Church presumed it had much to gain by eradicating such error.

The crucial involvement of the Dominicans and Franciscans during this first Christian campaign against the Talmud is unmistakable. Nicholas Donin himself may have joined the Order of Friars Minor shortly after his conversion. The letter of Gregory IX ordering the original confiscation of the Talmud directed that all copies be handed over to the friars of the two orders, who in turn received instructions personally to direct the burning of those books found to contain doctrinal error. Thomas of Cantimpré, writing only two decades after the disputation of Paris, wrote that not Donin but a Dominican named Henry of Cologne persuaded Louis IX to confiscate and burn the Talmud.[45] Henry's energies, as well as the king's general tendency to support the efforts of the friars and the Inquisition, probably explain why of all the monarchs of Europe Louis alone complied with the papal instructions. (His mother, Blanche of Castile, who was probably instrumental in convening the disputation between Donin and Yeḥiel, also lent considerable support to the mendicants' efforts in France.)[46] Moreover, partic-

45. Thomas of Cantimpré, *Bonum universale* 1.3.6, p. 17: "Deuotissimus in principibus Rex Francie Ludovicus, anno circiter ab incarnatione Domini, MCCXXXIX, instigante fratre Henrico, dicto de Colonia, ordinis Praedicatorum, praedicatore peroptimo, sub poena mortis congregari fecit Parisiis nefandissimum librum Iudaeorum, qui Thalmud dicitur, in quo inauditae haereses et blasphemiae contra Christum, et matrem eius, locis plurimis erant scriptae. Huius itaque libri diversa exemplaria ad comburendum Parisios allata sunt." On Henry's ecclesiastical career, see Merchavya, *The Church*, p. 239, n. 41.

46. Jean de Joinville, *Histoire* §§ 657, 668, 691–92, pp. 360–61, 368–69, 380–83; L. K. Little, "Saint Louis' Involvement with the Friars," *Church History* 33 (1964), 125–48; Charles Homer Haskins, "Robert le Bourge and the Beginnings of the Inquisition in Northern France," in *Studies in Medieval Culture* (1923; repr., New York, 1965), pp. 242–43; and Marie-Humbert Vicaire, "Une nouvelle forme de vie religieuse: Les ordres mendiants," in *Le siècle de Saint Louis* (Paris, 1970), pp. 250–51.

ularly since most of the Latin sources never mention Nicholas Donin, the eventual condemnation and burning of the Talmud emerge more as the result of a concerted group effort on the part of the mendicants than that of any one individual's personal animus.[47] The Hebrew sources confirm this impression. Rabbi Yeḥiel relates that Donin "brought his false charges against us to the king, the Dominicans, the Franciscans, and the episcopal judges," and that with regard to the Talmud Donin "said to himself, 'I shall ransack all of its treasures . . . with the help of the idolatrous Franciscans.'" Rabbi Joseph ben Nathan Official, in his epilogue to the Hebrew protocol, likewise lists both mendicant orders among the judges at the debate.[48] Bishop Eudes's long letter to Innocent IV explaining the renewal of the judgment against the Talmud specifically mentions that Godfried de Blevel, in 1240 the Dominican confessor to Louis IX and later the confessor to Innocent himself, was one of the presiding judges at the original inquest in Paris. The long list of signatories to Eudes's second condemnation reveals the active participation of the friars in the inquiry.[49] And most copies of the Latin *Extractiones de Talmut* mention a Dominican, Thibaut de Sézanne, as the chief editor and translator; some scholars identify him as a provincial subprior of the Order of Preachers in Paris and a professor of Hebrew at its first language *studium* there.[50]

Whereas in the Maimonidean controversy, the friars of the Inquisition intervened in a matter, albeit important, of passing concern to the Jewish community, their attack on the Talmud struck at the very foundation of European Jewry's existence. It was an entirely new development in the Christian theology of the Jew, one

47. See Merchavya, *The Church*, pp. 246–47; the only ensuing reference to Nicholas occurs in a manuscript dated 1403 entitled *Judeorum repressio*, in which reference to thirty-five articles of a Nicholas de Rufila appears in a list of anti-Jewish polemics. Cf. Y. Baer, *A History*, 1:150; Grayzel, "The Talmud," pp. 224, 226.

48. *Wikkuaḥ*, p. 1; *Sepher Joseph ha-Mekane*, p. 141.

49. On Godfried see Grayzel, *The Church and the Jews*, pp. 276–77, n. 3; cf. Jacques Quétif and Jacques Echard, *Scriptores Ordinis Praedicatorum*, 2 vols. (1719–21; repr., New York, 1959), 1:127–29. The list of signatories to Eudes's condemnation appears in Denifle, *Chartularium*, 1:211; see also Eckert, "Hoch- und Spätmittelalter," p. 231; and Merchavya, *The Church*, p. 357.

50. Daniel Mortier, *Histoire des maîtres généraux de l'Ordre des Frères Prêcheurs*, 8 vols. (Paris, 1903–14), 1:430; Browe, *Die Judenmission*, pp. 206, 270; Andre Berthier, "Les écoles de langues orientales fondées au XIIIᵉ siècle par les Dominicains en Espagne et en Afrique," *Revue africaine* 73 (1932), 86–87; Klapper, "Ein florilegium"; J. M. Rosenthal, "The Talmud," p. 74; *SRH*, 9:278, n. 30; and Merchavya, *The Church*, p. 239. Cf. Erich Klibansky, "Beziehungen," pp. 457–58, who rejects the identification of Thibaut de Sézanne with Theobald the subprior of Paris.

fraught with great dangers for European Jewry at large. Rabbinic Judaism admittedly had come under Christian notice and attack in the West before the thirteenth century. Both Jerome and Augustine castigated the Jews for following rabbinic teachings that were of human, rather than divine, origin and alien to the true spirit of Scripture. Convinced that a genuine, unadulterated appeciation of Scripture would persuade the Jews of the truth of Christianity, the Emperor Justinian in 553 banned the public, homiletical explication of readings from the Bible by Jews according to their traditional rabbinic interpretation (*deuterosis*). An oath for Jewish converts to Christianity in Visigothic Spain in 637 similarly included a promise to surrender all nonbiblical or apocryphal works to the Christian authorities. In his famous epistle *De Iudeorum superstitionibus atque erroribus*, Agobard of Lyons pointed to the postbiblical Jewish tradition, including beliefs expounded in various mystical tracts, as giving rise to Jewish blasphemy against Christianity and a host of other noxious practices.[51] In the twelfth century, Peter Alfonsi and Peter the Venerable of Cluny attacked Judaism for the absurdity of many talmudic midrashim. Yet most of these attacks on rabbinic Judaism came at the hands of those who in ignorance of Hebrew had little or no firsthand knowledge of it. Their basic approaches to the question of the Jews in Christian society still derived from the tolerant theological posture of Augustine, with the issue of rabbinic and postbiblical teachings playing at most a very small role in their polemics. No one had accused medieval Jews of deliberately forsaking the literal biblical Judaism of their ancestors, and no one had maintained that it was illegitimate for Jews as Jews to preserve the Talmud and live according to its teachings. Nobody had indicted the constantly evolving legal tradition (*halakhah*), which regulated the conduct of every facet of Jewish life, for posing a heretical challenge to the authority of the Old Testament; only the homilies of the ancient rabbis, the *aggadah*, had come under attack. Few if any Christians had presumed to decide for the Jews the particulars

51. Jerome, *Epistola* 121.10, *In Esaiam* 8.11–15, 59.12–15; Augustine, *Contra adversarium legis et prophetarum* 2.12; *Iustinianae novellae* 146.1.2, in *Corpus iuris civilis*, ed. Paul Krueger et al., 3 vols. (Berlin, 1900–1905), 3:716. The most recent consideration of Justinian's intentions, including a review of past interpretations, is that of Albert I. Baumgarten, "Justinian and the Jews," in *Rabbi Joseph H. Lookstein Memorial Volume*, ed. Leo Landman (New York, 1980), pp. 37–44. The Visigothic oath appears in Jean Juster, "La condition légale des Juifs sous les rois visigoths," in *Etudes d'histoire juridique offertes à Paul Frédéric Girard*, 2 vols. (Paris, 1913), 2:306, n. 1. And see Agobard of Lyons, *Epistola* 8, MGH Epist. 5:185–99, passim.

of truly Jewish belief and ritual. Not even the bitter Peter the Venerable had called for the destruction of Jewish books.

Only in the thirteenth century did the Church, with the friars at the forefront, undertake a systematic study of contemporary Judaism and Jewish literature and endeavor to demonstrate in public, officially conducted disputations with real Jews that the rabbinic tradition of medieval European Jewry could not be tolerated in Christendom. No longer did Christian anti-Jewish polemic aim primarily at fortifying popular Christian belief, simply portraying the Jew as one whose obstinate adherence to a literalist interpretation of the Old Testament prevented his acceptance of Jesus as messiah and God.[52] Capitalizing upon the vastness and strangeness of post-biblical Jewish literature, which they now for the first time gained the ability to scrutinize, the friars of the Inquisition attacked the general authority of the *halakhah* as well as many of its specific provisions. The Church now depicted the "living" Judaism of its own day as a heresy and perversion, a pernicious oral tradition of religious law and doctrine, a gross deviation from the religion of the Old Testament. The Talmud not only, in the words of Gregory IX, held "the Jews obstinate in their perfidy" but also, with the equation of the talmudic *goy* and the medieval Christian, proffered a real threat to Latin Christendom. Toleration consequently gave way to the harassment of daily Jewish life, and the Jew in Christian theology, formerly a relic or artifact, at once became real and incurred immediate and direct suspicion and hatred. Over the course of time, the Christian fear of heresy and misunderstanding of what was thought to be the Jews' life of perversity came more and more to dominate Europe's conception of its Jewry.[53]

52. See, for example, the definitions adduced by Raymond de Peñaforte, *Summa* 1.4.1 (Verona, 1744), p. 24; the (presumably authentic) Jews are among those "qui male colendo Deum inhonorant," and they are defined as those "qui legem Mosaicam ad litteram tenent."

53. The degree of objective fairness involved in this tactical change in Christian polemic is happily not a major concern of this book. Nevertheless, the reader might gain helpful insight into the psychological underpinnings of medieval religious polemic from the comments of N. Daniel, *Islam*, p. 2, on Christian anti-Muslim arguments of the thirteenth century.

4

The Spread of
Inquisitorial Activity

As the Inquisition grew during the thirteenth and fourteenth centuries, so did its preoccupation with the Jews and Jewish life. Although the Inquisition ostensibly developed solely for the prosecution of heresy, in 1285 one Friar William of Auxerre appears mentioned in a source cited by Henry Charles Lea as "Inquisitor of Heretics and Apostate Jews in France." Documents concerning the Jewry of Pamiers led Lea to the rather sweeping conclusion that by 1297 the Inquisition had gained complete control over the Jews of Languedoc.[1] Whether or not Lea exaggerated, the extant sources do manifest a definite trend: while the interference of the Inquisition in the Maimonidean controversy and the disputation of Paris in 1240 had constituted major developments in the relationship of the Church and the Jews, by the end of the thirteenth century such intrusions into the daily religious life of European Jewry by the friars were by no means unusual. Endeavoring to convey the significance of such developments, I have admittedly used the term and notion of inquisitorial activity somewhat loosely. As was mentioned earlier, one encounters difficulty in trying to pinpoint the beginnings of the mendicant Inquisition in southern France, and the same often holds true for other areas into which the Inquisition subsequently moved. Even after one can safely assert that inquisitorial activity had begun in a particular region, it frequently remains impossible to isolate the bureaucratic machinery and personnel of an institution called the Inquisition. Thirteenth-century Europeans themselves lacked a clear-cut conception of such an organizational and institutional entity.[2] In the ensuing discussion, therefore, spe-

1. Lea, A History, 2:64, 96n.
2. See, for example, Richard Kiekhefer, *Repression of Heresy in Medieval Germany* (Philadelphia, 1979), pp. 1–10.

cific instances of inquisitorial activities of the friars cannot always be linked to the formal Inquisition. Yet it is the sort and the spirit of the ecclesiastical intervention in the internal affairs of the Jewish community with which my primary concern lies; for these are what serve to substantiate the pervasive effects of the friars' attack upon the Jews.

The Implications of 1240

The initial condemnation of the Talmud in Paris introduced two new elements into the relationship between the Church and the Synagogue: the attack on rabbinic Judaism and the holding of public, officially sponsored religious disputations between Christians and Jews for the express purpose of undermining contemporary Jewish life. Much of the Church's anti-Jewish activity during the thirteenth and early fourteenth centuries carried on in the footsteps of Nicholas Donin and his mendicant associates, in either one or both of these new arenas. The campaign against rabbinic literature struck at the Jews from many different directions. The Franciscan theologian Alexander of Hales attacked the Talmud in his *Summa theologiae*. The books of the wealthy Jew David of Oxford were confiscated upon his death in 1244 before his widow could inherit his estate. An angry mob burned the books of the Jews in the French city of Bourges in 1251.[3] Numerous tracts entitled *Pharetra fidei contra Iudeos super Talmut* (The quiver of the faith against the Jews concerning the Talmud) began to appear during this period, works that reviewed the charges leveled at the Talmud in Paris and often included collections of offensive talmudic quotations; by the fourteenth century, Latin translations of (undoubtedly parts of) the Talmud had in fact been catalogued in at least three European libraries.[4] In 1320, a Jew named Baruch, who had been baptized

3. Alexander of Hales, *ST* 2–2.3.8.1.1.2.1, 5 vols. (Florence [Quaracchi], 1924–48), 3:729; Roth, *The Jews of Medieval Oxford*, p. 124; and William Chester Jordan, *Saint Louis and the Challenge of the Crusade* (Princeton, 1979), pp. 116, n. 72.

4. See, for example, a brief summary of the *Pharetra* of one anonymous fourteenth-century Dominican in Quétif, *Scriptores*, 1:738; see also Berthold Altaner, "Zur Kenntnis des Hebräischen im Mittelalter," *Biblische Zeitschrift* 21 (1933), 297, nn. 2–3; Heinz Pflaum, "Ein französischer Dichter des 14. Jahrhunderts über Raschi," *MGWJ* 76 (1932), 580–83; and Max Manitius, *Geschichte der lateinischen Literatur des Mittelalters*, 3 vols. (Munich, 1911–31), 3:138. And cf. the fifteenth-century Spanish work *Censura et confutatio libri Talmud*, described by Isidore Loeb, "Polémistes chrétiens et juifs en France et en Espagne," *REJ* 18 (1889), 231–37.

under pain of death by a band of French Pastoureaux (crusading shepherds), confessed to the inquisitorial tribunal of Bishop Jacques Fournier of Pamiers that the Talmud prescribed most degrading rites of readmission for a baptized Jew who wished to return to Judaism.[5] And the fourteenth-century Dominican Petrus de Pennis, who had no real knowledge of rabbinic literature and authored an anti-Jewish treatise based almost entirely on biblical testimony to the truth of Christianity, still could proclaim unhesitatingly to his readers, "The entire text [of the Talmud] is heretical."[6] Alexander IV reminded the king and powerful barons of France of the anti-Jewish legislation enacted at the Fourth Lateran Council and then ordered that all copies of the Talmud be confiscated because of its anti-Christian blasphemy.[7] A decade later, Clement IV bemoaned the allegiance of Aragonese Jewry to the Talmud in *Dampnabili perfidia Iudeorum*.

We have heard with sorrow and now relate that the Jews of the Kingdom of Aragon, having neglected the Old Testament which the majesty of the creator of all conferred through his servant Moses, falsely pretend that the Lord handed down a certain other law or tradition which they call the Talmud. In its huge volume which is said to be larger than the text of the Old and New Testaments, are contained innumerable abuses and detestable blasphemies against the Lord Jesus Christ and his most blessed mother, the relation or hearing of which can hardly be undertaken by anyone without the onset of

5. Jean Duvernoy, ed., *Le registre de l'inquisition de Jacques Fournier, évêque de Pamiers (1318–1325)*, 2 vols. (Toulouse, 1965), 1:178: "Dixit tamen quod baptizati qui ad iudaismum revertuntur sic revertuntur iuxta doctrinam Talmutz: quod secant eis ungues manuum et pedum, et raduntur pili capitis, et deinde totum corpus abluitur in aqua currenti sicut secundum Legem purificabatur mulier alienigena quando debebat duci a iudeo in uxorem, quia ipsi reputant quod baptismus polluit ipsos qui recipiunt ipsum." On Baruch's deposition in particular and on Jacques Fournier and the Pastoureaux in general, see also Solomon Grayzel, "The Confession of a Medieval Jewish Convert," *HJ* 17 (1955), 89–103; J. M. Vidal, L'émeute des Pastoureaux en 1320," *Annales de Saint-Louis des Français* 3 (1898–99), 121–74; Yerushalmi, "The Inquisition," pp. 328–33; Annette Pales-Gobilliard, "L'Inquisition et les Juifs: Le cas de Jacques Fournier," in *JJL*, pp. 97–114; and Bath Sheva Albert, *The Case of Baruch: The Earliest Report of the Trial of a Jew by the Inquisition (1320)* [Hebrew] (Ramat Gan, 1974).

6. Shulamit Shahar, "Dialogus inter Judeum et clericum [Hebrew]," *Michael* 4 (1976), 56; Petrus even entitled his work something approximating *Liber contra Judeos nomine Thalamoth*—see pp. 34, n. 7, 37, 60.

7. Isidore Loeb, ed., "Bulles inédites des papes," *REJ* 1 (1880), 1:117: "Ad hec omnibus Iudeis predicte terre auferri facias libros qui thalmuth vulgariter appellantur, in quibus continentur errores contra fidem catholicam ac horribiles et intollerabiles blasphemie contra dominum nostrum Jhesum Xpum et beatam Mariam virginem matrem eius."

extreme shame and horror. The worst curses and horrible oaths, which are made daily against the Christians by these same ungrateful and perfidious Jews, are recorded in this law or damnable tradition. What more need be said? Such and other detestable things most damnably written in this law or profane tradition are reckoned to be the main reasons why this foolish, unfaithful people has for a long time stood obstinate in its perfidy.[8]

Clement proceeded to order that King James I of Aragon and the archbishop of Tarragona confiscate all copies of the Talmud, have them examined by the Dominicans and Franciscans, restore to the Jews those books free of blasphemy, and await further instructions from Rome as to the others. In a letter (*Nimis in partibus*) to the prelates of England probably solicited by the Franciscan archbishop of Canterbury, John Peckham, Honorius IV in 1286 began his list of complaints concerning the abuses of the Jews with a similar indictment of the Talmud.[9] And in 1320, John XXII, after reiterating the charges of Clement and Honorius, added a new complaint: Christians were actually studying the erroneous teachings of the Talmud and thereby being drawn closer and closer to Judaism. He therefore directed the archbishop of Berry to impound all talmudic manuscripts, searching well so as to prevent the Jews from hiding any, and to give them to the friars for examination; dangerous volumes should again be consigned to the flames.[10]

Echoing these sentiments, various French and Spanish monarchs reinforced the papal efforts with decrees of their own. Louis IX of France, after responding to the appeals of Gregory IX and Nicholas Donin in 1239, renewed the order to burn the Talmud in an ordinance of 1254. Louis's two successors, Philip III and Philip IV, both followed suit during their own regimes; each of their decrees to the French royal bureaucracy in this matter ordered complete cooperation with the inquisitors. Louis X, when in 1315 he readmitted the Jews and their books into France, specifically excepted the Talmud.[11]

8. Ripoll, *Bullarium*, 1:487.
9. Sbaralea, *Bullarium*, 3:590. On Peckham's role in soliciting this bull and his hostility toward the Jews, see Solomon Grayzel, "Bishop to Bishop 1," in *Gratz College Anniversary Volume*, ed. I. D. Passow and S. D. Lachs (Philadelphia, 1971), pp. 131–45.
10. See John's bull *Dudum felicis recordationis* in Cesare Baronius and Odericus Raynaldus, eds., *Annales ecclesiastici*, 34 vols. (Lucca, 1738–56), 24:138.
11. See Eusèbe de Laurière et al., eds., *Ordonnances des roys de France de la troisième race*, 21 vols. (Paris, 1723–1849), 1:75, 596; and Douais, *L'Inquisition*, pp. 357–58, 360–61.

In Aragon in 1263, James I ordered the Jews to surrender all the works of Moses Maimonides known as "Soffrim"—probably meaning "Shofeṭim," the last book of the *Mishneh Torah*, dealing in part with the reign of the messiah—because they blasphemed against Jesus. Two other decrees commanded the Jews to submit all of their books to the Dominican Pablo Christiani and several other friars for inspection and even to defray the friars' expenses incurred in carrying out such examinations. A decade later, James imposed a fine for each individual blasphemy that might be found in the books of the Jews.[12] In 1326, James II submitted various books confiscated from Jews—including a Hebrew Bible, volumes from the Talmud, and Rabbi David Qimḥi's book on biblical diction, *Sefer ha Shorashim* ("librum vocatum sarasin")—to a Franciscan Hebraist named Raymond de Miedas, encouraging his investigation of them for heresy.[13] And Alfonso X of Castile included a law against noxious Jewish literature in his *El fuero real*.[14] While not all of these anti-talmudic measures led to further burnings, some surely did; John XXII's bull *Dudum felicis recordationis* alone probably induced the autos-da-fé in Bourges, Toulouse, Paris, Pamiers, and Rome early in the fourteenth century.[15]

12. Heinrich Denifle, "Quellen zur Disputation Pablo Christiani mit Mose Naḥmani zu Barcelona 1263," *Historisches Jahrbuch* 8 (1887), 235: "Omnibus Iudeis nostri districtus in vestris [James is writing to the various members of his royal bureaucracy] vicariis comorantibus ex parte nostra districte precipiatis, ut omnes libros, qui vocantur Soffrim, compositos a quodam Iudeo, qui vocabatur Moyses filius Maymon egipciachus sive de Alcayra, Ihesu Christi blasfemias continentes, vobis . . . ostendant et tradant, quos mox in conspectu populi causa blasfemarum exposita comburi faciatis." See also pp. 235–37; and J. Lee Shneidman, "Protection of Aragon Jewry in the Thirteenth Century," *REJ* 121 (1962), 54. On Pablo Christiani and the Jews, see below, Ch. 5.

13. Antonio Rubió y Lluch, ed., *Documents per l'historia de la cultura catalana migeval*, 2 vols. (Barcelona, 1908–21), 2:50.

14. *El fuero real* 4.2.1, in Alfonso X (el Sabio) of Castile, *Opusculos legales*, 2 vols. (Madrid, 1836), 2:118. Cf. the curious interpretation of this law by J. N. Hillgarth, *The Spanish Kingdoms, 1250–1516*, 2 vols. (Oxford, 1976–78), 1:164–65, who construes it as a sign of Alfonso's enlightened, benevolent attitude toward the Jew: the king is alleged to have "extended the same protection to Jewish orthodoxy as he did to Christian dogma," a provision that according to Hillgarth "would have been inconceivable outside the [Iberian] peninsula."

15. Solomon Grayzel, "The Talmud and the Medieval Papacy," in *Essays in Honor of Solomon B. Freehof*, ed. Walter Jacob et al. (Pittsburgh, 1964), p. 233. To sense the seriousness of the blow which these later burnings of the Talmud were to the Jewish communities involved, see the reaction of Qalonymos ben Qalonymos ben Meir in *Even Bohan*, ed. A. M. Haberman (Tel Aviv, 1956), pp. 116, 161; Heinrich Graetz, "Burning the Talmud in 1322," *JQR*, o.s. 2 (1890), 104–6; and Peter Browe, "Die religiöse Duldung der Juden im Mittelalter," *Archiv für katolisches Kirchenrecht* 118 (1938), 56.

The second novelty in the Paris trials of the 1240s was the official ecclesiastical and royal sponsorship of a public disputation between Jewish and Christian clergy. Whereas before the thirteenth century most religious debate comprised either private conversation between individuals or simply fictions employed in literary polemic, real encounters between the friars and the Jews now became an important element in the attack of the Church upon Judaism. Both Dominic and Francis had preached among heretics and infidels, and instruction and disputation were significant weapons in the arsenal of the Inquisition.

Probably as early as the 1230s, Rabbi Meir ben Simeon of Narbonne was required to dispute publicly with a Dominican friar, dubbed "the preaching prostitute" (*ha-qadesh ha-doresh*) in Meir's apologetic work *Milḥemet Miṣwah*. The two debated not only the correct exegesis of biblical *testimonia* but also the validity of such mainstays of contemporary Jewish life as moneylending. From Meir's description, it is apparent that the Dominican had headed a Christian delegation that entered the main synagogue of Narbonne and had delivered a speech to the Jewish congregation who were compelled to listen; the rabbi had no choice but to respond.[16] In 1242, James I of Aragon became the first king to compel Jewish submission to such mendicant preaching by law, a measure which drew considerable praise from Innocent IV and which James renewed in 1263.[17] Edward I in 1280 similarly ordered English Jewry to listen peacefully to the sermons of the Dominicans, and James II of Aragon in 1296 even required the Jews to respond publicly to the challenges of the preaching friars.[18] In 1278, Pope Nicholas III for-

16. Henri Gross, "Meir b. Simon und seine Schrift Milchemeth Mizva: Analekten," *MGWJ* 30 (1881), 297. On Meir and his polemical tract see Siegfried Stein, *Jewish-Christian Disputations in Thirteenth-Century Narbonne* (London, 1969); Ch. Merchavya, "Concerning the Date of R. Meir ben Simeon's *Milḥemet Miẓva* [Hebrew]," *Tarbiz* 45 (1976), 296–302; Robert Chazan, "A Jewish Plaint to Saint Louis," *HUCA* 45 (1974), 287–305; and Chazan, "Anti-Usury Efforts in Thirteenth-Century Narbonne and the Jewish Response," *PAAJR* 41–42 (1973–74), 45–67. Some of the debates recorded in the *Milḥemet Miṣwah* were conducted between Meir and Archbishop Guy Fulcodi of Narbonne, later to become Pope Clement IV, the author of *Turbato corde* and *Dampnabili perfidia Iudeorum*; see Robert Chazan, "Archbishop Guy Fulcodi of Narbonne and His Jews," *REJ* 132 (1971), 587–94.

17. For the text of the decree, see its confirmation by Innocent IV in 1245, Grayzel, *The Church and the Jews*, p. 256; the edict renewing the provision appears in Denifle, "Quellen," pp. 234–36.

18. Thomas Rymer and Robert Sanderson, eds., *Foedera, conventiones, litterae, et cujuscunque generis acta publica . . .* , re-ed. Adam Clarke and Frederick Holbrook, 4 vols. (London, 1816–69), 1, 2:576; Rubió y Lluch, *Documents*, 2:11.

mally made preaching to and missionizing among the Jews part of the apostolate of both the Dominican and the Franciscan orders.[19] Not surprisingly, a sixteenth-century collection of papal bulls concerning the Inquisition, prepared by the Holy Office itself, included Nicholas's decree of *Vineam Soreth*, underscoring its lasting importance for inquisitors.[20]

We order your discretion by apostolic writ that, trusting in him whose is the prerogative to lavish special graces, through your own efforts and those of other friars in your order whom . . . you shall know to be suitable and whose industry and theological wisdom, implanted as gifts from the Lord, may shine dauntlessly for the Catholic faith and not falter in their clarity but enlighten confused souls by the repercussion of their rays and overcome the obstinacy of the perverse Jews, you be zealous, according to the grace given you by the Lord, in leading back to the way of clarity such people in the province entrusted to you who have been cut off by the darkness of the shadows. Summon them to sermons in the places where they live, in large and small groups, repeatedly, as many times as you may think beneficial. Inform them of evangelical doctrines with salutary warnings and discreet reasoning, so that after the clouds of darkness have gone, they may shine in the light of Christ's countenance, having been reborn at the baptismal font.

Although *Vineam Soreth* ordered the friars to deliver "salutary" warnings to the Jews, the anti-Jewish zeal of the mendicants in its practical application far traversed the boundaries set upon it by the laws regulating the Inquisition, including those compelling the Jews to submit their books to censorship or themselves to missionary sermons. Reports of excesses are corroborated in royal and even ecclesiastical decrees, probably issued in the wake of Jewish complaints, calling for restraint on the part of the friars. Only four days

19. The numerous copies of this bull, *Vineam Soreth*, issued to both orders vouch for its universal applicability among Franciscans and Dominicans alike. See the various rescensions cited in Sbaralea, *Bullarium*, 3:332–33 (to the Franciscan provincial minister in Austria), 371–72 (to the Franciscan minister in Sicily); F.-M. Delorme, ed., *En marge du bullaire franciscain* (Paris, 1938), pp. 36–38 (to the Franciscan minister in Aquitaine); Augustus Potthast, ed., *Regesta pontificum romanorum inde ab a. post Christum natum MCXCVIII ad a. MCCCIV*, 2 vols. (Berlin, 1874–75), 2:1729, no. 21383 (to the Dominican prior in Lombardy); and the *Septimi decretales* 5.1.2 (to the entire Dominican order). Cf. also L. Erler, "Die Juden des Mittelalters. Die Päpste und die Juden," *Archiv für katholisches Kirchenrecht* 50 (1884), 3, n. 2; and Synan, *The Popes and the Jews*, pp. 119–20.

20. *Litterae apostolicae diversorum romanorum pontificum pro officio sanctissimae Inquisitionis* (Rome, 1579), pp. 36–37.

after King James I of Aragon in 1263 renewed his decree allowing the Dominicans to compel Jewish attendance at their sermons, he partially reversed himself by strictly limiting the circumstances and locations in which such compulsion could take place. Five years later, James added that friars who entered synagogues to debate could not take Christian laymen with them, for fear that they might be incited to riot.[21] Peter III in 1279 reiterated his predecessor's stricture, revealing that friars still engaged in this dangerous practice. James II reprimanded several inquisitors for persecuting Jews against his wishes. He informed the Dominican Sanccio de Torralba, for example, that he was acting against canonical regulations, and the inquisitor Guillelmo Costa that his attack on rabbinic literature threatened the very existence of an entire Jewish community. Peter IV of Aragon found it necessary to censure Dominicans and Franciscans for delivering anti-Jewish sermons so inflammatory that they led to the murder of Jews and the destruction of their property.[22] And Philip IV, who expelled the Jews from France in 1306, on three earlier occasions warned his bailiffs and seneschals not to cooperate with mendicant inquisitors unlawfully attempting to prosecute Jews beyond the jurisdictional limits of the Inquisition—for example, in cases involving usury. The excesses of the friars must have been great to cause Philip at one point to distribute among his officials copies of Gregory X's rendition of *Turbato corde*, explaining that inquisitorial authority over the Jews could not exceed the limits laid down therein.[23] The papacy itself on more than one occasion had to react negatively to this extreme zealousness of the Inquisition. Boniface VIII, for example, forbade inquisitors to receive anonymous depositions against Jews, and John XXII, at the appeal of the bishop-elect of Trani, ordered the

21. Denifle, "Quellen," p. 237; Jean Régné, *History of the Jews in Aragon: Regesta and Documents, 1213–1327*, ed. Yom Tov Assis and Adam Gruzman (Jerusalem, 1978), p. 69 (no. 386). Grayzel, "Popes, Jews, and Inquisition," pp. 164 and n. 57, alludes to similar relaxations of James's decrees against rabbinic literature. To be sure, the Jews clamored strenuously for such protection and often obtained it by means of outright bribery; cf. Y. Baer, *A History*, 1:160.

22. J. E. Martínez Ferrando, *Catálogo de la documentación relativa al ántiguo reino de Valencia*, 2 vols. (Madrid, 1934), 2:153, nos. 684–86; Heinrich Finke, ed., *Acta aragonensia*, 3 vols. (1908–22; repr., Aalen, 1966–68), 2:859, 862, 870; Rubió y Lluch, *Documents*, 2:81; Yitzhak Baer, *Die Juden im christlichen Spanien, Erster Teil*, 2 vols. (1929–36; repr., Farnborough, Eng., 1970), 1:327–28.

23. Gustave Saige, *Les Juifs de Languedoc antérieurement au XIVe siècle* (1881; repr., Farnborough, Eng., 1971), p. 232. Cf. de Laurière, *Ordonnances*, 1:317, 346; and see above, Ch. 2, n. 39.

friars to desist from all dealings with the Jews except at the express request of the prelate.[24]

Although many of these restrictive decrees may have derived from the selfish interests of monarchs in safeguarding the welfare of "their" Jews, they still shed light upon the general trend of inquisitorial behavior. Wherever they could, the friars encroached upon the daily religious lives of the Jews. Burning or editing the books needed to sustain rabbinic tradition, invading the privacy and sanctity of the synagogue, and instilling fear through mob violence all pointed toward the same end: inducing the Jews to accept Christianity, thereby destroying the Jewish community in Christendom. At times the restrictions placed upon the inquisitors had no effect whatsoever.

From Harassment to Destruction

The Jewish communities of Apulia in southern Italy had flourished for several centuries, beginning in the late Carolingian period. Recognizing the cultural importance of these settlements for all of European Jewry, the great twelfth-century Rabbi Jacob Tam had punned on the famous messianic prophecy of Isaiah 2:3, "For out of Bari shall go forth the Torah and the word of the Lord from Otranto."[25] Yet at the end of the thirteenth century, most traces of a Jewish community in Apulia vanished, at least temporarily; the cause of the disappearance lay in the enthusiastic anti-Jewish campaigns of the Dominican Inquisition, especially those of the inquisitor general Friar Bartolomeo de Aquila.[26] Even before his inquisitorial activity began in 1278, the Inquisition had actively tried to strike

24. For these and similar instances, see Grayzel, "Popes, Jews, and Inquisition," pp. 185–88; and Grayzel, "References to the Jews in the Correspondence of John XXII," *HUCA* 23, 2 (1950–51), 74.

25. Jacob ben Meir Tam, *Sefer ha-Yashar: Ḥeleq ha-She'eilot weha-Teshuvot,* ed. Ferdinand Rosenthal (1898; repr., Jerusalem, 1965), p. 90.

26. Helpful if incomplete reconstructions of what transpired appear in Umberto Cassuto, "Ḥurban ha-Yeshivot be-'Italyah ha-deromit ba-Me'ah ha-13," in *Studies in Memory of Asher Gulak and Samuel Klein* (Jerusalem, 1942), pp. 139–52; and Joshua Starr, "The Mass Conversion of Jews in Southern Italy 1290–1293," *Speculum* 21 (1946), 203–11. An earlier version of Cassuto's study appeared as "Un ignoto capitolo di storia ebraica," *Judaica: Festschrift zu Hermann Cohens siebzigsten Geburtstage* (Berlin, 1912), pp. 389–404. For the extensive privileges granted Bartolomeo by King Charles I of Anjou, see Nicolo Toppi, ed., *Biblioteca napoletana* (Naples, 1678), p. 378.

at the Jewish communities in the lands of the Angevin kings. At the prodding of a baptized Jew named Manuforte, King Charles I in 1270 ordered that the Talmud and other offensive works of rabbinic literature be confiscated from the Jews under the supervision of the Dominicans and Franciscans. The charges of anti-Christian blasphemy echoed those of the condemnations of Paris, similarly referring as well to various collections of midrashim and prayers.[27] Perhaps capitalizing on the ruling Angevins' dependence on papal good will in southern Italy, the Inquisition also induced Charles II to expel the Jews from his French domains of Maine and Anjou in 1288.[28] The economic importance of Apulian Jewry, however, probably mitigated against expulsion in its case, and several extant decrees of Charles II do demand that inquisitors adhere to the canonical limitations of their jurisdiction over Jews. Another decree merely imposes a moderate fine on a Jewish notable of Naples indicted by Bartolomeo for causing the relapse of a baptized Jew, undoubtedly slighting the Dominican and his zeal.[29] Nevertheless, Bartolomeo and his colleagues persevered and eventually overcame all royal opposition to their designs.

Exactly how the inquisitors managed to rid Apulia of its Jewish community remains in question. Apparently taking advantage of both the tendency of many Jewish converts to Christianity to relapse and the broad jurisdiction of the Inquisition in cases of judaizing, the friars succeeded in harassing the Jews sufficiently so that most accepted baptism. This inquisitorial endeavor achieved success gradually during the last decade of the thirteenth century,

27. Giuseppe del Giudice, ed., *Codice diplomatico del regno di Carlo I°e II° d'Angiò*, 3 vols. (Naples, 1863–1902), 3:200–203: "Manufortis olim judeus et judeorum Synagoge Magister et iamdiu ad fidem Christianam reversus fidelis noster nobis exposuit quod nonnulli judei libros aliquos quorum unus vocatur talmuct alius Carrboct et alter Sedur penes se habere noscuntur in quibus libris multe blasfemie Jhesu Christi filii dei vivi et beate marie semper virginis continentur. Cum igitur hec non debeamus nec velimus aliquatenus sustinere fidelitati vestre etc. quatenus ad requisitionem eiusdem manufortis de consilio prioris patrum [fratrum?] predicatorum vel Guardiani minorum aut prelati loci ubi vos duxeritis requirendum de libris eisdem diligentius inquiretis et omnes libros huiusmodi penes quoscumque inveneritis capiatis illosque incontinenti per fides nuncios ad nostram Curiam destinetis."
28. Cassuto, "Ḥurban," p. 142.
29. Del Giudice, *Codice*, 2:345–46n., 3:203n.; Gennaro Maria Monti, "Da Carlo I a Roberto di Angiò: Richerche e documenti," *Archivio storico per le province napoletane* 59 (1934), 174; cf. Starr, "The Mass Conversion," pp. 205–6. Charles also protested against inquisitorial maltreatment of the Jews of Avignon; see Léon Bardinet, "Condition civile des Juifs du Comtat Venaissin pendant la séjour des papes à Avignon, 1309–1376," *Revue historique* 12 (1880), 7.

when the Jews began to convert en masse. In 1290, Charles II granted the request of some prominent Neapolitan converts to have a synagogue building, supposedly built by their recent ancestors in violation of canon law prohibiting such construction, given to them for use as a church.[30] Two years later the crown prince, Charles, who served as his father's viceroy in southern Italy, communicated to royal officials his approval of Bartolomeo's actions concerning a synagogue in Salerno. The friar had proved to the prince that Jews used the synagogue to induce the apostasy of Christians; they had recently dared to circumcise a Christian named Moses and ritually to annul the baptism undergone by a Jew, Azarias. Bartolomeo first ordered the synagogue destroyed, as canonical regulations apparently entitled him to do. But when on the next day all the Salernitan Jews suddenly recognized the truth of Christianity, the Dominican chose instead to sell the synagogue and use the proceeds to aid impoverished converts. A manuscript in the Vatican Library confirms the conversion of a great number of Apulian Jews by Bartolomeo and two colleagues in 1292.[31] And Neapolitan documents dating from 1294, which grant tax exemptions to newly baptized Jews, reveal that thirteen hundred Jewish families in Apulia had converted—probably a total of at least eight thousand proselytes. Other contemporary sources relate that many Jews fled from Apulia at this time, causing the Jewish community in at least some cities to vanish completely; in Trani, for example, the Dominicans

30. See the Neapolitan archive published for the first time by Cassuto, "Ḥurban," pp. 151–52.

31. Monti, "Da Carlo I," pp. 175–76: "Exposuit Excellencie nostre religiosus vir frater Bartholomeus de Aquila ordinis fratrum Predicatorum inquisitor heretice pravitatis in Regno Sicilie per Sedem Apostolicam constitutus quod cum pridem per legitimos testes sibi plene conscientie quod si sinacoga maiori Judeorum de Salerno scientibus et consencientibus Judeis Judayce salernitane ad quos predicta sinacoga spectabat plures heretici apostate a fide Christi receptati faciant in ea et quidem Christianus nomine Moyses fuerat circoncisus ibidem et quidam alii Judeorum heresim profexi et in puteo vel fonte ipsius sinacoge quidam nomine Azarias a fide Christi potestate in iniuriam baptismatis per Judeos Judaice predicte fuerat ablutus. Ideo sinacogam eamdem iuxta canonicas sanctiones auctoritate sibi conmissa mandaverit funditus dirui reservata tamen in potestate ipsius super predicta sinacoga et bonis eiusdem ut possit aliter de ipsis disponere si promocioni fidei foret expediens. Sed quia sequenti die divina gracia Judei Judayce predicte universaliter fere illuminavit lumen catholice fidei inter quos maior pars male primitus paupertatis sentenciam de predicta sinacoga diruenda conmutans et disponens de ipsa sinacoga ut in pecunia convertatur de qua in sacro baptismate provideatur pauperibus." And see Vat. MS Lat. 10511, f.° 185b, quoted in Marco Vattasso, *Le due Biblie di Bovino ora codici vaticani latini 10510–10511 et le loro note storiche* (Rome, 1900), p. 39.

received permission to take possession of the Jewish cemetery in 1302.[32]

Although the documents allow the inference that the Inquisition exploited the relapse of Jewish *conversi*, prosecuting to the fullest extent possible the Jews who consorted with the *relapsus* too, Prince Charles's letter of 1292 in particular indicated that such judaizing legally warranted the destruction of a synagogue in Salerno, not the eradication of Salernitan Jewry. How did Bartolomeo and his colleagues justify to the Angevin government their program of doing away with the Jewish community? Two traditions that supply answers have survived. In 1304 the Italian Dominican preacher Giordano da Rivalto told the story of how Bartolomeo had approached King Charles II with a charge of ritual murder against the Jews. Charles in turn ordered the arrest of all Apulian Jews and compelled them to choose baptism or death. With an assortment of variations, the same report reached the sixteenth-century Hebrew chronicler Solomon ibn Verga.

> In the year of the aforementioned expulsion [from England—1290], the two large [Jewish] communities of Naples and Trani were compelled to convert, and most [Jews in them] did. . . . I have heard reported by the elderly that a priest quarreled with a certain Jew from Trani and wanted to vent his wrath on them all. He placed a wooden statue of Jesus in the garbage. . . . When the secular authorities saw that their forces were not sufficient to resist them [the infuriated Christian mob] because they were very numerous, they advised the Jews to convert and be rescued. . . . Most did convert, but some fled to Naples with the Gentiles in pursuit. The citizens of Naples also . . . rose up against Neapolitan Jewry, demanding that they surrender the refugees or themselves be killed. They [the Jews] saw themselves in great danger. . . . Some were forced to convert . . . , and the rest departed for distant lands.

Two other sixteenth-century Jewish writers voiced a different explanation: the king, who owed the Jews a kindness, was convinced by his advisers—perhaps the friars—that converting the Jews constituted the greatest act of piety toward them.[33]

32. Cassuto, "Ḥurban," pp. 147–48. See, for example, the grant to the converts of Salerno in A. Marongiu, ed., "Gli Ebrei di Salerno nei documenti dei secoli X-XIII," *Archivio storico per le province napoletane* 62 (1937), 265–66.

33. Giordano da Rivalto, *Prediche*, 2 vols. (Florence, 1831), 2:230–31; Solomon ibn Verga, *Shevet Yehudah* [Hebrew], ed. Azriel Shohat (Jerusalem, 1946), pp. 66–67; Samuel Usque, *Consolaçam ás tribulaçoens de Israel* 2.3.11 (Coimbra, 1906–8), pp. xa–

Giordano's explanation preceded those of the three Jewish chroniclers, but either of the two traditions is plausible. Whatever really happened, the episode helps to reveal the aggressiveness as well as the true objectives of many Dominicans and Franciscans with regard to the Jews. Through preaching, implanting fear, and extending their inquisitorial authority beyond the limits set by canon law, the mendicants seemed to be trying to rid Christian Europe of its Jewish population. Amazingly, the mendicants' persecution of Judaism did not end there but continued even after the disappearance of the Jews from various areas of Europe.

Bernard Gui

Because his attitude to Judaism both exemplifies the anti-Jewish designs of the friars and itself marks a noteworthy development in the evolution of their ideology, one Dominican inquisitor in particular deserves special consideration. Born in 1261 or 1262 in the French town of Royère, Bernard Gui made his solemn profession in the Order of Preachers in 1280. After devoting the next decade to the study of logic, physics, and theology, Gui taught at Dominican *studia* from 1290 until 1294 and then occupied various administrative positions in the order until 1307. He served as the papal inquisitor in Toulouse from 1307 until 1320, when he became bishop of Tuy; one year later, Pope John XXII transferred him to the see of Lodève, which remained his until his death in 1331. Throughout his life, Gui performed many special missions for the papal curia, further revealing the strength and energy of his orthodoxy. An extremely prolific writer as well, in his thirty-four known works Gui dealt with theology, liturgy, hagiography, the history of Church councils, the lives of popes and emperors, the history of France and her kings, French geography, the annals of the Dominican Order, the local history of Toulouse, and the Inquisition.[34] In his book on the last, the *Practica inquisitionis heretice pravitatis* com-

---

xib; Joseph ben Joshua ha-Kohen, *'Emeq ha-Bakha*, ed. M. Letteris (1885; repr., Jerusalem, 1967), pp. 64–65.

34. On Gui's life and work, see Léopold Delisle, "Notice sur les manuscrits de Bernard Gui," *Notices et extraits des manuscrits de la Bibliothèque Nationale et autres bibliothèques* 27, 2 (1879), 169–455; and Antoine Thomas, "Bernard Gui, Frère Prêcheur," *HLF* 35 (1921), 139–232. An excellent study of Gui's treatment of the Jews appears in Yerushalmi, "The Inquisition."

pleted in the 1320s, Gui expressed his views on the Jews and their religion.

Gui's *Practica* offers fascinating insight into the workings of the Inquisition and the inquisitor, but is also long and unwieldy, moving from item to item with little explanation or commentary. Its five parts consist of (1) twenty-eight formulae concerning the citation and capture of heretics, (2) fifty-six acts of grace or commutations of punishments, (3) forty-seven formulae for sentencing, (4) a discussion of the powers and duties of the inquisitor, and (5) methods for finding and interrogating different sorts of enemies of the Church.[35] From these different sections of the work, three distinct points of contact between Gui's inquisitorial handbook and Judaism emerge.

First, since the Inquisition's most immediate concern with and access to the Jews lay in the prevention of judaizing by Christians— especially those recently converted from Judaism—the *Practica* explains how the inquisitor ought to deal with *relapsi* and their Jewish compatriots. In this regard, Gui prescribes the formula for imposing penance on a Jew who has helped to receive a judaizing Christian into the Jewish community. Because the Inquisition could not force the Jew to perform acts of Christian piety, the Jew, upon confessing his wrongdoing, had to pay a fine of one hundred Turonian pounds to be spent by the inquisitor for the promotion of pious causes. The Jew received a warning that he would suffer imprisonment for future offenses.[36] Two virtually identical formulae then explain how to release a Jew from incarceration imposed for repeatedly consorting with *relapsi*. The Jew must swear "on the Law of Moses" that he will never commit such an offense again; rather, he will report all such judaizing directly to the Inquisition or subject himself to the same penalties prescribed for the *relapsi*. Again the Jew had to pay a fine, but the Inquisition retained the right to return him to jail or to increase the fine without having to show cause.[37] The *Practica* also dictates the exact questions to be used in beginning the interrogation of Jews and *relapsi* as well as

---

35. In the citations that follow, Celestin Douais' edition of the *Practica inquisitionis heretice pravitatis* (Paris, 1886) has been used for the first four parts of Gui's work; and G. Mollat's edition of *Manuel de l'inquisiteur*, 2 vols. (Paris, 1926–27), for the final part. On the contents and composition of the *Practica*, see Delisle, "Notice," pp. 351–62; Thomas, "Bernard Gui," pp. 203–9; and Mollat's introduction to Gui's *Manuel*, 1:viii–lxvi.

36. *Practica* 2.13, pp. 49–50.

37. Ibid. 2.1,4, pp. 35–36, 39–40.

the oaths of abjuration to be sworn by them.[38] In addition to promising not to aid in the judaizing process, the Jew had to swear not to blaspheme against Jesus, Mary, or the Christian faith.

The role of Jews in tempting or aiding Christians to become heretics was, according to canon law, the most justifiable reason for inquisitorial jurisdiction over them. Gui conveniently rationalized his concern with the Jews in such terms, quoting the relevant canon in the *Liber sextus*:

> The perfidious Jews try, when and where they can, secretly to pervert Christians and drag them to the Jewish perfidy, especially those who were previously Jews and converted and accepted baptism and the Christian faith, especially those who are of special concern or related to them. It has therefore been decreed that just as one should proceed against Christians who go over or return to the Jewish rite . . . as against heretics, so one should proceed against those who aid them as against those who aid heretics.[39]

Of note, however, is the fact that, like most of the material in the *Practica*, the passages cited thus far are general formulae, which leave blanks for the names of the inquisitor and accused. None allude to any specific incidents or individuals, and the records of the Inquisition in Toulouse during Gui's tenure indicate that he prosecuted only two cases of judaizing during his entire career. Yet when these passages regarding judaizing are contrasted with other more specific excerpts in the *Practica* which do refer to actual events, one gains the impression that Gui's real "Jewish" interests lay not merely with the Jews who aided *relapsi* but with Jewish books and beliefs.[40]

The second concern of the *Practica* for Judaism, then, lay with the Talmud. Gui included in his manual six letters which he wrote in January 1310, trying to begin an extensive campaign against offensive Jewish books, a program that may well have culminated in the burning of the Talmud.[41] Gui first wrote to one Iohannes de

38. *Manuel* 5.5.3, 9–10, 2:10–13, 46–51.

39. Ibid. 5.5.1, 2:6–7.

40. *Liber sententiarum inquisitionis tholosanae*, printed as the second volume of Philip van Limborch, *Historia Inquisitionis*, 2 vols. (Amsterdam, 1692), 2:167, 230. Cf. Yerushalmi, "The Inquisition," pp. 325–26.

41. On the real date of these letters, which themselves read 1309, see Yerushalmi, "The Inquisition," p. 323, n. 19. The Talmud had been burned in Paris only a month earlier; see Henri Duplès-Agier, ed., *Chroniques de Saint-Martial de Limoges* (Paris, 1874), p. 144.

Crespeyo, the royal superintendent for Jewish affairs in Toulouse, demanding under the threat of excommunication that he deliver to Gui for inspection all Jewish books found in his domain. Gui also dispatched similar, although less harshly worded, instructions to the royal seneschal at Agen, requested that the prior of the Dominican convent there supervise the roundup of the books and hold them for Gui's personal examination, and issued sentences of excommunication for those Christians who might refuse to surrender these books to the Inquisition.[42] (Elsewhere in the *Practica*, Gui includes one blanket formula for condemning the Talmud, but owing to its mention of John XXII's judgment against the Talmud, it can probably be dated in the 1320s.[43] Gui himself again burned the Talmud in Toulouse in 1319, an example which may well have induced the papal condemnation and which was followed two years later in Paris and by Bishop Jacques Fournier in Pamiers.[44])

To a certain extent, Yosef Yerushalmi is correct when he asserts, "The charges against the Talmud repeated in most of these forms are of little interest, for they simply parrot the stereotyped accusations found in the papal bulls since the time of Gregory IX."[45] For example, in the sentence of excommunication against those who would not surrender their books, Gui explained: "It is expedient and necessary for the orthodox faith that all books of the Jews containing theological errors and blasphemies against the name of the Lord Jesus Christ and his most holy mother the virgin Mary to the dishonor of that orthodox faith, be removed from circulation and justly burned."[46] Gui indicted the Talmud on the same basis on which it was condemned of 1240: doctrinal heresy and anti-Christian blasphemy. In his letter to Iohannes de Crespeyo, he even supported his charges with the fact that the Talmud "had long ago been condemned by the sentence of the lord Eudes, cardinal-legate in France."[47]

Nevertheless, despite Yerushalmi's contention, Gui's attack upon the Talmud has several instructive nuances. Most strikingly, Gui

42. *Practica* 2.48–50, pp. 67–71. The sixth letter of January 1310 releases Iohannes de Crespeyo from the threat of excommunication when official business necessitated his departure from Toulouse.

43. *Practica* 3.47, p. 170–71; here Gui mentions "speciale mandatum sanctissimi patris ac domini nostri summi pontificis domini Johannis pape XXII directum et factum tali inquisitori ut omnes et singulos libros tales comburi faciat."

44. *Liber sententiarum*, p. 273; Yerushalmi, "The Inquisition," p. 327.

45. Yerushalmi, "The Inquisition," p. 352.

46. *Practica* 2.50, p. 69.

47. Ibid. 2.48, p. 67.

totally omits the third of Nicholas Donin's major accusations: that the Talmud caused grossly unethical behavior on the part of medieval Jews toward Christians. This omission in turn derived from the limited scope of Gui's charges and correspondence. The former struck solely at Jewish books, not at Jews; the latter was directed entirely to Christian addressees. Whereas in 1239, Gregory IX ordered the confiscation of the Talmud from the Jews while they were praying in their synagogues, in 1310 Gui made no mention of Jews or synagogues. In fact, Jews no longer lived in royal France, having been expelled by King Philip IV in 1306.[48] Gui must have believed that the mere presence of rabbinic literature left behind by the exiled Jews posed a serious threat to the Christian community.[49] Accordingly, he thought it "most expedient and necessary for the purity of the orthodox faith that doctrinal errors and heresy should be eradicated not only from the hearts of the errant but also from books."[50]

In much the same way as any form of Christian heterodoxy, talmudic Judaism in the opinion of the Inquisition now constituted an ideational danger to the Church even without the presence of practicing Jews. Consequently, Bernard Gui endeavored to record all the dangerous aspects of rabbinic Judaism that he could, hoping that the knowledgeable inquisitor could better combat them. Hence the third interest of the *Practica* in Judaism: understanding Jewish beliefs and rites that might have had a bearing on Christianity and Christendom. The *Practica* first describes "the Jews' rite and manner for rejudaizing baptized converts [to Christianity] who return to the vomit of Judaism."[51] According to Gui's description, the *relapsus* must first proclaim his willingness to undergo "tymla," supposedly a Hebrew name for a ritual of immersing the body in flowing water ("in aqua currente"). The Jew presiding over the ceremony then dubs the *relapsus* a "Baaltussuna" or penitent. The latter then has his head shaved, his nails cut until they bleed, and his body scrubbed with sand—especially those parts which had

48. Yerushalmi, "The Inquisition," pp. 351–52, n. 79, thus corrects the century-old belief that Gui merely copied these pronouncements from a mid-thirteenth-century French inquisitorial handbook; cf. Robert, "Catalogue," p. 214; and Grayzel, *The Church*, pp. 341–43.
49. See Yerushalmi, "The Inquisition," p. 323; and *SRH*, 9:271–72, n. 15. Cf. Robert Anchel, *Les Juifs de France* (Paris, 1946), p. 110, n. 1; and Lewin, "Die Religionsdisputation," p. 209, which question the date of 1310 simply because French Jewry had been expelled in 1306.
50. *Practica* 3.47, p. 170.
51. *Manuel* 5.5.2, 2:6–9.

been anointed with baptismal chrism. He next proceeds with the ritual immersion; after he has dipped his body in the flowing water, the other Jews present recite: "Blessed are you, God, king of the universe, who has commanded us to be sanctified on that water or bath which is called 'tymla' in Hebrew."[52] The penitent emerges, confesses his belief in Judaism, and reenters the Jewish community with the acceptance of the other Jews. With regard to Christian-born converts to Judaism, Gui subsequently adds two details to the judaizing process: The Jews, he writes, circumcise Christian converts only partially, not completely removing the foreskin as they would from their own children. The new proselyte also received a certificate identifying him as a Jew, without which other Jews would neither eat nor drink with him.[53]

Owing to his concern with the substance of rabbinic Judaism, Gui also sought in the *Practica* to expose its anti-Christian blasphemy as best he could. First he accused the Jews of saying regularly in their prayers, "Blessed are you, God our Lord, king of the universe, who has not made me a Christian or a Gentile." Another benediction implored: "May there be no hope for apostates or converts to Christianity; may all heretics, infidels, collaborators, and informers be destroyed immediately; may all the enemies of Israel speedily be killed; and may the kingdom of evil rapidly be vanquished, broken, and destroyed in our own day. Blessed are you, God, who destroys enemies and vanquishes the wicked."[54] A third prayer praised God for not making the Jews like the idolatrous Christians and asked that the practice of all such idolatry speedily be obliterated.[55] Gui similarly attacked the Jews for their "cematha," a caustic liturgical poem for the Day of Atonement which branded Jesus the illegitimate son of a prostitute and Mary a woman of lust

52. Ibid., p. 8: "Benedictus Deus, Deus, rex seculorum, qui precepisti nobis sanctificari super istam aquam seu balneum, quod vocatur tymla in hebreo."
53. Ibid. 5.5.3, 2:12.
54. Ibid. 5.5.4, 2:14.
55. Ibid., pp. 14–16: "Super nos est adlavandum Deum super omnia ad dandam magnitudinem creatoris principii, qui non fecit nos sicut sunt gentes vel gentiles terrarum . . . qui illi inclinantes ad vanitates vanitatum et adorant ad Deum non valentem neque salvantem. Super hoc speramus tibi, Deus, Dominus noster, ad vincendum cito seu velociter in pulcritudine virtutis tue ad transeundum vel expellendum sculptilia, id est ymagines quas christiani de terra adorant ad honorem Christi. . . . Et omnes filii carnis invocant in nomine tuo ad revertendum ad te. . . . Restitues omnibus eorum jugum regni tui et regnabis super eos velociter, jugum in perpetuum, quia regnum est tibi in seculum seculi, regnabis in gloria sicut scriptum est in lege tua: 'Deus regnabit in eternum et in seculum seculi.'"

and luxury.[56] Finally, the *Practica* indicted various medieval rabbis for their commentaries on the Bible and the Talmud: Rabbi Solomon ben Isaac (Rashi), the most widely cited and respected Jewish biblical exegete, employed many talmudic absurdities in his commentary, denied the divine and messianic nature of Jesus, and labeled Christians heretics and infidels; Maimonides in his *Mishneh Torah* and Rabbi David Qimḥi in his commentary on Psalms expounded in the same fashion; the former even asserted that Jesus had committed greater misdeeds than Muhammad, placing most of the world in doctrinal error.[57]

Vindictive as all of Gui's accusations might be, they are remarkable for their accuracy; the inquisitor clearly intended to give a faithful representation of contemporary Jewish practice. The account of the rejudaizing rite is highly plausible in all its detail. The threefold immersion (what Gui dubbed *tymla*) and accompanying benediction conform almost exactly to the ancient practice of dipping (*ṭevilah*) in the ritual bath of flowing water (*in aqua currente*) still in use today for converts to Judaism. Especially in view of various medieval Jewish attitudes toward the apostate as one who indeed had left the fold, it makes sense that such a rite would have been prescribed for the *conversus* who later returned as a penitent (*ba'al teshuvah* = Gui's *Baaltussuna*). The Bible itself (Deuteronomy 21:10–13) requires the shaving of the head and manicure in the conversion of a Gentile woman taken captive in war, and other medieval sources, both Christian and Jewish, confirm that such rituals must have existed. Rabbinical courts to this day issue certificates of conversion, and while it is difficult to imagine how partial (*semiplene*) circumcision would have sufficed for the Jews, at least the Inquisition's belief in the existence of this practice finds corroboration in another thirteenth-century source.[58] With regard to Gui's liturgical citations, all of them represent accurate quotations from the Jewish

56. Ibid., pp. 16–19.
57. Ibid., p. 18.
58. See Katz, *Exclusiveness and Tolerance*, pp. 67–76 (esp. 73 n. 3); and Netanyahu, *The Marranos*, pp. 5–22. A forced Jewish convert to Christianity gave a similar description of this rite to the Inquisition at Pamiers in 1320; see above, n. 5. For further confirmation, in both inquisitorial and rabbinic sources, see Yerushalmi, "The Inquisition," pp. 369–76; and Joseph Shatzmiller, "Converts and Judaizers in the Early Fourteenth Century," forthcoming in the *HTR*. I am grateful to Mr. Shatzmiller for providing me with a copy of his essay in advance of its publication. On partial circumcision, cf. the anonymous *Tractatus de haeresi pauperum de Lugduno* in *Thesaurus novus anecdotorum*, ed. Edmund Martène and Ursinus Durand, 5 vols. (1717; repr., New York, 1968), 5:1794.

prayerbook, except insofar as they mention Christians;[59] Gui himself admits that Christians are not mentioned, and he has simply included his inferences in his translation.[60] The three rabbinic exegetes adduced by Gui all naturally bore hostility toward Christianity, sentiments that previous Christian polemicists had already noted.[61]

The attitude of Friar Bernard Gui toward Judaism has a twofold importance in the history of the relationship between the medieval Church and the Jews. On the one hand, his *Practica*, which quickly gained and for a long time commanded respect as a guide for inquisitors, rendered concern with the Jews a permanent aspect of the operations of the papal Inquisition. The zealousness of a Nicholas Donin or a Bartolomeo de Aquila in trying to rid Christian civilization of infection by contemporary Jews, a zealousness that derived from the initiative of the individual friar, could now be communicated to any inquisitor simply through the reading of Gui's manual. In this sense, Gui did not innovate; he merely institutionalized. On the other hand, his approach to the Talmud and rabbinic Jews constituted a revolutionary development. If other inquisitors before him had viewed the Jews as a noxious element in Christendom because of postbiblical rabbinic ideas, Gui now attacked rabbinic literature even in the absence of Jews. In no way did he feel the Church could tolerate Jewish theology.

The Inquisition and the Jews

Less than a century elapsed between the friars' first intervention in the controversy over the works of Maimonides and Bernard Gui's composition of the *Practica*. Yet much of the force of Augus-

59. For Gui's three quotations from the daily Jewish liturgy, see S. Baer, *'Avodat Yisra'el*: the blessing of God "who has not made me a Gentile," p. 4 and n.; "May there be no hope for apostates," p. 93 and n. (and see above, Ch. 3, n. 42); and the praise of God for not making Jews idolatrous, the *'Aleinu* prayer, p. 131 and n. On the *Shamta* (Gui's *cematha*), see Ch. Merchavya, "The Caustic Poetic Rebuke (*Shamta*) in Medieval Christian Polemical Literature [Hebrew]," *Tarbiz* 41 (1971), 95–115; and Yerushalmi, "The Inquisition," pp. 360–63.

60. *Manuel* 5.5.4, 2:16: "Notandum autem quod in predictis verbis Judei intendunt imprecari christianis, quamvis expresse non nominent christianos set sit per circumloqutionem, quamvis ipsi expresse intendant et intelligant de populo christianorum."

61. Merchavya, *The Church*, p. 419, gives a complete listing of the citations of Rashi in the Latin anthology of talmudic quotations compiled in the wake of the trials in Paris. In the 1270s, Raymond Martini already quoted the thirteenth-century David Qimhi's books in his *Pugio fidei*; see below, Ch. 6. For Maimonides' definition of Christianity as idolatry, see his *MT*, Laws of Idolatry, 9.4.

tine's call for toleration of the Jews because their survival and that of their beliefs could be put to good use by the Church had vanished in mendicant circles. Although canon law still technically protected Jews' lives and property, Judaism came to be treated in practice as a pernicious heresy, a religion with no legitimate place in Christian society. The friars of the Inquisition may have paid lip service to the canons protecting the Jews and their niche in Christendom, but men so zealous as these were not easily thwarted. They wisely chose to attack the rabbinic Judaism of the Talmud, which did indeed hold the Jews steadfast in their beliefs, and perhaps they exploited the blanket provision in canon law making any Jew who consorted with judaizers also subject to inquisitorial jurisdiction. Simultaneously, the friars encroached upon the actual practice of Jewish life, forcibly entering synagogues and subjecting Jews to offensive harangues, participation in debates whose outcomes had been predetermined, and the violence of the mob. The intent of the friars was obvious: to eliminate the Jewish presence in Christendom—both by inducing the Jews to convert and by destroying all remnants of Judaism even after no Jews remained.

This constituted the change in the Jewish policy of the Church hinted at by Pope Innocent IV when he condemned the Talmud: an offensive against the religious life of the Jew. I shall explore the underlying causes of this development at the conclusion of this book. Suffice it to note here, however, that although the zeal of the mendicants, the efficient cause of the change, at first may have contravened the spirit of traditional ecclesiastical protection of the Jews, the Church quickly rallied behind the friars. In his commentary on the *Decretales*, Innocent IV asserted the right of the papacy not only to compel Jews to listen to conversionist sermons but also to police the internal religious affairs of the Jewish community.

> Indeed, we believe that the pope, who is the vicar of Jesus Christ, has authority not only over Christians but also over all infidels, since Christ had authority over all. . . . Therefore, the pope can judge the Jews, if they violate the law of the Gospel in moral matters and their own prelates do not check them, and also if they invent heresies against their own law. Induced by this rationale, Popes Gregory and Innocent ordered the books of the Talmud, in which there were contained many heresies, to be burned, and they commanded that those who followed or taught these heresies be punished.[62]

62. Innocent IV, *Commentaria . . . super libros quinque decretalium* ad X.3.34.8, 2 vols. (Frankfurt, 1570), 1:430: "Sed bene tamen credimus, quod Papa qui est vicarius

S. W. Baron has interpreted this passage as part of the papal endeavor to support the curia's claims—as opposed to those of the Holy Roman Emperor—to lordship over the Jews, who had been condemned to perpetual servitude in Christendom.[63] The reality of any such papal-imperial conflict notwithstanding, Innocent here has not alluded to Jewish servitude. Rather, in an ex post facto justification for the burning of the Talmud, he has assumed for the papacy supreme doctrinal authority in the internal religious affairs of all peoples, not only those of Christian communities. In other words, he has proclaimed the unwillingness of the Church to tolerate any heresy whatsoever, especially such a heresy—in this case orthodox Judaism—as might impede the Christianization of Europe.

Innocent's line of thought quickly became the common opinion of thirteenth- and fourteenth-century canonists.[64] It apparently guided the friars of the papal Inquisition. By the second half of the fourteenth century, the Dominican inquisitor Nicholas Eymeric considered it a direct mandate to the Inquisition to defend genuine Judaism against internal heresy and thereby to bring Jews closer to an acceptance of Christianity.[65] For the period under consideration

---

Iesu Christi potestatem habet non tantum super Christianos, sed etiam super omnes infideles, cum enim Christus habuerit super omnes potestatem. . . . Item Iudaeos potest iudicare Papa, si contra legem evangelii faciunt in moralibus, si eorum praelati eos non puniant, et eodem modo, si haereses circa suam legem inveniant, et hac ratione motus Papa Gregorius et Innocentius mandaverunt comburi libros talium [probably "Talmut" or "Talmuti"], in quos multae continebantur haereses, et mandaverunt puniri illos, qui praedictas haereses sequerentur, vel docerent. . . . Item licet non debeant infideles cogi ad fidem, quia omnes libero arbitrio relinquendi sunt, et sola Dei gratia in hac vocatione valeat . . . tamen mandare potest Papa infidelibus, quod admittant praedicatores Evangelii in terris suae iurisdictionis, nam cum omnis creatura rationabilis facta sit ad Deum laudandum . . . si ipsi prohibent praedicatores praedicare peccant, et ideo puniendi sunt."

63. Baron, "'Plenitude of Apostolic Power,'" pp. 294, 528; cf. James Muldoon, *Popes, Lawyers, and Infidels: The Church and the Non-Christian World, 1250–1550* (Philadelphia, 1979), p. 154.

64. See the decretal commentaries of Hostiensis, Ioannes Andreae, and Franciscus Zabarella which mention the Talmud by name; and Muldoon, *Popes*, pp. 23–26.

65. Eymeric, *Directorium* 2.46.3–4, pp. 244–45: "Quaedam alia sunt nobis Christianis, et iudaeis communia, per quae a nobis Christianis non distinguuntur, nec iudaei sunt nec habentur: utpote, credere Deum unum esse, et illum creatorem omnium, et similia. Et si iudaei in his ab eorum priori credentia discedant, et ea abnegent esse vera, heretici et in priori promissa fidelitate, et in eorum theologia seu lege, et communi iudaeorum extimatione sunt, et habentur. Et quia in his nobiscum conveniunt, et talia negare, est legem Christianam directe agitare; ideo a Christianis, et fidei Christi iudicibus Episcopis, et Inquisitoribus arctandi sunt ea credere; et fidem, quam Deo in his credendo promiserunt, firmiter observare. Si

in this book, it also characterized the attitudes of most other Dominicans and Franciscans who left written records of an interest in Judaism: missionaries, academic orientalists, and local preachers. The activities of the Inquisition had provided the most common and immediate locus for the clash between the mendicants and the Jews. But it remained for these other friars to perceive the theoretical nuances underlying the inquisitorial sort of anti-Jewish hostility, to develop them into a working ideology, and then to apply that ideology to the extent of its logical conclusions.

---

ergo inveniantur iudaei in his, quae nobis Christianis et eis sunt communia, delinquere, verbo vel facto ea abnegando, ut si asserant verbo, Deum non unum esse, vel facto, demonibus sacrificando quod est facto asserere demonum fore Deum, et similia perpetrare, praesertim in praesentia Christianorum, debent ut haeretici in eorum lege, et ut fautores haereticorum contra legem Christi, et inductores, arctari et puniri per episcopos, et inquisitores iudices fidei."

PART TWO

Ideological Refinements

5

The School of Raymond de Peñaforte: Pablo Christiani

Most of the confrontations between the friars and the Jews already considered in this book occurred north and east of the Pyrenees; but we must now turn to the work of a group of Dominicans on the Iberian peninsula in order to view a second stage in the development of the new anti-Jewish polemic. Spain was unique during the Middle Ages, both in the history of Latin Christendom and in the history of the Jews. The early centuries of Muslim domination and the Christian reconquest that began almost as soon as the Moorish invasion ended made Spain the main point of convergence between medieval Judaism, Christianity, and Islam. Medieval Spain displayed an enlightenment and a sophistication unknown to the rest of the continent; her palaces, her schools, and even her highways were frequented by travelers from all over the Mediterranean world, facilitating a highly complex and variegated cultural exchange. The various products of this interaction—in literature, art, architecture, philosophy, and science—all bore the singular stamp of an Iberian culture, which alone seemed capable of overcoming the narrowmindedness and provincialism that characterized most of Christian Europe.[1]

The Jews in particular benefited from the cosmopolitan aspects of medieval Spanish society. As a legal minority under Muslim as well as Christian rule, they possessed the cultural and social wherewithal to adapt successfully to either, and each warring party recognized the value of the Jews in dealing with the enemy. Jews

---

1. Cf. Hillgarth, *The Spanish Kingdoms*, 1:155.

took a leading role in the cultural symbiosis that occurred in medieval Spain, enriching their own civilization at the same time as they facilitated increased contact between the others. And Jews were constantly employed by Muslim and Christian princes as colonizers, diplomats, finance ministers, spies, and tax collectors. They enjoyed a tranquility (by medieval standards) that suffered disturbance only on rare occasions.

One of these disturbances was the persecution of the Jews by the Almohade Berbers in the middle of the twelfth century, which drove many Jews out of the Iberian peninsula and put an end to the famous "Golden Age" of Spanish-Jewish history. By the thirteenth century, however, the forces of the *Reconquista* had broken the power of the Almohades, and prosperity returned to the Jews of Spain, certainly in comparison to their situation elsewhere in Christendom.[2] It is noteworthy that the friars pursued and even refined their anti-Jewish program under these circumstances; if the favorable status of the Jews in Spain perhaps hampered the friars' ability to proceed against them, it may also have served to stimulate the mendicants to greater vehemence. In any event, the Jewish community of medieval Spain did not embark upon its permanent decline until after several generations of pronounced anti-Jewish activity on the part of the friars, activity that will be examined in this chapter and the one to follow.

Raymond de Peñaforte

One Dominican conspicuously appears in the midst of many of the mendicants' activities previously mentioned, both those directed specifically at the Jews and those pertaining to the general state of the Church and its fight against heresy. Raymond de Peñaforte was born near Barcelona in the small village of Villafranca del Penades between 1175 and 1180. For several years he taught at the cathedral school in Barcelona, where he himself had studied, and then in 1210 he left to study at the University of Bologna. Having received his doctorate and *licentia ubique docendi* in 1216 and returned to Barcelona, he instructed at the seminary for clergy there,

2. On the favorable treatment of the Jews in thirteenth-century Spain, especially in Aragon where the friars enjoyed greater influence than in Castile, see ibid., 1:161–214; Y. Baer, *A History*, 1:111–242; and J. Lee Shneidman, *The Rise of the Aragonese-Catalan Empire, 1200–1350*, 2 vols. (New York, 1970), 2:417–58.

and in 1222 he entered the Order of Preachers. In 1230, Gregory IX summoned Raymond to the curia and chose him as his confessor. There Raymond remained until 1238 when he became Master-General of the Dominicans, a post he relinquished only two years later in order to return to his convent in Barcelona, where he resided until his death in 1275.[3]

Raymond de Peñaforte's life accordingly combined careers of scholarship, service to the Church and the Dominicans, and contemplation, in a way that allowed him to pursue directly many of those goals for which his order had been founded. While at Rome, he edited the collection of *Decretales* promulgated by Gregory IX with the aim of rendering the workings of ecclesiastical government stronger and more uniform. During his tenure as Dominican Master-General, Raymond instituted a revision of the order's constitutions, which like the *Decretales* remained in large part in effect until the early twentieth century.[4] But most of all, Raymond's zealousness manifested itself in his efforts to uphold orthodoxy within Christendom by fighting heresy and to expand the dominion of the Roman Church by converting the infidel. He worked closely with the archbishop of Tarragona to regularize procedures in the battle against heresy in Aragon, and he himself convinced King James I to permit the establishment of the Inquisition in his domains.[5] Toward the end of his life, Raymond prevailed upon Thomas Aquinas to compose his *Summa contra gentiles* as a means of attracting converts to Christianity.[6]

3. A. Teetaert, "Raymond de Penyafort (Saint)," *Dictionnaire de théologie catholique*, ed. A. Vacant et al., 15 vols. (Paris, 1908–50), 13,2:1806–9; Mortier, *Histoire des maîtres généraux*, 1:255–85; José Giménez y Martínez de Carvajal, "San Raimundo de Peñaforte y las Partidas de Alfonso X el Sabio," *Anthologica annua: Publicaciones del Instituto español de estudios eclesiasticos* 3 (1955), pp. 302–14; Fernando Valls-Taberner, *San Ramón de Penyaforte* (1936; repr. as Obras selectas 1,2, Madrid, 1953), pp. 213–87.

4. See *Rex pacificus*, Gregory's bull of promulgation for the *Decretales*, in Ripoll, *Bullarium*, 1:69; and Hinnebusch, *A History*, 1:172.

5. On Raymond's role in founding the Aragonese Inquisition, see the letters of Gregory IX in Franciscus Balme and Ceslaus Paben, eds., *Raymundiana*, Monumenta Ordinis Fratrum Praedicatorum historica 6, 2 fascs. (Rome, 1900), 2:41–46; Celestin Douais, "Saint Raymond de Peñafort et les hérétiques: Directoire à l'usage des inquisiteurs aragonais, 1242," *Le Moyen Age* 12 (1899), 305–25; and, for the view that in this connection Raymond composed most of the first manual of inquisitorial procedure, Antoine Dondaine, "Le Manuel de l'inquisiteur (1230–1330)," *AFP* 17 (1947) 96, 131–32. Raymond's influence over King James is described by Petrus Marsilius, *Cronicae illustrissimi regis Aragonum domini Iacobi victoriosissimi principis* (1312), cited in Balme and Paben, *Raymundiana*, 1:12.

6. Petrus Marsilius, *Cronicae*, cited in Thomas Aquinas, *Liber de veritate catholice fidei contra errores infidelium*, ed. Peter Marc et al., 3 vols. (Tours, 1961–67), 1:73.

In the concerns of this book too, Raymond holds a place of considerable importance. Because he had great influence at the curia in the 1230s, one writer has gone so far as to suggest that "the moving spirit . . . of Gregory IX in all that affected the Jews was, no doubt, the famous Raymund de Peñaforte."[7] In his desire to eradicate heresy, the Dominican may well have induced Gregory to respond cooperatively to the anti-talmudic designs of Nicholas Donin. As a councillor of King James I in the next decade, Raymond, it is not unlikely, inspired the initial decree compelling the Jews of Aragon to attend the friars' conversionist sermons.[8] Yet by far the most significant effects his activities had on the Jews derived from the missionary programs which he himself inspired and directed but which he implemented through the efforts of two other Dominicans, Pablo Christiani and Raymond Martini.

As committed as he was to converting the infidel, Raymond de Peñaforte adhered firmly to the maxim of Gregory the Great included in Gratian's *Decretum* that non-Christians had to be converted "soothingly" (*blandimentis*).[9] To proselytize effectively, the missionary had to appeal to the infidels on their own terms—that is, with sources and arguments they themselves would consider authoritative. Aquinas in the *Summa contra gentiles* explained the rationale thus:

> To proceed against individual errors, however, is a difficult business, and this for two reasons. In the first place, it is difficult because the sacrilegious remarks of individual men who have erred are not so well known to us that we may use what they say as the basis of proceeding to a refutation of their errors. This is, indeed, the method that the ancient Doctors of the Church used in the refutation of the errors of the Gentiles. . . . In the second place, it is difficult because some of them, such as the Mohammedans and the pagans, do not agree with us in accepting the authority of any Scripture, by which they may be convinced of their error. Thus, against the Jews we are able to argue by means of the Old Testament. But the Mohammedans and the pagans accept neither one nor the other. We must, therefore, have recourse to the natural reason, to which all men are forced to give their assent.[10]

7. Williams, *Adversus Judaeos*, p. 242.

8. See Graetz, *Geschichte*, 7:119; and Y. Baer, *A History*, 1:147; Baer maintains that Raymond was also the personal confessor of James I. Cf. Joseph F. O'Callaghan, *A History of Medieval Spain* (Ithaca, 1975), p. 465.

9. Raymond de Peñaforte, *Summa* 1.4.1, p. 24; *Decretum*, D. 45, c. 3.

10. Thomas Aquinas, *Liber de veritate* 1.2, 2:4; in Thomas Aquinas, *On the Truth of the Catholic Faith* 1, trans. Anton C. Pegis (Garden City, N.Y., 1955), 62. On the

Yet to convince the Muslims and the Jews of the truth of Christianity, one also had to have a command of their languages. Raymond consequently founded Dominican *studia* to teach Arabic and Hebrew, schools designed especially for the missionary which issued not the usual teaching license (*licentia docendi*) to their graduates but rather a permit to dispute matters of faith (*licentia disputandi*). By 1250, Raymond de Peñaforte had dispatched a carefully selected group of friars to establish a *studium arabicum* in Tunis; a school in Murcia soon commenced instruction in both Arabic and Hebrew, and by the end of the century other schools had opened in Jativa, Valencia, and Barcelona.[11]

Through the study of Hebrew, Raymond intended to overcome the obstinacy of the Jews. As an anonymous fourteenth-century biographer of his reported,

> With his advice and approval, certain friars were thus instructed in the Hebrew language, so that they could overcome the malice and the errors of the Jews, who might no longer, as they had been accustomed to do in the past, audaciously deny the true text and the glosses of their own sages which agree with our own saints in these matters

novelty of this missionary approach of the Dominicans—the blend of scholastic rationalism with adaptation to the culture to which a mission was directed—see Burns, "Christian-Islamic Confrontation," pp. 139/ff.

11. Petrus Marsilius, *Cronicae*, cited in Thomas Aquinas, *Liber de veritate*, 1:73: "Studium linguarum pro fratribus sui ordinis Tunicii et Murciae statuit, ad quae fratres Cathalanos electos destinari procuravit. Qui in multum fructum animarum profecerunt, et in suae decoratum nationis." A fifteenth-century hagiographer named Theobald embellished this story considerably; see Alberto Collell, ed., "Raymundiana: Appéndice a un diplomaterio," *Analecta sacra tarraconensia* 30 (1957), 88–89: "Ostense fuit sancto Raimundo a Domino visio quadam vice quod fratres predicatores deberent inter gentes facere magnum fructum, et quod deberent ad conversionem infidelium operam dare. Propter quam visionem, accepta auctoritate a magistro ordinis et a regibus Castelle et Aragonie elegit XX fratres ydoneos et industrios, quos studere fecit in linguis scilicet abraica [sic] et arabica in quibus in brevi tempore profecerunt in tantum quod magistros suos primo converterunt ad fidem et postea plusquam decem milia saracenorum de Yspania et de Africa fidem receperunt et baptizati sunt et per illos divulgata est in illis partibus veritas fidei christiane. Erat enim sancto Raimundo cura sollicita circa neophitos conservandos in fide." On the growth and nature of the *studia* see Berthier, "Les écoles de langues orientales," pp. 88–96; Burns, "Christian-Islamic Confrontation," pp. 1401–10; Altaner, *Die Dominikanermissionen*, pp. 91ff.; Altaner, "Die fremdsprachliche Ausbildung der Dominikanermissionare während des 13. und 14. Jahrhunderts," *Zeitschrift für Missionswissenschaft und Religionswissenschaft* 23 (1933), 223–41; J. M. Coll, "Escuelas de lenguas orientales an los siglos XIII y XIV," *Analecta sacra tarraconensia* 18 (1945), 58–89, 19 (1946), 233–39; Coll, "Las disputas teológicas en la Edad Media," ibid. 20 (1947), 77–101; Coll, "San Raymundo de Peñafort y las misiones del Norte Africano en la Edad Media," *Missionalia hispanica* 5 (1948), 417–57; and Valls-Taberner, *San Ramon*, pp. 314–19.

pertaining to the Catholic faith. Moreover, [the friars studied Hebrew] so that the falsehoods and corruptions which they [the Jews] had inserted in many places in the Bible to hide the mysteries of the Passion and other sacraments of the faith, might be revealed through their authentic scriptural texts—which is all meant to confuse them [the Jews] greatly and confirm the Christian faith.[12]

Regrettably, no records remain of any significant disputations between the Jews and Raymond himself.[13] Nevertheless, the similarity of tactics that two of his disciples brought to their anti-Jewish polemics serves well to elucidate his own ideology.

The Disputation of 1263

During the summer of 1263, King James I of Aragon summoned Rabbi Moses ben Naḥman (Naḥmanides) of Gerona to debate with Friar Pablo Christiani before the royal court in Barcelona. Born a Jew in Montpellier, Pablo had originally been named Saul, and he had studied Jewish literature under the direction of Rabbis Eliezer ben Emmanuel of Tarascon and Jacob ben Elijah Lattès of Venice. But probably as early as 1229, when Raymond de Peñaforte had preached and missionized in Provence, Pablo converted to Christianity and quickly joined the Order of Preachers. In accordance with the objectives of the great Dominican master who had converted him, he devoted the rest of his life to proselytizing among his former coreligionists. In the view of at least one modern scholar, Pablo had already debated the distinguished Rabbi Meir ben Simeon of Narbonne several years before the great disputation at Barcelona, which was probably not his first meeting with Naḥmanides either. After his encounter with Naḥmanides in 1263, Pablo carried his mission beyond the Pyrenees to the Jews of northern France; he died in 1274.[14]

12. Balme and Paben, *Raymundiana*, 1:32.

13. At the conclusion of his account of his disputation with Pablo Christiani in Barcelona in 1263, Moses Naḥmanides relates (Chavel, 1:319–20) that eight days after the debate had ended, King James and a group of Dominicans interrupted Sabbath services in the Barcelona synagogue in order to preach to the Jews. Raymond de Peñaforte was then the first to speak for the Christians, and delivered a sermon on the Trinity; no other such instance has come to my attention.

14. Very little is known concerning the details of Pablo's life. A late thirteenth-century Hebrew polemic which reviews some of the proceedings of 1263 mentions Pablo as "an apostate from Montpellier . . . who has already debated against Rabbi Moses ben Naḥman before the king of Aragon in Barcelona." See Judah M. Rosen-

The disputation of Barcelona lasted through four sessions, conducted between Friday, July 20, and Friday, July 27, 1263. Having learned of the designs of his opponents, Naḥmanides remained in Barcelona through the Sabbath of August 4 to argue again with James and Pablo when they came to preach in the main synagogue of the city, and he returned to Gerona on the following day.[15] Between August 26 and 29, apparently motivated by what transpired at the debate, James issued four decrees pertaining to the

---

thal, ed., "A Religious Disputation between a Jew Called Menaḥem and the Convert Pablo Christiani [Hebrew]," in *Hagut Ivrit ba'Amerika: Studies in Jewish Themes by Contemporary American Scholars* 3, ed. Menahem Zohori et al. (Tel Aviv, 1974), 62. The sixteenth-century Jewish chronicler Isaac de Lattès in his book *Sha'arei Ṣion* mentions a Jewish convert to Christianity named Paul who had once studied under Eliezer ben Emmanuel of Tarascon and later debated with Rabbi Mordekhai ben Joseph of Avignon; the apostate later died in a place called in Hebrew *Tavar Mina*. For the identification of this Paul with Pablo, see Henri Gross, *Gallia judaica*, trans. Moïse Bloch, ed. Simon Schwarzfuchs (Amsterdam, 1969), p. 4, and for the various alternatives for the locality of his death, p. 5; cf. also Ernst Renan and Adolph Neubauer, "Les rabbins français du commencement du quatorzième siècle," *HLF* 27 (1877) [repr. in separate volume, Farnborough, Eng., 1969], 564–69; and Cecil Roth, "The Disputation of Barcelona (1263)," *HTR* 43 (1950), 143, n. 41. Both manuscripts of the bitter invective sent to a Friar Paul—commonly assumed to have been Pablo Christiani—by Jacob ben Elijah Lattès of Venice conclude: "This is the letter sent by Rabbi Jacob to Saul, renamed Paul . . . , who had been his student before his conversion." See Jacob's "'Iggeret (Wikkuaḥ)," ed. Joseph Kobak, *Jeschurun* 6 (1868), 31; and for the identification of the addressee with Pablo, see Kobak's n. 1 on pp. 1–2 of the "'Iggeret"; and Jacob Mann, "Une source de l'histoire juive au XIIIᵉ siècle: La lettre polémique de Jacob b. Elie à Pablo Christiani," *REJ* 82 (1926), 363–77. For the suggestion that Pablo converted in 1229 because of Raymond de Peñaforte's missionizing, see Williams, *Adversus Judaeos*, p. 244; and Roth, "The Disputation," p. 120. Despite the sound objections of Merchavya, "Concerning the Debate," p. 298, n. 11, Chazan's claim that Pablo was the "preaching prostitute" (*ha-qadesh ha-doresh*) who debated with Meir ben Simeon in Narbonne is especially tempting because Guy Fulcodi (then Archbishop of Narbonne), when he later became Pope Clement IV, issued a bull (*Dampnabili perfidia Iudeorum*) recommending Pablo as a highly qualified censor of Jewish literature; see Robert Chazan, "Confrontation in the Synagogue of Narbonne: A Christian Sermon and a Jewish Reply," *HTR* 67 (1974), esp. 445, 451–53, 457. At the very least, Chazan's emendation of the printed Hebrew text of the 1263 disputation to state that Pablo had previously preached to the Jews in Provence and elsewhere is undoubtedly correct; see "Confrontation," p. 452, n. 50. Finally, both Latin and Hebrew accounts of the disputation of 1263 indicate that Pablo had debated with Naḥmanides in Gerona prior to their meeting in Barcelona; see Y. Baer, "The Disputations," p. 185; and Chavel, 1:320.

15. This is the account of Naḥmanides himself—Chavel, 1:319–20—although the Latin protocol describing the disputation recorded that Naḥmanides fled from Barcelona in the king's absence before the debate could be completed; see Y. Baer, "The Disputations," p. 187. Because the rabbi has given a report of the actual dialogue in the synagogue, even if he slanted it in his own favor, and because the text of Naḥmanides' sermon delivered after the Christian contingent left the synagogue survives, his story appears the more credible.

Jews: he ordered the Jews to attend Dominican sermons, demanded that blasphemous passages be expurgated from Jewish books, established a censorship commission to achieve that purpose, and especially empowered Pablo to missionize among the Jews. Meanwhile, Naḥmanides in Gerona composed and distributed his own written account of the disputation, quite naturally unfavorable to the Dominicans. As a consequence, King James ordered him exiled for two years and his pamphlet burned. The Dominicans, dissatisfied with such a lenient punishment, again brought Naḥmanides before the king in 1265, this time on charges of blasphemy, but James accepted the rabbi's defense that a license of free speech had been granted him at the disputation. The persistent friars appealed to Rome, and Clement IV responded in 1266 with a letter to James I calling for royal diligence in suppressing Jewish audacity, especially that of Naḥmanides. The latter left Aragon for Palestine soon thereafter.

As in the case of the disputation of Paris in 1240, both Latin and Hebrew documents report what took place in Barcelona, the former a brief summary drawn up by the Dominicans and confirmed by James I soon after the debate and the latter the much longer and more detailed pamphlet of Naḥmanides. Yet unlike the proceedings at Paris, the disputation of 1263 had no catastrophic aftermath comparable to the burning of the Talmud, and its "outcome" is difficult to discern; the Dominican notary and Naḥmanides each claimed an uncontested victory. Modern historiography has produced many attempted reconstructions of the disputation, the stratagems employed therein, and its aftermath, often composed with the intent of determining who in truth emerged the victor.[16]

16. On the background, events, and aftermath of this disputation, see Graetz, *Geschichte*, 7:119–26; Denifle, "Quellen," pp. 225–31; Isidore Loeb, "La controverse de 1263 à Barcelona entre Paulus Christiani et Moise ben Nahman," *REJ* 15 (1887), 1–18; Dubnow, *Weltgeschichte*, 5:95–96; Y. Baer, *A History*, 1:150–62, and "The Disputations," pp. 180ff.; J. M. Millás Vallicrosa, "Sobre las fuentes documentales de la controversia de Barcelona en el año 1263," *Anales de la Universidad de Barcelona: Memorias y comunicaciones* 1940, 25–44; Coll, "Escuelas," 19:217–33; *SRH*, 9:83–87; Roth, "The Disputation"; M. Cohen, "Reflections," pp. 157–92; and Daniel, *Islam*, p. 184. Most recently, Robert Chazan has studied the forensic tactics and ploys of each disputant, highlighting the immediate objectives of Pablo Christiani in staging the disputation and the efforts of Naḥmanides to make himself appear victorious. See his "The Barcelona 'Disputation' of 1263: Christian Missionizing and Jewish Response," *Speculum* 52 (1977), 824–42. James's edicts appear in Denifle, "Quellen," pp. 234–43; cf. Régné, *History*, pp. 40–42, 47, 58–59 (nos. 209, 212, 215–17, 249, 323). Most scholars assume the identification of Bonastruc de Porta in James's edict of 1265 with Naḥmanides (Denifle, pp. 239–40; Régné, pp. 58–59 [no. 323]), but there

The worth of such endeavors is itself questionable given the obvious biases pervading both the documents under examination, and specifying the winner and loser of the debate happily does not concern us presently. Yet despite the abundance of modern descriptions of the events of 1263, historians have never adequately explored the underlying theological approach taken by the Dominicans to Judaism at the disputation, and it is precisely this attitude that I shall attempt to elucidate.

Fortunately, both Latin and Hebrew sources agree as to the basic agenda of the disputation. According to the Latin protocol, Pablo intended to prove to Naḥmanides the truth of four propositions: "(1) that the messiah, which means Christ, whom the Jews have been awaiting, has undoubtedly [already] come; (2) that the same messiah, as had been prophesied, should at once be divine and human; (3) that he in fact suffered and died for the salvation of the human race; [and] (4) that the legal or ceremonial [provisions of the Old Testament] terminated and were supposed to terminate after the arrival of the said messiah."[17] Pablo structured the debate around a dozen biblical texts and rabbinic homilies which he claimed proved his propositions. Unlike the Latin notary,

---

is still disagreement over whether one Astrug de Porta, appearing in three royal decrees (Régné, pp. 49, 57 [nos. 262, 315–16]), who had been recalled from an exile imposed for offensive remarks made at a disputation, was Naḥmanides. For both points of view, see M. Kayserling, "Die Disputation des Bonastruc mit Frai Pablo in Barcelona" *MGWJ* 14 (1865), 308–13; and Heinrich Graetz, same title, ibid., pp. 428–33. Finally, the reader might wish to take note of the interesting, though altogether spurious story that as a result of the disputation Naḥmanides converted to Christianity and then helped in the conversion of many of his former coreligionists; this account is reported as fact in the *Enciclopedia universal ilustrada europaeo-americana*, 70 vols. (Barcelona, 1907–30), 8:1582. (I am grateful to my student Steven Gershbein for calling this reference to my attention.) The Latin protocol of the disputation appeared most recently in Y. Baer, "The Disputations," pp. 185–87; it has been translated in Robert Chazan, ed., *Church, State, and Jew in the Middle Ages* (New York, 1980), pp. 266–69. The charge of Loeb, "La controverse de 1263," p. 7, that the Latin protocol is a distorted account of the debate written as much as two years after the event, is unfounded and unfair, especially if one realizes that its author intended it not as a transcript but merely as a summary. Naḥmanides' Hebrew account of the debate is in Chavel, 1:297–320. Annotated English translations appear in Oliver Shaw Rankin, ed., *Jewish Religious Polemic* (Edinburgh, 1956), pp. 157–235, and Moses ben Naḥman, *Writings and Discourses*, trans. Charles B. Chavel, 2 vols. (New York, 1978), 2:651–96. For a translation of both Hebrew and Latin accounts into German, with notes and commentary that comprise a thorough review of the pertinent secondary literature, see Hermine Grossinger, "Die Disputation des Nachmanides mit Fra Pablo Christiani, Barcelona 1263," *Kairos*, n.s. 19 (1977), 257–85, 20 (1978), 1–15, 161–81.

17. Y. Baer, "The Disputations," p. 185.

Naḥmanides gives a chronological account of the four sessions which comprised the disputation, and it is from his pamphlet that the following schema of Pablo's arguments has been compiled.

First session

   (1) Genesis 49:10 and TB Sanhedrin 5a—The Jews' loss of political power proves that the messiah has already come.
   (2) Midrash *Lamentations Rabbati* 1.57—The messiah was born on the day the temple was destroyed; he therefore has come.
   (3) Isaiah 52:13—The Suffering Servant was the messiah who suffered and died to save mankind.
   (4) TB Sanhedrin 98a—Elijah told Rabbi Joshua ben Levi that the messiah has come and is in Rome.

Second session

   (5) Isaiah 52:13 and Midrash *Yalquṭ* on Isaiah § 476—The messiah is greater than Abraham, Moses, and the angels; he therefore must be divine.
   (6) A homily of Rabbi Moses ha-Darshan—The messiah was meant to accept punishments to atone for Israel's sins.
   (7) Daniel 9:24ff. and Midrash *Yalquṭ* on Hosea § 518—Daniel's prophecy of seventy weeks proves that the messiah must have come.
   (8) Tractate *Derekh Ereṣ Zoṭa*, ch. 1—The messiah entered the Garden of Eden; he must therefore have already come.

Third session

   (9) Incorrect quotation of *MT*, Shofeṭim—The messiah will die, but his son will rule after him.[18]

Fourth session

   (10) Psalm 110:1 and a homily of Rabbi Moses ha-Darshan—The messiah sits with God; he must be divine.
   (11) Leviticus 26:12 and Midrash *Yalquṭ* on Leviticus § 672—God will walk like a human being with the righteous.
   (12) Midrash *Genesis Rabbah* 2.5—The divine spirit hovering over the waters of creation is the messiah.

The Latin protocol specifically mentions only the passages discussed in the first session, claims that Naḥmanides made several very

18. See Lieberman, *Shkiin*, p. 80.

embarrassing admissions naturally not mentioned by the rabbi in his story, and passes over all Pablo's other arguments with the statement that Naḥmanides was convinced "through many talmudic proof-texts" (*per multas auctoritates de Thalmut*).[19] In no way, however, does the Latin protocol contradict the impression gained from Naḥmanides of the particular texts discussed by the disputants.

From a logical point of view, for Pablo to argue the second, third, and fourth of his four propositions on his agenda, he had to establish the first: that the messiah had indeed come. Accordingly, most of Pablo's textual evidence intended to prove just that. The fifth and the last four texts adduced by the friar sought also to establish the second proposition, the divine as well as human nature of the messiah. The third, fifth, and sixth texts at least began to argue that the messiah suffered and died for the sake of humanity, the third of Pablo's propositions. Most surprisingly, however, neither account of the disputation mentions any debate over the fourth proposition: that the authority of Mosaic Law terminated with the coming of the messiah. If Pablo did in fact hope to convert the Jews through his missionary and forensic efforts, proving this final proposition constituted the key to his success. The Jews had to be shown that their religion had become obsolete. For even though a Christian polemicist could point to messianic allusions in biblical and rabbinic sources, he still had to define and establish the significance and ramifications of these allusions for the Jews of his day— namely, that bespeaking the truth of Christianity, they invalidated contemporary Jewish observance—before the Jews would accept conversion. In his own account of the proceedings, Naḥmanides charged Pablo with precisely this task at the very beginning of their discussion.

> Friar Pablo began by saying that he would prove from our Talmud that the messiah of whom the prophets testify has already come. I replied that before we should argue on that I would request that he show and tell me how this could be possible. For since the time that he had gone to Provence, I heard that he had made such a statement to many Jews in numerous places, and I am very surprised at him. Let him [thus] respond to me on this point: Does he wish to say that the sages of the Talmud believed that Jesus was the messiah and that he was totally man and yet truly God, according to Christian doctrine? Is it not known to be true that the episode of Jesus [his life] transpired

19. Y. Baer, "The Disputations," p. 186.

during the period of the second temple, that he was born and killed before the destruction of the temple? But the sages of the Talmud lived after the destruction, like Rabbi Aqiva and his colleagues. And those who taught the Mishna, Rabbi [Judah the Patriarch] and Rabbi Nathan, lived long after the destruction [of the temple], and how much more so Rav Ashi, who compiled the Talmud and reduced it to writing, who lived about 400 years after the destruction. Now if these sages believed in the messianic character of Jesus, that he was true [truly God and the messiah] and that his beliefs and teachings were true, and if they wrote these statements from which Friar Pablo states he will prove these assertions—if so, why did they persist in the religion and ancient practice of the Jews . . . , they, their children, and their students who heard their teachings directly from them?[20]

If the rabbis of the Talmud knew the messiah had come and still practiced Judaism, how did Pablo's fourth proposition follow from his first? Why should medieval Jewry forsake its religious observances and convert to Christianity?

Would the friars, who had requested that James I convene this disputation, have allowed it to pass without at all meeting this challenge? One wonders why the accounts of the debate contain no explicit discussion of it. To be sure, the exigencies of the discussion and Naḥmanides' counterarguments did not permit Pablo to proceed at the desired pace. Perhaps this accounts for the Dominicans' consternation at not being able to continue their discussions with Naḥmanides after the king had ended the disputation. Nevertheless, one finds it hard to believe that a skilled debater like Pablo would have neglected to mention this most crucial issue throughout the four days of discussion.

The only alternative is to show that the friar did in fact try to demonstrate the invalidity of current Jewish observance but that he did so subtly, so as to allow for no direct refutation from Naḥmanides but to achieve the desired effect nonetheless. In describing the ostensive motivations of the friars, the Latin protocol of the debate hints at the method employed by Pablo to reach his objective.

Friar Pablo had previously decided with the lord king and certain Dominican and Franciscan friars who were present, that the faith of the Lord Jesus Christ—which on account of its certitude should not

20. Chavel, 1:303, with the emendation of Chazan mentioned above at the end of n. 14.

be debated—should not be disputed with the Jews like something in doubt. Rather, on account of the errors of the Jews which must be eradicated, the truth of his faith should be made manifest. And in order to gain the confidence of the Jews, who, when they could not defend their errors, used to say that the said Jewish teacher [Naḥmanides] could respond adequately to the general and specific questions that were put forth to them, he [Pablo] proposed to the said Jewish teacher that with the help of God, he would prove through texts common to and authoritative among the Jews, the following things. [There follow the four propositions of the agenda.][21]

As the Dominicans' protocol reveals, the role of Naḥmanides in Pablo's designs was apparently one of great importance. The rabbi of Gerona justifiably commanded the respect and admiration of all of Spanish Jewry for his erudition; if many Jews could not respond effectively to Christian polemic, they all believed that Naḥmanides could. Pablo knew very well that, were the rabbi discredited publicly, the Jewish community would lose much of its ability to withstand Christian missionary efforts. By summoning the rabbi to the disputation in Barcelona, Pablo forced him to serve as the defender of the faith of Spanish Jewry, as the symbol of contemporary Judaism. And by placing Naḥmanides in the position of having to deny classical rabbinic texts which supposedly proclaimed the advent of the messiah, those texts "authoritative among the Jews," Pablo endeavored to emphasize that Naḥmanides and contemporary Jewry had broken with the faith of their ancient ancestors. "That you are now addressed as 'rabbi (*maestre*)' is an error," Pablo told his adversary at the beginning of the disputation, "and falsely you assume that title."[22] True Judaism would have dictated an acceptance of Jesus; the current Judaism of Naḥmanides—the observance of Mosaic and rabbinic law—could thus not be orthodox. Simply by forcing Naḥmanides to respond to his arguments—that is, to reject the textual evidence—for the first three propositions of the agenda, Pablo hoped cleverly to prove the fourth and most important: continued practice of the Judaism of rabbinic law now constituted doctrinal error even for the most pious of Jews!

Both Hebrew and Latin accounts of the disputation make plain the dilemma confronting Naḥmanides. Accepting the rabbinic texts adduced by Pablo meant admitting that the messiah, who was both human and divine, had already come and suffered and died in

21. Y. Baer, "The Disputations," p. 185.
22. Chavel, 1:304.

order to redeem mankind. Refusing to accept Pablo's evidence, however, amounted to rejecting the authority of rabbinic tradition, hardly an option for a practicing Jew. Nor could the rabbi remain silent. The four stratagems comprising the course he followed reveal the precarious and delicate nature of his situation.

According to his own pamphlet, Nahmanides argued first that the heart of the problem lay not with his rejection of rabbinic texts but rather with Pablo's misunderstanding of them: (1) the texts in question did not really refer to the messiah, as Pablo had understood them to;[23] (2) they established the birth of the messiah but not his redemptive coming;[24] or (3) they in no way could apply to Jesus.

In his last response lay the second stratagem in Nahmanides' defense: attempting to veer the discussion away from the truth of rabbinic texts to an evaluation of fundamental Christian beliefs. Whenever he could, the rabbi answered his opponent's arguments concerning the messiah by showing their lack of conformity to the facts of Jesus' life.[25] And at one point, Nahmanides managed to interject a long speech that attempted to end discussion on Jewish messianism and to move to the consideration of Jesus himself. Addressing himself to King James of Aragon, Nahmanides argued that the issue of the messiah did not constitute the essential point of contention between Christians and Jews. Like James, observed the rabbi, the messiah is simply a king, special only because he enforces Jewish law on his subjects. And since a Jew in the Christian Diaspora must exert himself much harder to observe the commandments than he would have to under messianic rule, his reward is naturally greater; King James, quipped Nahmanides, is therefore worth more to the Jews than the messiah. Rather, the fundamental disagreement between Church and Synagogue lay in the Christian doctrine of the incarnation. "That the creator of the heaven and the earth . . . should become a fetus in the womb of a certain Jewess, grow there for seven months, be born an infant, then grow up, and later be delivered into the hands of his enemies, that they should condemn him to death and execute him, and that afterwards . . . he lived and returned to his previous abode—the mind of no Jew nor of any [other] man will accept this." With this

23. In this and the two succeeding notes, see Nahmanides' treatment of the various texts adduced by Pablo—as I have listed them previously—in the specified pages of Chavel, vol. 1: Text #1, pp. 304–6; #3, p. 307; #5, pp. 311–312; #7, pp. 312–15; #9, pp. 315–16; #10, pp. 317–18; #12, p. 319.

24. Text #2, Chavel, 1:306; #4, p. 307; #8, p. 315.

25. Text #2, Chavel, 1:306; #6, p. 312; #7, pp. 312–14; #11, pp. 318–19.

issue at stake, he asked, why should Naḥmanides and Pablo bother debating about the messiah?[26] Yet in his attempts to alter the agenda of the debate, Naḥmanides failed. The friars determinedly refused to submit Christian theology to debate; they insisted on keeping Naḥmanides on the defensive. And when the rabbi first tried to show that a rabbinic text adduced by Pablo could not have spoken of Jesus, an observer at the debate quickly admonished him: "We are not now discussing Jesus, but the question is, whether the messiah has come or not. You have said that he has not come, but this book of yours says that he has come."[27] The Christian disputants did not stop at pointing to rabbinic recognition of the messiah; they steered the discussion to emphasize Naḥmanides' rejection of that messianic belief.

Naḥmanides' third means of defense demonstrates well the severity of Pablo's attack upon the orthodoxy of contemporary Jewish observance. Shortly after the friar's announcement of his intention to prove with talmudic sources that the messiah had come, Naḥmanides voiced an objection to such a design.

> For all our practices today are based on the Talmud and on what we have witnessed talmudic scholars practicing and doing from the day it [the Talmud] was compiled until now. For all of the Talmud is meant only to teach us the observance of the Torah and [its] commandments—and how our ancestors in [the days of] the temple observed them according to [the instructions of] the prophets and our teacher Moses, may peace be upon him.[28]

Pablo had not even mentioned the current religious practices of Jews; why did Naḥmanides? Moreover, one would think that the binding authority of the Talmud among medieval Jews explains exactly why Pablo extracted his evidence from rabbinic literature; why then did Naḥmanides ostensibly have to repeat precisely the same argument in his own response? As explained above, however, Pablo's pitting of Naḥmanides against rabbinic homilies concerning the messiah impugned the orthodoxy of the observance of the rabbi from Gerona. The latter's proclamation of the continuity of talmudic Judaism even until his own day aimed to affirm that

---

26. Chavel, 1:310–11. On the lasting theological implications of this speech of Naḥmanides, see Solomon Schechter, *Studies in Judaism* (New York, 1896), p. 105; and Williams, *Adversus Judaeos*, p. 246.
27. Chavel, 1:306; cf. Y. Baer, "The Disputations," p. 185.
28. Chavel, 1:303–4.

orthodoxy. Pablo, not contemporary Jews, argued Naḥmanides, destroyed talmudic teaching, which dealt primarily with "the practice of law and precept"—the target of the fourth proposition on Pablo's agenda—and not with the homiletical messianic exegesis of biblical verses.

Fourth, because Naḥmanides in the defense of his own orthodoxy was thus forced to downplay the importance of talmudic homilies or *aggadot,* he had to justify on theological grounds how he could choose to value one aspect of talmudic teaching over another. For though he had argued vigorously that Pablo had in fact misinterpreted all the *aggadot* he adduced, the blatant messianic implications of many of them had forced Naḥmanides to exclaim twice on the first day of the debate, "I do not believe in that *aggadah!*" Regarding at least two other *aggadot,* one of which Pablo also adduced on the first day, Naḥmanides had to contrast his own exegesis of a biblical verse with that of the rabbis of the Talmud.[29] At the first instance of such rejection by Naḥmanides, Pablo quite understandably proclaimed in triumph: "Behold how he denies their own writings!"[30] Accordingly, on the second day of the debate, Naḥmanides began the proceedings with a long explanation for his self-incriminating arguments, a speech that exhibits the pressures the rabbi was undoubtedly experiencing.

> Friar Pablo asked me if the messiah of whom the prophets spoke has already come, and I said that he has not come. So he [Friar Pablo] adduced an aggadic work in which it is said that on the very day of the temple's destruction the messiah was born. And I stated that I do not believe this. . . . You should know that we have three categories of writings: One is the Bible, and we all believe in it unquestioningly. The second is called Talmud, and it is a commentary on the commandments in the Torah; for in the Torah there are 613 commandments, and not one is left unexplained in the Talmud. And we believe it [the Talmud] in its interpretation of the commandments. We have yet a third class of writing called midrash, that is to say homiletic literature (*sermones*), like that produced if the bishop were to rise and deliver a sermon and one of those listening were to like it and write it down. As for this class of writing, if anyone believes it, it is fine, and if anyone does not believe it, no harm is done. We have sages who wrote that the messiah will not be born until shortly before the end of

---

29. Concerning text #1 on the list above, see Chavel, 1:306; texts ##3–4, p. 307; #8, p. 315.
30. Chavel, 1:306.

days, when he will come to deliver us from exile. I therefore do not believe this book inasmuch as it said that he [the messiah] was born on the day of the [temple's] destruction.[31]

With this speech, Naḥmanides' account of the argument over the authority of *aggadot* suddenly ends, and it is indeed possible that Pablo did not and perhaps felt no need to say more. Forcing his opponent to deny, however reasonably, the authority of talmudic *aggadot* might have sufficed perfectly for the friar. He thereby made the point that contemporary Jewish observance, that which Naḥmanides exemplified, represented a break with classical Judaism; faithful adherence to the latter thus demanded a renunciation of traditional rabbinic observance. Pablo had established, at least to his own satisfaction, the essence of the fourth proposition on his agenda: the invalidity of Jewish law in the Christian era.

Naḥmanides' distinction between talmudic law, binding upon all orthodox Jews, on the one hand, and midrash, which any Jew could freely reject, on the other, appears to diverge sharply from his otherwise essentially anti-rationalist outlook. Throughout his biblical commentaries and mystical writings, Naḥmanides commonly assumed and asserted the basic truth of the *aggadah*, in order to justify his typological understanding of history and his kabbalistic theology. Moreover, he insisted that *aggadot*, like Scripture, never be interpreted completely allegorically, so as to detach their symbolic interpretation from their literal meaning in obvious preference for the former. Rather, as Amos Funkenstein has recently observed, Naḥmanides moved toward the opposite extreme; he believed that what for the Maimonidean rationalists constituted the hidden realm of allegory in interpreting a text actually belonged to—and did not negate—its *peshaṭ*, or primary literal intention. The true kabbalist, not the philosopher, would know how to resolve the resulting problems in understanding the Bible and to reconcile ostensibly contradictory *aggadot*.[32]

31. Chavel, 1:308.
32. The question of the significance of Naḥmanides' denial of the binding authority of *aggadot* is not a new one. In 1931, Y. Baer, in "The Disputations," p. 184, argued that Naḥmanides had thereby compromised his own essential religious beliefs. Several years later, Lieberman, in *Shkiin*, pp. 81–83, attempted to prove that Naḥmanides could indeed find ample support in rabbinic literature for his controversial statement. Nevertheless, Lieberman did not address the question of Naḥmanides' personal consistency—i.e., whether or not he compromised his own beliefs at the disputation. And even if Naḥmanides managed to appease his own conscience with his disclaimer, it is not certain that he communicated its subtlety to his listen-

Naḥmanides' basically mystical and anti-rationalist temperament must have been well known not only to the Jewish community of Spain but also to the Dominicans, who had taken an active part in the recent Maimonidean controversy. Pablo in particular, who had grown up as a Jew in Montpellier where the controversy had exploded, would have been sensitive to the great emotional and ideological commitments of the opposing factions as well as the havoc which the controversy had wreaked among the Jews.[33] He apparently concluded that eliciting a public renunciation of what for Naḥmanides constituted an essential doctrine was a highly effective way of discrediting both the rabbi and the Jewish observance for which he stood. Not surprisingly, then, Naḥmanides' rejection of the binding authority of *aggadot* provides the Dominicans' description of the disputation with a definite climax.

> Although he was not willing to confess the truth unless compelled to do so by the force of authoritative textual evidence, when he could not refute such evidence he said publicly that he did not believe in those texts which had been adduced against him, even though they are in ancient and authentic Jewish books, because they are *sermones*, in which their doctors very often lied for the sake of exhorting the people. He thereby impeached [the authority of] both the doctors and the scriptures of the Jews.[34]

ers, either Christian or Jewish; for he had indeed used this explanation to justify his rejection of more than one talmudic homily. The Latin protocol shows clearly how the Dominicans understood the rabbi, and the need for Naḥmanides to preach as he did to Barcelona Jewry suggests that the Jews might have shared the Dominicans' understanding. More recently, Baer's position has found support in Gershom G. Scholem, *Les origines de la Kabbale*, trans. Jean Loewenson (Paris, 1966), pp. 416–37, which deals in general terms with the anti-rationalism of the Kabbalists of Gerona, and, more specifically with regard to the disputation of 1263, in Roth, "The Disputation," p. 128, and Haim Hillel Ben-Sasson, "Rabbi Moshe ben Naḥman: 'Ish be-Sivkhei Tequfato," *Molad*, n.s. 1 (1967), 363–64. Yet the most convincing statement on the subject is that of Amos Funkenstein, "Nachmanides' Typological Reading of History [Hebrew]," *Zion*, n.s. 45 (1980), 43–47, which aptly concludes (p. 47): "*In foro externo* there appears before us a different Naḥmanides than *in foro interno*."

33. On the widespread influence of Naḥmanides and the rapid dissemination of his beliefs on the proper interpretation of sacred texts, see Efraim Gottlieb, *Studies in the Kabbala Literature* [Hebrew], ed. Joseph Hacker (Tel Aviv, 1976), pp. 88–90. That the Dominicans' study of Hebrew texts included as current a work as Naḥmanides' commentary on the Pentateuch is evidenced by Raymond Martini's quotation from it; see, for example, *Pugio*, 3.3.16.37, p. 866. For the view that Pablo might have consciously been exploiting the issues of the Maimonidean controversy to embarrass his opponent, see Rankin, *Jewish Religious Polemic*, p. 169; and M. Cohen, "Reflections," p. 171. Dinur, *Israel in the Diaspora*, 2, 2:515, 653, n. 5, has even suggested that the Maimonidean controversy had actually caused Pablo to apostasize in the first place.

34. Y. Baer, "The Disputations," p. 187.

Naḥmanides sensed so great a threat in this charge that he felt bound to refurbish his reputation in the eyes of the Jewish community. When a week after the disputation the king and a delegation of Dominicans came to preach to the Jews of Barcelona during their Sabbath morning services, the rabbi of Gerona delivered a lengthy sermon entitled "The Torah of the Lord Is Untainted" (*Torat ha-Shem Temimah*) to the congregation upon the visitors' departure.[35] The sermon was probably intended above all to restore the morale of Barcelona Jewry after the harrowing disputation. But it is no accident that Naḥmanides devoted over half of it to expounding some of the great lessons of the biblical account of creation, often alluding to the importance of rabbinic traditions concerning that story. By harping on the ever-present miracles of nature, he clearly endeavored to give the Jewish community a more accurate picture of his anti-rationalist theology. (The remainder of the sermon appropriately emphasized the eternal authority and legitimacy of the Mosaic commandments as the proper guide to religious observance for Jews.)

Such was the crucial element in Pablo's attack on Naḥmanides: the demonstration of the heresy—the "errors of the Jews which must be eradicated" mentioned in the Latin protocol—inherent in the current religious observance both of the rabbi and, by extension, of the Jewish community at large. Ingeniously constructed, Pablo's arguments forced Naḥmanides to argue on the subject of the messiah in such a way as to challenge his own orthodoxy; the friar subtly, although threateningly, thereby advanced the proposition that contemporary Jewish life had lost its validity. Naḥmanides futilely tried to alter the course of the discussion and bypass the dilemma. Failing to do so, he pleaded for his own orthodoxy as best he could and responded in kind to Pablo's *ad hominem* attack: while Naḥmanides had preserved the true Jewish faith, Pablo, the apostate from the Jewish community, had distorted it. Pablo it was who had misunderstood the biblical and rabbinic texts which were discussed, perverting their true meaning, even attempting to fabricate evidence.[36] On the last day of the disputation, for example, Naḥmanides turned upon Pablo and exclaimed:

35. The text of the sermon commences in Chavel, 1:141–75, and is completed in Ephraim Kupfer, ed., "The Concluding Portion of Nachmanides' Discourse Torat ha-Shem Temima [Hebrew]," *Tarbiz* 40 (1970), 64–83; on the date and setting of the sermon, see Chavel, 1:139; and Kupfer, pp. 66, n. 10, 8on. For an annotated English translation, see Moses ben Naḥman, *Writings and Discourses*, 1:25–139.
36. Concerning text #9 on the list above, see Chavel, 1:315.

Are you the clever Jew that discovered this novel interpretation and apostasized because of it? Are you the one who proposes to the king to gather the Jewish scholars for you, so that you can debate with them concerning the novel interpretations you have found? Have we never heard of this matter before now? There is not a monk or child who will not pose this question to the Jews! This question is ancient indeed.[37]

In dealing with the theological implications of Scripture, he said, weakness of conviction and lack of resiliency, as opposed to any revolutionary exegetical discovery, had led to Pablo's apostasy. But on a doctrinal level too, Naḥmanides argued that Pablo had misconstrued the real continuity between classical and medieval Judaism, with the result that the friar and not the Jews had fallen into heresy. If the rabbis of the Talmud knew that the messiah had come, asserted Naḥmanides,

Why did they not apostasize and turn to the religion of Jesus as has done Friar Pablo, who has understood from their words that the faith of the Christians is the true one—God forbid!—and has gone and apostasized on the basis of what they said? Yet they and their disciples who received the law directly from them lived and died as Jews, just as we are today. . . . For if they believed in Jesus and his religious teaching, why did they not do as has done Friar Pablo, who understands their words better than they themselves?[38]

As in the disputation over the Talmud in 1240 in Paris, the argument came down to the question of who, the rabbi and exponent of talmudic law or the Jewish convert to Christianity, had fallen away from real Judaism into a life of doctrinal *innovatio*.

Pablo's Approach to the Talmud

Especially in view of the outright condemnation of the Talmud by ecclesiastical authorities only two decades earlier, Pablo's use of and attitude toward rabbinic literature appear to be complex and to warrant further explanation. The polemical stance Pablo took in 1263, however, assumes much greater significance if appreciated as the concerted effort of a whole school of Dominican missionaries

37. Chavel, 1:317.
38. Chavel, 1:303–4.

and polemicists, that of Raymond de Peñaforte, in which Pablo was but one very active and important member. Pablo's attitude did not merely express the animus of a single vindictive convert from Judaism.[39] The Latin account of the Barcelona disputation opens by specifying that Naḥmanides "had been summoned from Gerona by his majesty the king at the insistence of the preaching friars." The agenda for the debate had been determined by a group of friars who also attended the actual proceedings. Naḥmanides likewise notes that various Dominican and Franciscan scholars were present at the debate, including Arnold of Segarre, the Dominican prior of Barcelona.[40] At the beginning of the fourth and final day of the debate, Naḥmanides requested royal permission to withdraw from it; he explained that many Jews and even influential Christian clerics, a Franciscan named Peter of Genoa in particular, urged him to do so out of fear of "the Dominicans, who spread terror throughout the world."[41] Whatever the motives of Peter of Genoa, Naḥmanides' appeal hints at the great stake which the Dominicans as an order must have had in the debate. More revealing are Naḥmanides' two references to Raymond de Peñaforte. Naḥmanides reports that when the debate commenced, he made his liberty to speak freely a condition of his participation: "I said: 'I shall carry out the royal command [to debate with Pablo] if you give me permission to speak as I wish. I request the permission of the king and that of Friar Raymond de Peñaforte and his associates who are present.'" Along with King James, Raymond presided over the disputation, and Naḥmanides accordingly acknowledged him as the leading clerical authority among the Christians present. A week after the disputation ended when, according to Naḥmanides, "the king and the Dominicans desired to come into the synagogue on the Sabbath," Raymond was the first of his delegation to speak, delivering a sermon on the Trinity.[42]

Inasmuch as Raymond de Peñaforte had conceived of the disputation with Naḥmanides and employed Pablo therein because of the latter's training in Hebrew and rabbinics, perhaps one can understand the Christian approach to the Talmud in 1263 better when it is seen in terms of the goals and programs of the former Domini-

39. Cf. the latter impression given by Chazan, "The Barcelona 'Disputation,'" pp. 830–31.

40. Y. Baer, "The Disputations," p. 185; Chavel, 1:308, 314. For the identification of Arnold of Segarre, see M. Cohen, "Reflections," p. 163.

41. Chavel, 1:316; cf. the Latin protocol in Y. Baer, "The Disputations," p. 187.

42. Chavel, 1:302, 319–20.

can Master-General. As his biographer related, Raymond valued the use of Hebraists in anti-Jewish polemic for two reasons. First, with a knowledge of Hebrew, friars could prevent Jews from denying the support given by various biblical verses and rabbinic glosses to the tenents of Catholic doctrine. And second, Hebrew would enable friars to disclose the falsehoods and corruptions with which the Jews had consciously concealed the biblical revelation of Christianity. Raymond thus approached rabbinic literature partly in a utilitarian manner but otherwise quite negatively. Assuredly, he believed, not even the ancient rabbis could prevent the acknowledgment of Christianity, so blatantly prefigured in the Old Testament, from entering their literature; their glosses offered a potentially invaluable means for converting the Jews. Nevertheless, the Jewish sages stubbornly refused to accept the truth of Christ which they themselves had recognized; instead they tried to obscure and falsify christological passages in the Bible and continued to practice Judaism, even though they knew the Old Testament to be obsolete and invalid. From here derived the subtle and ingenious argument that continued practice of rabbinic Judaism constituted heresy, the charge that underlay the structure of the discussions between Pablo and Naḥmanides. And here lay the answer to the challenge Naḥmanides had hurled at his Dominican adversary as the disputation began: how could the rabbis of the Talmud have acknowledged the coming of the messiah and still continued their observance of Judaism? They too left the fold of orthodoxy, refusing to yield to the dictates of reason and textual evidence from Scripture.

That in Raymond's estimation these elements of heresy and a willful rejection of the true messiah comprised talmudic Judaism appears still more plausible if one recalls his presence at the Roman curia as papal confessor when Nicholas Donin first leveled such charges against the Talmud in 1236, eventually eliciting a sympathetic reaction from Gregory IX. Furthermore, we have already noted that Raymond and Thomas Aquinas shared the same views on how best to convert the infidel, an affinity between the two men which allowed Raymond to solicit the composition of the *Summa contra gentiles*. Perhaps then it is no mere coincidence that in contrast to most Christian theologians in the West from Augustine through the end of the twelfth century, who castigated the Jewish sages at the time of Jesus for not recognizing him as the messiah when they should have, Aquinas taught that those sages knew that Jesus was the messiah and crucified him in spite of that knowledge.

The disbelief of the Jews derived, therefore, not from ignorance, but from a deliberate defiance of the truth.[43]

Pablo's structuring of the Barcelona disputation around rabbinic texts should thus not mislead the reader into concluding that the friar thereby displayed a positive attitude toward the Talmud. Instead, he translated his ideology into a direct attack on Naḥmanides with great skill. The immediate aftermath of the disputation as well as the remainder of Pablo's polemical career substantiates the conclusion that he shared Raymond de Peñaforte's general aversion to the religious beliefs and practices of the rabbis of the Talmud. We have already mentioned the anti-Jewish edicts of James I issued only several weeks after the disputation. One of them ordered the burning of the last volume of Maimonides' code of Jewish law, which Pablo himself had tried to quote during the debate.[44] Another edict empowered Pablo to missionize among all the Jews of Aragon, demanding that they submit all their books to him for inspection. A third decree established a commission to purge Jewish books of blasphemy within three months; the panel consisted of Pablo, Raymond de Peñaforte, and Arnold of Segarre, the three Dominican notables present at the disputation.[45] Issued in the same spirit that originally had led to the summoning of Naḥmanides to Barcelona, these royal enactments evidently jibed with the wishes of Raymond de Peñaforte and his associates, bespeaking their true feelings for rabbinic literature.

The remaining documentary evidence, both Latin and Hebrew, concerning Pablo's anti-Jewish polemic confirms that he was hostile toward the Talmud. In his famous letter of reproof to Pablo, Rabbi Jacob ben Elijah of Venice devoted a great deal of space and energy to defending the crucial importance of the Talmud in orthodox Judaism, justifying both its legal enactments and its homiletical *aggadot*. He wrote to the Dominican: "You have struck out at the Talmud."[46] In 1267, when he attacked the Talmud and urged the king and clergy of Aragon to have all Jewish books censored, Clem-

---

43. Thomas Aquinas, *ST* 3.47.5, 54:68: "Dicendum quod Judaeos quidam erant majores, et quidam minores. Majores quidem, qui eorum principes dicebantur, sicut et daemones cognoverunt, eum esse Christum promissum in lege: omnia enim signa videbant in eo quae dixerant futura Prophetae." See also my forthcoming "The Jews as the Killers of Christ: A Religious Motif in Historical Perspective."

44. Régné, *History*, p. 40 (no. 212); and cf. text #9 on the list above (Chavel, 1:315).

45. Régné, *History*, p. 41 (nos. 215–16). On the spirit of these decees, cf. also Grayzel, "Popes, Jews, and Inquisition," pp. 163–67.

46. Jacob ben Elijah, "'Iggeret," pp. 1–13.

ent IV in his *Dampnabili perfidia Iudeorum* specifically mentioned Pablo as one highly qualified and suitable to direct such an operation. The language of the bull even allows for the possibility that Pablo himself initially approached the pope with an appeal against the Talmud.[47] A Hebrew polemical treatise of the same period, compiled in reaction to Pablo's subsequent activities in northern France, prefaced a summary of the Barcelona disputation with a description of the friar as "a skeptic concerning the *aggadot* in our Talmud."[48] Yet another contemporary Hebrew source from northern France depicts Pablo as considering Parisian Jews heretics, and therefore worthy of burning.[49] And an anonymous Parisian chronicler of the late thirteenth century similarly described the approach the friar took when preaching to the Jews of the French capital: "He preached to the Jews—who came by royal order—showing them that their law was null and worthless, that they had in fact not observed it for a long time, that indeed they deviated daily from all its precepts."[50]

The far-reaching implications of the approach of Raymond de Peñaforte's school to contemporary Judaism will be discussed fur-

47. Ripoll, *Bullarium*, 1:488: "Ad hoc autem dilectus filius Frater Paulus, dictus Christianus, de Ordine Fratrum Predicatorum, lator presentium, creditur non modicum profuturus, tum quia ex judeis trahens originem, et inter eos litteris hebraicis competenter instructus, linguam novit, et legem antiquam, ac illorum errores, tum etiam quia de sacro fonte renatus zelum habet fidei Catholice, ac eruditus occurrit laudabiliter in Theologica facultate."

48. J. M. Rosenthal, "A Religious Disputation," p. 62. Rosenthal's claim that this Hebrew treatise records the arguments of an actual encounter between Pablo and a rabbi named Menahem has been effectively challenged by Joel E. Rembaum, "A Reevaluation of a Medieval Polemical Manuscript," *Association for Jewish Studies Review* 5 (1980), 81–99.

49. Adolph Neubauer. "Another Convert Named Paulus," *JQR*, o.s. 5 (1893), 714. Although the Paul described in the ms. fragment here published by Neubauer is dubbed a *ḥovel*, usually the epithet for a Cordelier or Franciscan, the facts that he came from Spain, argued on the basis of talmudic texts ("'al pi ha-Talmud"), and had converted to Christianity from Judaism all make his identification with Pablo likely, a conclusion also accepted by Roth, "The Disputation," p. 143, n. 41, and Chazan, *Medieval Jewry*, p. 152.

50. Léopold Delisle, "Notes sur quelques manuscrits du Musée britannique," *Mémoires de la Société de l'histoire de Paris et de l'Ile-de-France* 4 (1877), 189: "Eodem ano [1269], circa Penthecosten, venit quidam frater de ordine Fratrum Predicatorum, nomine [   ], de partibus Lumbardie, qui fuerat judeus, et erat optimus clericus in lege mosayca et in lege nostra, et publice in curia regis Parisius et in curia Fratrum Predicatorum predicabat Judeis, qui de mandato regis veniebant ibidem, ost[endens eis] quod lex sua nulla erat et quod non valebat, quod etiam [a longo tempore] eam non tenebant, immo ab omnibus ejus articulis [quotidie] deviabant." For the identification of the friar and the translation, see Chazan, "Confrontation," p. 455.

ther at the end of the next chapter. Suffice it to note here that the career of Pablo Christiani itself heralded dangers for the Jews of Spain and France which both incorporated and exceeded those accompanying the growth of the papal Inquisition. As we have seen, Pablo stressed the heresy inherent in contemporary Jewish observance. He attacked Jewish books themselves too, calling at times for their destruction and at times for their censorship. He succeeded in forcing the Jews of Aragon and portions of France to attend his sermons. He managed to dispute publicly with renowned Jewish leaders such as Naḥmanides, Mordekhai ben Joseph of Avignon, Samuel ben Abraham of Dreux, and perhaps Meir ben Simeon of Narbonne.[51] He elicited decrees from King Louis IX of France enforcing the anti-Jewish legislation of the Fourth Lateran Council and even requiring the Jews to respond publicly to his arguments whenever he so desired.[52] And he may even have begun the inquisitorial practice of disinterring *relapsi* and other Jewish converts to Christianity from their Jewish graves[53]

All these means of harassing the Jews were employed by other mendicant inquisitors, and the tactics often resulted in a considerable number of conversions. But Pablo added to the friars' anti-Judaism the tremendous missionary zeal of the school of Raymond de Peñaforte, a commitment not only to defend the religious purity and orthodoxy of Christendom by punishing the heretic but also to convert the infidel at virtually any cost. The various extant Hebrew tracts that respond to Pablo's arguments—the long letter of Jacob ben Elijah, which upbraids Pablo for proselytizing, especially

51. On Mordekhai of Avignon, see the report of sixteenth-century Isaac de Lattès in his Shaʿarei Ṣion, cited in Gross, *Gallia Judaica*, p. 4. With reference to Samuel of Dreux, see Neubauer's discussion in "Another Convert," pp. 713–14. And on the possibility that Pablo debated with Meir ben Simeon, see above, n. 14. Marc Saperstein, "R. Isaac b. Yedaʿya: A Forgotten Commentator on the *Aggada*," *REJ* 138 (1979), 44 and n. 106, and *Decoding the Rabbis: A Thirteenth-Century Commentary on the Aggadah* (Cambridge, Mass., 1980), p. 198, makes the essentially undocumented suggestion that Pablo also disputed with Rabbi Isaac ben Yedaʿyah of Béziers in the early 1260s.

52. De Laurière, *Ordonnances des roys*, 1:294, cites a decree of Louis IX providing for strict enforcement of the Lateran canon demanding that Jews wear a distinctive sign on their clothing; the royal decree was issued "ad requisitionem dilecti nobis in Christo fratris Pauli Christini [sic]." See also the manuscript cited by Chazan, "The Barcelona 'Disputation,' " p. 830 and n. 24; and cf. Robert, "Catalogue des Actes," p. 216, no. 40.

53. See Jacob ben Elijah, "'Iggeret," p. 20; and Joseph Shatzmiller, "Paulus Christiani: Un aspect de son activité anti-juive," in *Hommage à Georges Vajda: Etudes d'histoire et de pensée juives*, ed. Gérard Nahon and Charles Touati (Louvain, 1980), pp. 203–17.

among Jewish children, as well as for attacking the Talmud, the aforementioned polemic written in response to his mission to northern France, and the theological treatise *The Reinforcer of the Faith* (*Maḥaziq ha-'Emunah*) of Mordekhai of Avignon—all witness the great missionary pressure the Dominican exerted. Not lightly did Hebrew chroniclers write of Pablo as a missionary that "he came . . . to destroy the remnant of Israel" or "he wanted to uproot everything."[54] Yet the depth and essence of this attack upon the Jews cannot be fully understood prior to an examination of the *magnum opus* of Raymond de Peñaforte's school's mission to the Jews, written by Pablo's confrere and associate.

54. See Chazan, "Confrontation," pp. 452–53, 455–56; Neubauer, "Another Convert," p. 714; and Solomon ibn Verga, *Shevet Yehudah*, p. 148.

6

The School of
Raymond de Peñaforte:
Raymond Martini

The most thorough exposition of the mendicants' new attitude toward the Jews appears in Raymond Martini's *Pugio fidei*, whose annotated printed edition exceeds one thousand pages in length, a book that has not unjustifiably been termed "the most learned and best documented polemic against Judaism which the Middle Ages produced."[1] Its author, born between 1210 and 1215 near Barcelona, entered the Dominican Order between 1237 and 1240. Selected by Raymond de Peñaforte to participate in the founding of the first *studium arabicum*, Martini went to Tunis in 1250, but he returned to Spain by the end of 1262, and in 1264 James I named him to the panel of friars responsible for censoring Jewish books in Aragon. In 1266 he may have gone to the Dominican *studium* in Murcia, and in 1268 he again traveled to Tunis. A year later, however, he was back in Europe serving as Raymond de Peñaforte's emissary to Paris, where he persuaded Louis IX to wage a crusade against Muslim North Africa and may have asked Thomas Aquinas to compose the *Summa contra gentiles*. Martini spent the remainder of his life in Barcelona; in 1281 he undertook supervision of the *studium hebraicum* there. He died between 1285 and 1290.[2]

1. Amos Funkenstein, "Gesetz und Geschichte: Zur historisierenden Hermeneutik bei Moses Maimonides und Thomas von Aquin," *Viator* 1 (1970), 173.
2. This reconstruction of Martini's biography generally follows Peter Marc in his edition of Thomas Aquinas, *Liber de veritate*, 1:53–57, 243, 369–71, 609–12; cf. also André Berthier, "Un maître orientaliste du XIIIᵉ siècle: Raymond Martin O.P.," *AFP* 6 (1936), 267–78; Joseph Jacobs, *An Inquiry into the Sources of the History of the Jews in Spain* (New York, 1894), pp. 15 (#193), 17 (#230); and Quétif, *Scriptores*, 1:396–97. Conjecture over various aspects of Martini's life has led to several outlandish as-

If the chronology of Martini's life remains largely obscure, its character does not; an avid follower of Raymond de Peñaforte, Martini devoted himself to converting the infidel. His travels to Africa attest to his role in the forefront of Dominican missionary efforts; his mastery of both Arabic and Hebrew, probably achieved at Dominican *studia*, bespeak the energy and commitment with which he followed his conversionist pursuits; and the key roles entrusted him by his master hint at his creativity and industriousness in advancing the cause of Raymond de Peñaforte's school and ideology.

---

sumptions. In his fifteenth-century polemic against his former Jewish coreligionists, the recently converted Bishop Paul of Burgos (Paulus de Santa Maria) quoted "Raimundus Rab. tuus in suo pugione"; see his *Scrutinarium scripturarum* 1.8.15 (Mantua, 1475), f.° 105v. Here commenced the tradition that Martini had been a learned Jew and then had converted to Christianity, a belief maintained even today in *SRH*, 9:298, n. 9. Yet both the early chronology of Martini's life, which does not seem to allow the time necessary for him to have become a learned rabbi, and the cogent arguments of Lieberman, *Shkiin*, pp. 2, 43–45, that Martini's writings demonstrate a lack of familiarity with the Talmud in the original, testify against the likelihood of his Jewish origin. Perhaps Paul of Burgos merely based his statement on Petrus Marsilius' *Cronicae*, cited by Quétif, 1:396—which labels Martini a "magnus Rabinus in Hebraeo." This means no more than a great Hebrew teacher, which Martini evidently was. And while an important affinity clearly existed between Pablo Christiani and Raymond Martini, scholars have embellished the picture of their relationship with details unsupported by the extant sources. Rankin, *Jewish Religious Polemic*, pp. 160–61 (cf. Graetz, *Geschichte*, 7:150), maintains that Martini received his Hebrew instruction from Pablo. Martini's appointment to James I's censorship commission working with Pablo in 1264 has led some to suggest that Martini was present at Pablo's disputation with Naḥmanides and may even have participated in it; see, *SRH*, 9:281, n. 35; Roth, "The Disputation," p. 122, n. 10; and Peter Marc's comment in Thomas Aquinas, *Liber de veritate*, 1:54. Y. Baer, "The Disputations," p. 180, ascribes the authorship of the Latin protocol of the 1263 debate to Martini, a claim that results, no doubt, from Baer's improbable view that Martini indiscriminately forged textual evidence with which to substantiate his arguments; see below, n. 15. At least Marc's statement that Martini participated in the disputation derives from Johann Christoph Wagenseil's edition of Naḥmanides' account of the debate in *Tela ignea Satanae* (Altdorf, 1681)—although Marc admits, "I did not see this work"—where Wagenseil, pt. 4, p. 2, himself errs by stating that the rabbi debated against both Pablo and Martini. Naḥmanides' account mentioned the Dominican notables present as well as others besides Pablo who entered the discussion. Why would he have intentionally omitted Martini? The fact that Martini joined the royal censorship commission in March 1264 and not in August 1263, when James I first created the panel, itself suggests that Martini was not in Barcelona during the summer of 1263. Moreover, Marc argues that Martini debated with Naḥmanides on the basis of Raymond Lull's description of the friar's exchanges with an unnamed rabbi in Barcelona. I have argued differently in "The Polemical Adversary of Solomon ibn Adret," *JQR*, n.s. 71 (1980), 48–55. Marc's view that Martini solicited the composition of the *Summa contra gentiles* has elicited heated opposition in the review of Marc's book in *RLT* 2 (1967), 51–56, and Alvaro Huerga, "Hipótesis sobre la génesis de la 'Summa contra gentiles' y del 'Pugio fidei,'" *Angelicum* 51 (1974), 533–57, cited in *RLT* 9 (1974), 82–83.

The Corpus of Martini's Polemic

Martini expressed himself not only in action but also in writing. He wrote prolifically, and his works reflect the breadth of his activities as well as the development of his missionary capabilities and sophistication. In 1257, during his first sojourn in Tunis, he composed his *Explanatio simboli apostolorum*, a tract addressed to all infidels which endeavored to prove the twelve articles of the Apostles' Creed primarily with quotations from Scripture.[3] To aid in converting the Muslims, Martini also composed a summa against the Koran and an Arabic lexicon entitled *Vocabulista in arabico*, and his influence and instruction gave rise to the compilation of an anti-Muslim polemical guide now often called the *Quadruplex reprobatio*.[4]

It was in his anti-Jewish writings, though, that Martini demonstrated the greatest advances in polemical methodology. In 1267 he wrote the *Capistrum Iudeorum*, a work that not only proffered prophetic evidence to establish the advent of the messiah but also refuted Jewish objections to such argumentation taken from rabbinic literature. The *Capistrum* revealed signs of a growing recourse to propaedeutic rational argumentation on Martini's part, an approach entirely lacking in the earlier *Explanatio*. Similarities between the *Capistrum* and the *Summa contra gentiles* have led some scholars to the conclusion that Aquinas consulted Martini's work while writing his own, finding the method of using sources currently regarded as authoritative by the infidel a very helpful technique. Martini, however, himself found the *Capistrum* ineffective for converting the Jews, apparently because they refused to accept as evidence biblical or rabbinic sources adduced in their Latin translation.[5] The friar consequently compiled the *Pugio fidei adversus Mauros*

3. The text has been published by Joseph M. March, "En Ramón Marti y la seva 'Explanatio simboli apostolorum,'" *Institut d'estudis catalans—Anuari*, 1908, pp. 443–96.

4. Quétif, *Scriptores*, 1:397; Burns, "Christian-Islamic Confrontation," pp. 1411–12; N. Daniel, *Islam*, p. 13.

5. Berthier, "Un maître orientaliste," pp. 287–91, 299–300; Thomas Aquinas, *Liber de veritate*, 1:55–56, 65–72; F. Cavallera, "L''Explanatio symboli apostolorum' de Raymond Martin O.P.," in *Studia mediaevalia in honorem ulmodum reverendi patris Raymundi Josephi Martin* (Bruges, 1948), 201–20; Tomas and Joaquín Carreras y Artau, *Historia de la filosofia española: Filosofia cristiana de los siglos XIII al XV*, 2 vols. (Madrid, 1939–43), 1:153–54; and Thomas Murphy, "The Date and Purpose of the *Contra Gentiles*," *Heythrop Journal* 10 (1969), 408–9. Mss. of the still unpublished *Capistrum* are in the Bibliothèque Nationale of Paris (MS Lat. 3643) and the Biblioteca Universitaria of Bologna (MS 1675, attributed to Thomas Hispanus).

et Iudeos, a work completed in 1278, which marked the climax of his polemical career. The book had both defensive and missionary objectives, which Martini defined thus:

> It has been enjoined upon me, that from those books of the Old Testament which the Jews accept and even from the Talmud and the rest of their writings authoritative among them, I compose such a work as might be available like a dagger (*pugio*) for preachers and guardians of the Christian faith—at some times for feeding to the Jews the bread of the divine word in sermons; at other times for confront-ing their impiety and perfidy, and for destroying their pertinacity against Christ and their impudent insanity.

Despite the full title of the *Pugio,* Martini specifies that he has written this work "principally against the Jews, and then against the Saracens and other various enemies of the true faith."[6]

The *Pugio fidei* embodied several specific advances over Martini's other polemical writings. Most obvious is the enormous extent of the *Pugio*'s argumentation, especially when compared with those of the *Explanatio simboli apostolorum* and the *Capistrum Iudeorum.* The first part of the *Pugio,* containing twenty-six chapters, endeavors to refute common philosophical objections to a revealed religion such as Christianity, trying thereby to establish some of the latter's basic theological beliefs: the creation of the world, the primacy of revela-tion over reason, the extension of divine providence to individuals, and the resurrection of the human body. Although Martini often quotes the Old Testament in this part of the *Pugio,* at one point cites Maimonides' *Guide of the Perplexed,* and on another occasion even adduces two passages from the Talmud,[7] he clearly directs his arguments not at Jews but at pagan and Muslim philosophers. Accordingly, I will not consider the first section of the work here. The remainder of the *Pugio,* however, speaks almost exclusively to the Jews. Part two seeks to prove that the messiah has already come. Martini devotes considerable attention to several outstand-ing messianic prophecies of the Old Testament—Daniel 9:24, Genesis 49:10, and Daniel 2:31–45—arguing that they already had to have been fulfilled and that they, as well as all other such bibli-cal allusions to the messiah, can refer to no one else but Jesus. Even the Talmud could be shown to acknowledge the advent of the

---

6. *Pugio,* prooemium 3, p. 2. At 2.10.2, p. 395, Martini explains that "nunc" is 1278.
7. Ibid., 1.14.6, pp. 233–34; 1.22.6, p. 246.

messiah. Martini then discusses dozens of Jewish objections to his christological reading of biblical prophecy and the Jews' reasons for rejecting Jesus in particular, ostensibly refuting them all. The third and concluding part of the *Pugio* deals with the Trinity and contains three sections (*distinctiones*). The first seeks to prove the existence of the Trinity with evidence drawn from Jewish sources that allegedly bespoke a plurality in the godhead of the Jews. The second *distinctio* argues that this Trinity created man in its own image but that primeval man then fell from his state of grace, transmitting his original sin to all of his posterity and sinking into a sinful state from which only one both divine and human could redeem him. Atonement for sin as great as that of Adam and all of mankind which followed him required the sacrifice of the most righteous of all men; even so, since God had originally endowed man with grace, only God could restore him thereto. The agent of redemption, the messiah, therefore had to fulfill both roles. The third *distinctio* analyzes the actual occurrence of the redemption, or the incarnation of Christ. Martini seeks to demonstrate that every aspect of Jesus' life conformed to the career of the messiah as described in biblical prophecy and that Jesus did actually redeem mankind. Martini again devotes special attention to answering the objections of the Jews to the very notion of the incarnation of God in a human being and his birth of a virgin. Finally, the last three chapters of the *Pugio* describe the reprobate state of the Jews, their punishment for having rejected and crucified God and Christ.

The methodology of the *Pugio* was innovative in various noteworthy ways. In his previous writings Martini had quoted the Bible and rabbinic literature simply in a Latin translation, but in the *Pugio* all Jewish texts—and sometimes even quotations from the New Testament—appear first in Hebrew or Aramaic and only then in Latin.[8] Thereby having eliminated all opportunity for Jews to claim that a language barrier prevented them from understanding his textual evidence, Martini then sought to prevent any Jewish assertion that *he* had misunderstood the sources he quoted. Particularly in the case of biblical quotations, he informs his reader that he has taken great pains in translation, often abandoning the renditions of the Septuagint or of Jerome in favor of a more lit-

8. *Pugio*, 3.3.10.5, p. 772; 3.3.13.1, p. 818; 3.3.14.1, p. 825. On Martini's Hebrew translation of New Testament texts in particular, and on medieval Hebrew versions of Christian Scripture in general, see Pinchas E. Lapide, *Hebräisch in den Kirchen* (Neukirchen-Vluyn, 1976), pp. 27–29, 33–68.

eral translation.⁹ Most important, however, is the great use to which Martini put rabbinic literature in the *Pugio*. In the *Capistrum Iudeorum*, he had quoted rabbinic texts in order to identify Jewish objections to his christological arguments, objections that he then proceeded to refute. In the second and third parts of the *Pugio*, he draws upon rabbinic sources extensively; exhibiting a remarkable familiarity with the Talmud, various collections of midrashim, and even the philosophical and exegetical works of important medieval Jewish scholars, Martini used them not only to define Jewish opposition to his own arguments but also as evidence in his own behalf. By the time he wrote the *Pugio*, he evidently had come to share Pablo Christiani's view that the Talmud and midrash, as well as the Bible, could be used to convince the Jews of the truth of Christianity.

Before proceeding to a closer examination of Raymond Martini's attitude toward the Jews and Judaism, we might note that despite the magnitude of the *Pugio fidei* and the influence it had on the anti-Jewish polemic of the late medieval, Renaissance, and Catholic Reformation periods,¹⁰ modern scholars have paid very little attention to its attack on the Jews. Christian historians have tended to emphasize its importance as a philosophical work, concentrating almost entirely on part one, which did not concern the Jews. After demonstrating the maturation of Martini's propaedeutic approach to converting the infidel and the parallels between the *Pugio* and Aquinas's *Summa contra gentiles*—indicating the reliance of the

9. *Pugio*, prooemium 10, p. 4: "Caeterum inducendo authoritatem textus ubicumque ab Hebraico fuerit desumptum, non septuaginta sequar, nec interpretem alium; et quod majoris praesumptionis videbitur, non ipsum etiam in hoc reverebor Hieronymum, nec tolerabilem linguae Latinae viabo improprietatem, ut eorum quae apud Hebraeos sunt, ex verbo in verbum, quotiescumque servari hoc potuit, transferam veritatem. Per hoc enim Judaeis falsiloquis lata valde spatiosaque subterfugiendi praecludetur via; et minime poterunt dicere non sic haberi apud eos, ut a nostris contra ipsos, me interprete, veritas inducetur." See also §§ 11–15, pp. 4–6. On the original format of the *Pugio*, at some variance with that of the printed edition, see Ch. Merchavya, "The Hebrew Versions of 'Pugio Fidei' in the Saint Geneviève Manuscript [Hebrew]," *KS* 51 (1976), 283–88.

10. Williams, *Adversus Judaeos*, pp. 248–49; Antonio Pacios Lopez, *La disputa de Tortosa*, 2 vols. (Madrid, 1957), pt. 1, chs. 2, 4, 5, passim; Francois Secret, "Notes pour une histoire du Pugio fidei à la Renaissance," *Sefarad* 20 (1960), 401–7; Y. Baer, *A History*, 1:167, 185, 331, 434, n. 8, 2:172, 181; Eusebio Colomer, "Die Beziehung des Ramon Llull zum Judentum im Rahmen des spanischen Mittelalters," in *JIM*, p. 206; Kenneth R. Stow, "The Burning of the Talmud in 1553, in the Light of Sixteenth Century Catholic Attitudes toward the Talmud," *Bibliothèque d'Humanisme et Renaissance* 34 (1972), 435–59, passim; and Ch. Merchavya, "The Talmud in the *Additiones* of Paul of Burgos," *JJS* 16 (1965), 115–19.

former on the latter—these scholars pass over the bulk of the *Pugio* with at most a cursory glance.[11] Jewish scholars, on the other hand, have generally confined their concern with the *Pugio* to the question of Martini's honesty and reliability in quoting rabbinic sources; for so great is the wealth of rabbinic material quoted that Martini's credibility would constitute an important factor in determining the worth of variant readings he adduces. Debate over this question has continued for the past century, carried on most recently by Yitzhak Baer and Saul Lieberman. Baer has castigated Martini as an indiscriminate forger of evidence, pointing to the lack of correlation between readings in the *Pugio* and those in the common Jewish versions of the same works, to discrepancies among multiple citations of the same text by Martini, and to inconsistencies between quotations and translations in the *Pugio* itself.[12] Lieberman, however, has responded convincingly that especially when viewed in terms of medieval standards of accuracy, Martini was faithful in his transmission of rabbinic material. A Christian who never received a traditional rabbinic education, Martini had to have worked from anthologies of talmudic passages, which in turn had drawn from different Hebrew manuscripts containing numerous textual variations.[13]

11. Berthier, "Un maître orientaliste," pp. 299–304; Thomas Aquinas, *Liber de veritate*, ed. Marc, 1:61–65; Carreras y Artau, *Historia de la filosofia*, 1:157–62; Marcelino Menéndez y Pelayo, *Historia de los heterodoxos españoles*, 2d ed., 7 vols. (Madrid, 1911–32), 3:250–55. The one exception to this rule seems to be J. Nicks, "La polémique contre les Juifs et le Pugio fidei de Raymond Martin," in *Mélanges d'histoire offerts à Charles Moeller*, 2 vols. (Louvain, 1914), 1:519–26, which summarizes Martini's anti-Jewish arguments but offers little penetrating analysis.

12. Yitzhak Baer, "Ha-Midrashim ha-Mezuyafim shel Raymundus Martini u-Meqomam be-Milhemet ha-Dat shel Yemei ha-Beinayim," in *Studies in Memory of Asher Gulak and Samuel Klein* (Jerusalem, 1942), pp. 28–49. See also A. C. Jennings and W. H. Lowe, eds., *The Psalms with Introductions and Critical Notes*, 2d ed., 2 vols. (London, 1884–85), 2:250–52; S. M. Schiller-Szinessy, "The Pugio Fidei," *Journal of Philology* 16 (1888), 131–52; and Ludwig Levy, "Rabbi Rachmon im Pugio fidei," *Zeitschrift für hebraeische Bibliographie* 6 (1902), 30–31.

13. Saul Lieberman, "Raymund Martini and His Alleged Forgeries," *HJ* 5 (1943), 87–102; and *Shkiin*, pp. 43–98. See also Leopold Zunz, *Die gottesdienstlichen Vorträge der Juden, historisch entwickelt* [Hebrew], ed. Ch. Albeck (Jerusalem, 1947), pp. 144–45; Adolph Neubauer and S. R. Driver, eds., *The Fifty-third Chapter of Isaiah According to Jewish Interpreters*, 2 vols. (Oxford, 1876–77), 2:xxix–xxxv (E. B. Pusey's introduction to the translation); *The Book of Tobit*, ed. Adolph Neubauer (Oxford, 1878), pp. xviii–xxiv; Neubauer, "Raymundus Martini and the Rev. Dr. Schiller-Szinessy," *The Academy*, 17 Sept. 1887, pp. 188–89; and "Jewish Controversy and the 'Pugio Fidei,'" *The Expositor* 7 (1888), 81–105, 179–97; Isidore Loeb, "La controverse religieuse entre les Chrétiens et les Juifs en France et en Espagne," *Revue de l'histoire des religions* 18 (1888), 137; Abraham Epstein, "*Bereschit-rabbati*. (Handschrift der prager jüdische Gemeinde.) Dessen Verhältniss zu Rabba-rabbati, Moses ha-Darschan, und Pugio

In any case, the question of Martini's honesty does not have much bearing on the underlying ideology of his polemic. Only one brief attempt has been made to penetrate the morass of material compiled by Martini and to discern the nature of his approach to Judaism, and although it discusses some important questions and insights, the brevity of the study, its resultant omissions, and some questionable conclusions mean that an analysis of Martini's polemical ideology still remains to be undertaken.[14]

A New Scheme of Jewish History

Such an analysis might well begin with the observation that the arguments of the *Pugio fidei* follow almost exactly the agenda set by Pablo Christiani for his disputation with Moses Naḥmanides in 1263. Like Pablo in Barcelona, Martini begins his attack upon the Jews with evidence for his claim that the messiah has come; he then proceeds to argue for the trinitarian nature of God and the need for a messiah both divine and human; and he concludes with a discussion of the incarnation and life of Christ, as the messiah who suffered and died to save mankind. And just as the fourth and most important argument on Pablo's agenda—that the Jews' adherence to their ritual law no longer represented a legitimate *modus vivendi* before God—underlay the entire structure of his

Fidei," *Magazin für die Wissenschaft des Judenthums* 15 (1888), 65–99; Epstein, *Moses ha-Darschan aus Narbonne: Fragmente seiner literarischen Erzeugnisse* (Vienna, 1891); George Foot Moore, "Christian Writers on Judaism," *HTR* 14 (1921), 203–5; Ch. Albeck, ed., *Midras Beresit Rabbati ex libro R. Mois Haddarsan* [Hebrew] (Jerusalem, 1940), pp. 1–6; Moses ha-Darshan, *Commentaire de la Genèse de R. Moïse de Prédicateur*, ed. Jean Joseph Brierre-Narbonne (Paris, 1939), pp. 5–19; A. Diez Macho, "Acarca de los midrašim falsificados de Raimundo Marti," *Sefarad* 9 (1949), 165–96; Ch. Merchavya, "Regarding the Rashi Commentary to 'Helek' [Hebrew]," *Tarbiz* 33 (1964), 259–86; and Merchavya, "Additional Information Concerning the Rashi Commentary to *Helek* [Hebrew]," *Tarbiz* 35 (1966), 278–94.

14. R. Bonfil, "The Nature of Judaism in Raymundus Martini's *Pugio Fidei* [Hebrew]," *Tarbiz* 40 (1971), 360–75. See also the brief and scattered, though often perceptive, remarks of Kurt Schubert, "Das christlich-jüdische Religionsgespräch in 12. und 13. Jahrhundert," *Kairos*, n.s. 19 (1977), 161–86. As this book was going to press, a long-awaited copy of Ina Willi-Plein and Thomas Willi, *Glaubensdolch und Messiasbeweis: Die Begegnung von Judentum, Christentum und Islam im 13. Jahrhundert in Spanien* (Neukirchen-Vluyn, 1980), finally reached my desk—too late for any meaningful consideration here. Nevertheless, it should be noted that ch. 2 (pp. 21–83) deals with "Der 'Pugio Fidei' des Raymond Martini als ein exemplarischer Versuch kirchlicher Auseinandersetzung mit dem Judentum," an essay that generally comports well with—but does not duplicate—my own ensuing analysis.

debate, so a similar line of reasoning permeated the fabric of the *Pugio fidei*, clearly conveying to the reader the essence of Martini's attitude toward contemporary Jewry. Martini's much longer and more explicit expression of this assertion, however, provides a better test for our impressions of the polemical stance taken by Raymond de Peñaforte and his school.

Following Pablo's example, Martini tried to prove this most central of his arguments by means of reference to a plethora of texts culled from rabbinic literature. Since he realized that rendering these texts in their original and employing them extensively in support of Christian doctrines constituted a radical tactical innovation in anti-Jewish polemic, he prefaced the *Pugio* with a justification for his method, which constitutes an important disclosure of his overall approach to the question of the Jews.

> The substance of this *Pugio*, especially inasmuch as it pertains to the Jews, is twofold: first and foremost, the *authoritas* of the law, of the prophets, and of all of the Old Testament; second, certain *traditiones*, which I found in the Talmud and midrashim—i.e., glosses—and traditions of the ancient Jews and which I most gladly raised up like pearls out of a very great dungheap. With the help of God I shall translate them into Latin and adduce and insert them in their proper places, insofar as shall seem wise to me.
>
> These *traditiones*, which they [the Jews] call *torah shebbe-'al peh*—oral law—they believe and state that God gave to Moses along with the law on Mount Sinai. Then Moses, they say, transmitted them to his disciple Joshua, Joshua to his successors, and so on, until they were committed to writing by the ancient rabbis. Yet it seems that to believe this, that God gave Moses all that is in the Talmud, should be deemed—on account of the absurdities which it contains—nothing other than the insanity of a ruined mind.
>
> Certain [*traditiones*], which know the truth and in every way reveal the doctrine of the prophets and holy fathers, wondrously and incredibly bespeak the Christian faith too, as will become obvious in this book. They destroy and confound the perfidy of modern Jews, and I do not think that one should question that they successively managed to make their way from Moses and the prophets and the other holy fathers to those who recorded them. For in no way other than from the prophets and fathers do we think that such things descended, since traditions of this sort are entirely contrary to those regarding the messiah and so many other matters which the Jews have believed since the time of Christ even until now.
>
> Such things of this sort were thus not meant to be rejected, since

nobody sane would reject what he finds in places like the law and the prophets, even though both these are rejected among those so perfidious [the Jews]. For a wise man never despises a precious stone, even if it might be found in the head of a dragon or a toad. Honey is the spittle of bees, and how could there be anything less worthy of those having a poisonous sting! Indeed he is not to be deemed foolish who knows how to render it fit for his own beneficial uses, as long as he knows to avoid the harm of the sting.

We therefore do not reject such *traditiones* but embrace them both for those reasons already mentioned and because there is nothing so capable of confuting the impudence of the Jews; there is found nothing so effective for overcoming their evil. Finally, what would be more joyous for a Christian than if he could most easily twist the sword of his enemy from his hand and then cut off the head of the infidel with his own blade or just like Judith butcher [the infidel] with his own stolen dagger?[15]

Martini here appears to have made primarily a methodological point: one can most effectively defeat the Jews in debate by using their own literature against them. Throughout the *Pugio* he returns to this message. Christian disputants can exploit Jewish books the majority of whose arguments are obviously false. Jewish collections of blasphemous tales concerning Jesus, for example, at least acknowledged the fact that he performed miracles.[16] More often than not, arguments against Christianity adduced by the Jews from their own literature can be turned against them on behalf of the Church; the Jews thus hurt themselves more than anyone else by debating with Christian clerics.[17] The key to success for the Christian debater lay in gaining a familiarity with Hebrew; only then could he wrest the spears of the Jews from their own hands, exulting in spoiling the very bedrock of Jewish perseverance in their ancient ways and beliefs.[18]

The constantly offered, often very detailed advice to the reader as to how to react to particular turns of argument, the abundance of alternative proof-texts with instructions for their use in support

15. *Pugio*, prooemium, 5–9, pp. 2–4.
16. Ibid. 2.6.4, p. 315; 2.8.8, p. 364.
17. Ibid. 2.13.8, p. 444; 3.3.11.27, p. 792. See also 2.13.1, p. 440.
18. Ibid. 2.14.4, p. 448: "Hinc igitur animadverte, lector, quam sit utile fidei Christianae, literas [sic] non ignorare Hebraicas. Quis enim unquam nisi ex suo Talmud sua posset in eos pro nobis jacula contorquere?" See also 3.3.2.13, pp. 655–56: "Gloriosus tamen, ac melius reputabitur, si quasi proprio eorum pugione de manu eorum violenter erepto falsitatis suae nequitias valeas jugulare."

of any specific contention, and the attempt to prepare in advance for all possible arguments Jews might offer in rebuttal—all serve to forward the proclaimed purpose of the book. Martini was writing a manual of strategy for those charged with defending Christendom against the infidel and then with converting him. As a zealous disciple of Raymond de Peñaforte, he subscribed to the view that converting the infidel required mastering his language and his literature, and having completed that arduous task himself, he attempted to provide his readers with the fruits of his labor, eliminating the need for them to duplicate it. Martini's zeal can well be understood in terms of the evolution and character of the Order of Preachers, as described in chapter two. The quoted portion of Martini's introduction to the *Pugio*, however, strongly suggests that this Dominican and his colleagues had not only a forensic message to convey but an important theological one as well.[19]

In the introductory passage, Martini distinguishes three different genera of expressions of Jewish belief. First, he speaks of the law and prophecies of the Old Testament, which along with their correct interpretations would, albeit prefiguratively, establish the truth of Christianity. These interpretations or *traditiones* were preserved by the Jews of the Bible as part of their oral tradition, which eventually came to be recorded by the rabbis of the Talmud. Such correct interpretations of Scripture must be extracted from rabbinic literature "like pearls out of a very great dungheap." Second, in contradistinction to these select few *traditiones*, the vast majority of talmudic teachings are described as the aforementioned dungheap, the head of a dragon or toad, or the venomous sting of the bee. This body of literature, replete with "absurdities," propagates the false beliefs "regarding the messiah and so many other matters which the Jews have believed from the time of Christ." Third, Martini identifies his present enemy, "the perfidy of modern Jews," which expresses itself as both "impudence" and "evil." It is against this third brand of Judaism that he intends to direct the christological *traditiones* of the first.

The polarity between the true and false components of Jewish literature is mentioned rather frequently throughout the *Pugio*.[20] It plays a thematic role of great importance for Martini; in it lies the

19. The remark of Colomer, "Die Beziehung des Ramon Llull," p. 206, that "the novelty of the *Pugio fidei* lies not in its ideas but in its methodology" exemplifies the lack of attention paid by scholars to the ideational depth of Martini's work.
20. *Pugio* 2.14.8, p. 450; 2.14.13, p. 452; 3.3.1.8, p. 633; 3.3.6.2., p. 728; 3.3.6.13, p. 733.

key to his approach to the Jews of his own day. Each of the three repositories of Jewish belief or expression mentioned in Martini's introduction represents a particular group of Jews in history. In the respective characters of these three groups and the relationships between them, as evaluated by Martini through their actions, their literature, and their attitudes toward their predecessors, lies the basic theological message of the *Pugio fidei*.

The first group consisted of the Hebrews of the Old Testament. Despite the fact that God gave Moses and the Israelites the law of the Pentateuch, the Jews of that period lived in a state of spiritual depravity, having inherited the original sin of their forefather Adam; until the redemptive advent of Christ, such was the state of all mankind. This condition of perpetual, inescapable guilt before God constantly manifested itself in the lives of the Israelites. "Before the advent of our savior, there was an abundance of idolatry and false prophets in the world, not only among the Gentiles but also among them [the Jews]." Moreover, Martini instructs his reader to "note that the Jews have always provoked God even more with words and blasphemies than with their evil deeds." In particular, they committed several especially heinous crimes for which God punished them with periods of exile and captivity. First they sold their brother Joseph into slavery for twenty pieces of silver, for which God punished them with 210 years of slavery in Egypt. Later, the ten tribes of Israel doubted the divine sponsorship of the house of David, broke away from the Davidic kingdom, and proceeded to worship idols; as a result, God permitted Assyria to destroy the kingdom of Israel. Subsequently, in the kingdom of Judea, Jews sacrificed their own infant children, bringing upon themselves the seventy years of Babylonian captivity. Nor did this tendency to sin exist merely among the masses of uneducated, spiritually insensitive Jews; with an excerpt from the midrash on the Song of Songs, Martini pointed out that even the three patriarchs of the Jews and their prophets had sinned. Moses himself had sinned on many occasions, once actually attempting to dedicate his first son to a life of idolatry. In short, "all the fathers of [this] era, even the holy men, were culpable and liable before God."[21]

The fallen state of man during this period accords with the quality of the prevalent law of the Old Testament. Specifically, Martini isolated seven deficiencies in the system of Mosaic commandments:

21. Ibid. 3.2.7.1, 5–6, 10, pp. 591, 594–8, 601; 3.3.13.11, p. 821; 3.3.16.6, 13, pp. 845–46, 849. Cf. *Song of Songs Rabbah* 1.4a.1.

In its time, no one either entered paradise or could avoid hell. It showed the way of repentance to sinners only through the obscure and imperfect signs of physical sacrifices, not in an outright and explicit manner. It afforded the Jews only an incomplete knowledge of God. It gave an unsatisfactory explanation of the nature of the human soul and its cognition. It included imperfect legal ordinances which do not allow for a viable religious life. It offered only temporal rewards to those who obeyed it. And it contained no trace of any belief in resurrection. The greatest significance of these criticisms of the Old Testament lay in Martini's insistence that one therefore had to distinguish between it and the truly salvific covenant of the messiah. For the law of Moses proffered no way for man to overcome his fallen state and achieve salvation. If it made all of its promises to the Jews conditional upon their obedience to its commandments, their sinful state and consequent inability to fulfill the demands of the law insured that they would never enjoy the rewards their prophets described to them.[22]

The reader might well ask, why then did God give the law of Moses to the Jews? While Martini never responds directly, he implies at least parts of an answer. The fact that the law of Moses was imperfect neither negated its value for the Jews entirely nor eliminated its ability to play an important role in the divine plan of human salvific history. Many benefits must have accrued from having a corpus of law, which regulated the workings of society, wield authority in a community of naturally sinful men.[23] A corollary of this point is of great importance for understanding Martini's scheme of Jewish history. The Jews of the Bible accepted the law of Moses as authoritative and binding in their community. In other words, however much their fallen state might have facilitated both their transgression of the law and their resultant failure to achieve salvation, the Jews before Jesus recognized the Old Testament for what it was—those commandments by which God had instructed them to live. Martini never accuses the Jews of this period of collectively denying God or his law or falling into heresy. Although every individual Jew may have sinned, the Jewish community at

---

22. *Pugio* 2.15.1–9, pp. 465–70; 3.3.20.15, pp. 891–92; on the infinitesimal chances Jews had of achieving salvation, see 2.11.22, p. 423: "Per Talmud sit evidenter ostensum quod non omnes Judaeos Messias salvare debuerit; sed unum de civitate, et duos de cognatione, sive duos de sexcentis millibus: Et quod se, atque suos nec ab illusionibus, nec a suppliciis, seu tormentis defendere debuerit, ut supra est tam per textum, quam per Talmud probatum." Cf. 2.11.1–2, p. 405; 2.11.21, p. 421.
23. Cf. Thomas Aquinas's evaluation of the Mosaic law in his *ST* 2.1.98.1.

large remained the chosen people and a vital part of God's plan for saving mankind. For the most important function of the Mosaic Law, a task it hardly could have fulfilled without having been given to the Jews, was to prefigure the perfect New Testament of Christ, which would accompany his incarnation and redemption of humanity.

One can now appreciate the paradox in Martini's statement that even the holy men or saints (*sancti*) among the Jews of the Bible— the patriarchs, Moses, the prophets, for example—were doomed to hell before Christ's advent.[24] How could saints merit such a punishment and still retain their holiness? Having inherited Adam's fallen nature, these men sinned; without God's redemptive grace, they could not be saved. Nevertheless, they received, transmitted, and of necessity understood the message of God which pointed to the future redemption and the covenant of grace. Their functioning *within* the divine economy of salvation allows Martini to justify his strategy of finding proof of Christianity in the literature of the Jews—not only in the God-given law and prophecies of the Old Testament but also in the correct christological interpretations of such passages found in rabbinic literature. "For in no other way than from the prophets and the fathers [these 'holy men'] can we think that such things descended." Accordingly, Martini habitually vouches for the credibility of the texts that he adduces from rabbinic literature in his own behalf as representing "the interpretation of the most ancient of the Jews" (*expositio antiquissimorum Judaeorum*).[25] Sinful as they may have been, these Jews before the time of Jesus followed God insofar as the fallen state of men allowed them.

Apart from the contention that the most ancient Jews' impressions of the coming of the messiah appeared in rabbinic literature as well as in the Old Testament, Martini's characterization of these Jews differed little from that of most Christian writers before him.

---

24. *Pugio* 3.2.7.10, pp. 600–601. On Isaiah 53:5–6 ("Et ipse vulneratus propter culpas nostras, attritus propter peccata nostra; disciplina pacis nostrae super eum, et in livore ejus medicatum est nobis. Omnes nos sicut oves erravimus. . . ."), Martini comments: *"omnes nos,* nullo excepto usque ad Redemptoris adventum. . . . Et *peccata nostra* non solum originale, sed etiam actuale, tollunt nos in hoc mundo, ut dictum est; et animam post mortem ad inferos, licet differenter. Nam impiorum animas tollebant, et tollunt daemones propter peccata sua ad aeternum supplicium: justorum vero animae propter originale peccatum, etsi aliud non erat, ducebantur, ad alium quendam infernum, ad locum scilicet tenebrosum. . . ."

25. *Pugio* 3.3.5.5, p. 718; cf. the references to "Judaei Antiqui" in 3.3.6.2, p. 728, and the *Antiqui sapientes Judaeorum* in 3.3.15.5, p. 838.

Only in its discussion of the Jews of the Talmud, who lived during and after the life of Jesus—the second key period in their history— does the *Pugio fidei* truly begin to explicate the new mendicant conception of Judaism. Although Christ substituted the New Testament, his perfect Gospel, for the imperfect law of Moses and offered man his redemptive grace, the Jews did not forsake their fallen nature.[26] Rather, the same propensity for sin which had led them to sell their brother Joseph into slavery, to doubt the divine promise of redemption made to the patriarchs, and to engage in idolatry and human sacrifice in the first temple now led them to commit a new series of crimes, the offer of redemption extended to them by Jesus notwithstanding.

> What was the evil in those Jews' actions, for which God expelled them from his home—i.e., from Jerusalem—and the land, where his home was, and for which he will never cherish them as long as they remain Jews? The first villainy in the Jews' actions causing that final expulsion was the reprobation, reproaching, and repulsion of our messiah, as well as the persecution of him, the pointless hatred with which they have hated him until now and hated him then. . . . The second villainy of the Jews' deeds on account of which God expelled them from his home—i.e., the temple—and from Jerusalem was that after rejecting the messiah—namely, the Lord Jesus Christ—they accepted a false messiah, Bar Cosba. . . . The third villainy in the Jews' deeds and the greatest insanity of all was that after forty-eight and one-half years had elapsed since the destruction of the temple and the death of their aforementioned false messiah Bar Cosba they produced another no less false one named Ben Cosba.[27]

In punishment for all these various misdeeds, God destroyed the Jews' cult and religious community through the power of Rome. The Jews no longer could offer sacrifice; they had lost all vestiges of political independence; and they remained without anyone to offer them proper spiritual guidance. They had rejected not only the

26. As might have been expected, the New Testament had seven aspects of perfection which corresponded to the seven flaws of the Mosaic law; see *Pugio* 3.3.20.16, pp. 892–93.

27. *Pugio* 3.3.21.2, 7, 9, pp. 895, 904, 907. On the first crime, cf. 3.3.16.6, p. 846. In the second and third accusations, Martini alludes to Simon bar Kozevah, often dubbed Bar Kokhba, the leader of the Judean revolt against Rome from 132 to 135. The notions, however, that another Bar Kozevah lived during the destruction of the second temple and that only 48½ years elapsed between the temple's destruction (70) and the Bar Kokhba rebellion (132) are entirely unfounded; I hope to pursue their origins on another occasion.

messiah but God himself, and he therefore deprived them of his love, refusing to hear their prayers. Simultaneously befitting both the teaching that the rituals of Mosaic Law would be abrogated upon the advent of the messiah and the wretchedness of the Jews' crimes, God's punishment also included the harsh decrees of the Hadrianic persecution in Palestine, which outlawed adherence to basic Mosaic commandments like circumcision and the Sabbath.[28]

What then happened to the Jews? Before the thirteenth century, Christian writers continued to view the Jews who lived after Jesus essentially as they had viewed those who preceded him. In other words, the Jews of the first century, after blindly refusing to accept Jesus as Christ, remained persistent in their observance of Old Testament law and still awaited the messiah, just as they had done before Jesus. Yet because they retained the Old Testament, which God indeed had revealed to them, they still had a part to play in the divine direction of the destiny of mankind. Augustine himself had allotted them important functions in witnessing the truth of the Bible and in the future fulfillment of divine prophecy. He wrote in *The City of God*:

> The Jews, who killed him [Jesus] and would not believe in him, because he must needs die and rise again, were ravaged still more miserably by the Romans and were utterly uprooted from their kingdom, where they had already been ruled by foreign-born rulers; and they were scattered throughout the lands—for indeed there is no place where they are not found—and so by means of their own Scriptures they bear witness on our behalf that we have not forged the prophesies about Christ. . . . When they do not believe in our Scriptures, their own Scriptures, to which they are blind when they read, are fulfilled in them. . . .
>
> After admonishing them [the Jews] to remember the law of Moses (for he foresaw that for a long time to come they would not take it, as they should have, in a spiritual sense), the prophet continued: "And behold, I will send you Elijah the Tishbite, before the great and shining day of the Lord shall come, and he shall turn the heart of the father toward the son and the heart of man toward his neighbour, lest perchance in my coming I utterly shake the earth [Malachi 3:23–24]." That in the last days before the judgement, by means of this great and wonderful prophet Elijah and his explanation to them of the law, the

28. *Pugio* 3.1.4.12, p. 495; 3.3.4.5, p. 689; 3.3.11.12–22, pp. 778–89; 3.3.21.15, p. 911; 3.3.23.1–2, pp. 953–54.

Jews are to believe in the true Christ, that is, in our Christ, is a frequent topic on the lips and in the thought of believers.[29]

The view that Judaism had simply remained stagnant since the time of Jesus conditioned the character of anti-Jewish polemic in early medieval Christendom. Attacks on the Jews harped almost entirely on the christological interpretation of the Old Testament. And the gap in reality between the Jews in the Bible and the Jews of medieval Europe, as well as the positive functions allotted the Jews in Christendom, helped to preserve the theoretical nature of such polemic, keeping it devoid of practical consequences for the European Jewish community.

Martini, on the other hand, evidently shared Thomas Aquinas's novel opinion that the rabbis of the first-century Jews were blameworthy for their deliberate rejection of Jesus.[30] Their own law *and exegetical teachings* pointed to him as their savior! Their hatred for him, then, derived not from blindness, but from a rejection of God which radically altered the character of their Judaism from the divinely ordained, albeit imperfect, religion of the Old Testament to a wicked and heretical perversion thereof. Martini viewed the Jews of the rabbinic period as having distorted the character of Mosaic law completely, for they contended that the Old Testament itself constituted the perfect expression of divine wisdom and thus had eternally binding authority over them. Finding no legitimate support in any source, such a claim epitomized the irrationality of the Jews, who "moved by the most impudent folly go out of their minds" to espouse it. Martini found it difficult to understand how any human being could persist in such a belief: "Note that every

29. Augustine, *De civitate Dei* 18.46, 20.29, 6:48–49, 432–33.

30. See above, ch. 5, n. 43. While Martini never accuses the ancient rabbis of deliberate and willful rejection of the messiah in the explicit way that Thomas Aquinas does, the charge nevertheless appears to underlie his basic attack on rabbinic Judaism, just as it did that of Pablo Christiani. If the truth of Christianity were evident in the Talmud, how could the rabbis have failed to understand it?—hence the responses of Naḥmanides to Pablo, and Martini's own claims (to be discussed presently) that the rabbis deviously corrupted the text of Scripture to conceal their perversity. Parkes, *Conflict*, pp. 100–103, points out how various passages from the apocryphal Gospels similarly accuse the Jews of having recognized the divinity and messiahship of Jesus and having rejected him nonetheless, in violation of the teachings of the Old Testament. The writers of these ancient passages, however, did not have adequate historical hindsight—inasmuch as they lived during the talmudic period—to proceed to view postbiblical Judaism as a rabbinic heresy. In any event, the implications of such passages were generally ignored in the West until the thirteenth century.

Jew, unless inwardly he be less than a beast, here ought to concede that this wisdom or law of God, which loves those who love him, is something rational because it is the wisdom of God, and it is not the law of Moses, which is not capable of love or hate, just like other inanimate things which are written on the hides of rams or bucks" (a reference to the Torah scroll).[31] On account of this distortion of the character of the Old Testament, Rabbi Aqiva and the other rabbinic martyrs of the Hadrianic persecution of the Jews deserved to die. These men died at the hands of the Romans not because they kept the law of Moses but because they forsook it, by supporting two false messiahs in succession, inciting rebellion against Rome, and denying that Jesus was the messiah. By rejecting God as their savior, the Jews of the Talmud destroyed the whole system of divine prophecy in the Old Testament, implying its uselessness and falsity.[32]

This point was a central one in Martini's polemic. It actually began the whole treatment of the Jews in the body of the *Pugio fidei*; the second part of the work, although it ostensibly aims to establish the past advent of the messiah, opens with a discussion of the divisiveness of ancient Jewry. In the days of Jeroboam, the ten tribes of Israel broke away from Judah, rejecting their Davidic heritage and erecting idols to worship in place of God, for which crimes Assyria conquered and dispersed them. Similarly in the days of Jesus, most of the Jews rejected the divine and Davidic messiah, espousing false ones in his place and meeting punishment at the hands of Rome. They thereby forsook their biblical heritage, left the fold of God's chosen people, and transferred their allegiance to the devil.[33] It was a "demonic" insanity that had led the Jews to reject Jesus, a state of mind which perversely caused them to ascribe his miracles to "Beelzebub, the prince of the demons." The devil convinced the Jews to follow Bar Cosba as their messiah, and Rabbi Aqiva "was thus a martyr for the devil and not for God." The legendary *bat qol* of rabbinic homilies, the voice that according to Jewish belief came down from heaven to express the will of God, was in truth not a heavenly voice but a satanic one.

31. *Pugio* 3.1.7.1, 18, pp. 511, 519.
32. Ibid. 2.4.27, p. 329: "Non ideo interfecti sunt quia in lege Mosis studebant; sed potius, quia contra legem Moysis, et Prophetas duos falsos Messias unum post alium [Akiba] fecerat . . . , et quia contra Romanos surrexerat, et Judaeos insurgere fecerat, et cum eis Dominum Jesum fuisse Messiam negaverat." See also 3.3.1, p. 661.
33. Ibid. 2.1–2, pp. 260–65.

Most important, the devil returned the Jews to the observance of the Mosaic commandments which God had intended to nullify through the Roman persecution; the devil thus lay at the root of the Jews' heresy and irrationality.

> Besides the spirit of fornication which is in their midst—that is, in their hearts—of whom ought it more appropriately to be said than of the devil Bentamalyon, that he restored to them circumcision, the Sabbath, and the other rituals which God removed through the agency of the Romans? The devil undoubtedly . . . misled them and deprived them of a sense of understanding the truth, so that they are less intelligent than asses as regards divine scriptures.[34]

Because the Jews of the Talmud had abandoned both reason and God, the Christians had replaced the Jews as God's chosen people. The Jews, whom Martini identified with the eschatological force of evil named Magog, now adhered to the cult of the devil rather than the cult of God. This new status quite naturally colored and characterized the literature of the talmudic rabbis, for after substituting Jesus' apostles for the previous rabbinic leadership of his people, God deprived the rabbis of all divine inspiration; he "removed the spirit of prophecy, and he allowed their sages to be infatuated by the devil and spiritually blinded." The demonic heresy of the rabbis of the Talmud accordingly pervaded all their teachings, and the rabbis went so far as to assert that transgressions against their own legal ordinances warranted more severe punishments than those against biblical commandments, the enactments of God himself.[35]

Martini adduces many sorts of arguments and much documentation in support of these general accusations. He castigates the rabbis of the Talmud both for stupidity in their skeptical interpretation of messianic prophecies in the Old Testament and for deliberate distortions in attempting to deny and conceal biblical allusions to Jesus. Numerous talmudic arguments remained embarrassingly lacking in supporting evidence.[36] Still more shamefully, the rabbis

---

34. Ibid. 3.3.21.23, p. 918. See also 2.4.26–27, p. 329; 2.6.6, p. 352; 2.8.5, p. 362; and 3.3.7.4, p. 741. The connection in the medieval mind between the rabbis' deliberate rejection of Jesus and their alliance with the devil has been discussed briefly—without reference to the *Pugio fidei*—by Cecil Roth, "The Medieval Conception of the Jew," in *Essays and Studies in Memory of Linda R. Miller*, ed. Israel Davidson (New York, 1938), pp. 172ff.

35. *Pugio* 2.14.20, p. 457; 3.3.12.8, p. 807; 3.3.21.19, p. 914; 3.3.22.4, p. 924.

36. See, for example, ibid. 2.3.8, p. 277; 3.1.9.4–5, pp. 530–31; 3.3.2.13, p. 655; 3.3.3.6, p. 667; and 3.3.18.7, p. 878.

dared actually to alter the text of the Old Testament, thereby corrupting its meaning, in their use of the device known in rabbinic literature as "scribal emendation" or *tiqqun soferim*. Martini here refers to rabbinic glosses which indicate to him that the present reading of various passages of the Hebrew Bible represents a rabbinic distortion of a previous, authentic reading, alterations which Martini asserts crept into the text at some point between the times of Josephus Flavius and Jerome.[37] The rabbis also changed the meaning of important texts both by varying the pointing or vocalization (*niqqud*) of the consonants in Hebrew words, whereby slight changes could greatly alter a word's meaning, and by establishing traditions of substituting different words to be read (*qeri*) out loud in place of those encountered in the written text (*ketiv*).[38] The Old Testament, Martini argues, originally contained many more proofs for the mystery of God's incarnation, but the Jewish sages either deleted them entirely or managed to distort them.[39]

Not only did the rabbis of the Talmud in Martini's view corrupt the text and meaning of Scripture, but the corpus of their writings— the *torah shebbe-'al peh* or oral tradition—was quintessentially stupid,

37. Ibid. 2.3.9, pp. 277–79; 3.4.11, pp. 695–96; 3.3.16.16, p. 850; 3.3.16.27, pp. 859–60; 3.3.16.32, p. 864. Modern as well as medieval biblical scholars have shown that *tiqqun soferim* was very possibly simply the rabbis' way of noting that Scripture itself had spoken euphemistically. At most, all that was ever altered was a single letter of a word, and that only for the sake of the honor of God's name. See W. Emery Barnes, "Ancient Corrections in the Text of the Old Testament," *Journal of Theological Studies*, o.s. 1 (1900), 387–414; and Saul Lieberman, *Hellenism in Jewish Palestine*, 2d ed. (New York, 1962), pp. 28–37. The conclusion that Martini's argument manifests a new stage in the development of anti-Jewish polemic finds additional support in the use of *tiqqun soferim* made by a Jewish disputant in his own behalf, without fear of reproach by Christian opponents. Although this anonymous writer was Martini's contemporary, he clearly belonged to the earlier breed of polemicist. See *The Jewish-Christian Debate in the High Middle Ages: A Critical Edition of the Niẓẓaḥon Vetus*, ed. David Berger (Philadelphia, 1979), Heb. p. 72, line 65; and cf. Berger's comments on the *Pugio*, p. 36, n. 104. Martini did not invent the notion that Jews had interfered with the true reading of the Hebrew Bible. Yet while Justin Martyr (second century), Paulus Alvarus (ninth century), and Peter of Blois (twelfth century) had all voiced such sentiments before him—see Williams, *Adversus Judaeos*, pp. 33, 225, 402–403—none had developed the idea as succinctly or extensively as Martini did, nor did it figure in their polemics in so crucial a fashion. To my knowledge, Martini was the first Christian Hebraist to air this charge and the first to link it with *tiqqun soferim*.

38. *Pugio* 3.3.4.11, pp. 696–98. On these variations between the written text and that to be read out loud, see Harry M. Orlinsky, "The Origin of the Kethib-Qere System: A New Approach," *Supplements to Vetus Testamentum* 7 (1959), 407–15.

39. *Pugio* 3.3.4.15, pp. 705–6: ". . . quae a Scribis, et sapientibus Judaeorum de sacra pagina, vel omnino abrasa sunt, vel loco eorum alia substituta, vel punctando perperam, vel aliter scribendo interius, aliter exterius, a veritate, quia indigna multa, et impossibilia Deo videbantur attribuere, deviata. . . ."

blasphemous, and heretical. Martini stresses the absurdity of count-less talmudic *aggadot*. Some such homilies were simply ridiculous fables, like the story that the messiah was born on the day that the temple was destroyed, the superstitions concerning how to avoid the angel of death, tales describing the nature and lives of demons, and the legend of the death of King Og of the Bashan.[40] A second sort of homily not only possessed the foolishness of the first but also revealed the terrible state of moral depravity in which the rabbis supposedly lived and functioned. Martini is duly horrified at the Talmud's frankness concerning matters of sex—the legend that Adam copulated with demons after leaving the Garden of Eden; the explanation of Noah's curse of his grandson Canaan (Genesis 9:21–25) as a response to having been either castrated or raped by his son Ham (Canaan's father); the description of the cultic orgy staged by Zimri ben Salu for which he merited slaughter at the hands of Phineas the priest (Numbers 25:6–8, 14); or mention of Samson's great sexual potency. Equally terrible was the talmudic statement that Abraham taught his son Isaac everything, even sor-cery. Martini concludes: "Know that countless evil and most im-pudent lies of this sort are in the Talmud and their other books, with which I no longer wish to soil my parchment. It is sufficiently obvious from these how fetid was the doctrine of the scribes—i.e., the teachers of the Jews—from the time that our savior came."[41] The most dangerous talmudic fables, however, dealt with various as-pects of God's activities: that during each of three nightly watches he roars like a lion and bemoans the destruction of the temple and the dispersion of his people; that daily at sunset he receives the sun as a king would a subject at court; that God spends his day studying, judging the world, feeding the world, playing with the leviathan, and teaching schoolchildren; or that God had to console the moon for his having made the sun brighter.[42] Such anthropo-morphic *aggadot* manifested the terrible heresy of the rabbis of the Talmud; their god could not possibly be the omniscient and omnipotent lord of the universe, the same God in whom the Jews of the Bible had believed.

It should be noted that for yet another reason the Jews are said not to have a true God or God of truth—namely that when they say that they believe in and worship the God of Abraham who made heaven

40. Ibid. 2.2.6, p. 352; 3.3.22.24–27, pp. 937–40.
41. Ibid. 3.2.5.16, p. 573; 3.3.22.15–18, pp. 932–33.
42. Ibid. 3.3.22.9–13, pp. 928–31, passim; cf. also 2.15.15, p. 473.

and earth, it is not he; but rather they are fashioning and inventing some monster for their god. For they say many things [as in the aforementioned fables] concerning their god—whom they worship and for whom they observe the Sabbath, practice circumcision, pray, build huts [the *sukkot* or booths of the autumnal festival], and do other things of this sort—from which it necessarily follows that he is neither God nor any living being but only some figment of their imagination which is not, was not, and never will be.[43]

The heresy and depravity of the Talmud, moreover, extended into its enactment of law as well. Martini chastises the rabbis for their practice of granting absolutions from vows, for instance, decrying the liberties they thereby took in contravening biblical commandments, and pointing to the resulting punishment God afflicted on them.[44] Another law that for him exemplified the wretchedness of talmudic Judaism and its distortion of the Bible was the rabbinic prescription that the ritual circumcision ceremony include the oral suction of blood from the infant's wound.

> Behold, reader, how God, in view of their crimes, placed the Jews in a terrible state of perception, so that they do what ought not to be done and is not becoming. And with what great guilt is that most abominable mouth, which quite often has blasphemed the Lord Jesus Christ, infected and punished! For as often as they circumcise an infant or an adult, they suck the penis orally for as long as blood emerges from it, desiring to obey the aforementioned mandate of the rabbis. They excuse this by saying that if this would not be done, all their infants would die, which is false. For the Saracens circumcise their infants and never do this abominable act.[45]

Yet worst of all were rabbinic opinions that in certain cases countenanced the discriminatory treatment of Gentiles by Jews, or homilies that seemed to call for the slaying of the best of the Gentiles. This iniquity removed all room for doubt in Martini's evaluation of rabbinic literature. "Let your prudence take note, reader, that the Talmud, which teaches them to cheat so perniciously and to kill

43. Ibid. 2.15.15, pp. 472–73.
44. Ibid. 3.3.22.1, pp. 920–21.
45. Ibid. 3.3.11.18, p. 786. That even medieval Jews believed that this practice truly derived from medical necessity may be seen from its inclusion as such in Maimonides, *MT*, Laws of Circumcision 2.2, and Maimonides' general prescription of oral suction for the cleansing of wounds in his *Treatise on Poisons and Their Antidotes* 1.1.1, ed. Suessman Munter (Philadelphia, 1966), p. 9.

Christians, is not the law of God but the artifice of the devil. The best indication of this is the nonsense and insanity recorded here."[46]

The third group of Jews in history, the *Iudei moderni* of Martini's own day, maintained the perverse beliefs of the rabbis who preceded them, inheriting and persisting in all the vices and insanities of talmudic Judaism. By contending that the promises of God to the Jews in the Old Testament were eternally binding and not made conditional to the fulfillment of his commandments and total abstinence from sin, modern Jews too mistook the Mosaic law for God's redemptive logos or permanent covenant of grace and so continued in the heresy of their talmudic predecessors. Martini warns his reader that contemporary Jews imitate their ancestors' evil, contradicting what has already been proven of Christianity beyond any doubt.[47] Failing to learn from the bad example of the talmudic rabbis, modern Jews continue to live a life of sin, extending the list of crimes in punishment for which God has kept them in perpetual dispersion and captivity: "The fourth villainy of the Jews' action was that despite the ruse by which they had been seduced so basely into [accepting] the first two false messiahs, they have created [advocated false belief in] a third messiah, whom modern [Jews] still most foolishly await, even though more than a thousand years have elapsed since the day of the destruction of the temple, when they pretend he was born."[48] Contemporary Jews have thereby incurred the same guilt and responsibility for having necessitated the destruction of the temple, and by persevering in the observance of the Mosaic commandments which God had the Romans outlaw, they similarly preserved the rabbinic alliance with the devil. "There is no greater rejection of the Jews' confusion," writes Martini, "than to demonstrate to them . . . that the observance of circumcision, of the Sabbath, and of the other ceremonial precepts after the messiah has come is not, as has been proven many times, the service or worship of God, but the cult of the devil."[49]

Martini finds many different sorts of manifestations of modern Jewry's continued heretical distortion of the Old Testament. Its scholars author numerous false interpretations of messianic allusions in the Bible so as to conceal their real christological meaning.

46. *Pugio* 3.3.22.21–22, pp. 935–36.
47. Ibid. 2.15.11, p. 471.
48. Ibid. 3.3.21.10, p. 908. Cf. 3.3.21.2,7,9, pp. 895, 904, 907.
49. Ibid. 3.1.14.24, p. 461; 3.3.11.25, p. 791; 3.3.21.2, p. 898.

Their rejection of interpretations in the ancient Targum—the Aramaic translation of the Old Testament—constitutes a great offense (*nefas*) from a Jewish perspective.[50] They too engage in trying to alter the correct reading of the text of the Bible, both by changing the spelling of words and by falsifying their real pointing or vocalization. They persist in recognizing as legitimate the phenomenon of *tiqqun soferim* and do not hesitate to exploit the textual corruptions thereby produced.[51] Moreover, they have no scruples when they debate with Christians concerning the true meaning of biblical passages; they feign ignorance, deny incontrovertible argumentation, and impetuously advance the most ridiculous conclusions. "In contradicting us and the truth, the Jews are borne by such great malice that they distort the meaning of individual words completely, without any hint of shame."[52]

Accepting all of their rabbinic heritage indiscriminately, modern Jews also believe in the foolish and blasphemous talmudic *aggadot* considered above. Although some Jews might claim that these *aggadot* are in truth allegorical and not meant to be understood literally, their entirely literal interpretation by no less an authoritative Jewish commentator than Rabbi Solomon ben Isaac of Troyes proves such a claim deceitful and false.[53] And in affirming the Talmud's anthropomorphic homilies concerning the deity—for example, that every night he laments the destruction of the temple and the dispersion of Israel—modern Jews find themselves on the horns of a dilemma, which proves that they do not worship the true God. For concerning the god of the Jews who grieves over their captivity, Martini demands that one of two things be conceded: either this god desires to liberate the Jews and cannot, in which case he is not the true God, or he can liberate them but does not desire to do so, so that his grief is pointless and foolhardy. "Hence it follows that the god of the modern Jews is not the true God; for the God of Abraham and the other holy fathers was said to be wise and pow-

---

50. See, for example, ibid. 2.3.8, p. 275; 2.9.12, p. 381; 3.1.10.9, 15, pp. 537, 539; 3.3.4.3, p. 684; and 3.3.4.8, p. 693. Martini displays a remarkable familiarity with the exegetical and speculative writings of Solomon ben Isaac of Troyes or Rashi, Abraham ibn Ezra, Moses Maimonides, David Qimḥi, and even the same Moses Nahmanides who debated with Pablo Christiani.

51. *Pugio* 2.3.9, p. 379; 3.3.7.6, p. 743; 3.3.16.24, 27, pp. 855, 860.

52. Ibid. 3.1.10.1, p. 534; 3.2.8.3, p. 605; 3.3.2.11, p. 650. And see, for example, Martini's account of their denial of man's having been created in God's image, ibid. 3.2.1.3, p. 551.

53. Ibid. 3.3.22.10, p. 928.

erful."[54] Obdurate in their refusal to submit to all rational argument, and not even desirous of ridding themselves of their wicked disdain for God, the Jews of medieval Europe emerge in the *Pugio fidei* as heretical and blasphemous.[55]

It was therefore fitting, the Dominican contended, that they had never escaped the punishment which God had imposed on the rabbis and their followers. The terrible prophecy of Deuteronomy 28:28 now applied to them: "May the Lord strike you with madness, blindness, and bewilderment." They remain in exile, and because they have forsaken the law of God, they are ruled by others.[56] Although the Jews say that the virgin (really young woman—'*almah*) of Isaiah 7:14 was an adulteress, their synagogue is the real adulteress, condemned to hell, for whom the gates of prayer have been eternally locked.[57] The Jews live on with no peace from the domination of the devil, and although they assume that they will soon repossess their ancient patrimony, Martini states with confidence that "as long as they shall be such—i.e., Jews—they never are meant to be freed."[58]

Ideological Conclusions

By thus taking his reader through the course of Jewish history and considering each of these three genera of Jews, Martini has returned to the fourth and most crucial item on Pablo Christiani's agenda for the debate with Moses Naḥmanides. In order to argue with the Jews successfully so as to convert them, one had to con-

54. Ibid. 2.15.15, pp. 473–74: "Ex istis, et multis aliis his similibus de Talmud, quae fastidio prolixitatis abjeci, liquet aperte Judaeos non habere hodie verum Deum. De moderno enim Judaeorum Deo qui taliter dolet, et tristis est propter captivitatem ipsorum, oportet concedere alterum e duobus; videlicet, vel quod ipse vult liberare Judaeos, sed non potest; vel potest quidem sed minime vult. Si primum dederint, talem non esse verum Deum nulli sani capitis poterit ese ambiguum. . . . Quod si alterum dixerint, scilicet, quod valet quidem eos liberare, sed non vult: tunc necessario summae fatuitatis, et extremae stultitiae notam incurrit. Stultissimus namque; et mentis inops etiam apud homines censeretur ille, qui supradicto morbo tristitiae tabesceret, cujus causam posset sibi solo nutu subtrahere: sicque modernum Judaeorum Deum non esse verum sequitur evidenter: Deus quippe Abrahami, et aliorum sanctorum Patrum sapiens praedicatur, et potens."

55. See ibid. 3.3.2.13, p. 654; 3.3.21.22, p. 916.

56. Ibid. 3.3.2.13, p. 654; 3.3.21.15, p. 912; 3.3.22.19, pp. 933–34.

57. *Pugio* 3.3.7.4, pp. 740–41; the entire verse reads, "A young woman ['*almah*] is with child, and she will bear a son, and will call him Immanuel."

58. *Pugio* 3.3.16.6, p. 846: "Quamdiu tales fuerint, i.e. Judaei, nunquam sunt liberandi"; 3.3.21.16, p. 912; 3.3.23.2, p. 954.

vince them not only of the christological meaning of the Old Testament prophecies, but also that their continued observance of Jewish law was wrong in the eyes of God. Unveiling this heresy which contemporary Judaism entailed made anti-Jewish Christian polemic a much more relevant and formidable challenge. It struck far deeper than the old standard argument that at one particular point in ancient history the Jews had blindly failed to recognize Jesus as their messiah and that their descendants thus still clung to the law of the Old Testament. Just as Pablo had done in 1263, Martini argued that contemporary Jewry had broken away from its heritage of the divinely revealed faith of the Bible. For although the rabbis of the Talmud could not bar the correct interpretation of Scripture from entering their literature altogether, talmudic Judaism, still maintained by the Jews of medieval Europe, constituted a willful rejection of the divine ordinance to the Jews. Like Pablo, Martini exploited the revealing exegetical admissions of rabbinic literature to the utmost extent, but in no way that prevented him from condemning talmudic Judaism as severely as Nicholas Donin had condemned it some forty years earlier.

In 1263 the setting of a formal disputation had necessarily put several constraints on Pablo's expression of his own sentiments regarding the Jews. He could not forget that every contention voiced explicitly would encounter immediate refutation from Naḥmanides. Nor could he afford to alienate his Jewish audience with overly hostile and castigating references to contemporary Jews, if in truth he hoped to convert them. Martini, however, addressing the *Pugio fidei* to Christian missionaries who would in turn dispute with the Jews, had no such need for discretion. The practical ramifications of Raymond de Peñaforte's ideology concerning the Jews, the dire need to suppress the heresy of modern rabbinic Judaism and convert the infidel to Christianity, which became evident in the various activities of Pablo Christiani's career, found full expression in the text of the *Pugio fidei*.

Asking the reader's forgiveness for the length of his arguments, Martini underscored the threat contemporary European Judaism posed to the purity of the Christian faith. "May I be pardoned," he wrote, "for being oppressive in this prolixity of words. For I have not been able to dispel the many and diverse, lengthy and broad insanities and wiles of the Jews with a few brief arguments. And they [the insanities and wiles] could have bewitched a great many simple men, if they had remained unrefuted."[59] By maintaining that their ritual law is still binding, "the Jews are like the scorpion, always armed, so as to injure the soul even more than the body, and in this way they have never ceased from contradicting the truth." In a more immediate sense too, the presence of Jews in Christendom posed a great danger to the society at large. Following Nicholas Donin's example, Martini identifies the talmudic injunctions against Gentiles as deliberate attacks on Christians. Modern Jews, he maintains, are thus permitted by their law to cheat Christians and deceive them in court. And relying on the Talmud, the Jews "even now are prone to kill Christians, to hurl their children in pits and wells, and even to cut them to pieces, when they can [do so] secretly."[60]

Although any sane and rational human being would admit that Jesus Christ, the messiah, has already redeemed mankind, the Jews retain their alliance with the devil, threatening the welfare of the Christian public. In response, God has extended his aid against the force of this enemy, and he will ultimately emerge completely victorious.

> Against the enemies of the human race—the demons as well as the Jews of this time who endanger the public safety—God extended his hand—i.e., his son—who is his virtue, his wisdom, and his word . . . , when he sent him to be the messiah. . . . This fastening and conjunction of divine with human nature—that is, the incarnation of the son of God—the Jews will understand at the end of days.[61]

From here derives the twofold necessity and intention underlying Martini's polemic: "To establish the faith of the Christians in their [the Jews'] hearts and to refute the Jewish depravity," thereby protecting Christendom and perhaps even hastening the final redemption.[62]

Martini viewed his task as a particularly urgent one. Even if the Jews will convert at the end of days, Martini never draws the conclusion that the Jews of his time must remain a part of Christian society, witnessing the truth of biblical history to the Gentiles and

59. Ibid. 2.3.33, p. 294.
60. Ibid. 3.11.14, p. 782; 3.3.22.21, 22, pp. 935, 936.
61. Ibid. 2.12.16, p. 436; 3.3.23.4, p. 956.
62. Ibid. 3.3.16.1, p. 841: "Christianorum fidem in cordibus eorum confirmare, et Judaicam confundere pravitatem . . ."

eventually fulfilling Old Testament prophecy with their final conversion. Rather, for Martini the Jews have no positive function in
Christendom. They constitute the worst enemy of the Church, and
Martini explains why the importance of converting them outweighs
even that of the Christian mission to the Muslims. "For according
to the opinion of Seneca, there is no enemy more capable of inflicting injury than a familiar one, and there is no enemy of the Christian faith more familiar and more unavoidable for us than the Jew."[63]
This is a radical departure from the long-standing official attitude
of the Church toward the Jews—that they merit toleration precisely
because they live peacefully among Christians—expressed, for instance, by Iohannes Teutonicus in his ordinary gloss on Gratian's
Decretum: "Jews and Saracens are our neighbors, and it is true that
they ought to be loved by us as we [love] ourselves."[64]

A Jewish Response: Solomon ibn Adret

The centrality of the argument that contemporary Jewish observance constituted a pernicious deviation from true biblical Judaism
in Martini's polemic is best corroborated by the responses of contemporary Jewish polemicists, just as Naḥmanides' arguments had
manifested the real concerns of Pablo Christiani in 1263 and Yeḥiel
ben Joseph's claims those of Nicholas Donin in 1240. It would be at
least somewhat surprising and certainly unfortunate for historians
had Martini's novel and severe attack upon the Jews of his own
day left no trace in extant Hebrew sources of the period. In the
nineteenth century, Joseph Perles and Heinrich Graetz maintained
that Martini personally debated with Rabbi Solomon ben Abraham
ibn Adret (ca. 1235–1310) of Barcelona and that the latter recorded
his responses in a collection of commentaries on talmudic *aggadot*;
Perles published the text of these arguments as an appendix to his
brief biography of ibn Adret.[65] But except for occasional similarities

---

63. Ibid., prooemium 2, p. 2. Williams, *Adversus Judaeos*, p. 250, n. 1, points out
that this homily is not from Seneca but from Boethius, *De consolatione philosophiae*
3.5.

64. Ad *De poen.* D. 2, c.5, § 4, in Gratian, *Decretum*, 2 vols. (Venice, 1600), 2:1606:
"Ergo Iudei et Sarraceni proximi nostri sunt, et diligendi a nobis ut nos."

65. Joseph Perles, *R. Salomo b. Abraham b. Adreth: Sein Leben und seine Schriften*
(Breslau, 1863), pp. 54–56; Graetz, *Geschichte*, 7:151–52; cf. also the concurrence of Y.
Baer, *A History*, 1:281. Ibn Adret's polemic begins in Perles, Heb. pp. 24–56; and is
continued in Solomon ben Abraham ibn Adret, *Sefer She'eilot u-Teshuvot ha-Rashba*, 4
(1883; repr., Jerusalem, 1970), 53–54.

in subject matter between the *Pugio fidei* and ibn Adret's polemical tract, neither Perles nor Graetz could adduce any evidence establishing that a confrontation between Martini and the great rabbi of Barcelona ever occurred. On the basis of external evidence, however, I have elsewhere argued that Martini did engage in debate with ibn Adret on several occasions during the friar's later years in Barcelona.[66] A close reading of ibn Adret's work lends credence not only to this claim but also to the danger that the thirteenth-century Jewish community perceived in a work such as Martini's. Ibn Adret does not simply reproduce the arguments of any particular debate or discussion between himself and a Christian cleric. His approach is topical and analytical and not strictly narrative; he sets out to extrapolate from contemporary Christian polemic the most central and threatening arguments, so that he might respond to them. Yet he clearly based his tract on the experience of real confrontations with a Christian disputant. Ibn Adret often presents his consideration of specific points of contention in dialogue form, and in the second half of the work, topical organization and structure gradually give way to a series of exchanges between the rabbi and his opponent over the interpretation of different talmudic *aggadot*, a series that does not exhibit the continuity of one extended disputation. Because they do not comprise a continuous literary unit, one can conclude that he did not fabricate these debates simply for the sake of writing his polemic in dialogue form, as early medieval writers might have tended to do.

At the very outset, ibn Adret explains the objective of his work.

> Because human minds are weak by nature, they do not understand the essentials of things. And one who will not investigate problems properly may be overcome when debating with the enemy, who will prevail over him. . . . Therefore I have undertaken to collect in a treatise several arguments, in order to strengthen the hands of our colleagues, and so that they might know the meaning of what appears in some *aggadot* in the Talmud and our collections of midrashim.[67]

Ibn Adret here indicates that the "enemy" presently attacking the Jews was using talmudic *aggadot* to bolster his arguments, just as Raymond de Peñaforte's disciples were wont to do. In much the same way as the *Pugio fidei* began with a classification of all men

66. See my "Christian Adversary."
67. Perles, *R. Salomo*, Heb. p. 25.

into those believing in a divinely revealed law and those not, so ibn Adret writes that all men fall into one of two religious categories. Some, like the philosophers who deny the existence of any truth other than that discovered by the human intellect, reject all of Scripture. The others accept divinely revealed religion; this group includes Jews, Muslims, and Christians, who all acknowledge the truth of Mosaic prophecy and law.[68] Yet rather than defining or characterizing Christianity according to its beliefs in the past advent of the messiah and in the Trinity, those beliefs around which Raymond Martini structured the *Pugio fidei*, ibn Adret concentrates almost entirely on Christianity's approach to the commandments of the Old Testament.

> None of these peoples [in the second class] will subvert this [belief—that is, in the truth of the Old Testament] except for one people [the Christians] who have divided the commandments into three categories. They have specified one group to bear chosen allegorical and figurative meanings . . . ; they strip them of their evident intentions and dress them with false connotations. The second class they have understood literally, but they have placed a time limit upon them . . . and decreed that they are symbols of the future, and when the time comes, that which was symbolized will be revealed and the symbol will be canceled. . . . And the third category they left without any time limit, and yet they still altered their meanings.[69]

These three classes of commandments provide ibn Adret with the basis for organizing his treatise. Except insofar as they relate to the interpretation of specific talmudic texts, the rabbi of Barcelona does not take up the issues of Christian belief in Jesus as the messiah, the Trinity, or the incarnation of Christ.

Responding to the first Christian claim that some Mosaic commandments were never literally binding but intended merely as parables and metaphors, ibn Adret raises several theological and logical objections. As the greatest of all prophets, Moses could have expressed his prophecy in whatever way God desired; other prophets received their prophecy in parabolic visions, but nothing prevented Moses from prescribing the divine precepts in their primary and literal sense. Why would God have desired him to teach

68. Ibid., Heb. pp. 25–26. Cf. *Pugio* 1.1.1–3, p. 192: "Viam verae fidei et veritatis errantium turba, licet quodammodo sit incomprehensibilis, et infinita, potest tamen quodammodo sub duplici distinctione concludi. Quicunque enim a fidei veritate exorbitant, vel sunt habentes legem, vel minime legem nisi naturalem habentes. . . ."
69. Perles, *R. Salomo*, Heb. p. 26.

in confusing figures of speech? It is also inconceivable that Moses would have been inconsistent in his prophecy, speaking metaphorically concerning one precept and literally concerning the next. Nor could what the commandments symbolized have been entirely unrelated, as the Christians claimed it was, to the essence of the commandments themselves—for example, those pertaining to forbidden foods—whose primary meaning God never intended to annul entirely. Such annulment would permit human discretion in defining the real meaning of divine ordinances, implying that the wisdom of man exceeded that of God and his prophet, a claim tantamount to blasphemy and heresy. Finally, and most significantly, ibn Adret argued that the Jews' continued observance of the Mosaic Law just as it had been ordained in the wilderness of Sinai constituted the best possible proof of their rectitude in understanding the commandments as they did.[70] For if their present understanding of the law was incorrect, either the Jews had never observed the law correctly, in which case Moses had forsaken his duty to teach and instruct his people, or they had changed their understanding of the commandments since the time of Moses. If this change was unintentional on the part of the Jews, how did it go totally unchallenged by all rabbinic authorities? If Jews intentionally perverted the correct understanding of the law, why is there no record of the great assembly that must have convened to effect such change? In other words, the Jews' eternal constancy in their mode of religious observance offers proof of their conception of the intent and nature of the Old Testament. However much the Christians have tried to demonstrate that the Jews corrupted the text of the Bible, they have only managed to point to the rabbinic term of *tiqqun soferim*, which, as will be explained shortly, in ibn Adret's opinion did not denote any emendation of the biblical text at all. Even *tiqqun soferim* applies only to eighteen words in the entire Old Testament; what of the rest of Mosaic prophecy whose text in all opinions has remained uncorrupted? "Indeed, we the people of Israel have not swerved in our consistent observance of all the commandments, from the days of Moses our teacher, may he rest in peace, to [those of] Joshua, to [those of] the elders, to [those of] the great assembly, and even today."[71]

70. Ibid., Heb. p. 29.
71. Perles, *R. Salomo*, Heb. p. 30. The "great assembly" is in the Jewish tradition considered the repository of religious legal authority in the Jewish community in the days of the second temple from Ezra until the high priest Simon the Just.

At this point in the text, ibn Adret's Christian opponent makes his first appearance and proposes a slightly different, and intriguing, classification of the Mosaic commandments:

> A Christian scholar answered me that in truth they [the Jews] did practice [the law] consistently in the days of Moses and for a while thereafter. And yet the commandments were still divided into three categories: one pertaining to holiness, one pertaining to the functioning of the polity, and one for training and education—i.e., as on a calf or ass still untrained in bearing a burden, men will lay a heavy load so that he will grow accustomed not to stumble and afterwards they will lighten the load and give him the suitable burden. Thus when the law was given to you, you were new and far ahead of other nations in [the observance of] commandments, and to accustom you [to such observance], he [God] burdened you with commandments like [the ban on] eating pork, the ban on mixing species, and the like, and after the training these were annulled.[72]

Such a breakdown of the Mosaic commandments immediately brings to mind that of Thomas Aquinas: "It is necessary to divide the precepts of the old law into three classes: the moral precepts. . . , ceremonial precepts . . . , and judicial precepts." The one didactic function which ibn Adret's opponent ascribes to ceremonial commandments of the Old Testament also resounds with the rational approach to them taken by Aquinas in the *Summa theologiae*.[73] Ibn Adret thus leads us to infer that the Christian scholar in his treatise has come under the influence of the great angelic doctor of Paris. In ibn Adret's account, the same Christian leveled the charges, based on instances of *tiqqun soferim*, that the Jews had corrupted the text and meaning of the Old Testament. The rabbi responds that the term *tiqqun soferim* does not mean that anyone actually changed the biblical text but rather that the Bible itself was understood by the ancient Jewish scribes (*soferim*) as having spoken euphemistically and that this understanding constituted a sort of emendation (*tiqqun*).[74]

Returning to the Christians' categories of Mosaic commandments, ibn Adret deals next with the second genus, those which are binding temporarily until such time as what they prefigured should

72. Ibid., Heb. p. 30.
73. Thomas Aquinas, *ST* 2.1.99.4, 29:44–45: "oportet tria praecepta legis veteris ponere; scilicet moralia . . . caeremonialia . . . et judicialia"; 2.1.101–2, passim.
74. Perles, *R. Salomo*, Heb. pp. 32–34.

become a reality. The rabbi contends that no commandments except those explicitly prescribed for a limited period of time can be considered temporary. Even those laws which assume the Jews possess the land of Israel and operate the temple in Jerusalem are now not in effect only because these prerequisite conditions do not exist. Jews will resume observance of them as soon as they repossess the land and rebuild the temple. That these commandments cannot presently be observed does not imply that they have lost their validity forever. On the contrary, the true messianic redemption will include their restoration. And although God has punished the Jews with a particularly lengthy period of exile, their fate has derived from their failure to keep the Mosaic commandments and not from a continued observance of them—that is, not from an incorrect interpretation of the law's nature and intent. Arguing from a specific piece of scriptural justification, ibn Adret concludes: "Behold how he [the prophet he has just quoted] has testified that there will not be punishment except for abandonment of the covenant which he [God] struck with us at Sinai with respect to the commandments in their totality, and [punishment was] not [foretold] for our going astray to espouse a new religion which we were not commanded at Sinai."[75] The dispersion of the Jews has not resulted from their having fallen into an innovative doctrinal heresy through which they misconstrue the nature of the Mosaic commandments and continue to observe them. Ibn Adret then discusses various rabbinic homilies adduced by his Christian opponent to prove the temporary character of this second class of commandments; quite a few of these *aggadot* appear in the *Pugio fidei* as well.[76]

Ibn Adret does not deal explicitly with the third category of Mosaic commandments in the Christian classification—those which were meant to endure eternally but whose meanings would change in time. (Had he done so, he probably would merely have repeated the arguments already expressed regarding the first two classes:

---

75. Ibid., Heb. pp. 35–44 (quotation on p. 36). Cf. the similar claims of the Jewish polemicist in the "additions" to Joseph Qimḥi's *Sefer ha-Berit*, in *The Book of the Covenant and Other Writings* [Hebrew], ed. Frank E. Talmage (Jerusalem, 1974), pp. 62–63; on the probable thirteenth-century date of this passage, see Talmage's introduction to his English translation of *The Book of the Covenant* (Toronto, 1972), p. 18, n. 45.

76. Cf. Perles, *R. Salomo*, Heb. p. 37, and *Pugio* 3.3.11.13, pp. 781–82; Perles, Heb. p. 38, and *Pugio* 3.3.11.20, p. 787; Perles, Heb. p. 40, and *Pugio* 2.12.16, pp. 434–35; and Perles, Heb. p. 41, and *Pugio* 3.3.21.2, pp. 895–96.

that God intended for the Jews (1) to understand the commandments literally and (2) to observe them forever; otherwise he would have said so in no uncertain terms.) Instead, ibn Adret offers answers to his Christian opponent's use of certain *aggadot* to argue for the truth of various tenets in Christian theology: the Trinity, the advent of the messiah, the incarnation of Christ, and the imperfect nature of the Old Testament. In this part of the argument the majority of rabbinic texts discussed are among those quoted by Martini in the *Pugio fidei*.[77] At one point in the discussion, the Christian disputant interestingly refuses to accept a philosophical argument of ibn Adret's as admissable in debate over the Trinity. "He said, 'These are philosophical arguments, and you will not ascertain religious truth by means of philosophy; for from philosophy originate several logical difficulties for all religions.'" Such an attitude brings to mind a story told by ibn Adret's contemporary and acquaintance in Barcelona, the Franciscan tertiary Raymond Lull, in which Raymond Martini argued before both a Saracen king and a Jewish rabbi of Barcelona (probably ibn Adret himself) that the doctrines of Christianity were not subject to rational proof and understanding.[78]

Two important conclusions emerge from this consideration of Solomon ibn Adret's polemical treatise. First, if one tries to identify his opponent, various factors all point in the same direction. Ibn Adret felt the most threatening Christian attack on contemporary Judaism to be that based on the use of talmudic *aggadot* in behalf of Christianity; his adversary had a good command of rabbinic sources. Ibn Adret's initial classification of genera of religions duplicates that in the *Pugio fidei*, and many of the specific *aggadot* quoted by the rabbi, as well as the question of *tiqqun soferim*, also are discussed in the *Pugio*. This Christian disputant classified Mosaic commandments almost exactly as Thomas Aquinas had done, suggesting a Thomistic influence upon him. And just as Raymond Lull described Raymond Martini doing, so ibn Adret's unnamed Chris-

77. Cf. Perles, *R. Salomo*, Heb. p. 44, and *Pugio* 3.3.3.2, p. 662; Perles, Heb. p. 46, and *Pugio* 3.1.7.13–16, pp. 516–18; Perles, Heb. p. 49, and *Pugio* 3.2.9.4, p. 621; Perles, Heb. p. 52, and *Pugio* 3.1.4.11, p. 494, 3.1.11.16, p. 548; and Solomon ibn Adret, *Sefer She'eilot u-Teshuvot*, 4:53, and *Pugio* 2.14.4, p. 447.

78. Perles, *R. Salomo*, Heb. p. 45. See Raymond Lull, "Le *Liber de acquisitione Terrae Sanctae*" 3.1, ed. Ephrem Longpré, *Criterion* 3 (1927), 276–77. For the identification of Martini and ibn Adret in the story, cf. Ephrem Longpré, "Le B. Raymond Lulle et Raymond Marti, O.P.," *Bolletí de la Societat arqueologica luliana* 49 (1933), 269–71; and my "Christian Adversary."

tian refused to accept philosophic argumentation as conclusive proof of theological assertions. If ibn Adret did not debate with Raymond Martini himself, he unquestionably was responding to Martini's anti-Jewish polemic, perhaps voiced by a student or colleague.

Second, ibn Adret's own priorities in this treatise accord with our impression of the stance taken toward Judaism in the *Pugio fidei*. Martini might have organized those parts of the *Pugio* concerning Jews around issues such as the advent of the messiah, the Trinity, and the incarnation, just as Pablo Christiani had structured the disputation in Barcelona in 1263. But the underlying attack upon the Jews, around which ibn Adret, like Naḥmanides before him, felt pressed to organize his response, lay in the charge that contemporary Judaism constituted a perversion of the religion of the Old Testament. In claiming that the Mosaic law embodied the most perfect revelation of God whose authority was to endure forever, the Jews who lived after Jesus, it was charged, deliberately distorted the true character of the commandments, a pursuit that even led them to corrupt the text of the Bible. Ibn Adret did all he could to advance the notion of the constancy of Judaism and Jewish observance throughout all of history, a claim entirely antithetical to Raymond Martini's schema of Jewish history. In ibn Adret's words, the Dominican identified contemporary Judaism as "a new religion which we were not commanded at Sinai." As the rabbi of Barcelona perceptively recognized, charging contemporary Judaism with heretical *innovatio* on the basis of rabbinic texts embodied the most effective means of dulling the resistance of the medieval Jew and ultimately of converting him.

The Legacy of Raymond de Peñaforte

Although Raymond de Peñaforte did not engage personally in much anti-Jewish polemical activity, he managed to wage an attack on contemporary Judaism through the careers of his disciples, which he directed toward very definite objectives. He himself probably attracted Saul of Montpellier to become Pablo Christiani, and his supervisory role at the disputation of 1263 betrays his ultimate responsibility for the staging of the debate and the Dominican strategy employed therein. His selection of Raymond Martini to undertake important missions to Tunis and Paris suggests that he also directed that friar's polemical pursuits, and he probably ordered the compilation of the *Pugio fidei*. Martini relates in his introduction, "It has been enjoined upon me, that . . . I compose such a work as might be available like a dagger for preachers and guardians of the Christian faith." In the next paragraph, he begs to be excused for "this rash and bold undertaking," partly because of the "not inappropriate refusal of the prelate's command," presumably a refusal to free Martini from this arduous task. The "prelate" who insisted upon the composition of the *Pugio* was in all likelihood Martini's master and teacher Raymond.[79]

Having considered the attacks of Pablo Christiani and Raymond Martini on the Jews, we can now view the "school" of Raymond de Peñaforte not only as a specific group of friars but also as a school of thought, the proponent of a particular anti-Jewish polemical ideology: rabbinic Judaism had no place in Christendom, and every effort thus had to be made to convert its Jewish adherents. It was no accident that Raymond Martini followed in the *Pugio fidei* the agenda for Pablo Christiani's debate with Naḥmanides, and that the same crucial point, the fourth proposition on Pablo's agenda, underlay both friars' positions: contemporary Jewish observance of the Mosaic commandments was inherently improper and heretical even for the Jews. God had never intended the Old Testament to be eternally binding, and rabbinic Judaism which construed it as such accordingly constituted a demonic perversion and rejection of the divine ordinance. Hardly coincidentally, Pablo and Martini both endeavored to prove this argument in the same way, by exploiting the few "correct" interpretations of Scripture which in their view had managed to infiltrate the rest of rabbinic literature, even though the rabbis of the Talmud themselves, in continuing to observe Jewish ritual, had deliberately refused to accept the true messiah and allied themselves with the devil. In fact, every rabbinic source Pablo quoted appears also in the *Pugio fidei*, as do many of the *aggadot* discussed by Solomon ibn Adret in his polemic and Naḥmanides in his sermon *Torat ha-Shem Temimah*, delivered to the Jews of Barcelona as a response to Pablo's arguments.

This use of rabbinic literature by the friars accords completely with Raymond de Peñaforte's twofold reason for promoting the study of Hebrew among his friars: to respond to the Jews, "who audaciously deny the true text and the glosses of their own sages

79. *Pugio*, prooemium 3–4, p. 2. Cf. Thomas Aquinas, *Liber de veritate*, 1:58.

which agree with . . . the Catholic faith," and so that "the false-hoods and corruptions, which they [the talmudic rabbis] had in-serted . . . in the Bible to hide the mysteries . . . of the faith, might be revealed." In his undoubtedly sincere Dominican zeal to convert the infidel and rid Christendom of any taint of heresy, Raymond de Peñaforte could not tolerate the existence in Christian society of the heirs to such a corrupt and hostile rabbinic tradition. Yet he wisely realized that the exploitation of rabbinic texts to prove Christian beliefs was potentially the key to reaching his goals. In no way did he thereby attribute any bit of theological legitimacy to the Talmud in general; he merely chose to be pragmatic and utili-tarian, to use the Talmud if it could aid him in securing its own condemnation and the conversion of the Jews.[80]

Such an understanding of these Spanish Dominicans facilitates the solution of a problem that has long intrigued historians of this period: how could the Church in general and the friars in partic-ular, who had begun to condemn the Talmud to the stake in the 1240s, suddenly begin, only a few decades later, to argue from the Talmud against the Jews? Most scholars have maintained that the approach of Pablo Christiani in 1263 and Raymond Martini in the *Pugio fidei* represented a radical break with the anti-talmudic pos-ture of Nicholas Donin and the clerical courts of Paris. Donin charged the Talmud with heresy, according to this interpretation, while Pablo and Martini claimed it proved the truth of Christianity. Some have ascribed this apparent shift to the different intellectual atmospheres then prevalent in northern France and Spain, others merely to the inclinations of the individual polemicists. But virtually all have agreed that the Barcelona disputation of 1263 marked a definite and drastic change in the attitude of the Church to rabbinic Judaism. As Amos Funkenstein has recently written:

Two main attitudes [of Christian theology towards postbiblical Jewish literature] were possible. . . . The one attitude . . . amounts to a systematic alienation of the Jew even from the position he had in Christian consciousness before, an alienation based on the hidden

80. See Balme and Paben, *Raymundiana*, 1:32. One finds an excellent example of the utilitarian nature of this approach to rabbinic literature in the respective uses Pablo and Martini made of one particular rabbinic homily. In the debate with Naḥ-manides, Pablo quotes the legend that the messiah was born on the day of the temple's destruction to prove the past advent of the messiah; Martini, however, devotes an entire chapter to the refutation of this belief and concludes that it mani-fests the devil's delusion of the Jews, *Pugio* 2.6, pp. 348–52.

assumption that he is not a Jew any more in the classical sense, that the Jews have changed. The other possible attitude was one . . . developed in the Disputation of Barcelona and in the *Pugio fidei* of Raymundus Martini; it was still the basis for Reuchlin's demand for the preservation of the Talmud, as it contains christological traditions and thus serves to refute the Jews from within.

Funkenstein asserts further that the Church felt pressed to desist from attacking the Talmud as heresy unfounded in Scripture after the middle of the thirteenth century, because it feared for the image of its own postbiblical traditions.[81]

The received opinion on this question is itself inherently problematic. The Church's attack on the Talmud as heresy did not cease in the thirteenth century but continued recurrently for hundreds of years thereafter. As described in an earlier chapter, the papal Inquisition condemned and burned the Talmud repeatedly throughout the thirteenth and fourteenth centuries, and men such as Bernard Gui campaigned against rabbinic Judaism even in the absence of Jews. Generations of canon lawyers in the later Middle Ages reiterated that Gregory IX and Innocent IV had burned the Talmud on the legitimate grounds of its heretical deviation from biblical Judaism. An anonymous Jewish apologist of the late thirteenth or early fourteenth century described the accusation of Christian polemicists, "that the Talmud distorts and spoils our entire Torah and prevents us from realizing the truth by leading us astray."[82] A curious component of papal coronation ceremonies which originated in the twelfth century, whereby the Jews of Rome would present the new pope with the gift of a Torah scroll, grad-

---

81. Funkenstein, "Basic Types," p. 379–81. The omissions in this paragraph, noted by ellipses, allude to Funkenstein's contention that these different polemical types first appeared in the twelfth century, an assertion discussed above in Chapter 1. For a more detailed analysis of the two allegedly different approaches to the Talmud, see also Funkenstein, "Changes," pp. 137–44. Other adherents of this view include Graetz, *Geschichte*, 7:120–21; Loeb, "La controverse religieuse," 18:135; Nicks, "La polémique," p. 521; Roth, "The Disputation of Barcelona," p. 122; *SRH*, 9:83–86, 105–8; Y. Baer, *A History*, 1:152; Herman Hailperin, *Rashi and the Christian Scholars* (Pittsburgh, 1963), p. 115; Eckert, "Hoch- und Spätmittelalter," p. 212; Bonfil, "The Nature of Judaism," pp. 360–61; Chazan, *Medieval Jewry*, p. 144: Kenneth Stow, *Catholic Thought and Papal Jewry Policy, 1555–1593* (New York, 1976), pp. 57–58; Schubert, "Das christlich-jüdische Religionsgespräch," p. 161; and *The Jewish-Christian Debate*, ed. D. Berger, pp. 30–31.

82. *The Jewish-Christian Debate*, ed. D. Berger, p. 230, Heb. pp. 163–64. See also above, Ch. 4, nn. 62, 64–65.

ually came to include the pope's damnation of contemporary Jewish observance along with his acceptance of the divinely revealed law. The *Ordo romanus* formally incorporated this denunciation of postbiblical Judaism into the liturgy in the fourteenth century, and the Church apparently had no desire to hide its contrast of rabbinic Judaism with the ordinances of Scripture when Agostino Patrizi compiled his *Caeremoniale romanum* for the papacy in 1488.

> Once the pontiff has reached Mt. Jordanus, the Jews come to meet him, and having genuflected, they offer the law to the pontiff, praising the law in Hebrew and urging the pontiff to pay homage to it. As they listen, the pontiff responds as follows: "The holy law, O Jews, being what was given by almighty God through the hands of Moses to your ancestors, we both praise and venerate. But your observance and vain interpretation [of the law] we damn and reject, since the savior, whom you still futilely await, the apostolic faith teaches has already come and declares [is] our Lord Jesus Christ, who, with the father and the holy spirit, lives and reigns as God for all eternity."[83]

Popes in the sixteenth century continued to campaign against the Talmud, banning its study and publication and again ordering it burned. The attack of the Church on rabbinic Judaism as heresy in fact endured throughout the late medieval and early modern periods with predominantly the same emphases as those first given it by Nicholas Donin.[84]

The war on the Talmud, moreoever, often went hand in hand with the exploitation of it for conversionary purposes. Pablo Christiani himself bitterly attacked the Talmud during much of his career, even in the immediate aftermath of the Barcelona disputation. The conclusions of some historians that he must have decided to reverse his polemical strategy after the encounter with Naḥ-

---

83. Agostino Patrizi, *Caeremoniale romanum*, ed. Jean Mabillon (1689; repr., Ridgewood, N.J., 1965), p. 17. Cf. *Ordo romanus* 13.20, in Jean Mabillon and Michael Germain, eds., *Museum italicum*, 2 vols. (Paris, 1724), 2:259. On the origin and development of this ceremony, see Franz Wasner, "The Popes' Veneration of the Torah," *The Bridge* 4 (1962), 274–93, and *SRH*, 4:10, 237, n. 7, 238, n. 10. A medieval Jew's description of a similar practice is cited by Saperstein, *Decoding the Rabbis*, p. 190.

84. Abraham Yaari, *Sereifat ha-Talmud be-'Italyah bi-Mle'ot 'Arba' Mei'ot Shanim la-Gezeirah* (Tel Aviv, 1953); Ch. Merchavya, "An Anti-Talmudic Pamphlet from the Period of the Burning of the Talmud in Italy [Hebrew]," *Tarbiz* 37 (1967–68), 78–96, 191–207; Stow, "The Burning of the Talmud." Cf. also Grayzel, "The Talmud," pp. 233–43; Browe, "Die religiöse Duldung," pp. 61–76.

manides appear both forced and unfounded.[85] At the famous disputation of Tortosa, convened in 1413 by the antipope Benedict XIII, the Christian disputants again challenged the Jews with rabbinic texts that allegedly demonstrated the truth of Christianity. This use of the Talmud, however, did not prevent Benedict from publicly indicting it for heresy at the disputation and subsequetly ordering it confiscated from its Jewish owners.[86]

The approach of Raymond de Peñaforte and his followers to rabbinic Judaism, then, represented no ideational break at all with the stance taken at the Paris trials of the 1240s, but rather a more sophisticated development of it. The attack of the mendicant Inquisition on contemporary Jewry relied on the claim that rabbinic Judaism, embodied in the Talmud, which had just become known to the Church, was heretical and evil. In their belief that all heresy threatened the proper order of a universal Christian society, and especially incensed by evidence of hostility toward Gentiles in the Talmud which they assumed applied to Christians, the friars began to see no place for the Jews in Christendom. Raymond de Peñaforte, Pablo Christiani, and Raymond Martini, who agreed wholeheartedly with this evaluation, did not stop at merely trying to extirpate manifestations of contemporary Judaism from Christian Europe. Instead they sought a more lasting and comprehensive remedy for the problem. For they were zealously committed not only to defending the faith but also to converting the infidel; and so they undertook an active program of missionizing among the Jews best serviced by the exploitation of certain rabbinic texts. After the inquisitors first scrutinized and then attacked the real, "living" Judaism of their own day, Raymond and his school developed that approach into an organized and aggressive Christian mission to the Jews, very much a novely in medieval Europe.[87]

85. Graetz, *Geschichte*, 7:124; Chazan, *Medieval Jewry*, pp. 152–53.

86. *SRH*, 9:87–92; Grayzel, "The Talmud," pp. 235–36. Cf. also Ch. Merchavya, "A Spanish-Latin Manuscript Concerning the Opposition to the Talmud in the Beginning of the 15th Century [Hebrew]," *KS* 45 (1970), 271–86, 590–606.

87. Kenneth Stow has recently—and it now appears incorrectly—argued that both the recognition that a generally heretical Talmud could be exploited for conversionist purposes and an organized, concerted ecclesiastical effort to convert the Jews were inventions of the sixteenth century. See both his "Burning of the Talmud" and his *Catholic Thought*, pp. xiii–xxviii, 3–59; as well as my review of the latter in the *Newsletter* of the Association for Jewish Studies 21 (October 1977), 12. On the ineffectual character of the Christian mission to the Jews before the thirteenth century, see Browe, *Die Judenmission*, pp. 13–18, 56–65; and Berthold Altaner, "Sprachstudien

Raymond de Peñaforte was not satisfied with simply ridding Europe of contemporary Judaism; he committed himself to making contemporary Jews believing Christians.

---

und Sprachkentnisse im Dienste der Mission des 13. und 14. Jahrhunderts," *Zeitschrift für Missionswissenschaft und Religionswissenschaft* 21 (1931), 129ff.

7

Synthesis and Diffusion:
Nicholas of Lyra

The mendicant Inquisition had initiated the attack on rabbinic Judaism by charging that the religion of medieval Jewry was not the biblical faith which according to Augustinian theology justified Jewish survival in Christendom. The Spanish Dominican school of Raymond de Peñaforte transformed that theological position into a working ideology, demonstrating how best to implement the new approach to contemporary Judaism in an organized campaign of polemic and proselytizing. We have yet to examine the extent to which the anti-Jewish program of the friars was indeed brought to bear and how it must be evaulated in the context of their overall impact on thirteenth- and fourteenth-century Europe. Part Three of this book will deal directly with these questions. Before we can move in that direction, however, there still remains the work of one Franciscan friar, whose polemical writings illustrate the diffusion of the new mendicant ideology, its continuing refinement, and its growing acceptance among the religious intelligentsia of Europe.

Whereas the *Pugio fidei*, the fullest expression of the attitude of Raymond de Peñaforte's school toward the Jews, hardly left room for addition or expansion, the great size of Martini's work actually decreased its utility and value in the daily activities of polemicists and missionaries. The medieval manuscripts of the *Pugio* filled huge tomes; the mass of material it contained not only made it too unwieldy to serve as a practical handbook for clerics but also tended to obscure its basic train of thought and its underlying theological considerations.[1] The arguments and ideas of the

1. Nicks, "La polémique," p. 525.

Pugio demanded reduction into a manageable form before they could exert a wide and enduring influence, and such a project was soon undertaken by the Franciscan Nicholas of Lyra.

The Christian Study of Hebrew

Nicholas's polemical writings warrant additional attention because they exemplify the interest in contemporary Judaism taken by a growing number of Christian Semitists, most of whom were friars. Christian Hebraic scholarship both contributed to and derived from a growing animus on the part of medieval Christians toward the Judaism of their own day. The Church did not consider burning or censoring Jewish books until it had the facility for scrutinizing their contents, and no one advocated a conception of Christian Europe without Jews before he had encountered rabbinic Judaism and concluded that it defied the positive mission which, according to Augustine, God had ordained for them. Hand in hand with the rising Christian knowledge of Hebrew came an increased respect for the truly literal meaning of the Hebrew Bible and, perhaps understandably, the expectation that the Jews were bound as Jews to remain faithful to it. In its turn the friars' portrayal of the Jews as having no proper place in Christendom stimulated the study of Jewish culture still further; if Europe were to be rid of its Jews through effective missionizing and polemic, the Jews had to be debated on their own terms and in their own language.

The study of Semitic languages in Christian Europe had already gained momentum in the twelfth century, most notably the study of Arabic at Cluny and that of Hebrew at the school of St. Victor in Paris.[2] But nonetheless, at the end of the twelfth century, training

2. For excellent treatment of these endeavors, see Kritzeck, *Peter the Venerable*; Beryl Smalley, *The Study of the Bible in the Middle Ages*, 2d ed. (1952; repr., Notre Dame, Ind., 1964), chs. 2–3; Aryeh Grabois, "The Hebraica Veritas and Jewish-Christian Intellectual Relations in the Twelfth Century," *Speculum* 50 (1975), 613–34; Raphael Loewe, "Alexander Neckham's Knowledge of Hebrew," *Medieval and Renaissance Studies* 4 (1958), 17–34; Loewe, "The Medieval Christian Hebraists of England: Herbert of Bosham and Earlier Scholars," *Transactions of the Jewish Historical Society of England* 17 (1953), 225–49; and Loewe, "The Medieval Christian Hebraists of England: *The Superscriptio Lincolniensis*," *HUCA* 28 (1957), 205–52. On the rarity of Christian Hebrew scholarship during the early Middle Ages, see Samuel Abraham Hirsch, "Early English Hebraists: Roger Bacon and His Predecessors," *JQR*, o.s. 12 (1900), 34–88 [repr. as book, London, 1905]; Judah M. Rosenthal, "Ha-Lashon ha-'Ivrit weha-Keneisiyyah ha-Noṣrit 'ad ha-Me'ah ha-15," in *Studies and Texts*, 1:214–19; and especially Thiel, *Grundlagen*.

in these languages was still limited to a very small handful of clerics. Only with the rise of the two mendicant orders and their missionary and scholarly pursuits did the study of Arabic and Hebrew become a more popular and significant activity.[3] In 1236 the Dominican general chapter in Paris called for the study of local vernacular languages by friars in all areas, and a faculty position in Hebrew was established at the order's *studium* in Paris.[4] One year later the Dominican prior in Palestine wrote Pope Gregory IX that his friars were studying foreign languages, especially Arabic, so that they might preach to the infidels around them.[5] And at the general chapters of 1255 and 1256 the Dominican master-general Humbertus Romanus issued encyclical letters decrying the ignorance of foreign languages—specifically Hebrew and Arabic—on the part of the friars and lauding those who did God's work by studying them.[6]

Although many more records remain concerning Dominican than Franciscan missionary efforts during this period, members of both orders became famous in connection with the study of Hebrew and Arabic. Throughout his writings, the thirteenth-century English Franciscan Roger Bacon frequently lamented the terrible state of all translations of the Bible; he vehemently advocated the study of Hebrew and even claimed that he could teach Hebrew to any intelligent student in the brief span of three days. Apart from aiding in the study of the Bible, Bacon wrote, clerical knowledge of foreign languages proffered many benefits to the Church, not the least important of which was their efficacy in the conversion of the

3. Raphael Loewe, "The Medieval History of the Latin Vulgate," in *The Cambridge History of the Bible*, ed. P. R. Ackroyd et al., 3 vols. (Cambridge, Eng., 1963–70), 2:148–52; Altaner, "Zur Kenntnis," pp. 293ff.

4. Benedictus Maria Reichert, ed., *Acta capitulorum generalium Ordinis Praedicatorum*, 1, Monumenta Ordinis Fratrum Praedicatorum historica 3 (Rome, 1898), 9; Mandonnet, *St. Dominic*, p. 78; Smalley, *Study*, p. 339.

5. *Chronica Albrici monachi Trium Fontium, a monacho novi monasterii hoiensis interpolata*, MGH SS 23: 942.

6. Benedictus Maria Reichert, ed., *Litterae encyclicae magistrorum generalium Ordinis Praedicatorum ab anno 1233 usque ad annum 1376*, Monumenta Ordinis Fratrum Praedicatorum historica 5 (Rome, 1900), 16–20, 38–42. The first encyclical speaks of a major goal of the Dominican Order, p. 18f., "scilicet ut per ministerium ordinis nostri et scismatici christiani revocarentur ad ecclesiasticam unitatem et nomen domini Ihesu Christi deferretur coram perfidis iudeis, coram sarracenis a pseudo propheta suo tanto iam tempore deceptis, coram paganis ydolatris, coram barbaris et gentibus universis, ut essemus testes eius, et salus omnibus usque ad ultimum terre. Sed effectui rei huius obviant duo quedam. Unum est defectus linguarum, quibus addiscendis vix ullus frater vult vacare, multis curiositatem multimodam utilitati preponentibus in studendo. Aliud est amor soli natalis. . . ."

infidels, particularly the Jews. Bacon criticized both Albertus Magnus and Robert Grosseteste for their ignorance of Hebrew, and he himself probably composed a basic Hebrew grammar. Among Bacon's disciples, the Franciscans William de la Mara, Gerard of Huy, and Henry of Cossey also demonstrated a good command of the Hebrew language and a familiarity with various rabbinic commentaries on the Bible.[7] Turning to the Order of Preachers, one finds in the English chronicle ascribed to Florence of Worcester that in 1275 a Dominican named Robert of Reading converted to Judaism, evidently as a result of having been well trained in Hebrew. In the next century the Spanish Dominican Alfonso Bonhomo used his extensive knowledge of Arabic not only to missionize in Muslim North Africa but also to translate or rework various Arabic tracts into Latin polemics against the Jews.[8] For our own purposes,

7. Roger Bacon, *Opus tertium* 20, in *Opera quaedam hactenus inedita*, ed. J. S. Brewer (1859; repr., n.p. 1965), p. 65; Bacon, *Opus maius* 3.13, ed. John Henry Bridges, 3 vols. (Oxford, 1897–1900), 3:120–21: "Nam in manibus Latinorum residet potestas convertendi. Et ideo pereunt Judaei inter nos infiniti quia nullus eis scit praedicare, nec scripturas interpretari in lingua eorum, nec conferre cum eis nec disputare juxta sensum literalem, quia et veram literam habent [et] suas expositiones antiquas secundum [sententiam . . .] et aliorum sapientum quantum literalis expositio requirit, et in universali quantum ad sensum spiritualem. Nam textus ubique spiritualiter sonat Messiam quem Christum dicimus, sicut ipsi Hebraei non ignorant, eo quod expectant ipsum venturum, sed in tempore sui adventus decepti sunt. O damnum ineffabile animarum, cum facile esset innumerabiles Judaeos converti! Quod esset pessimum quia ab eis fundamentum fidei nostrae incepit, et deberemus considerare quod sunt de semine patriarcharum et prophetarum, et, quod plus est, de eorum stirpe Dominus natus est et gloriosa Virgo et apostoli et innumerabiles [sancti] a principio Ecclesiae descenderunt." On Bacon's criticism of his colleagues, see Stewart C. Easton, *Roger Bacon and His Search for a Universal Science* (New York, 1952), pp. 89, 214. See also the editorial comments on Roger Bacon, *The Greek Grammar . . . and a Fragment of His Hebrew Grammar*, ed. Edmond Nolan and Samuel Abraham Hirsch (Cambridge, Eng., 1902), pp. 201ff., which appear to counter effectively the view of Moritz Steischneider, "Christliche Hebräisten," *Zeitschrift für hebräische Bibliographie* 1 (1896–97), 53. And on Bacon's disciples, see Smalley, *Study*, p. 336; Hailperin, *Rashi*, pp. 130–33; Roth, *Jews of Medieval Oxford*, p. 122, n. 3.

8. Florence of Worcester, *Chronicon ex chronicis*, ed. Benjamin Thorpe, 2 vols. (London, 1848–49), 2:214. Cf. Beryl Smalley, "Robert Holcot O.P.," *AFP* 26 (1956), 61–62, which speaks of this friar as John of Reading. On Alfonso's life and works see Atanasio López, *Obispos en el Africa septentrional desde el siglo XIII* (Tangiers, 1941), pp. 74–78; and G. Meersseman, "La chronologie des voyages et des oeuvres de frère Alphonse Beunhombre O.P.," *AFP* 10 (1940), 77–108. Alfonso claimed to have translated two polemical tracts from Arabic to Latin: *De adventu messiae praeterito liber*, supposedly written by a Moroccan Jew named Samuel who had converted to Christianity in the late eleventh century, and *Disputatio Abutalib Sarraceni et Samuelis Iudei, que fides precellit—Christianorum, an Iudeorum, an Sarracenorum*. Many writers have maintained, however, that the *De adventu messiae* was really a forged readaptation of an anti-Jewish tract written by a Jewish convert to Islam in the twelfth century, Samuel ibn Abbas, and have debated whether Alfonso or someone else committed

though, the significance of the increased study of Semitic languages by the friars is best conveyed through a detailed examination of one scholar in particular.

Nicholas and the *Postilla*

Born to Christian parents around the year 1270 in the Norman town of Lyre, Nicholas entered the Franciscan convent of Verneuil by the turn of the century. The study of theology soon took him to the University of Paris, where he received his doctorate in 1309. He proceeded to devote the rest of his life both to the study of theology and the Bible at Paris and to the service of his order. Appointed Franciscan provincial minister of royal France by 1319, he assumed the direction of the province of Burgundy as well by 1325. He died in 1349, having gained recognition as an excellent scholar, a man committed to Franciscan ideals, and a friar who worked hard to preserve the stability of his order in the wake of the crises that beset it in the first half of the fourteenth century. He was also a prolific writer. His extant works include the famous *Postilla litteralis super Biblia*, a less well known *Postilla moralis* on the Bible, a commentary on Peter Lombard's *Sentences*, a small treatise extolling Francis of Assisi, and two brief works concerning the Jews.[9]

---

the actual forgery. Already in the fifteenth century the Spanish rabbi Hayyim ibn Musa, in a list of anti-Jewish polemics, mentioned this work as "a book *attributed* to Rabbi Samuel (*sefer ha-meyuhas le-R. Shemu'el*)"; see ibn Musa's *Magen wa-Romah*, ed. Adolf Posnanski (Jerusalem, 1970), p. 1. The resolution of this question lies beyond the purview of the present study, since the *De adventu messiae* really belongs to the early medieval brand of anti-Jewish polemic, dwelling almost entirely on the figurative, christological interpretation of Old Testament passages and on the Jews' punishment of dispersion and captivity for having rejected and crucified Jesus. Its nature cannot be construed as proof of its early composition, however, since the old type of polemic never completely disappeared. The most thorough attempts to deal with this work, which include critical editions of it, are those of M. A. van den Oudenrijn, "De opusculis arabicis quae Latine vertit fr. Alphonsus Buenhombre, O.P.," *Analecta sacri Ordinis Fratrum Praedicatorum* 28 (1920), 32–44, 85–93, 163–68, which simply concludes, p. 41, regarding both of Alfonso's works that "utrumque tractatum non a iudaeo catechumeno sed a theologo christiano esse conscriptum"; and the published dissertation of Monika Marsmann, *Die Epistel des Rabbi Samuel an Rabbi Isaak: Untersuchung und Edition* (Siegen, W. Germany, 1971), which confidently concurs, pp. 15–23, in assigning authorship of the treatise to Alfonso. The text of the *De adventu messiae* appears also in PL 149: 333–68.

9. Already by the early fifteenth century, various reports had begun to circulate among both Christians and Jews to the effect that Nicholas of Lyra had been born Jewish, or that in their poverty his Christian parents had sent him to Jewish teachers for religious instruction at no cost. Both these stories undoubtedly originated to

In considering Nicholas of Lyra, I shall dwell mostly on these two treatises devoted exclusively to the Jews; they embody the straightforward expression of his anti-Jewish polemic. The *Postilla litteralis*, which because of its adherence to the progression of the biblical text did not allow for a systematic treatment of the Jews, nevertheless requires some attention, even beyond its exposition of the Old Testament passages normally cited by Christian polemicists as having special christological significance—Genesis 49:10, Isaiah 7:14, Psalm 110:1, and others—texts that I shall not review here. The *Postilla* has brought Nicholas of Lyra widespread recognition for his mastery and use of Hebrew and rabbinic literature in interpreting the text of the Bible; these skills comprised important elements of the basic methodology he employed in his commentaries, especially those on the books of the Old Testament. As Roger Bacon and others did before him, Nicholas decries the scribal corruptions of the text of the Vulgate as well as the distortions of meaning which invariably appear in any translation, justifying the need to resort to the *hebraica veritas*. And because many Hebrew words are themselves ambiguous, Nicholas writes in his second prologue to the *Postilla* that "in order to determine the literal sense, I intend to introduce the sayings not only of Catholic doctors but also of Hebrew ones—especially of Rabbi Solomon, who among the Hebrew doctors has spoken most reasonably."[10] Throughout the *Postilla*, Nicholas displays a noteworthy familiarity with (and a great debt to) the gloss of Solomon ben Isaac of Troyes (1040–1105, known as Rashi), which he quotes on virtually every page of the commentary of the Old Testament. He also exhibits an acquaintance with the works of other Jewish exegetes, philosophers like Maimonides, and collections of classical rabbinic midrashim. Nicholas appears to possess a good understanding of current Jewish

---

explain Nicholas's mastery of Hebrew and rabbinic literature, and the first report in particular has found and still finds adherents among many scholars. For a summary of the important opinions with an effective demonstration of these stories' fictitious nature, and on Nicholas's life and work in general, see Henri Labrosse, "Biographie de Nicolas de Lyre," *Etudes franciscaines* 17 (1907), 480–505, 593–608; Labrosse, "Ouevres de Nicolas de Lyre," ibid. 19 (1908), 41–52, 153–75, 368–79; Charles-Victor Langlois, "Nicolas de Lyre, Frère Mineur," *HLF* 36 (1927), 355–400; Palemon Glorieux, *Répertoire des maîtres en théologie de Paris au XIIIᵉ siècle*, 2 vols. (Paris, 1933–34), 2:215–31; Hailperin, *Rashi*, p. 144; Blumenkranz, "Anti-Jewish Polemics," p. 135; and Rega Wood, "Nicholas of Lyre on the Church," M.A. thesis, Cornell University, 1971.
10. *Biblia sacra cum glossis, interlineari, et ordinaria, Nicolai Lyrani postilla, ac moralitatibus, Burgensis additionibus, et Thoringi replicis, etc.*, 6 vols. (Venice, 1588), 1:3GH.

beliefs and practices, knowledge that he exploits at numerous points in the *Postilla*.[11] And he assures his readers that he has taken great care to verify his readings and interpretations. He writes in his treatise *De differentia nostrae translationis et hebraicae litterae* that owing to his relative lack of skill in Hebrew, he has presented translations from Jewish sources only with the collaboration and approval of Hebraists more learned than he.[12] Herman Hailperin, author of the most extensive treatment of Nicholas's use of rabbinic biblical exegesis, showers praise upon him for the enlightened, impartial and objective spirit in which he made use of such tools. "He undoubtedly . . . sought the *proprietas* of the Hebrew not only as an aid to correct the Latin; Lyra was an intellectual person who saw the great need of the exegesis of the Hebrew Bible, in general, aside from the Vulgate." As regards the frequency with which Nicholas reflects the influence of Rashi's commentary, Hailperin adds that "there is no polemic in his use of Rashi"; the Franciscan's intentions were genuinely disinterested and scholarly.[13] Yet in view of the inevitably polemical nature of much medieval biblical exegesis—a christological reading of the Old Testament itself constituted an attack upon the Jews who rejected it—one wonders if Hailperin's evaluation of Nicholas and his *Postilla* is entirely fair. Medieval Jewish commentaries on the Bible themselves had a markedly polemical orientation deriving from the need to defend a rabbinic understanding of the Hebrew Bible against the challenges

11. See Hailperin, *Rashi*, pp. 145–246, for a thorough treatment of the similarities between the two glosses; cf. also W. Neumann, "Influence de Raschi et d'autres commentateurs juifs sur les Postillae perpetuae de Nicolas de Lyre," *REJ* 26 (1893), 172–82, 27 (1893), 250–62; and Abraham J. Michalski, "Raschis Einfluss auf Nicholas von Lyra in der Auslegung der Bücher Leviticus, Numerei und Deuteronomium," *Zeitschrift für die alttestamentliche Wissenschaft* 35 (1915), 218–45, 36 (1916), 29–63. For instances of Nicholas's familiarity with contemporary Judaism, see the *Postilla* on Dan. 6:10, *Biblia*, 4:307GH, and on Ezek. 1:1, 4:209F.

12. Quoted in Samuel Berger, *Quam notitiam linguae hebraicae habuerint Christiani Medii Aevi temporibus in Gallia* (Paris, 1893), p. 54. Nicholas's admission of not having real expertise in Hebrew has been construed by some to be important evidence for disproving the legend of his Jewish origin; see, for example, the medieval Jewish convert to Christianity, Paul of Burgos (Pablo de Santa Maria), *Additiones ad Postillam magistri Nicolai de Lyra super Biblia*, in *Biblia*, 1:6E, or PL 113:46; the conclusions of Graetz, *Geschichte*, 7:447; and Helen Rosenau, "The Architecture of Nicolaus de Lyra's Temple Illustrations and the Jewish Tradition," *JJS* 25 (1974), 303. Yet while Graetz is probably correct, 7:301, in inferring that Nicholas did receive aid from Jewish converts to Christianity—for there were few Christians better schooled in Hebrew than he—Nicholas's disclaimer of expertise in Hebrew proves nothing about his birth. He also admits a lack of expertise in Latin (see below), revealing that both statements establish nothing more than his own modesty.

13. Hailperin, *Rashi*, pp. 144–45.

of the Church, and scholars have singled out Rashi's gloss as a prime example of this sort of polemic.[14] If Nicholas used Rashi—whose teaching, he writes, "is deemed highly authoritative among modern Jews"[15]—as much as Hailperin has shown he did, the *Postilla* could not have avoided taking an opposing polemical stance with regard to numerous passages of the Old Testament. Moreover, it is quite likely that Nicholas did not merely succumb to this necessity but consciously conceived of an attack upon the Jews and their interpretation of Scripture as an important aspect of his commentary. As his modern biographer Henri Labrosse has written, "Nicholas is a polemicist above all. To convince the Jews [of the truth of Christianity]—that is his constant preoccupation, the constant and definite goal of all his work."[16]

Evidence of Nicholas's antagonistic stance in regard to the Jews appears right alongside his declaration of the great exegetical value of making reference to the Hebrew Bible and rabbinic commentaries, in the prologue to the *Postilla*. Immediately after justifying his use of the *codices Hebraeorum*, he adds a warning: "Yet in this, great caution must be taken with regard to the places in the text of the Old Testament that speak of the divine nature of Christ and its ramifications, several of which [texts] the Jews have falsified in the defense of their error, as I have demonstrated to some extent in a certain *quaestio* concerning the divinity of Christ and as I shall demonstrate more fully when such places occur, God willing."[17] Nicholas assures his reader that owing to these dangers involved in referring to Jewish sources, and "because I am not so experienced in either the Hebrew or the Latin language," he has made no statement for which he has not found blatant support either in Scripture itself or in the teachings of the Church. He invites both the Church and any pious reader of his work to correct him wherever he may have erred. And he declares his intention to maintain not only a defensive posture in regard to the anti-Christian aspects of Jewish sources but also an offensive stance, to exploit those sources in demonstrating the errors of Judaism. "Occasionally, although rather infrequently, I shall also insert plainly absurd

14. See, for example, Y. Baer, "Rashi"; E. I. J. Rosenthal, "Anti-Christian Polemics"; and J. M. Rosenthal, "The Anti-Christian Dispute." Cf. the helpful comments of Ruether, *Faith and Fratricide*, p. 121.

15. See the citation of Nicholas's *De differentia nostrae translationis* in Berger, *Quam notitiam*, p. 54.

16. Labrosse, "Oeuvres," p. 377.

17. *Biblia*, 1:3G.

sayings of the Hebrews, not in order to espouse or follow them, but so that through them might appear how great a blindness has come upon Israel."[18]

Various instances in the *Postilla* at which Nicholas acted upon his polemical intentions manifest a basic hostility toward the Jews. Commenting on Jeremiah 13:23, "Can the Nubian change his skin or the leopard its spots?" Nicholas observes: "Thus he speaks regarding the Jews, that they were not able to revert to good on account of an inclination to evil, since [this] inclination is [their] particular nature."[19] Elsewhere, Nicholas focuses his attack against the Jews on their traditions of biblical exegesis and midrash—that is, the conception of and attitudes to the Bible in rabbinic Judaism. The Jews, he contends, corrupt the explicit teachings of the Old Testament, falsely listing the generations of King David's descendants so as to exclude Jesus of Nazareth.[20] Such teachings of the rabbis in turn maintain Jewish laymen in their condition of theological error, preventing them from acknowledging the truth of Christianity. On Isaiah 29:12, "Give the book [of prophecy] to one who cannot read," Nicholas comments: "When mention of the past advent of Christ and of similar matters is made to the simple among the Jews, they say that they are not experienced in the law but that their teachers know how to respond to such things. To their [teachers'] errors they adhere most unyieldingly."[21] He does not hesitate to accuse Rashi of having fallen into grievous theological error.[22] On a considerable number of occasions, Nicholas adduces rabbinic fables and homilies from the Talmud and midrash to substantiate his claims concerning the absurdities of the Jews. He mocks the stories about the huge size of Og, king of Bashan and last of the gigantic Refa'im (Deuteronomy 3:11), the "false and puerile" tale of God lamenting the destruction of his temple, and several homilies concerning the leviathan. One of these in particular draws an indignant rebuke; it pertains to Genesis 1:21; "God then created the great sea-monsters."

The Hebrews here say that this sort of fish is of incredible magnitude, because of which if any of them [the fish] would multiply, the world

18. Ibid., 1:3H.
19. Ibid., 4:131A.
20. Ibid., 6:116G (on 1 Tim. 1:14).
21. Ibid., 4:54H.
22. See, for example, ibid., 4:409CD (ad Zach. 3:80, 1:315F,H ad Num. 28:15), and 4:54H (ad Isa. 29:11).

would be destroyed, since the sea would not be navigable nor could other fish exist in the sea. Therefore, after God had created this species in both masculine and feminine genders, he killed the female lest any would multiply, and he saved her for the just to eat in the world to come. Whence it is obvious that the Jews have fallen into the error of the Saracens, who define the beatitude of the future life as the corporeal delights of food and sex, which is deemed absurd not only among the Catholics, but also among the Gentile philosophers who view the beatitude of man in the works of his rational faculty.[23]

The tale that Adam cohabited with demons while he abstained from relations with Eve for three hundred years or that God dwells in the west are ridiculous because neither God nor any demon is corporeal, having any physical substance.[24] The statement of Ecclesiastes 24:5 that wisdom existed before the creation of the world is falsely interpreted by the rabbis to refer to the law of Moses, simply for them to avoid having to admit any distinction in the eternal deity between creator and created *logos*. The rabbinic understanding of Amos 1:3, that one can receive forgiveness from God three but not four times for the same sin "is erroneous and in opposition to Scripture."[25] And in connection with the Mosaic prescription for a sin-offering to be sacrificed on the day of the new moon, Nicholas tells the talmudic story of God needing to repent for having made the moon inferior to the sun and therefore requiring this particular sacrifice. "Whence is obvious the blindness even the insanity of the Jews, who believe God to have been in need of expiation and to have sinned."[26] The insanity of the Jewish tradition has perverted the Jews' whole understanding and appreciation of biblical prophecy. Their teachers have consequently failed consistently in projecting the date of the messiah's advent; and the redeemer whom they now expect at the end of the Roman Empire is really the Antichrist.[27]

Although the size and nature of the *Postilla* did not allow for a systematic exposition of many of these charges, the commentary nevertheless manifests elements of the new mendicant anti-Jewish polemic discussed in the preceding chapters. On the basis of his

23. Ibid., 1:278B,D; cf. 1:333FGH (ad Deut. 3:11); 3:77F (ad Job 40:10); 124B (ad Ps. 28:9); 241C (ad Ps. 103:26); and 4:43G (ad Isa. 22:5).

24. Ibid., 2:105C (ad 2 Sam. 7:14), 263F (ad Neh. 9:6).

25. Ibid., 3:411B, 4:395C.

26. Ibid., 1:315F,H (ad Num. 28:15).

27. Ibid., 2:65G (ad 1 Sam. 2:10), 4:54H (ad Isa. 29:11); cf. also 4:340B (ad Hos. 6:1).

own reading of Jewish sources, Nicholas charges the rabbinic tradition with falsifying both the text and the proper interpretation of the Old Testament in order to hide its straightforward revelation of Christianity. The absurdities of postbiblical Judaism have led the Jews to a blasphemous, anthropormorphic conception of God, a distorted, physical picture of the world to come, and other ridiculous beliefs. In their basically evil nature, the Jews have been deprived of any correct understanding of the Bible; their allegiance now lies with the Antichrist. A bibilical commentator himself, Nicholas focused his attack on the Jews around the rabbis' corruption of the Bible and biblical traditions; to examine this phenomenon more closely, he authored the two small treatises pertaining to the Jews, which usually appear in print as appendices to the *Postilla*.

The Two Anti-Jewish Treatises

The first treatise originated as a scholastic discourse in 1309 which Nicholas subsequently revised in the early 1330s and which has since assumed many different titles, ranging from those stressing its christological concerns (for example, *Quodlibetum de adventu Christi*) to others highlighting its polemical nature (*De Iudeorum perfidia*, for instance). The *Quodlibetum*, as I shall refer to it here, sets out to investigate "whether from writings accepted [as authoritative] by the Jews it can be proven effectively that our savior was both God and man."[28] Nicholas asserts that the Old Testament itself sufficiently demonstrates the truth of this proposition, both as regards the divine and human nature of Christ and as regards the whole mystery of his incarnation at a particular point in human history; but one might argue, states the friar, that if all this is so obvious, the Jews should have already forsaken their errors. Thus an examination of Jewish literature is required to provide an effective proof for the fundamental beliefs of Christianity and to demonstrate that the blame for the Jews' obstinacy lies only with themselves.

What books comprise the literature of the Jews from which Nich-

28. Ibid., 6:275E. For the date and titles of this work see ibid., 6:278B; Langlois, "Nicolas de Lyre," pp. 377–78; Bernhard Blumenkranz, "Anti-Jewish Polemics and Legislation in the Middle Ages: Literary Fiction or Reality," *JJS* 15 (1964), 136, n. 16, 137; and Hailperin, *Rashi*, p. 285, n. 28. The text of the work appears in *Biblia*, 6:275E–280D.

olas adduces his evidence? After listing the books of the Old Testament accepted by the Jews as canonical, he adds that the Jews have also transmitted their teachings in Aramaic and Greek, as in their several translations of the Bible. These texts are authoritative among the Jews, and the Jews often use them as commentaries, because they are occasionally clearer than the Hebrew and they frequently add an explanation to the literal translation. Christians must therefore have a knowledge of such writings in order to dispute ably with the Jews. And, like Raymond Martini, Nicholas proposes also to use the Talmud and midrashic works of the ancient rabbis, despite the erroneous nature of the Jews' oral law.

> Besides the canonical texts there are also other texts accepted by the Jews as equally authoritative—i.e., the Talmud. . . . [There follows an explanation of the Jews' belief in an oral tradition.] Likewise the teachings of the Hebrew doctors who glossed the Old Testament are much more authoritative among them than the teachings of Jerome and Augustine and other Catholic doctors are among us. . . . Although the texts of this sort—i.e., the Talmud and the glosses of the Hebrew doctors—are in large part false, with them we can still argue effectively against them [the Jews], since they are accepted by them in the manner described.[29]

Nicholas proceeds to consider three issues in the *Quodlibetum*: the plurality within the Godhead, the divine as well as human nature of the biblical messiah, and the past advent of this messiah. With regard to each question, he adduces a variety of corroborating passages from the Old Testament, then shows how their obvious trinitarian and/or christological implications are acknowledged in rabbinic sources, and finally encounters the objections of other Jews to his scriptural interpretations. In general, although not always, those rabbinic sources Nicholas cites on his own behalf belong to the classical rabbinic period—the first several centuries after Jesus—while the objections to Nicholas's arguments derive from the works of more recent Jewish writers. The brunt of his polemic, therefore, falls upon the bearers of the talmudic traditions of rabbinic Judaism, especially the Jews of his own day. Examination of several separate passages in the *Quodlibetum* will best serve to illustrate the substance of his attack.

In support of his arguments for the Trinity, Nicholas first refers to the Bible's use of a plural noun (*Elohim*) for God, as in the

29. *Biblia*, 6:275FG.

opening verse of Genesis, a noun often accompanied by plural adjectives and verbs. Although Jews deny the plural meaning of *Elohim*, Nicholas concludes that the "said excuse is false" (*praedicta evasio est falsa*).[30] He cites two midrashim, on Psalm 50:1 and Ecclesiastes 2:12, which contend that *Elohim* denotes three different creative properties of God or applies to God and the lords of his "council"; either will support the Christian belief in the divine plurality. Modern Jews, however, try to pervert the meaning of such midrashim.

> Hence it is clear that it is not against the intention of the ancient Hebrew doctors that some plurality might be placed in God or the Gods while the unity of the deity is still preserved, which unity the Catholics most truly affirm. This last response, which, as has been seen, contains the truth, later Jews distort, saying that divine knowledge, goodness, and power are those three properties in which God created the world. . . . But this response is not reasonable.[31]

Nicholas then shows why and goes on to explain that he would conclude his trinitarian argument here, if he had not recently found a Hebrew book that poses further objections; so the citation of the Bible and relevant glosses continues. He finally concludes his discussion of the Trinity with a scathing condemnation of Rashi for the false denial (*mendacium*) of evidence of God's plurality in Isaiah 48:16: "Thus it is evident that the argument of Rabbi Solomon is not only opposed to all the scripture and prophecy of the Old Testament . . . but also opposed to all the writings of the philosophers, as is clear from what has been said."[32]

Attempting to demonstrate the truth of the Christian belief in the incarnation—that the messiah in the Old Testament prophecies was both divine and human—Nicholas adds to the list of biblical passages and ancient rabbinic interpretations which medieval Jews have tried to deny. In this section of the *Quodlibetum*, several new elements also appear in Nicholas's accusations. One finds citations of a medieval rabbinic work, Maimonides' *Guide of the Perplexed*, in support of Christianity and of a classical midrash to demonstrate the absurdities of Jewish biblical exegesis. Arguing that Jeremiah 23:6 ("and this is the name to be given him [Israel's redeemer]: the Lord is our righteousness") refers to the messiah by the name of

30. Ibid., 6:276A.
31. Ibid., 6:276B.
32. Ibid., 6:276FGH.

the Lord, Nicholas counters the claims of Hebrew exegetes that the use of God's name in this verse does not equate the messiah with the deity. Citing Maimonides' *Guide*, Nicholas argues that while all the other names of God derive from divine works and therefore need not always refer to God himself, the name of the Lord, the tetragrammaton, denotes the divine essence and never appears in any other context.[33] And if a contemporary Jewish work could lend support to Nicholas, a classical text might also exemplify the Jews' foolishness. He adduces the allusion to the messiah in Micah 5:1, "whose roots are far back in the past in ancient days gone by," as testimony to the messiah's primordial origins and divinity—and cites the objection of the Jews based on their midrash that God had created seven things before the creation of the world, including the law, repentance, and the name of the messiah, the ostensive object of Micah's allusion. Yet this absurd teaching, Nicholas responds, does not even merit a response. The law could not exist outside of an intellect. And since the eternal intellect of God could not have anything new created within it, the creation of the law had to await the appearance of a human or an angelic intellect, neither of which existed before the creation of the world. Similarly, repentance, which presupposes the existence of sin, could not exist before the creation of the world and its sinful inhabitants. Nicholas claims that he could refute the remaining particulars of this midrash with equal facility, but he adds, "I desist, since their [the Jews'] teachings appear frivolous and altogether ridiculous."[34]

Following the example of *Pugio fidei*, Nicholas also accuses the Jews of distorting the sense of Scripture by interfering with the correct pointing or vocalization of Hebrew consonants.[35] But his most startling accusation posits that the present Hebrew text of the Bible varies from a more ancient, genuine one. Surpassing even Raymond Martini in this regard, Nicholas may well have been the first medieval Christian who used Hebrew not only to understand the Masoretic Text but also to allege that there existed more authentic "published" versions of the Bible. Many of his predecessors, most notably at the Parisian school of St. Victor, had respected the Jews for their faithful preservation of the *hebraica veritas*, but Nicholas apparently did not share that respect. In his eyes, the

33. *Biblia*, 6:277A.
34. Ibid., 6:277FG. For a series of medieval Jewish attempts to explicate this midrash, see Saperstein, *Decoding the Rabbis*, p. 219, n. 58.
35. *Biblia*, 6:277D.

Bible of medieval Jewry had ceased to be the most reliable text of Scripture. This accusation too appears in connection with Jeremiah 23:6, which according to Nicholas and the Vulgate clearly equates the messiah with "the Lord, our righteousness." In reply to the Jewish objection that Jeremiah in this phrase speaks not of the Davidic messiah but of God himself, who calls upon himself to redeem his people Israel—an interpretation apparently justified by the reading of the Masoretic Text—Nicholas says:

> Against this explanation there is no argument, unless it can be shown that they [the Jews] here pervert the true text and deny the truth just as they deny the divinity of Christ. This might best be done from ancient Bibles, which were not corrupted in this and other passages in which there is mention of the divinity of Christ, if they [these Bibles] can be had. In this way our predecessors used to argue against them [the Jews] over this and similar passages. Yet although I myself have not seen any Bible of the Jews which has not been corrupted, I have faithfully heard from those worthy by reason of their lives, consciences, and knowledge, who swear on oath that they have seen it thus in ancient Bibles.

If one could not acquire such uncorrupted biblical texts with which to argue, Nicholas would normally advocate turning to a biblical translation acknowledged by the Jews as authoritative, like the Septuagint. Yet Nicholas also believed that the original seventy translators of the Bible into Greek themselves had obscured prophetic references to a divine Christ so as not to invite charges of dualism from King Ptolemy. Hence his rather sweeping conclusion: "the *autoritas* [sic] of Jeremiah 23 . . . is effective for proving the divinity of Christ not according to the translation of Jerome but only from the true Hebrew."[36]

36. Ibid., 6:277BC. According to Nicholas, the Masoretic Text has distorted the vocalization of the word *yqr'w*, reading *zeh shemo 'asher yiqre'o, YHWH ṣidqeinu* ("this is his name by which he will call him—the Lord our righteousness") instead of the correct *zeh shemo 'asher yiqre'u YHWH ṣidqeinu* ("this is his name by which they will call [him,] the Lord our righteousness"). Interestingly, the seventeenth-century Jewish exegete Jedidiah Solomon Raphael ben Abraham Norzi, in his *Minḥat Shai,* mentions a printed version of the text which reads *yiqre'u,* although he emphatically states that such a reading is erroneous; I am grateful to David Berger for calling this reference to my attention. While the present-day reader might consider Nicholas's fiery exclamation well out of proportion to the nature of the discrepancy in question, the mere vocalization of one consonant, medieval and even Renaissance churchmen deemed the pointing of the Hebrew Bible just as sacred a component of God's revelation to Israel as the text itself; see Simon Federbusch, *Ha-Lashon ha-'Ivrit be-Yisra'el uva-'Amim* (Jerusalem, 1967), pp. 137–38.

From a tactical or methodological point of view, Nicholas departed little from the devices used to substantiate his first two major arguments in pursuing the third, the past advent of the messiah. In this section of his treatise, he simply adds to his repertoire of classical Jewish sources that serve as evidence of Christianity; he cites the books of the Maccabees, Josephus, and even the *Toledot Yeshu*, the collection of derogatory Jewish tales concerning the life of Jesus.[37] Then finally, at the end of the *Quodlibetum*, Nicholas seeks to analyze the Jewish mentality, both classical and contemporary: if the writings of the Jews offer irrefutable proof of Christianity, why did and do the Jews remain blind and unyielding to it? He responds that many at the time of Jesus and soon after his death did admit to the truth of his teaching; some, like the apostle Paul, actually converted. "And of the leaders [of the Jews] many believed in him but on account of the Pharisees did not admit it, lest as the chief priests and doctors of the law they be said to be expelled from the synagogue. Many legal scholars even after this period perceived this [the truth of Christianity], as has been said by Josephus, and likewise can it be said regarding many others." Why then have the Jews not yet converted? Nicholas can suggest three possible reasons. First, the Jews have always been greedy people, and they fear that by abandoning the promise of temporal reward in their law they would invite financial penury upon themselves. Second, "from the cradle they have been nurtured in the hatred of Christ, and they curse Christianity and the Christians daily in their synagogues." The suppositions upon which one is reared eventually become part of one's natural outlook, in this case perverting any rational, objective sense of judgment. And third, acceptance of Christianity demands subscription to difficult beliefs quite foreign to a Jewish mentality, like those in the Trinity, the dual nature of Christ, and transubstantiation; "indeed, in that sacrament of the Eucharist, they [the Jews] consider us the worst of idolaters."[38]

Nicholas completed his second anti-Jewish polemical treatise, sometimes entitled *Responsio ad quemdam Iudeum ex verbis Evangelii secundum Matheum contra Christum nequiter arguentem*, in June 1334.[39]

---

37. *Biblia*, 6:277H–280C.
38. Ibid., 6:280CD.
39. Ibid., 6:280B,D–285D; for the various titles of this work, see Langlois, "Nicolas de Lyre," p. 378; Blumenkranz, "Anti-Jewish Polemics," p. 135; and Hailperin, *Rashi*, 285, n. 29.

The particular motivation for the composition of this work lay in a tract written by a Jew and attacking the Gospel, which happened to come to Nicholas's attention after the completion of the *Postilla*. From the contents of the *Responsio*, this "tractate composed by a certain Jew" appears to have been Book XI of the twelfth-century Jacob ben Reuben's anti-Christian polemic, *The Wars of the Lord* (*Milḥamot ha-Shem*), either in its original or in a revised form. This portion of Jacob's polemic contains a list of excerpts from the book of Matthew and from several other Christian works, which Jacob endeavors to use in support of his attack on Christianity. Jacob's was one of the first and fiercest anti-Christian polemics written by a medieval Jew and the work elicited responses from several Christian writers; one can well appreciate the sense of urgency and thoroughness with which Nicholas undertook to refute it.[40]

With only two or three very minor omissions, Nicholas proceeds systematically through every argument of Jacob ben Reuben, citing each textual quotation, reviewing the Jewish objections, and offering what he deems adequate rebuttal. Just as he did in the *Quodlibetum*, he makes use of Scripture, classical rabbinic midrash, and contemporary Jewish writings with which to substantiate his conclusions. The questions considered in the *Responsio* are addressed to Christian texts, and Nicholas's methodology for answering the Jews departs little from that of the *Quodlibetum*; the *Responsio* accordingly does not add much to our understanding of Nicholas's attitude toward the Jews. Nevertheless, as Bernhard Blumenkranz has pointed out, the *Responsio* does portray Nicholas involved in a polemical struggle with the Jews of his day. Even though most of

40. On the identification of the "tractatus a Iudaeo quodam confectus" with *Milḥamot ha-Shem*, ch. 11, pp. 141–56, see Rosenthal's introduction to Jacob's polemic, p. xx; and Steinschneider, *Catalogus*, 2:2554–55. Bernhard Blumenkranz, in "Nicolas de Lyre et Jacob ben Reuben," *JJS* 16 (1965), 47–51, has objected, however, that because Nicholas responds to this Jewish *tractatus* on account of its potentially bad influence over uneducated Christians, it could not have been written in Hebrew, which the average Christian could not read; it rather had to have been a Latin revision of Jacob's work by a later Jewish author. Moreover, Blumenkranz points to the different order of the passages from Matthew in *Milḥamot ha-Shem* and in Nicholas's *Responsio*. Yet Blumenkranz fails to consider that few uneducated Christian laymen in the later Middle Ages could read Latin either. Nicholas might easily have felt obliged to respond to the Jewish *tractatus* simply because it represented a danger to Christians if it were circulating among Jews—as it apparently was—who might use the arguments contained in it. And as regards the ordering of the passages from Matthew, Nicholas in his *Responsio* simply dealth with them in order, just as they appear in the Gospel; he might well have undertaken such a reordering of Jacob's material himself.

French Jewry had been expelled by 1334, Nicholas came across a current edition of Jacob ben Reuben's work; as we have seen, he was certainly familiar with contemporary Jewish literature of many different varieties. And he introduces the *Responsio* with a statement justifying its composition: "Although his [the Jewish author's] attack is of no or of slight danger among the intelligent, since, however, the simple can be upset by it, I propose to refute such a rash denier of the truth, as much as the Lord will allow me."[41] Yet the reader must return to the friar's first treatise in order to analyze and appreciate his attitude toward the Jews. As Nicholas notes in the *Responsio*, he has dealt with these matters in great detail "in a certain quodlibetal *quaestio*."[42]

Because the *Quodlibetum* originated in the context of a scholastic disputation at the University of Paris in 1309,[43] and because there were then no Jews in France at whom such a treatise might be directed, both Bernhard Blumenkranz and Herman Hailperin have concluded that one may not rightly classify it as anti-Jewish literature. Nicholas's audience had to have been a Christian one, and he therefore intended the *Quodlibetum* for the internal use and guidance of the Christian scholarly community; the work could have no immediate missionary value.[44] Hailperin in particular has attributed to Nicholas's treatises on the Jews a tolerant, ecumenical attitude toward a rival religion which one would find admirable even in a modern theologian.

Now it is to be noted that these small polemical tracts are "anti-Jewish," for the most part only in the *academic, scholastic* sense; they are apologetic mainly; they attempt to clarify the Christian religion for Christians as well as Jews. We have found in these tracts but one passage that might be described as bitter and invective. . . . It may be said truly that although most of the anti-Jewish polemical writings of the Middle Ages are unscholarly and usually offensive to the Jews, these tractates of Lyra . . . are noteworthy for the moderation of the polemic and for the power of the argument. . . . It is no exaggeration to say that Lyra is serious, loyal, courteous, positive, and truly scientific.

41. *Biblia*, 6:280D; Blumenkranz, "Anti-Jewish Polemics," p. 138.
42. *Biblia*, 6:284C.
43. Langlois, "Nicolas de Lyre," p. 357.
44. Blumenkranz, "Anti-Jewish Polemics," pp. 138–39; Hailperin, *Rashi*, pp. 140–41, 286, n. 31.

Such a one-sided evaluation of Nicholas's *Quodlibetum* overlooks much of this little work's significance. Nicholas generally does avoid the biting, anti-Jewish calumnies of men like Nicholas Donin, Pablo Christiani, or Raymond Martini. And it is also true that both when Nicholas first delivered his discourse in Paris in 1309 and when he revised it in the early 1330s, there were no Jews in France whom he might have intended as its audience. Yet as we have seen, his two treatises dealing with the Jews embody a major indictment of the contemporary rabbinic understanding of Scripture. It appears noteworthy that Nicholas felt obliged to polemicize against Jewish biblical exegesis even after France had already expelled her Jews, along with their teachers and books. Moreover, it is misleading to evaluate the ideological importance of Nicholas's writings simply on the basis of their tone. Nicholas was not a missionary by trade, and we have no evidence that he ever disputed personally with Jews. Rather, he wrote in and for a scholarly community; no reason, either in the setting of his works or in the background of their author, existed for the bitter invective which one finds in a book such as the *Pugio fidei*. Nicholas's attitude toward the Jews should thus be evaluated according to the substance of his arguments and the methodology with which he developed them.

Hailperin himself admits that Raymond Martini's *Pugio fidei* influenced Nicholas in his frequent reference to rabbinic sources,[45] and close examination reveals that apart from the bitterness of Martini's tone, the attitudes of the two men to Judaism and Jewish literature are quite similar. Yet because Nicholas never had to apply his beliefs to the practical situations of debating against and missionizing among the Jews, he usually does not emphasize his sentiments as forcefully as Martini had done, thereby perhaps misleading his modern readers. Like the *Pugio fidei*, Nicholas's *Quodlibetum* sets out to prove three fundamental doctrines of Christianity—the past advent of the messiah, the Trinity, and the incarnation of Christ— with the aid of writings accepted as authoritative by the Jews. Following Martini's example, Nicholas introduces his work with a description of the basic textual components of rabbinic tradition and an explanation that although that tradition is essentially false, it can be exploited well for polemical purposes. Hailperin's attempt to minimize the antagonism in his view of rabbinic Judaism not-

45. Hailperin, *Rashi*, p. 287, n. 45; and cf. below, n. 47.

withstanding, Nicholas's frequent reference, both in the *Postilla* and in the two shorter treatises, to the absurd beliefs of the rabbis indicates that he shared Martini's opinion of the inanity and stupidity of rabbinic literature. The *Quodlibetum*—and to some extent the *Responsio*—follow the forensic tactics employed in the *Pugio*: biblical texts in conjunction with rabbinic glosses and homilies are used to encounter and overcome the objections of modern Jews to the doctrines of Christianity. Furthermore, Nicholas's arguments and methodology seem to display an acceptance of the three-tiered structural view of the evolution of Jewish history and literature underlying Martini's work. The obvious christological message of the Old Testament (stage 1) could not avoid leaving its mark in the literature of the most ancient rabbis. For many teachers of the Jews living at the time of Jesus (stage 2), as Nicholas remarks at the end of the *Quodlibetum*, recognized the divinity and messiahship of Jesus but feared to admit them publicly. To hide their rejection of him in whom the Bible was fulfilled, they reworked the original text of the Old Testament (the *hebraica veritas*), distorting many of those passages which foretold of Christ most explicitly. They introduced numerous absurd explanations of other telling passages into the Talmud and midrash, but, as much as they tried, they could not exclude evidence of Christianity from their literature altogether. Modern Jews (stage 3), whose objections to Christianity and whose biblical commentaries Nicholas refutes in the *Quodlibetum*, represent the spiritual heirs of the ancient rabbis and their perverse teachings. Led by men like Rashi, they continue to falsify and corrupt the correct understanding of the real Hebrew Bible. They have been brought up to harbor intense hostility against Christianity and the Church, every day cursing Christians in their prayers. And in their intellectual inadequacy to comprehend the truth of Christian beliefs, they deem Christians the worst of all idolaters. Like the friars of the Inquisition and the school of Raymond de Peñaforte, then, Nicholas of Lyra directed his anti-Jewish polemic at contemporary rabbinic Judaism. The rabbis of the Talmud had kept the Jews away from the truth and fulfillment of Jewish Scripture. Their descendants in the Middle Ages were thus no longer the Jews of the Bible, to whom the right of existence in Christendom had been guaranteed.

Given Nicholas's great reliance on the *Pugio fidei*, ought one to evaluate his stance in regard to the Jews merely as a replica of Raymond Martini's? In her landmark study of medieval Christian

Bible scholarship, Beryl Smalley has observed that Nicholas of Lyra "represents the culmination of a movement for the study of Hebrew and rabbinics."[46] By his time, the use of these tools in biblical exegesis had become widely respected; the *Postilla* constituted the natural climax of that trend, in its size, its depth, and its erudition. In much the same fashion, one would be wise to approach Nicholas's anti-Jewish writings as the natural outgrowth of the polemical trend begun by the friars of the Inquisition and the disciples of Raymond de Peñaforte, a trend itself predicated upon a direct confrontation with postbiblical Jewish writings. Nicholas's *Quodlibetum* does more than simply echo Martini's *Pugio*; it indicates that the new mendicant attitude toward contemporary Jewry was not restricted to inquisitors and missionaries personally involved in encounters with European Jews but had successfully entered the academic community as well. In view of Nicholas's stature, both in the Franciscan Order and at the University of Paris, his espousal of the new attitude is in itself significant, reflecting its growing acceptance in clerical and scholarly circles. The fact that he could not have addressed his treatises directly to a Jewish audience contributes still further to this significance. Like Bernard Gui's condemnation of the Talmud and rabbinic beliefs and practice while the Jews were absent from France, Nicholas's writings demonstrate the great extent to which the notion of the perversity of contemporary Judaism had penetrated the ecclesiastical world view. Nicholas, however, not only subscribed to the new approach of the friars, but he also refined it. Whereas the *Pugio fidei* was too unwieldy to become popular among many Christian disputants and missionaries in the field, Nicholas made his two treatises short and concise. Both the *Responsio* and the *Quodlibetum* proceed along tightly structured lines of scholastic organization. Each tract announces its plan at the outset and then analyzes one biblical text or doctrinal question after another with fine logic and clarity. Nor does the fact that a majority of Nicholas's citations of rabbinic sources also appear in the *Pugio fidei* detract from the scholarly nature or significance of his work.[47] An able academician, Nicholas was probably one of the

46. Smalley, *Study*, p. 355.
47. Hailperin, *Rashi*, p. 287, n. 45, correctly notes that "Lyra seems to have gotten many of his Jewish sources, especially in the field of polemics, from the *Pugio fidei* of Raymundus Martini. Although Lyra does not mention this work, it is certain that he borrowed therefrom." Yet Hailperin's lone example of such borrowing in the *Quod-*

few who could sufficiently master the contents of a potentially helpful tool like Martini's magnum opus in order to translate its message into a much more readable and systematically organized presentation.

The utility of Nicholas's *Quodlibetum*—the *Responsio* constituted a defense of the Gospel against Jewish attack—for Christian polemicists is manifest in the work's subsequent popularity and in the responses it elicited from Jews. There are seven extant manuscripts of the *Pugio fidei*, but over eighty manuscripts of the *Quodlibetum* have survived; the demand for it even led to its translation into Russian and employment against the Jews of Eastern Europe by the end of the fifteenth century.[48] Moreover, although Rabbi Solomon ibn Adret of Barcelona probably debated personally with Raymond Martini, neither he nor any other late medieval Jewish writer admits to a direct acquaintance with the *Pugio fidei*; yet several Jewish authors do mention Nicholas's *Quodlibetum* and reveal that they felt an obligation to respond to it. Profiat Duran, for example, a noted rabbi of Perpignan, in 1397 wrote *The Shame of the Gentiles* (*Kelimat ha-Goyim*), in which he refers on a number of occasions to Nicholas's anti-Jewish arguments. A century later, Isaac Abravanel likewise offered a rejoinder to Nicholas.[49] But the most noteworthy Jewish response to the *Quodlibetum* is *Shield and Javelin* (*Magen wa-Romaḥ*) by Ḥayyim ibn Musa, a Spanish physician and rabbi. This entire tract, written in 1456, is devoted to a systematic refutation of every argument and virtually every piece of evidence in the *Quodlibetum*.[50]

---

libetum fails to give an accurate impression of its extent. Although the list of sources cited in the *Quodlibetum* and appearing as well in the *Pugio* does not prove that Nicholas found them in Martini's work in every case, the frequent reference to clusters of sources used also by Martini in the same groupings vouches for Nicholas's considerable reliance on Martini. Such a list appears in the Appendix of this book.

48. Berthier, "Un maître," pp. 281–82; Blumenkranz, "Anti-Jewish Polemics," p. 137; Sh. Ettinger, "Jewish Influence on the Religious Ferment in Eastern Europe at the End of the Fifteenth Century [Hebrew]," in *Yitzhak F. Baer Jubilee Volume*, ed. Salo Wittmayer Baron et al. (Jerusalem, 1960), p. 237 and n. 53.

49. Profiat (Isaac ben Moses ha-Levi) Duran, "Kelimat ha-Goyim," ed. Adolf Posnanski, *Ha-Ṣofeh me-'Ereṣ ha-Ger* 3 (1913), 110, 178, 4 (1914), 86, 94, 95, 96; Langlois, "Nicolas de Lyre," p. 398, n. 3.

50. On ibn Musa see David Kaufmann, "Mikhtav ha-Rav Ḥayyim ibn Musa li-Vno R. Yehudah, Hu"l 'im He'arot u-Fetiḥah 'al Toledot ha-Meḥabber," *Bet Talmud* 2 (1882), 110–25.

A Jewish Evaluation of Nicholas's Polemic

Magen wa-Romaḥ vouches for the basic polemical orientation of Nicholas's *Quodlibetum* and the work's success in attacking contemporary Judaism. After opening his tract with the suggestion that many of the most dangerous anti-Jewish polemicists have been Jewish converts to Christianity, some of whom he lists by name, ibn Musa explains that his treatise will respond to the charges of Christian polemicists, so that the Jew should not be disheartened when they use the Bible and rabbinic literature to substantiate their claims. Toward this end, he proclaims his intent "to respond to the foremost of those who speak against us, Nicholas of Lyra, in the three parts of his polemical treatise," meaning the *Quodlibetum*.[51] There follow twelve methodological guidelines that ibn Musa proposes for Jewish disputants, which together comprise a rejoinder to the strategy adopted by Nicholas. Basically, ibn Musa counsels that the Jew should confine his exchanges with Christians to a discussion of the literal meaning of the Old Testament in its original Hebrew. Except when such references will aid him, he should not accept evidence from later translations of the Bible. Contrary to Nicholas's assertion, blanket acceptance of the Aramaic Targumim is not incumbent upon the Jews, since those translations contain numerous suspect interpretations. As for the Greek Septuagint, the Christians will seek to ascribe to it corrupt readings of the original Hebrew text, emendations which actually originated with Jerome. Naturally, the Jew should not accept proof from any work of Christian Scripture or literature, nor ought he to permit Christians to draw conclusive proof from ambiguous Hebrew words or to subject Scripture to the dictates of rational dialectic, or "external wisdom." The Jew must reject entirely the Christian notion that Jesus came to fulfill the law rather than detract from it; for the law of Moses can need no further fulfillment. Most important, the Christian disputant may not force his Jewish opponent to respond to nonlegal, homiletical passages from the Talmud and midrashim but only to the legal,

51. Ḥayyim ibn Musa, *Magen wa-Romaḥ*, p. 3; cf. the incorrect assertion of Loeb, "La controverse religieuse," 18:138, that Nicholas of Lyra as a polemicist made a negligible impression on Jewish writers.

halakhic teachings of rabbinic literature. Immediately, ibn Musa elaborates the rationale for this position.

> Even though you will see in this book that I demand the literal mean-
> ing of Scripture and that I do not want to accept [proof based on]
> homily and midrash from Christians, do not therefore suppose that I
> remove myself from a belief in all of the sages' teachings. Heaven
> keep me from the evil [of deviating] in any matter, slight or great; for I
> have chosen the way of belief. I shall cling to their [the sages'] words
> and bind them to me like crowns. But because the Christians make
> light of most of them and mock the rabbis and excerpt what they view
> as in agreement with themselves, denying the interpretation of them
> by the sages of Israel . . . , I tell them that when they bring a midrash
> or homily it will not be acceptable as evidence for either side. Decide
> on the basis of the scriptural verses according to their evident mean-
> ing![52]

Ibn Musa evidently considered Nicholas's use of rabbinic literature
for his own polemical purposes to pose a serious threat to the faith
of the average Jew, and he therefore rejected its validity outright.
Simultaneously, however, he felt bound to affirm his allegiance to
the same rabbinic tradition, to emphasize to the reader that that
tradition constituted the basis for authentic, orthodox Judaism.
Perhaps ibn Musa did not want to face the predicament into which
Pablo Christiani had forced Moses Naḥmanides in 1263.

Yet ibn Musa's repeated stress on the literal meaning of Scripture
(*peshaṭ*) hints that he recognized that Nicholas's attack upon contemporary Judaism consisted not only of the exploitation of rabbinic texts to prove Christian doctrine but also of the charge that
the Jews corrupted and deliberately misinterpreted the biblical text.
This supposition is borne out by the body of *Magen wa-Romaḥ*. As
ibn Musa proceeds through the *Quodlibetum* point by point, apply-
ing his twelve methodological guidelines to a refutation of its arguments, he constantly asserts that Nicholas, not the Jews, has
perverted the text and meaning of the Bible. The friar, writes the
rabbi, has often taken either words or whole verses out of their
proper context in order to adduce them as testimony on his behalf:
"I say to Nicholas, discard your commentators—and we shall
ours—into the sea, and we shall take all those [biblical] passages

52. *Magen wa-Romaḥ*, pp. 3–11 (quotation on p. 9).

where your evidence is found together with some verses above and below them, and we shall interpret them as reason shall dictate. And do not steal one word from a verse, or one verse from the rest of the text in order to support your proofs, because the context will disprove it [your argument]."[53] To Nicholas's contention that one need have recourse to the most ancient copies of the Bible in order to avoid Jewish distortions of Scripture, ibn Musa replies that he will accept the readings of none other than the present Hebrew (that is, Masoretic) text. For the Christians allege that the Septuagint—a copy of which, ibn Musa reports, he has never actually seen in their possession—reads differently only when they have difficulty corroborating their assertions. "As for his [Nicholas's] lengthy discussion of the Jews' distortion of the biblical text, behold he speaks falsely, since he himself is the forger." Ibn Musa thereby attempts to direct at postbiblical Christianity charges similar to those that Nicholas has leveled at the Jews. It is the Vulgate that abounds with deliberate corruptions of the true meaning of Scripture.[54] If Nicholas accuses the Jews of having committed various crimes over the course of their history, ibn Musa gives vivid descriptions of debaucheries committed by Christians, both clerics and laymen, in his own day.[55] And just as Nicholas uses rabbinic literature as a source of justification for his arguments, so ibn Musa refers to various works of Christian theology in his own behalf.[56]

Magen wa-Romaḥ appears hereby to aim at confining the Jewish-Christian dispute to the realm of understanding biblical testimonies correctly and removing it from the context of rabbinic and contemporary Judaism. Ibn Musa realized that the first sort of dispute was both an encounter in which the Jew had a better chance of placing his Christian opponent on the defensive and a more strictly academic exchange, one whose issues and outcome did not necessarily have a direct bearing on contemporary Jewry. The Christian attack on rabbinic Judaism and literature, however, struck at the daily religious life of the average medieval Jew. As epitomized for ibn Musa in the works of Nicholas of Lyra, it constituted a clear and present danger to the welfare of the contemporary Jewish community.

53. Ibid., p. 43.
54. Ibid., pp. 33, 35.
55. Ibid., p. 81.
56. Ibid., pp. 93, 97. On the exploitation of Christian theological literature by late medieval Spanish Jewish polemicists, see Netanyahu, *The Marranos*, pp. 84ff.

Nicholas of Lyra presented a scholastic systematization and re-finement of the theory behind the anti-Jewish efforts of Domini-cans and Franciscans. The idea that contemporary Jews and Judaism had no rightful place in Christian Europe was rapidly gaining ac-ceptance among the most prominent of friars, finding its way into the elite among missionaries and scholars. Yet several important questions remain to be posed. Beyond the mendicant activities and writings already discussed, how did the friars implement their new attitude? Could they communicate their ideas to enough strata of Christian society to influence the basic European conception of the contemporary Jew? Furthermore, apart from the unique circum-stances of a situation like the Maimonidean controversy or the vindictiveness of a man like Nicholas Donin, can one account for the evolution of this ideology in medieval Europe and for the key role of the friars in enunciating it?

PART THREE

The Ideology in Perspective: Its Applications and Its Significance

8

Raymond Lull

Of all the religious whose work this book has treated, the Franciscan tertiary Raymond Lull is probably the most well known and colorful figure. And it was he who attempted to apply the anti-Jewish ideology of the friars to the fullest extent of its logical conclusions: if the Jews of medieval Europe had no legitimate place in Christendom, Christians had the responsibility to rid Europe of their presence. Toward that end, Lull devised grandiose schemes for converting the Jewish community to Christianity, systematically and completely; as for those Jews who would ultimately persist in refusing baptism, he advocated their permanent expulsion from Christian society.

Born between 1231 and 1235 in the recently Christianized Catalan island of Majorca, Lull had joined the Aragonese court as a page by his fourteenth birthday; eventually he became the tutor of the crown prince, the future James II of Majorca. But in 1265, while composing a poem to one of his mistresses, Lull experienced the first of a series of visions of Jesus after his crucifixion, visions that initiated a painful and lengthy process of introspection. Lull's famous conversion actually spanned a period of ten years, culminating in 1275 when he placed his estate in the hands of an administrator, left his wife and children, and dedicated his life entirely to the task of converting the infidel to Christianity. In the words of his anonymous contemporary biographer, "The said revered master, now wholly enkindled in the ardour of love for the Cross, deliberated as to what greater or more pleasing act he could do than to convert infidels and unbelievers to the truth of the Holy Catholic Faith, and thereby place his person in the peril of death."[1] By 1275, Lull had completed a decade of concentrated study, con-

1. *A Life of Ramon Lull*, ed. E. Allison Peers (London, 1927), p. 4.

ducted most probably under the direction of Raymond de Peñaforte, who had convinced Lull not to travel to Paris for his education but to remain in his native Majorca, where the Dominican
convent in Palma might meet his spiritual as well as intellectual
needs. During the remainder of his life he did much traveling both
within and outside of Christendom. Yet his years at Palma set the
tone, for while there he began writing and he also engaged in debates with Jews and Muslims, activities that continued to fill his
time until his death in the winter of 1315–1316.[2]

Although when Lull decided to affiliate with the Friars Minor in
the 1290s his marriage necessitated his joining the Third Order of
Saint Francis, his career nevertheless exemplified many aspects of
the Franciscan ideal. Lull's conversion itself resembled that of
Francis; the latter would undoubtedly have approved of Lull's fear-
lessness in appealing to kings, popes, and prelates, his careless-
ness for matters of this world, his devotion to the conversion of
the infidel, and his eventual martyrdom in Muslim North Africa.
Lull's missionary work in general and, in the context of this book,
his mission to the Jews in particular clearly express the spirit of the
mendicant orders which pervaded Latin Christendom during the
thirteenth and fourteenth centuries.

Lull never enjoyed a leisurely schedule in which to pursue his
own research; yet during the last forty-five years of his life, he
managed to write at least 280 books and smaller treatises. The
modern scholarship that has grown up around Lull's work is accordingly quite enormous, and the ensuing discussion of his views
is not intended as a comprehensive review, either of his work or of
the pertinent secondary literature. Virtually every one of his writings touches in some way upon the conversion of the infidels. I
propose simply to demonstrate that Lull continued the development of the basic approach toward the Jews taken by Raymond de
Peñaforte and his disciples, by devising the practical means whereby he believed its goals might really be achieved. In view of Lull's
primacy in the missionary community of his day, that in itself
marked a major advance in this attitude's acceptance into the contemporary European religious consciousness.

2. Annotated, scholarly accounts of Lull's life may be found in E. Allison Peers,
Ramon Lull: A Biography (1929; repr., New York, 1969); and Armand Llinares, *Raymond Lulle: Philosophe de l'action* (Grenoble, 1963). On Lull's period of study and
conversion in Palma, see also the Latin version of his contemporary biography, *A
Life,* ed. Peers, p. 52; Erhard Wolfram Platzeck, *Raimund* Lull, 2 vols. (Rome, 1962–
64), 1:15, 48f.; and Ramon Sugranyes de Franch, "Le 'Livre du Gentil et des trois
sages' de Raymond Lulle," in *JJL,* p. 332.

The Art of Conversion

Lull's concern with the Jews must first be examined from the broader perspective of his efforts and methodology for converting all infidels. Toward this end, Lull developed his famous *Ars*, first elucidated in the early 1270s, which Etienne Gilson has rightly dubbed "a homemade method of apologetics which will infallibly bring about the conversion of unbelievers." The novelty of the *Ars* lay not in its ideas, which amounted to a pretty standard version of Bonaventurian-Augustinian philosophy, but rather in Lull's organization and application of them. Essentially the *Ars* consisted of a list of fundamental concepts or postulates, which Lull liked to inscribe in circles, and which when grouped together in various combinations and permutations offered his proof of the major tenets of Christian theology, metaphysics, and ethics. He hoped that the *Ars* would provide the foolproof means for converting the infidel, since if approached properly, no rational human being would reject its incontrovertible arguments.[3]

Lull was much concerned with what properly approaching and disputing with non-Christians entailed. Above all, Christian missionaries had to have a command of foreign languages, and Lull hoped to establish a number of missionary colleges to achieve that purpose. The first, founded at Miramar, Majorca, in 1276 with the approval of King James II and confirmation of Pope John XXI, opened with an enrollment of thirteen Franciscan friars intent on learning Arabic. Although Lull intended Miramar to be the first of many such colleges, circumstances forced its closing by the end of the century, and Lull spent the rest of his life vainly clamoring for the founding of similar schools.[4] He is commonly recognized as the guiding force behind Clement V's decree at the Council of Vienne in 1311 calling for the establishment of chairs in Hebrew, Arabic, and Aramaic at the papal curia and the universities of Paris, Oxford, Bologna, and Salamanca. Virtually no evidence remains, however, that the provisions of this decree were ever put into effect; one letter of John XXII in 1326 only inquires of Bishop Hugh of Paris as

3. Gilson, *History*, p. 351; J. N. Hillgarth, *Ramon Lull and Lullism in Fourteenth-Century France* (Oxford, 1971), ch. 1.
4. Peers, *Ramon Lull*, pp. 128–36; Berthold Altaner, "Raymundus Lullus und der Sprachenkanon (can. 11) des Konzils von Vienne (1312)," *Historiches Jahrbuch* 53 (1933), 190–219.

to what extent language studies had been organized at Paris in accordance with the decree.[5]

In addition to mastering languages, the Lullian missionary had to structure his confrontation with the infidel so as to induce the latter to convert of his own free will. For this reliance on the power of reason, as opposed to physical force, to effect his aims, Lull has elicited the praise of many modern writers. Although he did advocate compelling the infidels to listen and dispute with Christian preachers and toward the end of his life supported the waging of a military crusade against Islam—battle plans for which he himself undertook to prepare[6]—the emphasis on the *Ars* as the fundamental means of conversion never recedes from his writings. His forensic opponents in his works consequently often emerge his friends, as if Lull were able to draw a clear distinction between the ideas he opposed and the person espousing them.

As early as 1272 in his *Libre de contemplació*, Lull outlined in detail "how a man may perceive and understand which is the best and most truthful course to be taken in a disputation concerning the faith."[7] In this list of instructions for debaters, Lull stated that both parties to a debate must enter with entirely clear and unbiased minds, first establishing their mutual desire for truth and agreeing over common principles upon which they might proceed to build their arguments. They must meet only amiably and ought first to agree in writing as to what kind of argumentation they will admit, that based on sacred sources or that supported by logic. They must make a fair division of the time of the debate, allowing each disputant to correct his opponent's errors. As for the agenda of the debate, Lull advised the Christian missionary first to establish the existence and total perfection of God. Then he should examine each of the three religions based on a system of divine law—

5. Peers, *Ramon Lull*, pp. 350–61; Altaner, "Raymundus Lullus," pp. 207ff.; Llinares, *Raymond Lulle*, pp. 120–22; Ewald Müller, *Das Konzil von Vienne 1311–1312: Seine Quellen und seine Geschichte* (Münster, 1934), pp. 155–57. The decree appears in *Sexti decretales* 5.1.1. On its outcome, see Denifle, *Chartularium*, 2,1:293; cf. also Hailperin, *Rashi*, p. 134, where it is related that the Jewish convert to Christianity Jean Sauvé was sent to teach Hebrew at the University of Paris in 1319–20 in accordance with the Vienne decree; and Burns, "Christian-Islamic Confrontation," p. 1408.

6. See, for example, Berthold Altaner, "Glaubenszwang und Glaubensfreiheit in der Missionstheorie des Raymundus Lullus: Ein Beitrag zur Geschichte des Toleranzgedankens," *Historisches Jahrbuch* 48 (1928), 591, 603; Carl Selmer, "Ramon Lull and the Problem of Persuasion," *Thought* 23 (1948), 215–22; and Ramon Sugranyes de Franch, *Ramon Lulle: Docteur des missions* (Schöneck-Beckenried, Switzerland, 1954), pp. 84ff.

7. Raymond Lull, *Libre de contemplació*, ch. 187, in *Obres essencials*, 2 vols. (Barcelona, 1957), 2:546.

Judaism, Christianity, and Islam—together with its respective attributes and theological particulars. That law which best explicates the nature of God—which according to Lull would always be Christianity—is the only true one. The Christian disputant should have immeasurable patience with his opponent, allowing him as much time as necessary to recover from anger or embarrassment, to pose inquiries, and finally to acknowledge the truth.

How did the Jews enter into this Lullian conversionist framework? It must first be noted that Lull's estimation of Judaism is not entirely negative. In the *Libre de doctrina pueril*, Lull instructs his son that the Jews had always enjoyed the friendship of God because they did not practice idolatry and that God has punished them with servitude only for rejecting Christ. As a result of that divine friendship, which permitted Judaism the honor of giving birth to Christianity, the position of the Jews is superior to that of the Muslims, Lull affirms. At one point, he praises the self-discipline of the Jews over that of Christians, since the Jews pray in synagogues with a separation between men and women. Some scholars have long maintained that Lull was deeply influenced by the Spanish Jewish Kabbalah of the thirteenth century and drew heavily upon it in the formulation of his mystical ideas.[8]

Yet despite this respect for various aspects of Judaism, Lull considered the Jews infidels and usually grouped them as such along with the Muslims.[9] As a result, they too were prime targets of his missionary efforts. Lull himself probably debated extensively with individual Jews in Majorca and Barcelona, and in 1299 he received permission from James II of Aragon to enter Jewish synagogues on Sabbaths and festivals and compel the Jews to hear him preach.[10]

8. Lull, *Libre de doctrina pueril* 13.3, 13.7, 69.7–8, in *Obres doctrinales*, Obres de Ramon Lull 1 (Ciutat de Mallorca, 1906), pp. 29, 30, 123; *Disputatio Raymundi Christiani et Hamar Saraceni*, in *Opera*, ed. I. Salzinger, 10 vols. (1721–42; repr., Frankfurt a.M., 1965), 4:464; *Libre de Blanquerna* 3.71.7, Obres de Ramon Lull 9 (Palma, 1914), p. 258. On Lull and the Kabbalah, see J. M. Millás Vallicrosa, "Algunas relaciones entre la doctrina luliana y la Cabala," *Sefarad* 18 (1958), 241–53; Millás, "The Doctrine of the 'Lullian Dignities' and the Sefiroth [Hebrew]," in *Yitzhak F. Baer Jubilee Volume*, ed. Salo Wittmayer Baron et al. (Jerusalem, 1960), pp. 186–90; Joseph Leon Blau, *The Christian Interpretation of the Cabala in the Renaissance* (New York, 1944), pp. 117–18; and R. J. Z. Werblowsky, review of Raymond Lull, *El "Liber predicationis contra Judeos*," ed. J. M. Millás Vallicrosa [Hebrew], *Tarbiz* 32 (1963), 209–11.

9. Raymond Lull, *Liber de deo maiore et de deo minore*, in *Opera latina*, ed. Fridericus Stegmüller, 5 vols. (Palma, 1959–67), 1:489: "Impono istud nomen 'fidelis' Christiano, et istud nomen 'infidelis' Judaeo et Saraceno."

10. See Lull, *Petitio Raymundi in concilio generali ad acquirendam terram sanctam*, ed. H. Wieruszowski, in "Ramon Lull et l'idée de la Cité de Dieu," *Estudis franciscans* 47 (1935), 107; and Rubio y Lluch, *Documents*, 1:13f. Cf. also Colomer, "Die Beziehung," p. 213; and Peers, *Ramon Lull*, pp. 44, 45, and n.2.

Although Lull studied Arabic and not Hebrew, he did include Hebrew in the curriculum of his missionary colleges, and Hebrew was prominent in Clement V's decree at the Council of Vienne. Lull intended the graduates of his colleges to participate in a worldwide missionary program supervised personally by the pope and his cardinals, and he urged that as a part of this program, the Jews be compelled to hear the missionary sermons of such friars on a regular basis. They should be induced toward conversion with offers of alms and guarantees of permission to retain all their property.[11] Lull recognized that debate with the Jews concerning passages in the Hebrew Bible, for which each side would simply propose and then obstinately cling to its own interpretations, generally proved futile. He therefore asked that the pope institute a special college to train the Jews, who often tended to shy away from rational argument, in grammar, philosophy, and logic. Lull elaborated on this proposal in his *Liber de acquisitione Terrae Sanctae:*

> Jews are men without science, and when a Catholic disputes with them on the basis of reason, they do not understand the rational arguments. Therefore, it would be good for the pope through his college [of cardinals] to ordain (1) that they prepare themselves to respond to the rational arguments by learning science, (2) that they study not Hebrew but Latin or our vernacular, and (3) that they be addressed in the synagogues. If there shall be these provisions, they can be easily converted; and if finally they are not converted, [it would be good] for the pope to order that no one [of them] remain among the Christians. For they are more opposed to the law of the Christians than others, since they say assuredly that Christ is a rather evil man and that he never was nor will be. And daily they blaspheme him in the synagogues, and they say many terrible things, both concerning the blessed Mary and concerning the Apostles—for which reason wisdom, authority, and charity affirm: if they do not convert, let them be ejected from Christendom.[12]

11. Adam Gottron, *Ramon Lulls Kreuzzugsideen* (Berlin, 1912), pp. 67–73; Raymond Lull, *Blanquerna* 3.75.1, 4.80.3–13, pp. 268–69, 296–303. And on the Jews in the program, see also Lull, *Dictat*, in *Obras rimadas*, ed. Gerónimo Rosselló (Palma, 1859), p. 382; *Quae lex sit melior, major, et verior*, in *Vindiciae lullianae*, ed. Antonio-Raymundo Pasqual, 4 vols. (Avignon, 1778), 1:317: "et si noluerint per disputationem convenire aut liberam voluntatem, saltem praedicetur eis fides Catholica, et ad hoc per Christianorum Principes aut exercitus armis munitos compellantur"; *Tractatus de modo convertendi infideles*, in *Opera latina* ed. S. Galmés et al., 3 vols. (Palma, 1952–54), 3:104.

12. Lull, "Le *Liber de acquisitione Terrae Sanctae*," 2.3, p. 274. On the anti-rationalism of the Jews, see, for instance, Lull, *Liber super psalmum quicunque vult sive liber Tartari et Christiani*, Prologue, in *Opera*, ed. Salzinger, 4:348: "Ait illi [i.e., Tartaro] Judaeus: non est decens nec justum quod aliquis existat contra Fidem, ne amittatur

In the *Tractatus de modo convertendi infideles*, Lull explained how all this compulsion might effectively be brought to bear. The Jews in Christendom should be compelled to select representatives to study Latin, logic, and Christian philosophy, so that they might properly understand (and accept) the conversionist arguments of the Church. Jews who successfully completed their studies would engage in a religious disputation with Christian missionaries, to be, it was hoped, converted, so that they themselves might then proselytize in the synagogues. Not only would the Jewish community have to submit to the various aspects of this missionary campaign, but it would also have to finance it, by meeting the expenses of those who participated in the training program and by paying a heavy fine for all those who did not successfully complete it. In a similar vein, at the end of his *Liber de novo modo demonstrandi* Lull begged King Frederick of Sicily to publish his book, to compel the Jews to study it, and eventually to force them to respond to its arguments.[13]

Raymond Lull, like Raymond Martini, viewed the task of converting the Jews as a particularly urgent one; the mere existence of flourishing non-Christian communities posed a threat to the faith of individual Christians as they traveled about the world.[14] Lull therefore did not stop at stressing the importance of the Church's mission to the Jews and at making rather grandiose proposals as to how it might best be pursued. He was very much concerned with the actual arguments to be used against the Jews in disputations, both their substance and their tone. He gave detailed instructions for the use of his *Ars* in the conversion of the Jews, in two interesting and very different compositions: the well-known *Libre del Gentil e los tres savis* (Book of the Gentile and three wise men) and the relatively obscure *Liber predicationis contra Iudeos*.

The Gentile and the Three Wise Men

The *Libre del Gentil e los tres savis*, written during the early 1270s in Majorca, is one of those Lullian works often praised for their mod-

---

meritum; quia si aliquis cognosceret per necessarias Rationes, quod sua Fides esset vera, jam non haberet meritum; ergo utilius est tibi credere, et non intelligere nostram Fidem, ut in Lege Judaica habeas meritum in credendo."

13. Lull, *Tractatus de modo convertendi infideles*, p. 104; *Liber de novo modo demonstrandi* 5.3.10, in *Opera*, ed. Salzinger, 4:610.

14. See Lull, *Quae lex sit melior*, p. 316; and *Peticio Raymundi pro conversione infidelium*, ed. Wieruszowski, in "Ramon Lull," p. 101.

ern standards of tolerance and openmindedness.[15] It is the fictional account of a Gentile philosopher who, distraught at the thought of finding no life or salvation after his imminent death, undertakes a journey through an allegorical forest and there finds three sages—a Jew, a Christian, and a Muslim. The three had previously arrived at a spring irrigating five trees, which, according to a fair and beautiful maiden named Intelligence who there appeared to them, embodied in their various flowers the properties and virtues of God and different combinations of specific virtues and sins. The trees provided man with the rational means for discovering religious truth and solace. With the help of these trees, the sages had agreed to deliberate among themselves until they might discover the sole true law of God, under which all the peoples of the world could be united. Upon encountering the Gentile and learning of his atheism and despair, the sages in the first book of this work proceed to introduce their new acquaintance to religious belief, by means of the flowers of the five trees. The Gentile eagerly accepts a belief in an omnipotent, creator-God and in the resurrection of the dead, and he asks how he might best serve God. Each of the sages naturally wishes to convert the Gentile to his own faith, and in the next three books of the treatise each presents his most important beliefs to the Gentile, attempting to respond to the latter's questions. At the end of the work, the Gentile leaves the three sages without announcing which faith he plans to adopt. In this the sages delight, because they can continue their discussion in an entirely unbiased and objective manner. They resolve to meet again at an appointed time and place, and each then goes his separate way.

The cool and selfless nature of the three sages' discussion stands in strong contrast to the fierce religious zeal typical of many thirteenth-century clerics. When one sage had to speak for all three in teaching the Gentile the rudimentary principles of belief in God, virtues, and vices—the significance of the flowers of the five trees— each courteously wished to defer to his colleagues. They faced a similar problem when each had to explain the tenets of his own faith to the Gentile, and they agreed to present the religions in the

15. See Peers, *Ramon Lull,* p. 97f.; Llinares, *Raymond Lulle,* p. 278; Colomer, "Die Beziehung," pp. 224–25; Lull, *El "Liber predicationis contra Judeos,"* ed. J. M. Millás Vallicrosa (Madrid, 1957), pp. 20–21; and Sugranyes de Franch, "Le 'Livre du Gentil,'" pp. 319–35, passim. Cf. above, n. 6. The *Libre del Gentil e los tres savis* appears in *Obres essencials,* 1:1057–1138.

order of their antiquity: Judaism, Christianity, and then Islam. As each sage spoke, Lull had him present the articles of his own creed quite accurately. Most striking is the refusal at the end of the treatise on the part of the Gentile and of the sages to announce any kind of decision. The sages even apologized to one another in case anyone had offended another during the course of the preceding conversation. All this leads E. Allison Peers to conclude:

> From a superficial perusual of the work, the reader would hardly know which side is taken by its author. . . . The author wished each of the three faiths to stand on its own merits, so that the reader might choose for himself in a fair and unbiased manner. . . . In general it can be said that the arguments of each sage are set forth in similar fashion, with the same scrupulous care. There is no heat, no eloquence, no emotion . . . , and hardly a weakness in the argument on any one side which is not balanced by a weakness in each of the others.[16]

Yet to view the *Libre del Gentil* as an open-ended inquiry into the respective merits of different religions without ulterior motives on the part of its author constitutes a basic misunderstanding of Lull's writings in general and this work in particular. Lull was not an academic philosopher interested in the classification of different systems of belief, but a missionary, and he himself affirms the conversionist character and intention of this treatise. The prologue of the book begins thus:

> Since through activity of long duration we have come to know the conversation and the false and erroneous opinions of the infidels, in order that they themselves may praise our Lord God and arrive at the way of eternal salvation, I, a culpable, contemptible, poor, and sinful man, despised by all people, [I] whose name I reckon unworthy of being inscribed on this or another book, following the method of the Arabic book *Concerning the Gentile*, with all my strength wish to strive, confiding in the help of God, to investigate a new method and new rational arguments whereby the errant can be directed to endless glory and can escape infinite misery.[17]

16. Lull, *Libre del Gentil*, pp. 1060, 1072, 1138; Peers, *Ramon Lull*, pp. 97–98.

17. Lull, *Libre del Gentil*, p. 1057. The specific source for Lull's motif of the three-way dialogue, the *Liber Arabicus de Gentili*, is unknown. Some scholars have suggested Judah ha-Levi's twelfth-century *Kuzari*, while others have rejected this suggestion outright; see Peers, *Ramon Lull*, p. 100, n. 3; Colomer, "Die Beziehung," p. 224; Lull, *El "Liber predicationis,"* ed. Millás, pp. 23–24; and Sugranyes de Franch, "Le 'Livre du Gentil,'" pp. 330–31. It is also possible that Lull knew of Peter Abelard's

The *Libre del Gentil* embodied a demonstration of the new Lullian *Ars*, which, despite the lack of any definite outcome in the encounter in the allegorical forest, had very definite objectives. Even though the Gentile philosopher declined to reveal which faith he intended to espouse, he nevertheless acted as the agent of Lull's skillful and subtle religious polemic, as his discussion with the Jewish sage made clear.[18]

In response to the exposition of the Christian sage the Gentile limited himself to questions that enabled the Christian to elucidate beliefs such as those in the Trinity or incarnation, and he also appeared content with whatever answer he received from the Christian; but he exhibited no such reticence or satisfaction in regard to the Jew's presentation. Rather, concerning five of the eight articles of faith expounded by the Jew, the Gentile poses an objection or question which is usually identical with a common medieval Christian attack on Judaism.

Regarding the Jew's second article of faith, the belief in creation, the Gentile asks a handful of questions, one of which in particular warrants attention. He accepts that God created the earth, but he entreats the Jew to tell him, "What did God do before the earth was created, since God is of greater quality if he is eternal and acts eternally than if his activity had a beginning in time?" The Jew responds that he disagrees with pagan philosophers who claim to attribute greater honor to the world's first cause—that is, God—by stating that his creative action is from all eternity. He rather believes that God created the world in time but that previously God had fashioned in himself "an eternal operation, one loving and understanding him himself, glorying in himself, and understanding all extrinsic things."[19] This argument of the Jew's is astounding

---

Dialogus inter philosophum, Iudeum, et Christianum, PL 178:1609–84. Interestingly, Jewish polemicists of Lull's own generation themselves made use of this motif, although naturally with at least one key difference: the ultimate conversion of the inquirer to Judaism. See J. M. Rosenthal, "A Religious Disputation," p. 71; *The Jewish-Christian Debate*, ed. D. Berger, Heb. pp. 151–53; and Joseph Dan, "An Ashkenazic Story on the Conversion to Judaism of an Arab King [Hebrew]," *Zion*, n.s. 26 (1961), 132–37. Whatever the source upon which Lull drew, Rudolf Brummer, "Un poème latin de controverse religieuse," *Estudios lulíanos* 6 (1962), 275–81, has suggested that the Majorcan missionary may well have popularized this motif and facilitated its entrance into late medieval Latin poetry; see, for example, Hans Walther, *Das Streitgedicht in der lateinischen Literatur des Mittelalters* (Munich, 1920), pp. 227–29.

18. Lull's Gentile was no more receptive to Islam than he was to Judaism, but an account of his exchanges with the Saracen sage is not relevant here.

19. Lull, *Libre del Gentil*, p. 1078.

in that it embodied the basis for Lull's own proof of the Trinity, both as developed by the Christian in the *Libre del Gentil* and as emphasized repeatedly in the *Liber predicationis contra Iudeos:*[20] the elements of a creator (*gignens*), a creature (*genitus*), and a process of creation (*gignere*) are necessary components of the most perfect deity, since according to Lull and as the Gentile has here stated, "God is of greater quality if he is eternal and acts eternally than if his activity had a beginning in time."

The Jew next states his third belief, that the divine law was revealed to Moses on Mount Sinai, and the Gentile inquires if the Christians and Muslims also believe in this law. After explaining that although these two groups accept the fact of the Sinaitic revelation, they have added to and subtracted from the law of the Jews, the Jew concludes that they thus do not believe in it. Specifically, he notes, "we (and the Christians agree on the text of the *old* law, but we) disagree over [our respective] glosses and explanations, which contradict each other. Therefore, we cannot come to agreement by means of textual evidence, and we are searching for the necessary rational arguments which will make us agree."[21] Once again, the opinion expressed appears more like that of Raymond Lull than that of a real Jew, even one who would have been willing to dispute matters of faith with a Christian. No Jew would have referred to the law of Moses as "the old law"; and one notes that while elsewhere Lull castigates the Jews for their defective rational faculties and their unwillingness to debate with him according to the logic of his *Ars*, the Jew here offers a striking exception to that generalization, adhering fully to Lull's own opinions.[22]

The Jew proceeds to his fourth and most controversial article of faith, that the messiah will come at some time in the future; here too, the justification offered for this belief might lead the Gentile to espouse Christianity sooner than Judaism. The Jew asserts that if the law of God could not be observed in its entirety, it would betray a defect in the divine intelligence. And "since we are enslaved to all the nations on account of the sin of the first parents, and because of the slavery in which we now are held, we cannot rightly keep or fulfill the law which God gave us and which we would and could keep better, as ordained by command . . . , if we

20. Ibid., pp. 1090ff.; Lull, *El "Liber predicationis,"* pp. 73ff., passim.
21. Lull, *Libre del Gentil*, p. 1080, with the variant of the original Latin translation in *Opera*, ed. Salzinger, 2:50 (emphasis mine).
22. Cf. Lull, *"Le Liber de acquisitione Terrae Sanctae,"* 3.1, p. 277.

would be free. Thus it necessarily follows that God will send the messiah to redeem and free us from servitude and captivity." After the Jew has further related how the concept of divine charity, on account of which the Jews have survived for so long in captivity, will assure the coming of the messiah, a very interesting dialogue takes place. The Gentile asks about the length of and reason for the Jews' captivity, and the Jew replies: "We previously were in two periods of captivity; one that lasted for seventy years and the other four hundred. But this one, in which we now are, has lasted more than 1400. Regarding the first two periods of captivity, we know well the reason for which we were in them. Yet as to why we are in the present captivity we understand no reason." Although the Gentile has before this conversation never heard of Judaism (and still knows nothing of Christianity), he has a suggestion with which to relieve the Jew of his bewilderment: "Is it possible that you are in a certain [state of] sin, through which you are opposed to the goodness of God, that you do not believe you are in this sin, and that you do not seek forgiveness from the divine goodness, which accords with justice? Because of this justice, he [God] does not wish to liberate you, until you recognize your sins and ask forgiveness for them."[23]

No Jew ever interpreted the worldwide dispersion of his people as punishment for the sins of Adam and Eve; Jews rather explain the enduring diaspora in terms of the present state of the Jews, their religion, and the world. If God dispersed the Jews on account of Adam and Eve, why did not all other peoples, also descendants of the first parents, share in this punishment? And why then was there not one long uninterrupted period of captivity, beginning with the day of man's fall from the garden of Eden? Not only did rabbinic Judaism always spurn the concept of original sin, but it also never negated the value of Jewish religious observance in the diaspora, as Lull's Jew seems to do. The reader need only refer to the stance taken by Naḥmanides at the Barcelona disputation of 1263—with which Lull, who then had close ties to the Aragonese court, most probably was familiar—to ascertain that Iberian Jews did not always admit to looking forward to the messianic age as a period when the value of their religious lives would be enhanced.[24]

23. Lull, *Libre del Gentil*, p. 1081.
24. See above, Ch. 5, n. 26. On the emphasis of Sefardic Jewish messianism on political redemption in this world, see Gerson D. Cohen, "Messianic Postures of Ashkenazim and Sephardim," in *Studies of the Leo Baeck Institute*, ed. Max Kreutzberger (New York, 1967), pp. 117–56, passim.

And finally, few, if any medieval Jewish sages professed total ignorance of the reasons for their dispersion and would certainly have not accepted instruction from a Gentile in such matters.

Rather than adhering to a truly Jewish explanation of Judaism, Lull has had his imaginary Jewish sage open himself to the charges of a severe Christian polemical attack. The Jew first explains his present state of captivity just as a Christian theologian would: a result of still living in a state of sin inherited from Adam and Eve and, by implication, of not having opened himself to redemptive divine grace. In that state of captivity, the Jew adds in perfect Pauline fashion, he is incapable of observing biblical law as it should be observed. The Jews, the sage then remarks, have survived in dispersion only as a gift of divine charity, another statement characteristic of medieval Christian theology. And the Gentile's explanation of the present period of Jewish captivity—namely, that the Jews live in a fashion which makes them inimical to the goodness of God—which the Jewish sage silently accepts, reminds one of the basic charge of Raymond Martini: the allegiance of rabbinic (contemporary) Jews lies not with God but with his adversaries.[25] Can one then wonder if at the end of this fourth article of the Jewish faith, before he has heard the remaining four and before he has heard anything of Christianity or Islam, the Gentile expresses his opinion that to accept Judaism would be most foolhardy?

> If I, who am free, would become a Jew, would I be in the captivity in which you are? And in exchange for leaving my error, would I enter into slavery rooted in sin in which you say you are, because on account of that crime you have been placed in captivity? This does not seem fitting to me according to the ordinance which is suitable to be ordained by divine wisdom, goodness, power, and justice. For the ordinance would be better, and it would better suit the condition of the trees, if a man, who is sensually free insofar as his body is concerned and is in error as regards his soul, by deserting his error would arrive at corporeal liberty in which he can better observe his law, and if he would not pass from one error to another nor from one guilt to another.[26]

Even though at the end of the *Libre del Gentil*, the Gentile does not announce which faith he has chosen, he surely gives notice rather early in the book that he will not become a Jew.

25. Cf. Augustine, *De civitate Dei* 18.46; and above, Ch. 6.
26. Lull, *Libre del Gentil*, pp. 1082–83.

Moving on to the fifth article of his faith, the belief in resurrection, the Jewish sage tells the Gentile that among the Jews there exist three different opinions concerning this doctrine, and he offers a short summary of each. The Gentile responds immediately with the common Lullian claim that if the Jews were not so deficient in their command of logic and philosophy, they could more readily arrive at an apprehension of the truth. Their diversity of opinions in matters of theology underscores the irrational basis of their beliefs and their lack of concern for salvation by God. The Jew does not retort, as he might have done, that the Gentile, who only several minutes ago arrived at his own belief in resurrection, ought not to pass judgment too quickly on the ancient beliefs of others. Nor does the Jew marvel that the Gentile has leveled the same charge at Judaism as Christians have always done, that Judaism emphasizes the concerns of this world and ignores those of the next. Instead, he makes several startling admissions.

> We so much desire to regain the freedom which we were accustomed to have in this world and so much desire that the messiah should come and free us from the captivity in which we are, that we hardly consider the next world—all the more so, since we have been seized and forced to live among the nations who hold us in captivity and whom we pay annually great tribute, for otherwise they would not permit us to live among them. Moreover, you ought to know, something else impedes us, namely that our language and literature are in Hebrew which is no longer so much in use as it used to be, and are [thus] debased on account of ignorance. Therefore, we do not have so many books in the science of philosophy and other fields as we ought. There is nevertheless one science among us called Talmud; it is great and of great and subtle exposition. It is of so great and subtle exposition that it impedes us from taking note of the next world, especially since through it we incline to the law so that we might have our complement of temporal goods of this world.[27]

Had Raymond Lull wished to give a picture of a fair and friendly debate between three sages of different faiths, would he have portrayed the Jew as conceding what no medieval Jew would have admitted: the ignorance of the Jews in science and philosophy, the defects of Hebrew literature, the misleading nature of the Talmud, and above all the disregard of the Jews for the world to come? Furthermore, Lull himself elsewhere bemoans how to the infidels

27. Ibid., pp. 1083–84.

Christianity with all its various sects and heresies appears incon-
stant and unsure of the truth. He even laments how a Muslim once
chose Judaism over Christianity for precisely that reason.[28] In the
Libre del Gentil, however, one finds such a defect in Judaism alone.

In the discussion of the Jew's last three articles of faith, the
Gentile asks numerous questions but generally refrains from criti-
cizing the Jewish view of the final day of judgment, of paradise,
and of hell. The one exception occurs in the exchange concerning
the day of judgment. The Gentile asks the Jew how an invisible God
can pass sentence on those who appear before him corporeally.
The Jew responds that the same visible similitude of God which
appeared to Moses will hand down the sentences to those appearing for judgment. The Gentile, who speaks last in this piece of
dialogue, then reflects that the judgment would be more perfect if
God might assume some visible form himself and thus enable
those coming before him to see their judge. Although the Gentile
here falls short of mentioning the advantages of a belief in the
incarnation, the Christian sage, when he later explains his own
belief in the day of judgment, emphasizes that "it is right that he
who passes judgment be God and man."[29] Lull may well have deliberately left this point unresolved in the Gentile's discussion with
the Jew, so as to enable the Christian to harp on the superiority of
his own belief later.

If the *Libre del Gentil* indeed does exemplify the fairness and
equanimity of Raymond Lull's mission to the infidels, as many
have maintained, then perhaps that mission—at least insofar as it
was directed to the Jews—does not deserve all the praise it has
received for its tolerance and willingness to encounter opposing
viewpoints honestly and straightforwardly. It is true that the cordial relationship of the three sages—the willingness to defer to one
another in conversation, their pleasure at the Gentile's refusal to
announce his final decision to them, and their resolve to follow the
dictates of their rational conclusions in whatever direction they
might lead—would have been a most singular one in the thirteenth
century, given the atmosphere of religious dogmatism and mili-
tancy which generally prevailed. Yet that aspect of Lull's work is
fictional, or at best hypothetical; and Lull was neither a novelist
nor a theoretician by trade. He states at the outset that this work of
his has a decidedly missionary intent. He hoped to move its read-

28. Lull, "Le *Liber de acquisitione Terrae Sanctae*," 3.1, p. 277.
29. Lull, *Libre del Gentil*, pp. 1085, 1116.

ers along a very clear and predetermined path of action. He meant to convert Jews and Saracens to Christianity by means of the Lullian *Ars*, which ostensibly called for amiability and a lack of prejudice among those who disputed matters of faith.[30] Our own reading of the *Libre del Gentil*, however, suggests that the tolerance and impartiality of the Lullian method were not so real at all. Yet giving the impression that they were—by means of the veneer of the sages' mutual cordiality—constituted an important, subtle tactical ploy, a skillful attempt to convince the reader that the presentation of opposing religious viewpoints before him was entirely fair.

The Book of Preaching Against the Jews

Raymond Lull, unlike the heroes of the *Libre del Gentil*, would surely have been dissatisfied if completely objective rational argument led one to choose Judaism over Christianity. He clearly desired to convert the Jews and did and wrote everything he could to achieve that goal. For he viewed Judaism as possessing no inherent validity as a religion of God, an attitude that he developed more succinctly in the *Liber predicationis contra Iudeos*. Lull completed the *Liber predicationis*, which appears in manuscripts under various other titles as well, in August 1305 in Barcelona.[31] As opposed to the *Libre del Gentil*, where Lull portrayed a single exemplary debate between a Christian, a Jew, and a Muslim, both so as to influence non-Christian readers and to provide a model of how such discussions ought to be conducted, the *Liber predicationis* provides Christian missionaries with a host of different arguments which they can employ to prove the Jews in error. The book is essentially a compendium for the use of Christian clerics in implementing the Lullian call to compel the Jews (and Saracens) to listen to missionary sermons on a regular basis. As Lull explains, "In this book we therefore intend to place fifty [really fifty-two] sermons, so that in any week of the year a man can have a distinctly different sermon, and in any of them there will be many sermons suggested."[32]

30. This aspect of Lull's *Ars*, particularly as applied to the Jews, was not limited to the *Libre del Gentil*. Cf. his romance *Blanquerna* 4.81.1–2, pp. 296–97, where the cardinal instructs Jewish and Christian disputants in Rome that they must bear no ill will against each other and must remain friends; this was the only way for them to reason together constructively.

31. Platzeck, *Raimund Lull*, 2:47; Lull, *El "Liber predicationis,"* ed. Millás, pp. 32–33.

32. Lull, *El "Liber predicationis,"* p. 74. The arguments pertaining to the Trinity and incarnation Lull directs to both the Jews and the Saracens, but the inclusion of a

The sermons of the *Liber predicationis* attempt to demonstrate to the Jews the error in their own faith and the superiority of Christianity. Lull commenced with the observation that the Jews assert the authority and the truth of Mosaic law, that "the intellect is naturally the judge of reason," and that the Jews are noted for the Ten Commandments. He therefore proclaimed his intention to prove the errors of the Jews with texts from the Old Testament, with reason, and with reference to biblical commandments; in each sermon, Lull vowed, he would combine both *ratio* and *auctoritas*.[33] Thus emphasizing rational argument and yet taking into account the Jewish reliance on the Old Testament, the *Liber predicationis* presented the substance of the conversionist program which the Lullian *Ars* prescribed for the Jews. With the technical knowledge of the *Ars* and the specific arguments suggested by the sermons, Lull believed that a missionary could easily confound the infidels.[34]

Despite Lull's claim that the *Liber predicationis* provides the Christian preacher with a different sermon for each week of the year, the arguments of the entire work can be summarized under three headings. First, perhaps because of all Christian beliefs the Jews found that in the Trinity most difficult to accept, forty-three of the fifty-two sermons deal in some way with establishing that belief and with the sin of the Jews in rejecting it. In the first two sermons, Lull tries to substantiate his belief in the Trinity with both scriptural and logical arguments. The first sermon begins with the words of the Vulgate in Psalm (109) 110:3, "Before the first light I bore you (*ante luciferum genui te*)." Lull distinguishes in these words between the subject in the first person, the object in the second person, and the process of generation in the predicate. Since the generation occurred *ante luciferum*, it must have been an eternal process; and "since before *luciferum* no being was created," the generation had to have been part of God. Lull continues:

> By generation, however, we allude to the generator (*gignentem*), the generated (*genitum*), and the act of generating (*gignere*), without all of which there can be no generation. Thus it clearly follows that in God

---

number of sermons dealing with the errors in the Jews' understanding of the Mosaic commandments indicates that the prime targets of this missionary work were the Jews.

33. Ibid., p. 71.

34. Ibid., p. 97: "In sermone isto est datum exemplum per quod homo sciens Artem Generalem, sciet applicare profecias sive auctoritates Biblie cum proposicionibus necessariis, prout in isto sermone facimus, et talis doctrina est valde utilis ad confundendum infideles."

there is a plurality and a distinction—one [which existed] eternally—between *gigentem, genitum,* and *gignere.* The *gignentem* we call God the father, *genitum* God the son, and *gignere* is the act common to each one, in the father through activity and in the son through passivity. And since they love each other, we understand [the son] to be infused with life through love, which is the Holy Spirit.[35]

In the next sermon Lull offers corroborating logical argumentation based upon the premise that for God's goodness to be perfect, it can have need of nothing external to itself in order to exist.

God is by nature good per se, and he is fundamentally good through his goodness. Since because of his goodness there necessarily must be an activity—namely, to do good—it is clear that he should have a subject to which he may have the nature of doing good [he should have a recipient of his goodness], and that this [subject] be infinite and eternal, in order that the doing good itself may thus be infinite and eternal, as it is through the essence and nature of the divine goodness.

Him who does good (*bonificans*) Lull identifies as God the father, the recipient of this good (*bonificatum*) God the son, and their mutual relationship of goodness and love (*bonificare*) the Holy Spirit.[36] Although Lull did not himself conceive of this proof of the Trinity, he exploited it to the utmost in his anti-Jewish polemical sermons.[37] Besides the verse from Psalm 110 with which he began the *Liber predicationis,* he adduced many other Old Testament passages supposedly alluding to the Trinity; the Jews' denial of the Trinity accordingly amounted to an outright rejection of divine Scripture. Included in the fourteen biblical texts specifically cited to prove this assertion are God's identification of himself to Moses as "the God of Abraham, the God of Isaac, the God of Jacob" (Exodus 3:6); the exclamation of Isaiah that "holy, holy, holy is the Lord of hosts" (6:3); and the commandment to "love the Lord your God with all your heart and soul and strength" (Deuteronomy 6:5). With regard to virtually every such text, Lull accuses the Jews of blasphemy, since a refusal to accept the Trinity implied a denial of the

35. Ibid., p. 73.
36. Ibid., p. 74.
37. See Stanislaus Simon, *Mose ben Salomo von Salerno und seine philosophischen Auseinandersetzungen mit dem Lehren des Christentums* (Ohlau i. Schl., 1931), pp. 41–43; Lull, *El "Liber predicationis,"* ed. Millás, pp. 58ff.; and Platzeck, *Raimund Lull,* 2:155, n. 109.

veracity of God's word.[38] Thus he ends his discussion of Isaiah's trinitarian prophecy, " 'Shall I bring to the point of birth and not deliver?' the Lord says" (66:9), "We have therefore proven sufficiently clearly the most blessed Trinity of God, without which the prophecy could not be true. And inasmuch as the Jews and Saracens blaspheme it [the Trinity], they fall into a contradiction—namely, that the prophecy is true and that it is not true—whence it has been demonstrated that they are in error and in the anger of God."[39] The consistency of this error that the Jews made in understanding the Bible then led Lull to advance a more far-reaching assertion. After arguing that a rejection of the Trinity necessitates a denial of the biblical teaching that man was created in the image of God (Genesis 1:26–27), he concludes: "Thus the Jews and Saracens speak wickedly when they deny the divine Trinity; for in denying it they deny the aforementioned biblical text, and thus they are outside of the law (*extra legem*)."[40]

Denial of the Trinity also led the Jews to terrible logical conclusions concerning the nature of God. Since the Trinity is among the essential properties of God, unlike, for instance, his role as creator of the universe, refusing to believe in it connotes a rejection of the basic divine nature that even the Jews claimed to affirm. Because the three elements of the Trinity are necessary in order for God to be a perfect unity, the Jews' rejection of such a concept of unity logically permits the existence of numerous imperfect deities.[41] Yet even the Jews maintain that they believe God to be the ultimate in perfection, the *principium perfectum*; logic dictates that there then ought to be no quality which might have made him more simple (as in a perfect unity), more infinite or eternal, or more powerful and beneficent which he did not always have as an essential property of his existence. If the Trinity is indeed one such attribute, as Lull claims to have proved, then the Jew *as Jews* shoud be obliged to believe in it; such belief constitutes the only route of escape from their present philosophical error.[42] "If God did not have infinite and eternal power, he could not be a simple necessary being nor be infinitely and eternally active; and if he were not infinitely active, he would not necessarily exist. Whoever denies this is foolish, but

38. Lull, *El "Liber predicationis,"* pp. 77–79, 83–84, 89–91, 95–97, 105–6, 114–15, 118–19, 125–26, 142–43, 144–45, etc.
39. Ibid., p. 102.
40. Ibid., p. 93.
41. Ibid., pp. 76–77, 79–80.
42. Ibid., esp. pp. 85–86, 93–94, 98–99, 102–3, 116, 127–28.

the Jews and Saracens deny that God has the infinite and eternal activity of generation. They therefore agree with the fool who says in his heart, 'There is no God'" (cf. Psalm 14:1).[43]

After attacking the Jews' denial of the Trinity on both scriptural and logical grounds, Lull combines the two approaches in an effort to demonstrate that when they reject the Trinity, they contravene important Mosaic commandments. The injunction of the Ten Commandments to have no alien god (*deum alienum*) is disregarded by the Jews in three different ways, when they deny the trinitarian nature of God. For God not to be *alienus*, he must have been close to man and become incarnate, a direct result of his trinitarian nature. Moreover, even if God were not a Trinity, the three elements of the Trinity (*gignens, genitus, gignere*) still exist in every human being; there must then have been a *deus alienus* in whose trinitarian image man was created. Finally, if God himself taught in Scripture that he was not trinitarian and therefore not omnipotent, it would be absurd for any people to follow his commandments; the Jews must then contend that they obey the precepts of a different god, a deity inherently alien and false.[44] Rejection of the Trinity also makes the Jews spiritually responsible for the murder of their own souls; for when they deny the life-giving operation of the Trinity (*vivificans, vivificatus, vivificare*), their souls die in sin.[45] Because they really do not refer to God when they claim to, they take his name in vain, and they do not fulfill the commandment to love God with all of their hearts, souls, and strength. Denying God his trinitarian perfection, they also offer false testimony against him and steal from his glory.[46]

The second of the three major concerns of the *Liber predicationis* lies with the Jews' rejection of the Christian belief in the incarnation; not without reason was the book occasionally entitled *Liber de trinitate et incarnatione adversus Iudeos et Sarracenos*. Although Lull deals with the incarnation much less than, and often as a corollary

43. Ibid., p. 119.
44. Ibid., pp. 81–82: "Quia iudei et sarraceni talem operationem abnegant, sic habent Deum alienum et extraneum et etiam ydolorum, sicut si negarent quod Deus non esset prima causa, nec creator nec etiam dominator. Probatum est ergo satis evidenter quod iudei et sarraceni non [habent] Deum verum, sed fictum et falsum, et etiam quia non tenent predictum preceptum."
45. Ibid., p. 113: "Quia iudei et sarraceni negant et blasfemant ipsam, moritur anima eorum in peccato, et sic sunt contra mandatum, et per consequens, in errore et in ira Dei. . . . Cum iudei et sarraceni negent in divina bonitate vivificantem, etc., negando vitam supremam, anima eorum in peccato moritur."
46. Ibid., pp. 87–89, 103–5, 117–18.

to, the belief in the Trinity, his approaches to the two subjects follow similar lines. The incarnation provides the best conceptual framework for understanding a plethora of passages from the Old Testament, ranging from the commandment not to eat fish without fins and scales (Deuteronomy 14:10), to the exclamation of the Psalmist (33:5) that God's "love unfailing fills the earth," to Isaiah's vision (53:4) of the Suffering Servant who "bore our afflictions." The incarnation enables one to behold in God the greatest of human virtues; if it thus serves to enhance God's greatness it logically must be true. And because the incarnation increased man's feelings of emotional proximity to his neighbors, it facilitated better observance of the Ten Commandments' injunction against coveting. By denying the incarnation, the Jew deprived himself of all these benefits.[47]

Lull concluded that, in many ways, belief in the Trinity and in the Incarnation made Christianity an indisputably better faith than Judaism. The two articles of faith allow Christianity to proffer more love and knowledge of God, to give rise to more faith and hope in God, and better to demonstate the greater glory of God and his saints. The Trinity and incarnation make Christianity the faith which bespeaks the best things concerning God and has the best ability to preach about God, to teach about him, and to define his nature. On account of these beliefs, Christian theology demonstrates the greatest harmony between God's actions and his nature as well as the greatest concord between God and man. Interestingly, Lull contends that believing in the Trinity and the incarnation best predisposes man to observing the commandment against adultery, as evidenced by the chastity and asceticism of Christians in contrast to the luxurious and polygamous ways of the Jews (and Saracens).[48] For the sin of slandering and denying God incarnate and the Trinity, concluded Lull, the Jews rightly suffer eternal punishment.

> The Jews are and have been in sin; they indeed have been in sin, since for four hundred years they remained in captivity and again in another captivity for seventy years. Then, however, a remedy was implemented [for the captivities] on account of the penitence which they undertook. But [deserving to be punished] with this captivity in which

47. Ibid., pp. 122–25, 138–39, 140–41.
48. Ibid., pp. 107–8, 111–12, 119–22, 123–24, 130–32, 134–36, 137–38, 145–46, 148–50.

they are now . . . , they sinned inasmuch as they betrayed and killed Christ our God, hate and blaspheme him, and do the same [hate and blaspheme] to the Trinity. Whence it follows reasonably enough that all of them who die go to hell, since they die in sin.[49]

Finally, several of the sermons in the *Liber predicationis* stress neither the Trinity nor the incarnation but rather the sin of the Jews' misinterpretation of key Mosaic commandments. Honoring one's father and mother (Exodus 21:12, Deuteronomy 5:16), one of the few individual precepts of the Pentateuch accompanied by a promise of future reward, could not suffice to merit future salvation if understood literally and really must be interpreted as honoring God the father and the mother Church. The prohibition against eating animals who do not chew their cud or do not have split hooves (Leviticus 11:4, Deuteronomy 14:7) likewise ought to be explained only figuratively: chewing the cud—the process whereby an animal digests food only after having eaten it a second time—implies that observance of the new law surpasses that of the old in the attainment of cardinal and theological virtues; a split hoof stresses the distinction between one's corporeal and spiritual existence. On its surface, the injunction against eating pork (Leviticus 11:7, 14:8) contravenes an important motivation for God's creation of the physical world—nourishing man; one must therefore interpret it to apply not to eating pork but to imitating the base mode of behavior of the pig. Or why should God care to prohibit the planting of different species together (Leviticus 19:19, Deuteronomy 22:9)? Here too the precept aims at drawing distinctions—between corporeal and spiritual, imagination and intellect, or belief and understanding.[50] These examples demonstrate, in Lull's view, how the Jews misunderstood the real intent of the law and so do not observe it properly. As in the case of the commandment to keep the Sabbath, which since the redemption of humanity by Christ has been transferred from Saturday to Sunday, the Jews have not recognized the era of the new law, and they do not celebrate the Lord's day. For this reason they remain in captivity, vainly awaiting the messiah, destined to eternal damnation once they have died.[51]

To appreciate the nature of Raymond Lull's anti-Jewish polemic,

49. Ibid., p. 110.
50. Ibid., pp. 108, 128, 132–33, 147–48.
51. Ibid., pp. 99–100.

one ought to note that even though Lull did not know Hebrew or acquaint himself with rabbinic literature, the genre of philosophical argumentation embodied in the *Liber predicationis* impressed contemporary Jewish writers as posing a serious danger. In other words, although Lull did not follow the lead of Pablo Christiani or Raymond Martini in his choice of specific arguments, his writings fall into the new mendicant brand of polemic directed at the Jews of its own day for particular practical purposes. Unfortunately, no direct Jewish responses to Lull have remained with which this assertion might readily be substantiated. If it is considered, however, that Lull might be one of the several representatives of a new trend in anti-Jewish polemic whose writings have survived, the responses of Jewish polemicists to Lullian sorts of arguments advanced by other Christian clerics can still serve the same purpose.

In a preceding chapter, we noted how Lull's own contemporary and acquaintance, Rabbi Solomon ibn Adret of Barcelona, reacted vehemently against the charges of Raymond Martini that the Jews had abandoned the correct observance of the Old Testament, the third theme of the *Liber predicationis*. But the main thrust of the *Liber predicationis* was its logical assertion of the threefold operation inherent in God and men—*gignens, genitus, gignere, bonificans, bonificatus, bonificare*; or *intellectivus, intelligibilis, intelligere*—which Lull defined as the Trinity. A Jewish response to this type of argument appears in a pamphlet, simply entitled *Ta'anot* (Arguments), written by Moses ben Solomon of Salerno in the middle of the thirteenth century.[52]

The setting in which Moses ben Solomon lived and wrote, as well as the nature of his anti-Christian polemic, offers interesting parallels and insights to the work of Raymond Lull. Both Moses' Salerno and Lull's Majorca had advanced, highly cosmopolitan Mediterranean cultures which derived from intense contacts between Judaism, Christianity, and Islam.[53] Just as Lull intended his *Liber predicationis* to serve as a handbook for Christian preachers, so Moses' *Ta'anot*, written in Hebrew, aimed to offer advice and assistance to Jews who disputed with Christians.[54] The philosophical discussions

52. Published in part with a German translation by Simon, *Mose ben Salomo*.

53. Ibid., p. 47; Charles and Dorothea Singer, "The Origin of the Medical School at Salerno, the First University: An Attempted Reconstruction," in *Essays on the History of Medicine Presented to Karl Sudhoff*, ed. Charles Singer and Henry E. Sigerist (London, 1924), pp. 121–38; Peers, *Ramon Lull*, pp. 1–5; Llinares, *Raymond Lulle*, ch. 1, passim.

54. Güdemann, *Geschichte*, 2:230.

excerpted by Moses in the "Arguments" reflect a milieu of level-headed intellectual exchange between members of different faiths which Lull advocated and himself probably experienced in Spain.[55] And significantly, Moses reveals in his pamphlet that he engaged in this sort of argumentation with a large number of different Christian clerics, including friars, bishops, and Jewish converts to Christianity.[56] From this one may deduce that the particular arguments under discussion represented live, relevant, and pressing issues of the day as well as the anti-Jewish polemical approach common to many—perhaps a specific school of—Christian missionaries at the time.

Moses begins his pamphlet with an attack upon the Trinity based on a Maimonidean interpretation of Aristotle, according to which nothing immaterial can be said to have a finite number of specific properties. Therefore, as Moses relates he has proposed to various Christian disputants, God cannot be three.[57] Then Moses states, "After this introduction I am [now] going to prove that their faith is a faith of naught,"[58] and he devotes the entire pamphlet to the refutation of those Christian beliefs posing the greatest danger to Judaism—those in the incarnation and the Trinity. Apart from its emphasis on these two beliefs, most of Moses' treatise does not respond directly to the claims of Lull's *Liber predicationis*, but near its end the *Ta'anot* recounts:

55. Although I have here adduced the work of Moses ben Solomon to show how Jews felt threatened by the sort of argumentation used by Lull to prove his beliefs in the Trinity and incarnation, the affinity between the polemical controversies in which each author was involved can further be demonstrated—as by Simon, *Mose ben Salomo*, pp. 40–50—by the fact that Lull in his writings felt obliged to respond to anti-trinitarian arguments posed by Moses in the *Ta'anot*. Moses, for example, at p. x, contends that if the members of the Trinity are all the same entity, when one of the three became incarnate, so should the other two have entered human flesh, a logical conclusion rejected by the Christians. Or at pp. xi and xiii, Moses objects that the very idea of incarnation would put limits on God—a logical impossibility—by confining him in time and space. Lull counters those arguments in the *Liber super psalmum quicunque vult* 35.7–8, pp. 371–72, and the *Disputatio fidelis et infidelis* 4.8, in *Opera*, ed. Salzinger, 4:403.

56. Moses mentions that he had interchanges with a Dominican, Nicholas de Paglia of Giovenazzo (Simon, *Mose ben Salomo*, pp. i, 12, 52 and n. 4), a medical writer, Petrus di Birboa (pp. iv, 57 and n. 18), a "little friar" (a Minorite?) named Philip (p. v), an unnamed bishop (p. viii), a Christian teacher named Philip (p. ix), an apostate from Judaism named Philip of Tuscany (p. xviii; cf. Güdemann, *Geschichte*, 2:228), and a bishop named Mazio (Simon, p. xx).

57. Simon, *Mose ben Salomo*, pp. i–ii.

58. Ibid., p. ii.

Said Philip the apostate [Jewish convert to Christianity] from Tuscany, "Listen, O Jew. Behold, you have debated with Christians and yet refused to humble yourself to them, and you have not believed in the son of God. Now listen and understand that God does have a son; for the philosophers have already demonstrated that God is the intelligence, the intellective, and the intelligible. There are three—intelligence, intellective, and intelligible—and this is our Trinity."[59]

Moses then explains why he deems this Christian contention particularly important. "I the Hebrew have been obliged to review and write about this argument of this man, because the friars called *predicatores* have endeavored to prove the Trinity in just such a way as the philosophers have said that God is intelligence, intellective, and intelligible—this being the way of those that are foolish. . . ."[60] His response to this claim of the Dominicans interests us not nearly as much as the fact and significance of the claim itself: Lull's *Liber predicationis* must be viewed within the overall context of mendicant anti-Jewish polemic in the thirteenth century. It was fraught with real, practical consequences for contemporary European Jewry and accordingly elicited adamant refutation from the Jews.

The Lullian Option: Conversion or Banishment

How then can one understand the approach of Raymond Lull to the Jews and Judaism? Following the lead of the papal Inquisition and the school of Raymond de Peñaforte, Lull did not allot any proper place in Christian society to the Jews of his day. For the Jews no longer preserved the Old Testament, as Augustine had written that they must, but they were outlaws (*extra legem*), having forsaken completely the proper observance of the Bible.

The Jews lived in hostility to the divine goodness, and for this they were punished with physical, mental, and spiritual captivity, which they themselves prolonged by clinging to the errors of the Talmud and rabbinic Judaism. The Jews had lost the friendship of

59. Ibid., p. xviii.
60. Ibid., p. xix. On the use of this argument by Christian polemicists and Jewish responses to it, see Daniel J. Lasker, *Jewish Philosophical Polemics against Christianity in the Middle Ages* (New York, 1977), pp. 77–83. This trinitarian argument is also among those used against the infidel by Thomas Aquinas in the *Liber de veritate* 4.11, 14, 3:264–70, 273–76.

God which they once enjoyed, and Lull evidently felt justified in placing them in the same class of infidels as the Saracens. Their blasphemous rejection of Christian beliefs by failing to admit to the dictates of logic and reason *incumbent upon them even as Jews* made them, like the Saracens, a real threat to Latin Christendom, which Lull described as a continual attack upon Christ.[61]

In response to this hostility, the practical dangers to Christians which derived from it, and the inadequacy of existing methods for converting the Jews, Lull undertook—with a great sense of urgency—to devise a missionary program for them. Although the conversionist methodology he developed may well have called for amicable and low-keyed intellectual discussions between Christian and Jewish clergy, it nevertheless had as its goal the systematic conversion of the Jews, the elimination of the Jewish presence from Christendom. In other words, while Lull desired to train Jews in Latin, logic, and philosophy, so that they might debate constructively with Christian clerics, this was no more than a means to his ultimate objective. He indeed demanded that those Jewish trainees who eventually failed to convert to Christianity and to help proselytize among their former coreligionists be expelled from Christendom forever; their sin exceeded that of their brethren. And because Judaism had no proper place in a Christian world, Christians who permitted Jews to live in their community revealed an inadequate love for the various objects of Jewish blasphemy: God, the Trinity, and the virgin Mary. In the case of the latter Lull concluded:

> Therefore, since Jews exist among Christians and speak and commune with them, and [since] Christians let them houses in which they pronounce such great blasphemies concerning our lady, through this it is signified that Christians do not love our lady with the love with which they should love her and with which she is worthy of being loved. For, if Christians loved our lady perfectly, they would recall and understand and hate the insults which the Jews cause and speak against her, and they would preach to them and convert them. Or if this [converting the Jews] could not be done, they would not commune

---

61. Lull, *El "Liber predicationis,"* pp. 144–45: "Item iudei et etiam sarraceni sunt iniqui contra Christum Dominum nostrum eo quia blasfemant et vulnerant ipsum ponendo in ipso infamiam; adhuc iudei et sarraceni sunt iniqui contra Deum eo quia blasfemant in ipso divinam Trinitatem, quam pluries in hoc libro probavimus. . . . Amplius iudei et sarraceni . . . in tanta iniquitate consistunt contra Christum quod nolant rationes neque argumenta audire de Christo neque etiam supponunt quod sit possibile Deum esse trinum et unum et incarnatum."

with them, buy from or barter with them, nor sell nor rent them anything. And they would adopt any means whereby the Jews might be converted or among Christians might not dishonor our lady and her son whom they killed with the most vile and disgraceful death that they could.[62]

In the immediacy of his attack upon contemporary Jewry, Raymond Lull continued the trend represented by Nicholas Donin, Pablo Christiani, Raymond Martini, and others, but he also added to their legacy. Those before him harped on the theoretical and textual justification both for attacking rabbinic Judaism and for undertaking to convert the Jews, but Lull was more concerned with the practical operation of conversion. In the spirit of thirteenth-century scholasticism, he tried to develop the methodology of missionizing among the Jews into a foolproof technique which he hoped could not but succeed. His overriding concern for achieving that goal led to his demand that Jews who would not convert be expelled from Christian society. Lull's ideology and work, and in particular his ability to publicize such a demand, manifested the growing acceptance of the friars' new attitude toward the Jews; they also represented another stage in the refinement and implementation of that attitude. Not least significantly, his life and work reflected the impetuousness, the zealous devotion, and the unswerving piety of a Franciscan. As Lull wrote near the end of his life,

I was a married man, the father of a family, well-situated as to fortune, lustful and worldly. I renounced all that of my own accord, in order to be able to honor God, serve the public good, and exalt our holy faith. I learned Arabic, and went several times to preach to the Saracens. Arrested, imprisoned and flogged for the faith, I worked for five years to rouse the chiefs of the Church and the Christian princes on behalf of the common weal. Now I am old, now I am poor, but my purpose is the same, and I shall persevere in it, God willing, even unto death.[63]

62. *Libre de contemplació* 287.9, 2:887.
63. "Disputatio Petri clerici et Raymundi phantastici," ed. Marianus Müller, *Wissenschaft und Weisheit* 2 (1934), 312; trans. in Gilson, *History*, pp. 350–51. On missionizing as fulfillment of the Franciscan ideal, and on Lull's relationship to the Franciscan Order, see E. R. Daniel, *The Franciscan Concept*, ch. 6.

9

Involving the Laity: Mendicant Poetry and Preaching

The mendicant mission to the Jews constituted only one method of implementing the new anti-Jewish ideology, and by itself hardly an adequate one. Raymond Lull himself did not convert many Jews to Christianity, nor did the rulers of Europe carry out his elaborate proposals for training the Jews to dispute properly with Christian missionaries. In order to change the treatment and image of the Jews in Western Europe, the friars had to propagate their ideology among the Christian laity. We have already seen that in several instances they involved kings and princes in their designs—as in Paris in 1240 and Barcelona in 1263[1]—but that did not suffice for their purposes. The old Augustinian policy of toleration did not always yield immediately to the new, more hostile ideology. The success or failure of the mendicant program depended upon the ability of the Dominicans and Franciscans to instill a new picture of the Jew into the medieval mind, and this demanded the effective transmission of their attitudes to the rank and file of the European population.

Nevertheless, most of the anti-Jewish activities of the mendicants mentioned thus far had little effect upon the average Christian layman of the thirteenth and fourteenth centuries. Laymen may well have heard of a burning of the Talmud or may even have attended a disputation or sermon where friars endeavored to convert Jews to Christianity. The average Christian probably knew of the harassment of Jews by the Inquisition, especially in regions where its agents were active. But the layman was not likely to understand the polemical stratagems and subtleties operative in

1. On royal cooperation with (and occasional restriction of) the friars' anti-Jewish designs, see above, Chs. 3–4.

such confrontations, and he was still less prone to have had access to the revelatory writings of such men as Raymond Martini and Nicholas of Lyra. To achieve their goal the friars had to bring their ideology directly to the people—in terms the people could understand, in a manner befitting their perspective, and in their own language. While it is not possible here to quantify the extent to which the friars succeeded in this undertaking, especially during the early period in the orders' history, the fact that Jews were banished from most of Western Europe by the end of the Middle Ages suggests that it was adequate. My purpose in this chapter is rather to illustrate *how* the friars carried their anti-Judaism to the people, by offering three examples of mendicants who in various ways and in varying measures participated in this endeavor. The poetry of Matfre Ermengaud and the sermons of Berthold von Regensburg and Giordano da Rivalto may not by themselves have altered the status of medieval European Jewry in any momentous fashion. Yet these are the examples that have survived; they too bear witness to the wide dissemination of the new anti-Jewish ideology, and, if one reasons that there were similarly minded preachers whose teachings are no longer extant, they point to the far-reaching influence this ideology may well have had.

Matfre Ermengaud

Popular literature in the vernacular offered one possibility for communicating with the laity, although not many mendicants appear to have expressed their anti-Jewish sentiments in this fashion. Some Catalan works of Raymond Lull probably qualify as an attempt to reach a wider Christian audience, but one can find a better example in the poetry of Matfre Ermengaud, a troubadour of Béziers, whose life spanned the last third of the thirteenth century and the first several decades of the fourteenth. Matfre joined the Franciscan Order rather late in his life, apparently after completing his long and elaborate *Breviari d'amor*, but this encyclopedic poem of theology, religious history, and morals still manifests the sentiments and concerns of a man who inclined toward a mendicant apostolate.

Written in Provençal, the *Breviari d'amor* contains several passages in which the author berates the Jews for their obstinate refusal to accept the truth of their own Scriptures and acknowledge the validity of Christianity.[2] Admittedly, Matfre's major concern in the *Breviari* appears to be the justification of his own christological exegesis of the Old Testament, and as such his attack upon the Jews retains some basic characteristics of the early medieval polemics.[3] Yet the fact that he undertook to polemicize against the Jews in the vernacular reveals his desire to promote anti-Jewish feelings among a lay audience, and the *Breviari* clearly exhibits some tendencies of the new mendicant ideology with regard to the Jews. Not only does Matfre harp upon the blindness of the Jews—their inability to understand the Hebrew Bible—but he also accuses them of deliberately corrupting the text of the Old Testament in order to hide obvious references to Jesus. Such is the crime of the Jews that God "does not wish to soften their hardened hearts, nor to give them the light, nor to raise their hearts to the holy faith of Jesus, because they are not worthy of it, being so stubborn and so crafty that every day they seek a pretext for making their error appear trivial, as they forge and falsify the text of the Old Testament."[4] Like many of the friars already considered, Matfre complains of the hostility of contemporary Jews toward Christianity and Christians, expressed primarily in the blasphemous execrations they regularly uttered.

> It vexes me that God tolerates their blindness, for they pronounce blasphemies, outrages, and abominations against the glorious and precious holy virgin, mother of our savior, and against Jesus Christ her son; these sayings do not have the right to call Jesus Christ by his name. If someone could give proof of all of their [the Jews'] sins, they and anyone who would exonerate them would be condemned to the stake. And they commit yet another criminal act of folly; each day they utter certain curses against us.[5]

2. Matfre Ermengaud, *Breviari d'amor*, ll. 11,765–12,026 with texts, 12,397–472. Peter T. Ricketts of the University of Birmingham has graciously provided me with the relevant portions of his critical edition of the *Breviari*, now in progress, and it is to these that reference has been made. Readers may also consult the earlier edition of Gabriel Azaïs, 2 vols. (Béziers, 1862), 1:406–19, 433–36.

3. On Matfre Ermengaud, his *Breviari d'amor*, and its anti-Jewish polemic, see Paul Meyer, "Matfré Ermengau de Béziers, troubador," *HLF* 32 (1898), 16–56; Peter T. Ricketts, "The Hispanic Tradition of the *Breviari d'amor* by Matfre Ermengaud of Béziers," in *Hispanic Studies in Honor of Joseph Manson*, ed. Dorothy M. Atkinson and Anthony H. Clarke (Oxford, 1972), pp. 227–34; and Bernhard Blumenkranz, "Ecriture et image dans la polémique antijuive de Matfre Ermengaud," in *JJL*, pp. 295–317.

4. Matfre Ermengaud, *Breviari*, ll. 11,940–50.

5. Ibid., ll. 11,959–74.

On more than one occasion, Matfre denounces the Talmud as the source of the Jews' maledictions and of their perverse stubborness in clinging to the letter of their law.[6] And perhaps most notably, he revealed the practical dimension of his polemic by recording his scriptural evidence against the Jews in three languages—Hebrew, Latin, and Provençal—so that the Jews might not plead linguistic ignorance in denying its validity. Whether or not Matfre himself was an artist, the *Breviari* is replete with illustrations, a factor which undoubtedly contributed to its popularity and subsequent translations into Catalan and Castilian. In most of the extant manuscripts, the pictorial representations accompanying the biblical quotations in Hebrew commonly display a Jew being assaulted by the devil;[7] his continued allegiance to Judaism, therefore, did not derive from adherence to a divine covenant, but to a demonic perversion thereof.

As a work of literature, the *Breviari d'amor* enjoyed a wide audience and thus could publicize the friars' anti-Jewish polemic, but it was probably exceptional. Generally more effective than poetry as a means of disseminating the new mendicant ideology was the sermon, which could reach even the illiterate. Dominicans and Franciscans were much more highly acclaimed as preachers during the late Middle Ages than they were as poets, renown that occasionally led them into bitter conflict with the secular clergy of Christian Europe. Precisely how the friars may have conditioned the European mind to reject the legitimacy of Jewish life in Western Christendom becomes apparent in the extant sermons of two of the greatest mendicant preachers of the period.

Berthold von Regensburg

Scholars tend to describe the spiritual state of Germany—from a Catholic point of view—at the beginning of the thirteenth century as a sorry one, aggravated in particular by the ongoing conflict between papacy and empire. The moral standards of the people were low, heresy was rampant, and the local secular clergy could

6. Ibid., ll. 12,000, 12,458.
7. See the introduction to the series of quotations, ibid., ll. 12,001–26. And cf. Katja Laske-Fix, *Der Bildzyklus des Breviari d'amor* (Munich, 1973), pp. 59–64, 158; Bernhard Blumenkranz, *Le Juif médiéval au miroir de l'art chrétien* (Paris, 1966), p. 72; and *JJL*, figs. 5–6c, bet. pp. 352–53.

provide no effective guidance. Only the friars offered relief in this dire situation, as they enthusiastically taught and preached to the laity, transmitting their own religious devotion and passion to those who heard them.[8] The most widely acclaimed of these religious was the Franciscan Berthold von Regensburg, whose sermons many critics acknowledge as the zenith of premodern literary creativity in the German vernacular.[9] Born in the first decade of the century, Berthold began his preaching career in the 1240s and pursued it until his death in 1272, traveling through much of present-day Germany, France, Switzerland, Austria, and Czechoslovakia, and attracting huge audiences everywhere.[10] His sermons reflect a marked affinity with and sensitivity to the world and life-style of his listeners. He appealed to their own simple frame of reference, showing little interest in the works of important theologians or the rules of scholastic logic and rhetoric. Rather, he addressed blunt and basic religious messages to the people—harping on rudimentary Christian beliefs, the demands of Christian morality, and the avoidance of sin, but constantly expressing himself in images drawn from the social milieu of the lower classes.[11] Berthold's success in reaching the simple layman has led to his being labeled the high point of medieval German spiritual eloquence, the Elijah of his day, and "the greatest mission preacher of the whole Middle Ages."[12]

Berthold mentions the Jews frequently in his sermons, indicating that they constituted a real presence in thirteenth-century Germany, and his attitude toward them has two different aspects. On the one hand, he seems to portray the Jews as in a better spiritual state than pagans and heretics. For example, he states that if a pagan, a Jew, and a Christian commit the same sin, God punishes

8. R. Cruel, *Geschichte der deutschen Predigt im Mittelalter* (Detmold, 1879), p. 297; G. Schmidt, "Berthold von Regensburg: Ein christlicher Volksprediger des dreizehnten Jahrhunderts," *Theologische Studien und Kritiken* 37 (1864), 8–9; Freed, *The Friars,* passim.

9. See the introduction to Berthold von Regensburg, *Vollständige Ausgabe seiner Predigten,* ed. Franz Pfeiffer, 2 vols. (1862–80; repr., Berlin, 1965), 1:xviii. Berthold's acclaim is reflected in the many literary and linguistic studies of his sermons. Cf. also Max Scheinert, *Der Franziskaner Berthold von Regensburg als Lehrer und Erzieher des Volkes* (Dresden, 1896), pp. 26ff.

10. Karl Rieder, *Das Leben Bertholds von Regensburg* (Freiburg i. Br., 1901).

11. G. Schmidt, "Berthold von Regensburg," pp. 14–22; Cruel, *Geschichte,* pp. 307–8; Scheinert, *Der Franziskaner,* pp. 2–26.

12. Gustav Ehrisman, *Geschichte der deutschen Literatur bis zum Ausgang des Mittelalters,* 4 vols. (Munich, 1918–35), 4:417; Cruel, *Geschichte,* p. 322; G. G. Coulton, *Inquisition and Liberty* (1938; repr., Gloucester, Mass., 1969), p. 18.

the Jew more severely than the pagan, and the Christian most harshly, because of their ascending degrees of holiness and concomitant spiritual responsibility. Berthold asserts that the beliefs of heretics are far more absurd than those of the Jews.[13] Moreover, he instructs that God has always intended to preserve the free will of the Jews and not to compel them to convert; Christians should never attempt to baptize them by force.[14] On several occasions he praises Jews for being more scrupulous in their religious observance than most Christians, especially with regard to holy days, prayer, honoring one's parents, and sexual abstinence during a wife's menstrual period.[15] Christians should not cheat Jews, and recognizing that God created them too in his image, they certainly should not kill them. Berthold assigns to the German emperor the specific responsibility of protecting the Jews within the framework of the king's peace. They are to be preserved in Christian society because their mere presence serves as a reminder of Christ's martyrdom at their hands and also because they will convert at the end of days.[16]

On the other hand, the bulk of Berthold's references to the Jews betray a markedly aggressive and antagonistic stance. "Jews, heathens, and heretics," declares the friar, "never serve God; only Christians serve him. They imagine that they serve him, but it is for him a disservice and a displeasure."[17] Unlike Augustine, Berthold denied that the Jews are in any way fulfilling a divinely ordained mission. They have allied themselves with the devil and further his interests on earth; they enjoy no possibility of divine reward whatsoever.[18] False beliefs, entirely contrary to the tenets of Christianity, manifest these demonic ties. "You Jews, you heathens, you heretics, you can be recognized very well by your language, because you say everything which is against Christian doctrine, like your lord the devil, who for so long has inhabited the nether world and must inhabit it more and more everlastingly, [all] the while God is lord in heaven."[19] The Jews vainly persist at gnaw-

13. Berthold von Regensburg, *Das Wirken . . . gegen die Ketzer*, ed. Anton E. Schönbach, Studien zur Geschichte der altdeutschen Predigt 3 (Vienna, 1904), pp. 15, 41–42.
14. Berthold, *Vollständige Ausgabe*, 1:298, 439; 2:85–86, 228.
15. Ibid., 1:270, 323, 515; 2:216.
16. Ibid., 1:86, 363; 2:238, 254.
17. Ibid., 1:377.
18. Ibid., 1:1–2, 379, 529–30.
19. Ibid., 1:252.

ing the hard, tasteless rind surrounding the sweet kernel of God's covenant of grace, without ever tasting the goodness of the core. Along with those of pagans and heretics, their beliefs exemplify the teachings of Antichrist and the devil; they are all fated to be damned as punishment for their errors.[20] Accordingly, Berthold groups the Jews among the major enemies of Christendom. The papacy has the responsibility of fortifying the teachings of Christianity against possible encroachments by them; and if anyone within Christendom should disobediently challenge such teachings and weaken the strength of Christianity, the emperor must protect against the resulting possibility of attacks by the Jews from without.[21] In sum, all those endowed by God with power and authority must share in this obligation.

> I now want to tell you what is incumbent upon the emperor and the kings and the dukes and the barons and the counts and all worldly nobles, who are knights and lords, and all those to whom our Lord has given and entrusted authority and power on earth. For they also comprise one of the three [powers] to whom the almighty God has made the seven stones [classes, in terms of Berthold's allegory for this sermon] of people subordinate, in order that they [the people] should serve them. You [those in authority] therefore owe it to these children of God that you protect them from criminals and from robbers and from arsonists, from Jews, from heathens, and from heretics, from perjurers and from illegal violence.[22]

Berthold does not limit his attack to such generalizations: he elaborates to his listeners on both the actual nature of the Jewish error and the way Jews endanger Christendom. Just as Raymond Lull had done, Berthold criticizes Jews for not sharing one definite creed but maintaining a multiplicity of beliefs on crucial theological issues.[23] Such inconstancy not only precluded their entrance into the kingdom of heaven, a kingdom identical to Christendom precisely because of the latter's unity of faith,[24] but it also led Berthold to

20. Ibid., 1:3, 38, 44.
21. Ibid., 1:361–62.
22. Ibid., 1:144.
23. See, for example, Berthold, *Das Wirken*, p. 18, and *Vollständige Ausgabe*, 1:265.
24. Explaining the equation of Christendom and the kingdom of heaven, Berthold instructs, *Vollständige Ausgabe*, 2:186: "Daz ist darumbe, daz diu kristenheit alliu éinen gelouben hât und allez éin geloube ist. Swaz anderre geloube ist, die sint niht eines gelouben, heiden habent manigen gelouben, juden sint ouch niht alle éines gelouben."

attack the rabbinic tradition and leadership which governed the Jewish community. The friar accounts for variations in Jewish belief by noting that:

The Jews, who are most diverse in their faith, are not in harmony with the faith which their ancient forefathers believed. Whence they believe in one land many things regarding their faith which they do not in another—even in one city and not in another, and even in an individual home. The reason for this most diverse credulity of the Jews is that whatever their blind, modern teachers dream up and tell them to believe, they believe. And in order that they [the teachers] might receive greater honor from them [the Jews], they say that what a sage maintains is to be believed was given by God at Mount Sinai, so that people must believe [it]. Consequently, whatever this blind doctor says must be believed, [the Jews] immediately believe, and whatever a doctor of other [Jews] similarly says to his people must be believed they likewise believe, and thus in each individual case. Therefore, since one of the Jews' teachers says that one thing is to be believed and another teacher [says] another thing and a third [says] still another thing and so in many instances, there is a great diversity of belief among the Jews even in matters pertaining to the faith of the Old Testament.[25]

Like Nicholas Donin, Berthold here condemns the rabbinic tradition of medieval Judaism for its ridiculous inconstancy. He referred his audience to particular tales from the Talmud and midrash—for example, how those whom God rewards with eternal life will consume the flesh of the leviathan and how Adam cohabited with demons—in order to demonstrate Judaism's absurdities and irrationality.[26] Most significantly, he branded talmudic Judaism a hin-

25. Berthold, *Das Wirken*, p. 28.
26. Ibid., pp. 30–31: "Item, o judei, quam pulchra et rationabilis est fides vestra? respondete, et quid creditis? respondent: 'credimus unum Deum, creatorem celi et terre, sicut et vos.' respondeo: hoc est pulchrum; sed quid de illo? quomodo remunerat eum diligentes, intime et fidelissime servientes? debet eos diu valde secum tenere et postea adnichilare, et interim, cum secum sunt, dare piscem comedere? debeo propter hoc tantum eum diligere et tanta pati? immo, quia sine fine servio, debet remunerare sine fine. sed quid credis de creato Adam, quare fecit et dedit ei Evam, et quod genuit ei per triginta annos? item dic, quam vicine tibi attinet dyabolus ex Adam? si modo hoc diceremus etc. supra de vera. omnibus annis, quibus Adam fuit excommunicatus, genuit demones. . . . [There follows Berthold's account of the homily according to which Adam begat demons during the years he had no marital relations with Eve.] habent ex dictis Rabi Eleazar. sic: quid est quod scriptum est Gen. II: 'hoc nunc os ex osse meo'? Glossa: hoc nunc ergo animalibus coiverat cum aliquibus, que non placuerunt ei, ostendens, quod coivit Adam cum omnibus brutis, nec tamen cesserat appetitus ejus, donec Eva ei conjuncta fuit.—hec predicta

drance to the presence of God on earth, since belief in the Talmud constituted a gross violation of the Jews' covenant with God, amounting to no less than outright heresy.

> The Jews of one house believe what they do not believe in another. And he [the Jew] believes such terrible things concerning God, that he does not willingly tell [them even] to his children. Wherefore they have become heretics and break their covenant in every way. Their twelve [leaders?] hastily convened and composed a book, which is called Talmud. It is completely heretical, and it contains such damned heresy that it is bad that they [the Jews] live.[27]

Berthold deemed it bad that the Jews still lived in Christendom not simply because they symbolized the forces of Satan, but because their heresy and generally base character led them to proffer a real threat to the rank and file of Christian society. Daily Jewish behavior was itself dangerous: while the men engaged in the sinful practice of usury, the women dressed with ostentatious immodesty, detracting from the moral climate of Christian society.[28] So ingrained were these characteristics that Berthold reproves Christians who, in cheating their fellow or espousing evil beliefs, become Jews in deed and remain Christians in name only.[29] The worst threat of the Jew lay in his constant deprecation of Christianity and in his continual attempts to lead the faithful astray.

> A Jew wants to make conversation with you, so that you might thereby become weaker and weaker in your belief; therefore you should watch yourselves, you simple people. You always want to wage war on the Jews, [but] you are so unlearned, and they are well trained in Scripture. He [the Jew] has thought out well for a long time how he will converse with you, in order that you might thereby become ever weaker in your faith. For the same reasons, it is decreed by Scripture and the papacy that no unlearned man should speak with a Jew.[30]

Communing with the Jews—conversing with them, disputing with them, and even eating with them—was clearly dangerous to the

---

non dic in predicatione.—de hujusmodi stultitiis habent infinitas incredulitates, omni sapienti pro magna stultitia reputandas. aut ergo deserant aut virgam, id est fidem suam, eis aridam reddam, cum qua comburantur."

27. Berthold, *Vollständige Ausgabe*, 1:401.
28. Ibid., 1:27, 114–15, 281, 415, 438.
29. Ibid., 1:144, 418.
30. Ibid., 1:530, and cf. pp. 294–95.

welfare of Christian society, according to the Franciscan preacher. It is no wonder that he exhorted the emperor to insure that the Jews not become too numerous or powerful in Christendom to be effectively restrained from inflicting injury upon it.[31] For Berthold, it was even "bad that they live." Nor did he leave such conclusions to be inferred by his audiences but stated them explicitly and in a determined manner. In two of his sermons, Berthold compares the kingdom of God—Christendom—to a field in which a great treasure lies buried; whoever discovers the treasure will be perpetually endowed. The Jew, states the friar emphatically, has no rightful access to the field and its treasure; at best he represents a weed planted by the devil in the field, one which will, it is hoped, be removed.[37] In another sermon, Christendom is likened to the temple of King Solomon, complete with its magnificent architecture, draperies, and ornamentation. Calling particular attention to the four courtyards surrounding the temple, Berthold explains that they contain all those various groups who may not enter the temple itself: Jews, heathens, heretics, and those excommunicated for desecrating churches and monasteries, killing clerics, forging papal letters, and raping nuns. Who then, asks Berthold, may in fact enter the sanctuary? "They are Christians. The temple is Christianity; Jews and heathens cannot enter. And therefore a vessel stands before the temple, and whoever wants to enter the temple must wash his hands and feet, since no one may enter Christianity without being washed in holy baptism."[33]

Assessing Berthold's stance in regard to the Jews, one is struck not only by the friar's attack on the Talmud,[34] his charges of Jewish heresy, and his plaints of anti-Christian hostility, but also by his constant grouping of the Jews together with pagans and heretics. This linkage may well have had a profound impact on his listeners, since heretics and pagans had no rightful place whatsoever in medieval Christendom. Grouping the Jews, who practiced their Judaism openly within Christian society, together with these other en-

31. Ibid., 1:363; 2:19, 63, 238.
32. Ibid., 1:140, 357ff.
33. Ibid., 2:35–36.
34. The objection of Rudolph Piffl, "Einiges über Berthold von Regensburg," in *Programm des K.K. deutschen Obergymnasiums der Kleinseite in Prag* (Prague, 1890), p. 8, minimizing the significance of Berthold's attack on the Talmud because the friar mentions it only once, is not only partly untrue—cf. the separate references to rabbinic literature, above, nn. 25–27—but also misleading. On none of these occasions does Berthold merely allude to the Talmud; rather, he condemns the rabbis quite vehemently, even citing specific examples of talmudic heresy.

emies of Christendom made them an easily accessible target for the popular wrath normally reserved for pagans and heretics. While the provisions of both ecclesiastical and Germanic law prevented Berthold from publicly advocating the extermination of Judaism, his equation of the Jews with those already outlawed suggests his ultimate motives rather clearly.[35] To the average listener, whom the friar's sermons would have influenced much more directly than any papal bull, imperial charter, or conciliar canon, Berthold's impassioned attacks on contemporary Jewry must have outweighed his cool reminders not to inflict harm upon the Jews. How could simple folk remain passive while enemies of the society lived freely and prosperously in their midst?

It also seems reasonable to approach Berthold as representative of a group of preachers—perhaps its most able spokesman whose works have survived—and expressing a point of view that others undoubtedly shared. Berthold's eminent teacher and friend, for instance, the Franciscan David of Augsburg, similarly likened the Jews to pagans and heretics, who cause injury and insult to Christ and the virgin Mary, deceive simple Christians, and lead them along a path of damnation.[36] Such a view gains further credence

35. On the equation of Jews and heretics by Christian polemicists, see Raoul Manselli, "La polémique contre les Juifs dans la polémique antihérétique," in *JJL*, pp. 252–67. Most instructive is Manselli's observation on the danger seen by the Church in the possibility of Jewish and Muslim proselytism, p. 253: "The result was that Muslims and Jews were ultimately considered still more dangerous to the integrity of the faith and were placed on the same plane as the separatist heretics. The latter were guilty of shattering the inner unity of the faith; yet they [Jews and Muslims] were responsible for inducing Christians to give up their faith for another." Yet I must take issue with Manselli's approach to Christian religious polemics of the twelfth century, as if their use of similar lists of biblical *auctoritates* to confute both heretics and Jews marked a novel and significant development in attacks upon the Jews. As I endeavored to show in Ch. 1, such lists of *testimonia* comprised the hallmark of early medieval *adversus Judeos* literature, and Manselli himself admits, p. 262, that the allegedly new brand of polemic of the late twelfth century had little effect on the status and prosperity of European Jewry. Finally, Berthold's comparison of heretics and Jews appears to contradict Manselli's claim, p. 264, that the thirteenth century saw the end of this equation in Christian polemic.

36. See one of David's extant sermons in Franz Pfeiffer, ed., *Deutsche Mystiker des vierzehnten Jahrhunderts*, 2 vols. (Leipzig, 1845–57), 1:318–19: "Unde dar nâch, waz er scheltworte lîdet und sîn reinistiu muoter von dem vervluochten volke, den ungeslahten jüden, unde von den blinden heiden, unde noch lîdende wirt von den verdampten ketzern, die den rehten gelouben verkêrent unde die tôrahten liute verleitent nâch in ze der helle." Interestingly, some have attributed to David the compilation of an inquisitors' manual entitled *De inquisitione hereticorum*, which Bernard Gui used in amassing his own catalogue of the Jews' condemnable practices; see Yerushalmi, "The Inquisition," p. 375, n. 149; and, for an opposing view, Dondaine, "Le Manuel," pp. 180–83.

from the rapid appearance of attacks on both the Jews and their Talmud in secular German poetry toward the end of Berthold's career and soon thereafter.[37] Moreover, during the second half of the thirteenth century, with the redaction of the Bavarian law code, the *Schwabenspiegel*, the status of the Jews in Germanic law declined significantly. The *Schwabenspiegel* contains many more restrictions upon the Jews than the important German law code of the first half of the century, Eike von Repgow's *Sachsenspiegel*, including a law which in denying the Jew the right to be king likens him to heretics and pagans.[38] The law of the *Schwabenspiegel* in general manifests a concerted effort to exclude Jews from the mainstream of Christian society, a tendency which Guido Kisch has shown is epitomized in the denial of the Jews' right to bear arms. Kisch terms the treatment of the Jews in the *Schwabenspiegel* the "nadir" of their legal status during the Middle Ages. Significantly, he reveals that the *Schwabenspiegel* was composed by a Franciscan friar at the convent of Augsburg, the spiritual home of Berthold von Regensburg, and that the author of the code drew heavily upon the teachings of Berthold and his colleague David of Augsburg. "By this fact alone," Kisch concludes, "his attitude towards the Jews is unambiguously established."[39] Finally, because of the great influence of preachers

37. See Erwin Gustav Gudde, "Social Conflicts in Medieval German Poetry," *University of California Publications in Modern Philology* 18 (1934–36), 40–41, 72–75; for attacks on the Jews in general, and anti-talmudic references in particular, see Güdemann, *Geschichte*, 1:140ff.

38. Guido Kisch, ed., *Jewry-Law in Medieval Germany: Laws and Court Decisions Concerning Jews* (New York, 1949), pp. 38–39, 54–62—esp. p. 55(101.3).

39. Guido Kisch, *The Jews in Medieval Germany A Study of their Legal and Social Status*, 2d ed. (New York, 1970), pp. 38–41, 111–28, 159–68. Early in this century, Ludwig von Rockinger, "Deutschenspiegel, sogennanter Schwabenspiegel, Bertholds von Regensburg deutsche Predigten in ihrem Verhältnisse zu einander," *Abhandlungen der historischen Classe der königlich bayerischen Akademie der Wissenschaften* 23 (1906), 211–300, 473–536, rejected this common assertion that the compiler of the *Schwabenspiegel* relied on Berthold's sermons, and he posited the opposite: that Berthold drew upon the law of the *Schwabenspiegel*. Even if this is true, the fact that Berthold and the *Schwabenspiegel* originated in the same Franciscan circles—the matter of real importance to us here—still remains. Curiously, instead of Berthold's sermons, Rockinger maintained that Raymond de Peñaforte's *Summa de poenitentia* provided the editor of the *Schwabenspiegel* with his major theological source; see Rockinger's "Berthold von Regensburg und Raimund von Peniafort im sogennanten Schwabenspiegel," ibid. 13,3 (1877), 165–253. At p. 242–46, Rockinger asserts that this connection holds true particularly in the case of the proper treatment of the Jews. An equally interesting contention appears in Giménez y Martínez de Carvajal, "San Raimundo," passim, where the Spanish Dominican is viewed as a major influence on the Castilian Alfonso X's thirteenth-century law code, *Las siete partidas*; on Alfonso's treatment of the Jews, see Y. Baer, *A History*, 1:116ff.

like Berthold, some historians attribute to them the responsibility for the anti-Jewish violence in thirteenth and fourteenth-century Germany, a trend that reached a climax in the massacres of Jews which accompanied the Black Death.[40]

Giordano da Rivalto

The important role played by Berthold in the history of Christianity and the development of the *ars predicandi* in Germany was in many ways filled in Italy by the Dominican Giordano da Rivalto. Born around 1260 near Pisa, Giordano entered the Order of Preachers in 1280. During the next twenty years, he studied at various Dominican *studia*, including those at Bologna and Paris, and in 1302 he went to Florence to lecture on Peter Lombard's *Sentences* at the *studium generale* there. Giordano is most remembered for the many sermons he delivered over the next seven years in Florence, popular discourses that attracted huge crowds of listeners and had a profound impact on the spiritual climate of the city. He died en route to Paris in 1311.[41]

At the beginning of the fourteenth century, few, if any, Jews lived in Florence, and Jews understandably were the topic of Giordano's sermons only on occasion.[42] The friar told his listeners that in order to read the Old Testament in the original, he once received instruction in Hebrew from a Jew so virtuous that had he been Christian, he would have been worthy of walking with Jesus' apostles. Yet perhaps sensing the potential for the growth of a large Jewish community in Florence during the fourteenth century, he did devote one entire sermon on November 9, 1304, to the Jews.[43]

Giordano begins this sermon with a discussion of the sin committed by the Jews in killing Jesus and the series of divinely ordained punishments they consequently suffered, but he quickly

40. Cruel, *Geschichte*, pp. 620–21; Güdemann, *Geschichte*, 1:239–41. On the cooperation of German clerics with blood libels beginning in the second half of the thirteenth century—accusations that harped on the unnatural, satanic hostility of the Jews toward Christians—see Langmuir, "L'absence," p. 238.

41. On Giordano's life, see Carlo Delcorno, *Giordano da Pisa e l'antica predicazione vulgare* (Florence, 1975), pp. 3–28; on his contributions to the development of Italian language and literature, see ibid., pp. 29–237; and on his impact on Florence, see Robert Davidsohn, *Geschichte von Florenz*, 4 vols. (Berlin, 1896–1927), 4,3:64–76.

42. Umberto Cassuto, *Gli Ebrei a Firenze nell'età del Rinascimento* [Hebrew], trans. Menahem Hartom (Jerusalem, 1967), pp. 10–11; SRH, 10:275.

43. Giordano, *Prediche*, 2:220–32.

proceeds to consider the Jews of his own day. For the Jews, states the friar, continue to crucify Christ and—by extension—to attack Christianity whenever and however they can, perpetrating the most wretched of crimes against God and against all of humanity. In their minds and hearts, the Jews reenact the crucifixion through extensive blasphemy of Jesus and Mary, charges that Giordano claims to have verified himself.

> I say first of all that they repeat it [Christ's passion] in their hearts with ill will—wherefore they are evil at heart and hate Christ with evil hatred; and they would, were they able, crucify him anew every day and even thus they could not satiate themselves. For this reason they curse Christ continually—at least three times each day—at which three times they malign and blaspheme him; and they also curse the Virgin Mary every day. O behold this wicked people! And behold God who takes revenge on them in this world, who has brought them into the hatred of all peoples! There is not a nation, not a faction, which does not hold them in hatred, whence there is no people that wishes to meet them. They are hated throughout the world because they are evil toward Christ, whom they curse. Therefore, Friar Giordano has stated, having found it [evidence of these curses] in their books without their knowing it. God has brought them into hatred among all people.[44]

The Jews also maintain their offensive against Christ by purchasing Christian children in order to circumcise them and lead them away from the true faith. Such a crime is especially heinous because it shows that the Jews have broken their covenant with God completely. The Old Testament no longer belongs to them, and they now believe in a deity other than the true God.[45] In a much more direct fashion, the Jews kill Christ by frequently stealing the host and desecrating it as if they were attacking Jesus' body on the cross. On one such recent occasion, at which Giordano asserts he was present, the boy Jesus miraculously appeared on the scene and rallied the local Christian population to slaughter 24,000 Jews in punishment for their evil deed.[46] The Jews further reenact the passion of Christ by annually stealing a Christian child and crucifying him.[47] Just such a crime, explains the Dominican, enabled Friar

44. Ibid., p. 225.
45. Ibid., pp. 225–27.
46. Ibid., pp. 227–28.
47. Ibid., pp. 229–30: "L'altro modo onde rifanno la passione di Cristo, si è nella immagine sua; e questo è in due modi; l'uno si è nella persona d'alcuno uomo,

Bartolomeo de Aquila to convince the Angevin king Charles II to permit an inquisitorial attack on the Jews of Apulia, leaving them with a choice between baptism or exile.[48] Finally, the Jews persist in crucifying Jesus by abusing drawings and carvings of him; Giordano tells the story of one icon which miraculously produced real blood in response to Jewish torture of it, an event that led 40,000 Jews to convert.[49]

Most of the elements of Giordano's portrayal of the Jews in this sermon echo the new attitude toward the Jews expressed in the writings and pronouncements of other mendicants: the Jews' abandonment of God and the Old Testament, their adoption of heretical and idolatrous beliefs, the blasphemous nature of postbiblical Jewish literature, the anti-Christian hostility of contemporary Jewry, and the desideratum of converting the Jews to Christianity en masse. Like the sermons of Berthold von Regensburg, then, Giordano's discourse illustrates how the friars conveyed their ideology to the Christian laity, perhaps even managing to enlist lay support in their attack on the European Jewish community. Yet I have chosen to conclude the present survey of various mendicants' attitudes toward the Jews with Giordano da Rivalto, because his sermon manifests two nuances that provide this book with an appropriate conclusion. First, Giordano both echoed and contributed to the popular tendency to view the heresy and hostility of the Jew as giving rise to such satanic crimes as the desecration of the host and the commission of ritual murder. Although the papacy and the Empire often tried to protect the Jews from ritual murder charges during the thirteenth century and certainly never gave credence to these accusations,[50] Giordano, himself a well-educated teacher of theology, relates the stories of such incidents as if they were entirely factual. And second, unlike most of the other treatments of the Jews I have considered, Giordano's animus exhibits no trace of

---

perocchè ogni uomo è alla immagine di Dio, come dice Santo Paolo, e Moises; chè disse Iddio quando fece l'uomo: 'Faciamus hominem ad imaginem et similitudinem nostram'; sicchè ogni uomo è alla immagine di Dio: in questo altresì rifanno la passione di Cristo quando possono. Onde questo voglio che sappiate, e dovete sapere che ogni anno, se possono, purchè possano, che vegna loro fatto, e' pigliano e imbolano uno fanciullo de' cristiani, qualche poverello che non sia conoscinto, e sì'l mettono in croce come misero Cristo, e fannogli quella medesima passione e morte fare, che fecero a Cristo."

48. Ibid., pp. 230–31.
49. Giordano, *Prediche*, 2:231–32.
50. See, for example, Grayzel, *The Church*, pp. 262–71, 274–75; and cf. *SRH*, 11:146ff.

restraint or ambivalence. The friar offers his listeners no reason for preserving the Jews in Christian society. He displays no concern for the provisions of ecclesiastical and secular law which forbade inflicting violence upon them. Nor, as his various stories suggest, did he seek to rid Christendom of Jews solely through conversion. Like Raymond Lull, Giordano apparently advocated the expulsion of Jews from Christian society, and he accordingly praises Bartolomeo de Aquila for forcing Apulian Jewry to convert or flee. Giordano also rejoices over an incident he reports as having occurred in Greece, in which a Jewish father, along with many of his coreligionists, was burned for persecuting his son who had secretly converted to Christianity, and which culminated in the expulsion of all Greek Jewry.[51] Finally, Giordano did not even shy away from suggesting the extermination of Jews who exhibited hostility toward Christianity. His impassioned account of the Jews' desecration of the host ended with no other than Jesus instigating the retaliatory massacres. How should the average Florentine have reacted to Giordano's repetition of the cry that was raised on behalf of the sacrament and the body of Christ—"sieno morti i Giuderi," let the Jews die[52]—if not by harboring similar sentiments himself?

51. Giordano, *Prediche*, 2:228–29. On the history of this tale, its forms and variants, see Theodor Pelizaeus, *Beiträge zur Geschichte der Legende vom Judenknaben* (Halle, 1914); and Eugen Wolter, *Der Judenknabe* (Halle, 1879). Curiously, Giordano's rendition of the tale, more inflammatory than most earlier ones, escapes mention in these studies.

52. Giordano, *Prediche*, 2:228.

10

Conclusion: Mendicant Anti-Judaism and the Evolving Self-Consciousness of Latin Christendom

Condemning the Talmud in 1239 as a heretical deviation from the Jews' biblical heritage, Pope Gregory IX probably did not conceive of the important effects his pronouncements would have on the course of history. He could not have foreseen that he had sanctioned the commencement of an ideological trend that would justify attempts to eliminate the Jewish presence in Christendom, a radical shift from the Augustinian position that the Jews occupied a rightful and necessary place in Christian society. Yet Gregory's awakening to the discrepancy between the religion of contemporary Jews and that of the "biblical" Jews whom Augustine had wished to tolerate, coupled with the pontiff's exclamation that belief in the Talmud "is said to be the chief cause that holds the Jews obstinate in their perfidy," laid important groundwork for those who came after him. In the generations that followed the Paris disputation of 1240 and the initial burning of the Talmud in 1242, mendicant inquisitors throughout Europe continued to persecute rabbinic literature, compelled the Jews to submit to their inflammatory sermons, and where possible often worked toward the complete destruction of specific Jewish communities. Early in the fourteenth century, Bernard Gui burned the Talmud even in the absence of Jews. Meanwhile, as the attack on rabbinic Judaism became an ever-increasing concern of the Inquisition, the Spanish Dominican school of Raymond de Peñaforte masterfully developed the charges of heresy against the Jews and their Talmud into an ideology that called for the elimination, by conversion, of all of

European Jewry. Within several decades after Raymond Martini completed his *Pugio fidei*, its arguments were being synthesized and disseminated at the University of Paris, in the theological discourses of Nicholas of Lyra. Finally, still other Dominicans and Franciscans proceeded to act upon the new ideology, trying to infuse into the European consciousness the desideratum of excluding the Jews: Raymond Lull in his elaborate campaigns to convert the Jews and his call for the expulsion of those refusing baptism, Matfre Ermengaud in his illustrated book of romantic poetry, and Berthold von Regensburg and Giordano da Rivalto in their popular sermons.

Admittedly, these friars did not, in the mere span of a century, transform the way all Christians approached the question of the Jews. The medieval papacy never officially called for the expulsion or physical persecution of European Jewry. Some clerics still composed the old type of anti-Jewish polemic which had relatively little bearing upon the Jews and Judaism of their own day; even Dominicans and Franciscans occasionally produced polemical literature of this sort.[1] But the continued presence of the old attitude toward the Jews could not stifle the increasing acceptance and influence of the new. Although the papacy officially protected the Jews, it was bound to protect only those who conformed to the classical Augustinian conception of the bearers of the Old Testament; and that sort of Jew no longer existed. Innocent III, for instance, added to his own version of the traditional bull of *Sicut Iudeis*, which assured the Jews of their rights and liberties within Christian society, a noteworthy limitation: "We wish, however, to place under the protection of this decree only those who have not presumed to plot against the Christian faith."[2] In view of the friars' estimation of rabbinic Judaism, such a stipulation might have excluded a large portion, if not all, of European Jewry. By the fourteenth century, the *Sicut Iudeis* bull in particular and papal protection of the Jews in

---

1. See, for example, the work of Alfonso Bonhomo cited above, Ch. 7, n. 8; and the Dominican Gilbert of Tournai's *Disputatio Ecclesiae et Synagogae*, in *Thesaurus novus anecdotorum*, ed. Edmund Martène and Ursinus Durand, 5 vols. (1717; repr., New York, 1968), 5:1497–1506. On Gilbert's authorship of this work, see Heinz Pflaum, "Der allegorische Streit zwischen Synagoge und Kirche in der europäischen Dichtung des Mittelalters," *Archivum romanum* 18 (1934), 266–70; and Schlauch, "The Allegory," p. 456. See also Serper, "Le debat," pp. 207–33; and Heinz Pflaum, "Poems of Religious Disputations in the Middle Ages [Hebrew]," *Tarbiz* 2 (1931), 443–76.
2. Grayzel, *The Church*, pp. 94–95.

general had all but lost their practical effectiveness.[3] Or as Walter Pakter has recently shown, while the treatment of the Jews in the works of the canonists actually improved during the thirteenth century, it did so with regard to matters of little concern to contemporary Jews—for example, trading in non-Jewish slaves—and not in vital matters, such as the right to study and disseminate rabbinic literature.[4]

Some historians have characterized these developments as manifesting a gap between theory and practice in the Jewish policy of the late medieval Church, a contradiction that confused the rank and file of Christian society and moved it toward a much more violent treatment of the Jews.[5] My own findings, however, would lead to a redefinition of the contradiction as one between two differing ideological tendencies, that of Augustine and that of the friars. The late medieval attacks on contemporary Jewry did have their theological justification. Moreover, the mendicants stood in closer contact with the lay population of Europe than did the popes or the canonists. They had the opportunity not only to pursue their ideology in direct dealings with the Jews but also to transmit their sentiments to a wide and diversified audience.

From the thirteenth century onward, anti-Jewish violence increased throughout Europe. Only from this period were Jews portrayed as real, active agents of Satan, charged with innumerable forms of hostility toward Christianity, Christendom, and individual Christians. Blood libels (as distinct from the older accusation of ritual murder) and charges of host desecration first appeared in medieval Europe during the thirteenth century. In this century, the representation of Jews in Christian art became noticeably more hostile and demeaning, with the first examples of the infamous *Judensau* (portrayals of Jews sucking at the teats of a sow) and the frequent juxtaposition of the Jews and the devil. No longer were the Jews depicted like their Christian neighbors or as mere symbols in the drama of religious history; they had become pernicious enemies of Christians and the Church, and pictorially they often came to represent the archetypal heretics. Permanent expulsion of

3. Grayzel, "The Papal Bull," pp. 263ff.; and "The Avignon Popes and the Jews," *HJ* 2 (1940), 6–12.

4. Walter J. Pakter, "De his qui foris sunt: The Teachings of the Medieval Canon and Civil Lawyers Concerning the Jews," Ph.D. diss., Johns Hopkins University, 1974, esp. ch. 2.

5. Grayzel, *The Church*, pp. 81–82; Baron, *SRH*, 9:94–96.

European Jewries began in 1290. By the middle of the next century, it was almost inevitable that Jews were blamed for the Black Death and many of their communities in Germany completely and permanently exterminated.[6] And by the mid-1500s, most of Western Europe contained no Jews at all. In view of the great influence which religion wielded over the people of medieval Europe, it is difficult to believe that had the Church remained constantly committed to the Augustinian policy of tolerating the Jews, the Jewish presence in Western Europe could have been virtually eliminated. Surely, a change in Christian theological attitudes toward the Jews could not by itself exclude them from European society. The work of the friars was a vital prerequisite, one that eventually allowed other political, social, and economic trends to take their course.

Modern Jewish historiography has treated the plight of the Jews during the last centuries of the Middle Ages extensively, and a detailed account of the decline of the medieval European Jewish community would serve little constructive purpose here. Instead, I propose to conclude by considering the new anti-Jewish ideology of the friars in a somewhat broader context: Whence did it arise? What led to the theological attack on rabbinic Judaism by the mendicants in the thirteenth century? In an earlier chapter, we consid ered the possibility that since the friars often stemmed from and responded to the needs of the Christian middle class, they would have harbored natural resentment against the Jews, who had long dominated much of the commerce and moneylending in Western Europe (and were infidels besides). The very state of the Church at the beginning of the thirteenth century, in which the friars played

6. For lists and descriptions of the various accusations and outbreaks of violence, see Peter Browe, "Die Hostienschändungen der Juden im Mittelalter," *Römische Quartalschrift für christliche Altertumskunde und für Kirchengeschichte* 34 (1926), 167–97, and "Die Judenbekämpfung im Mittelalter," *Zeitschrift für katholisches Theologie* 62 (1938), 198–223; Joshua Trachtenberg, *The Devil and the Jews* (New Haven, 1943), passim; and James Parkes, *The Jew in the Medieval Community*, 2d ed. (New York, 1976), p. 237. On the worsening depiction of the Jews in Christian art, see Trachtenberg; Isaiah Shachar, *The Judensau: A Medieval Anti-Jewish Motif and Its History* (London, 1974), pp. 15ff.; and above all Blumenkranz, *Le Juif médiéval*. Although Blumenkranz asserts that the representation of Jews by Christian artists changed drastically after 1096 and the First Crusade, virtually all of his supporting examples date from no earlier than the thirteenth century. Finally, on the massacres of Jews during the Black Death, see Norman Cohn, *The Pursuit of the Millennium: Revolutionary Millenarians and Mystical Anarchists of the Middle Ages*, rev. ed. (London, 1970), pp. 86–87; George Deaux, *The Black Death, 1347* (New York, 1969), pp. 166–75; and Johannes Nohl, *The Black Death: A Chronicle of the Plague*, trans. C. H. Clarke (New York, 1969), pp. 181–206.

such a crucial role, lent itself to increased anti-Jewish hostility as well. Yet however near the truth these suggestions might be, they do not account for the ideational substance of the mendicant attack on the Jews. To be sure, the actual commencement of the confrontation between the friars and the Jews depended in large measure upon fortuitous circumstances: the rage of a single Jew who betrayed the works of Maimonides to the Inquisition in Provence or the vindictiveness of an apostate like Nicholas Donin. By the middle of the fourteenth century, however, the friars' attacks on the Jews were no longer fortuitous; they represented a deliberate effort on the part of groups of mendicants to rid Europe of contemporary Judaism. What in the religious and intellectual climate of the times both motivated and enabled the friars to break with the established Augustinian precedent and move in this direction? Or, if European Jews had always lived according to the teachings of the Talmud, as indeed they had, what suddenly led to the development and acceptance of the new attitude that rabbinic Judaism was heretical and had no place in Christendom?

One stimulus perhaps lay in a growing preoccupation with the notion of the imminence of the end of days and with different theories of successive ages in the salvific history of the world. Many important writers of the twelfth and thirteenth centuries revived the old patristic interest in the periodization of history.[7] Undoubtedly the most significant of these, Joachim of Flora (ca. 1135–1202), infused much of Christian Europe with the expectation of an impending transition to the final, perfect age of the spirit.[8] As Marjorie Reeves and others have shown, this sense of imminent change and crisis was inherited even by many of the chief opponents of Joachimite thought, including the Order of Preachers and those Franciscans who remained orthodox throughout the various doctrinal disputes of the period. The mild Roger Bacon and Nicholas of Lyra both reflected the influence of Joachim in their writings; Bonaventure, who himself defended the Franciscan Order

7. See Friedrich Heer, *The Medieval World: Europe, 1100–1350*, trans. Janet Sondheimer (Cleveland, 1962), pp. 231ff.; and Roderich Schmidt, "Aetates mundi: Die Weltalter als Gliederungsprinzip der Geschichte," *Zeitschrift für Kirchengeschichte* 67 (1955–56), 288–317.

8. On Joachim's thought and writings, see Morton W. Bloomfield, "Joachim of Flora: A Critical Survey of His Canon, Teachings, Sources, Biography, and Influences," *Traditio* 13 (1957), 249–311, passim; and Marjorie Reeves, *The Influence of Prophecy in the Later Middle Ages: A Study in Joachimism* (Oxford, 1969), pp. 16–27, 135–44.

against charges of Joachimism and attacked Joachim's views on many points, was, as Reeves notes, "a Joachite *malgré lui.*"[9]

Descriptions of the end of days such as those of Joachim and those to which Joachim's legacy gave rise usually included the conversion of all infidels to Christianity. Messianic expectations, therefore, naturally contributed to the general conversionist spirit exhibited by the friars during the thirteenth century.[10] Since of all the infidels the Jews were supposed to convert first, many probably viewed their conversion *en masse*—one means of ridding Christendom of Judaism—as a pressing task to be performed in order to pave the way for final redemption. Confuting the errors of the Jews thus took on a more aggressive character than it had had when intended chiefly for the internal consumption of the Christian community. Joachim himself, who ascribed especial significance to the conversion of the Jews in his own account of the end, explicitly drew this connection between polemic and eschatology. Introducing his own polemical *Adversus Iudeos,* he writes:

> Many have thought to act against the ancient stupidity of the Jews with texts from Scripture because, if there will not be one to resist those who assail our faith, opportunity will be given to the enemies of the cross of Christ to deride the simplicity of those believing in the Christian name. And these, who are weak in intelligence, will suffer the destruction of [their] faith. I, however, wish to oppose their [the Jews'] controversy and perfidy not only for this [reason], but also because I feel that the time for pitying them is at hand, the time of their consolation and conversion.[11]

Some have speculated that Innocent III's attacks on the Jews may have derived from his own expectations of the apocalypse. In his commentary on the Apocalypse, the Franciscan Spiritual Peter Olivi called upon the members of his order to missionize among the Jews. And because the Jews had traditionally been labeled the devotees of Antichrist, the presumed imminence of the final battle between the latter and the forces of Christ may well have added to anti-Jewish hostilities still further.[12]

9. Reeves, *The Influence,* pp. 46–48, 145–90, 228–41, 315–16.
10. Ibid., pp. 295–319, 395–415; Burns, "Christian-Islamic Confrontation," p. 1434.
11. Joachim of Flora, *Adversus Iudeos,* ed. Arsenio Frugoni (Rome, 1957), p. 1. See also Beatrice Hirsch-Reich, "Joachim von Fiore und das Judentum," in *JIM,* pp. 244ff.
12. See Allan Cutler, "Innocent III and the Distinctive Clothing of Jews and Muslims," in *Studies in Medieval Culture,* 3, ed. John R. Sommerfeldt (Kalamazoo, 1970),

The new attitude to the Jews, however, appears to have derived even more from a mounting trend in ecclesiastical circles to view the Church of Rome (*romana ecclesia*) not merely as the papal see or delimited jurisdiction of the pope in a Christendom governed jointly by spiritual and temporal swords, but rather as comprising the entire Christian *respublica* or *congregatio fidelium*. The idea of the Church as a supranational entity had always held a prominent place in Catholic theology, but it began to have its greatest effect upon the European consciousness only with the Gregorian reform and investiture controversy of the eleventh century. As the Church endeavored to model European Christendom along the lines of Gregory's perfect *societas christiana*, it also claimed universal headship of that society, relegating secular princes to a level of secondary authority and importance. All of society came to be viewed as an organic unity, whose *raison d'être* consisted of striving for and ultimately realizing the perfect unity of Christ on earth. Within such a unity, every component or constituent unit had to be measured from a teleological perspective: not only did each component of the whole have to further the ideals of the whole, but it also had to embody on a microcosmic level the ideals of the macrocosm. The Christian nature of this unity accordingly determined the necessity for its governance by those who best reflected that nature, and the fact that the whole society far outweighed in value and importance the sum total of all its members precluded any allowance for individualism or deviation within the society at large.[13] Otto Gierke thus describes

92–116; Raoul Manselli, *La "Lectura super Apocalipsim" di Pietro di Giovanni Olivi: Ricerche sull' escatologismo medioevale* (Rome, 1955), p. 216; and Cohn, *The Pursuit,* pp. 77–79.

13. For a general description of this world view, see Otto Gierke, *Political Theories of the Middle Age,* trans. F. W. Maitland (1900; repr., Boston, 1958), pp. 1–30; and Anton-Hermann Chroust, "The Corporate Idea and the Body Politic in the Middle Ages," *Review of Politics* 9 (1947), 423–52. And on the increasing prevalence of such sentiments from the time of Gregory VII, see Gerd Tellenbach, *Church, State and Christian Society at the Time of the Investiture Contest,* trans. R. F. Bennett (1959; repr., New York, 1970), pp. 126–61; Gerhart B. Ladner, "Aspects of Medieval Thought on Church and State," *Review of Politics* 9 (1947), 403–22; Ladner, "The Concepts of 'Ecclesia' and 'Christianitas' and Their Relationship to the Ideal of Papal 'Plenitudo Potestatis' from Gregory VII to Boniface VIII," in *Sacerdozio e regno da Gregorio VII a Bonifacio VIII* (Rome, 1954), pp. 49–57; Walter Ullmann, *The Growth of Papal Government in the Middle Ages,* 2d ed. (New York, 1962), chs. 9–10, 13; Brian Tierney, *Foundations of the Conciliar Theory* (1955; repr., Cambridge, Eng., 1968), pp. 37–46; and J. A. Watt, "The Theory of Papal Monarchy in the Thirteenth Century: The Contribution of the Canonists," *Traditio* 20 (1964), 279, 312–15.

those theocratic and spiritualistic traits which are manifested by the Medieval Doctrine of Society. On the one side, every ordering of a human community must appear as an organic member of that *Civitas Dei*, that God-State, which comprehends the heavens and the earth. Then, on the other hand, the eternal and other-worldly aim and objective of every individual man must, in a directer or an indirecter fashion, determine the aim and object of every group into which he enters.[14]

This conception of Christendom, together with its hierocratic implications, came closest to being realized during the first half of the thirteenth century, beginning with the pontificate of Innocent III. Innocent's attempts at reform of the Church and his campaigns against its various enemies all served to further the higher unity of Christendom under papal direction, and many have singled out Innocent as the pope who in his relations with temporal rulers enunciated the most far-reaching claims of papal lordship over the world. Yet however one evaluates Innocent's claims to temporal power, the pope's desire to unite Christian society clearly emerges in the ecumenical Fourth Lateran Council that he convened in 1215. Inviting not only Catholic clerics but also laymen and representatives of the four Greek Orthodox patriarchs to this synod, Innocent intended that it truly represent the totality of Christendom. In his bull of indiction of the council, *Vineam Domini Sabaoth*, he consequently assigned to the gathering the most extensive of responsibilities: the reform of Christian life, the suppression of heresy, the regulation of the clergy, the waging of a crusade, and "other matters too many to enumerate."[15] It is not surprising that Innocent's idealism and activities greatly strengthened the organic conception of Christian unity, allowing it to wield considerable influence over thirteenth-century Europe.[16]

An overriding concern with the properly ordered wholeness and functional unity of Christendom manifested itself in multifarious ways in the spiritual and intellectual climate of the period. Numer-

14. Gierke, *Political Theories*, pp. 7–8.
15. Innocent III, *Regesta* 16.30, PL 216:824.
16. On the monarchic character of Innocent's pontificate, see, for example, Ullmann, *A Short History*, pp. 208–26; Brian Tierney, "*Tria quippe distinguit iudicia.* Innocent III's Decretal *Per venerabilem*," *Speculum* 37 (1962), 48–59; and Watt, "The Theory," pp. 279–81. On the ecumenical nature and the breadth of the legislation of the Fourth Lateran Council, see Foreville, *Latran*, pp. 245–57, 287–306.

ous cultural historians have demonstrated how as an interest in a unifying synthesis overcame that in intellectual exploration and individualistic creativity, the humanism of the "renaissance" of the twelfth century gave way to the scholasticism of the thirteenth.[17] The *summa*, the complete synthesis and clarification of a field of learning in accordance with accepted philosophical and logical principles, quickly came to constitute the crowning achievement of scholastic writers.[18] Among theologians of the thirteenth century, there appears a trend of reinterpreting the traditional themes of nature and grace so as to place greater emphasis on life in this world. Whether one considers this phenomenon in terms of Francis of Assisi's attempt to live a life of evangelical piety without withdrawing from society, a way of life which laid great stress on the spirituality of nature, or of Thomas Aquinas's appreciation of the inherent goodness in nature, the new theological trend allowed for less bifurcation between the spiritual and mundane in daily life.[19] It rather induced an attempt to unify every aspect of one's existence in the pursuit of the religious ideal. Even the architectural style of the period, epitomized by the Gothic cathedral, reflects the new interest in synthesizing the totality of the human experience. According to one writer, "The cathedral is perhaps best understood as a 'model' of the medieval universe. It is the theological transparency of this universe that transformed the model into a symbol."[20]

17. Christopher Brooke, *The Twelfth Century Renaissance* (New York, 1970), ch. 7; Haskins, *The Renaissance*, passim; Urban T. Holmes, Jr., "The Idea of a Twelfth-Century Renaissance," *Speculum* 26 (1951), 643–51; and especially Heer, *The Medieval World*, passim.

18. Such indeed was Thomas Aquinas' primary objective, as he wrote in the prologue to the *ST*, 1:2: "Consideravimus namque hujus doctrinae novitios in his quae a diversis scripta sunt plurimum impediri, partim quidem propter multiplicationem inutilium quaestionum, articulorum, et argumentorum, partim etiam quia ea quae sunt necessaria talibus ad sciendum non traduntur secundum ordinem disciplinae, sed secundum quod requirebat librorum expositio, vel secundum quod se praebebat occasio disputandi, partim quidem quia frequens eorumdem repetitio et fastidium et confusionem generabat in animis auditorum. Haec igitur et alia hujusmodi evitare studentes, tentabimus cum confidentia divini auxilii ea quae ad sacram doctrinam pertinent breviter ac dilucide prosequi, secundum quod materia patietur." Cf. Martin Grabmann, *Introduction to the Theological Summa of St. Thomas*, trans. John S. Zybura (St. Louis, 1930), p. 70; and M.-D. Chenu, *Toward Understanding Saint Thomas*, trans. A. M. Landry and D. Hugh (Chicago, 1964), p. 299.

19. M.-D. Chenu, "Moines, clercs, laïcs au carrefour de la vie évangélique (XIIe siècle)," *Revue d'histoire ecclésiastique* 49 (1954), 59–89; Knowles, *The Religious Orders*, 1:121; Edward A. Armstrong, *Saint Francis: Nature Mystic* (Berkeley, 1973), pp. 5–17; Gilson, *History*, pp. 361–65, 379–81.

20. Otto G. von Simson, "The Gothic Cathedral: Design and Meaning," in *Change in Medieval Society: Europe North of the Alps, 1050–1500*, ed. Sylvia L. Thrupp (New

As men in every discipline of human intellectual creativity thus came to concentrate on the functional unity of their world—based, as it was, in the notion of the universality of the Roman Church—many saw fit to liken the totality of Christian society to the *corpus mysticum Christi*, the mystical body of Christ. The use of this metaphor to denote the society of all the faithful, rather than the body of Christ as mystically contained in the Eucharist, commenced during the twelfth century, as a result of a new stress on the doctrine of transubstantiation which caused the body of Christ in the sacrament simply to be labeled *corpus Christi*. By the thirteenth century, philosophers, theologians, and lawyers alike appropriated the image of Christ's mystical body to express their conception of Christendom; many soon came to describe the state in the same way. The term effectively captured the end, the true nature, and the ideal constitution of Christian society, as they had to be reflected in the society as a whole and in the functioning of each of its constituent members. In its opening canon, the Fourth Lateran Council suggested that it too shared this outlook.

There is one universal Church of the faithful, outside of which absolutely no one is saved, and in which Jesus Christ is himself at once both priest and sacrifice. His body and his blood are truly contained in the sacrament of the altar in the forms of the bread and the wine, the bread being transubstantiated into the body and the wine into the blood by the divine power, in order that to perfect the mystery of the unity [of Christ] we ourselves may receive from him what he received on our account. No one can perform this sacrament except a priest ritually ordained according to the [authority of the] keys of the Church, which Jesus Christ himself bestowed upon the apostles and their successors.[21]

York, 1964), pp. 168–87. Cf. also Erwin Panofsky, *Gothic Architecture and Scholasticism* (1951; repr., New York, 1957); and Seiferth, *Synagogue and Church*, pp. 123–40, who has attempted to demonstrate how during this period, even the artistic portrayal of the relationship of Ecclesia and Synagoga came to reflect the new conceptions of a universal Christendom: Ecclesia began to subsume Synagoga; whereas the two had always appeared together, the former often appeared alone. For if the Church were unified and universal, a separate representation of Synagoga was inappropriate. Rather, the Jews of the Old Testament whom Synagoga had represented had to take their place, albeit a carefully delimited one, within Christian society. Yet when the Church discovered that the Jews of Europe were not biblical Jewry, it could allow them no place whatsoever within the Ecclesia. On the generally unifying character of medieval symbolism, see Gerhart B. Ladner, "Medieval and Modern Understanding of Symbolism: A Comparison," *Speculum* 54 (1979), 223–56.

21. Alberigo, *Conciliorum*, p. 206. On the developing and changing uses of the term and notion of Christ's mystical body, see Henri de Lubac, *Corpus mysticum:*

Introducing its legislative program, the council simultaneously declared the universality and unity of the Church, linked that unity to the mystery of Christ's transubstantiated body, and stressed the primary role of the clergy in perfecting that unity.

The view, as expressed by Thomas Aquinas, that "the holy Church is called one mystical body by analogy with the physical body of man,"[22] assumed particular significance because its period of prevalence coincided with the reentrance of the concept of the organic corporation—that is, of the corporation as a fictitious person—into Western political and legal theory.[23] Inasmuch as anthropomorphic imagery befitted both the *corpus mysticum* and the corporation equally well, the former soon borrowed from the attributes of the latter, thus affecting more profoundly the particulars of conceptions of how Christendom should operate. Specifically, thirteenth-century decretalists, themselves also concerned with incorporating the proper order of the world into their legal system, used a concept of a corporate mystical body upon which to base their theory of papal monarchy: just as a body is governed by its head, so the universal *romana ecclesia* must be governed by its head, or Christ,[24] represented on earth by the pope. The logic of this power structure derived straightforwardly from the salvific goals of Christian society. The pope has the ultimate responsibility for the welfare of Christian souls; so to none other than his vicar should Christ have properly granted supreme authority on earth, in order that all Christian individuals and institutions might effectively contribute to the holy mission of the Church and the attainment of salvation for the faithful.[25]

The theory of the pope's *plenitudo potestatis* enunciated by the decretalists thus translated current ideas on the unity of Christen-

---

L'Euchariste et l'Eglise au Moyen Age, 2d ed. (Paris, 1949), chs. 1–5 and esp. pp. 281ff.; and Ernst H. Kantorowicz, *The King's Two Bodies: A Study in Medieval Political Theology* (Princeton, 1957), pp. 194–206.

22. Thomas Aquinas, *ST* 3.8.1, 49:54–55.

23. Ernst H. Kantorowicz, "*Pro patria mori* in Medieval Political Thought," *AHR* 56 (1951), 472–92; Tierney, *Foundations*, pp. 96ff.; Ladner, "Aspects," pp. 413–14.

24. Cf. Thomas Aquinas, *ST* 3.8.1, 49:54: "Christus dicitur caput Ecclesiae secundum similitudinem humani capitis."

25. Watt, "The Theory," pp. 273–81; Tierney, *Foundations*, pp. 132–53. Attempts to link the doctrine of the papal *plenitudo potestatis* with the treatment of the Jews in thirteenth-century Christendom appear in Baron, "'Plenitude of Apostolic Power,'" pp. 287–95, 526–28; and Grayzel, "Popes, Jews, and Inquisition," pp. 167ff. Yet owing, perhaps, to their failure to probe thoroughly the depth and background of this important theological concept, neither of these attempts is entirely convincing.

dom into law and political theory. During the thirteenth century, the internal organization of the Church did indeed come to resemble a monarchy. The administration of the papal curia was more centralized than the court of any European kingdom and assumed many of the trappings of royalty as well. Furthermore, the papacy demanded immediate submission from temporal rulers who thwarted its objectives; it did not hesitate repeatedly to depose and excommunicate the recalcitrant emperor Frederick II. Popes claimed supreme judicial authority not only over Christians but over infidels as well. And Pope Gregory IX in 1234 promulgated the first official code of canon law, the *Decretales*, to insure the smooth administration of his domains.[26] Although the popes were by no means unopposed in these efforts, their monarchic tendencies demonstrate how the government, in addition to the self-consciousness, of Christendom during the period derived from an ideal of universal Christian society on earth. Boniface VIII, whose bull *Unam sanctam* of 1302 perhaps enunciates most explicitly the medieval papacy's claim to power, in that bull himself drew this connection.

> That there is one holy, Catholic and apostolic Church we are bound to believe and to hold, our faith urging us, and this we do firmly believe and simply confess; and that outside this Church there is no salvation or remission of sins, as her spouse proclaims in the Canticles, "One is my dove, my perfect one. She is the only one of her mother, the chosen of her that bore her"; which represents one mystical body whose head is Christ, while the head of Christ is God. In this Church there is one Lord, one faith, one baptism. At the time of the flood there was one ark, symbolizing one Church. It was finished in one cubit and had one helmsman and captain, namely Noah, and we read that all things on earth outside of it were destroyed. . . . Therefore there is one body and one head of this one and only Church, not two heads as though it were a monster, namely Christ and Christ's vicar, Peter and Peter's successor.[27]

26. Geoffrey Barraclough, *The Medieval Papacy* (New York, 1968), pp. 118–40; Ullmann, *A Short History*, pp. 227–50; Tierney, *The Crisis*, pp. 139–57.

27. *Extravag. commun.* 1.8.1, in Friedberg, *Corpus*, 2:1245; trans. in Tierney, *The Crisis*, p. 188. Cf. the comments of Ernst Troeltsch, *The Social Teaching of the Christian Churches*, trans. Olive Wyon, 2 vols. (Glencoe, 1931), 1:227ff. For the understanding of *Unam sanctam* as the curia's reaction to the undermining of the organic conception of Christian society (as well as of papal sovereignty) by Aristotelian political theory, see Walter Ullmann, "Die Bulle Unam Sanctam: Rückblick und Ausblick," *Römische historische Mitteilungen* 16 (1974), 45–77.

At the time when Boniface VIII issued the bull *Unam sanctam*, the political realities of Western Europe did not comport with the ideal of a perfectly unified, papally dominated Christendom as described by the pontiff. The concept of distinct national states was rapidly on the ascendant. It has been argued, however, that during the previous century many had come to envision the "supremacy of unity over plurality"[28] in Christian society as a polity. If that is correct, one could expect them to have expressed their devotion to the ideals of Christendom in terms of sentiments resembling nationalism and patriotism. It is precisely during the thirteenth century that scholars discern the first appearance of nationalism and patriotism in Western Europe, in the law and the propaganda of the period.[29] By the end of the century, when the centralized, monarchic power of the papacy had already begun to decline, the term *patria* denoted specific national entities like England and France. Yet the notion of the *patria* and devotion thereto (patriotism) had always constituted important motifs in the theology of the Church; Ernst Kantorowicz accordingly urges that "one should at least consider the possibility whether—before the full impact of legal and humanistic doctrines became effective—the new territorial concept of *patria* did not perhaps develop as a resecularized offshoot of the Christian tradition and whether the new patriotism did not thrive also on ethical values transferred back from the *patria* in heaven to the polities on earth." More definitively, Kantorowicz has shown that like the theory of papal *plenitudo potestatis*, the emergence of feelings of patriotism on behalf of one's polity also derived from the current tendency to view Christendom as a corporate *corpus mysticum*.[30] Patriotism too emanated at least to some extent from the conception of the world as the unity of a universal Christian society.

In a society which was committed to an ideal of organic unity, which demanded of all its members a functional contribution to the achievement of that unity, which defined both its ideal and its mode of organization in terms of the mystical body of Christ, which operated (at least in theory) as the centralized monarchy of the earthly vicar of Christ, and which gave rise to intense feelings

---

28. Chroust, "The Corporate Idea," p. 429.
29. Halvdan Koht, "The Dawn of Nationalism in Europe," *AHR* 52 (1947), 265–80; Gaines Post, "Two Notes on Nationalism in the Middle Ages," *Traditio* 9 (1953), 281–96; Kantorowicz, *The King's Two Bodies*, pp. 232–58.
30. Kantorowicz, *The King's Two Bodies*, p. 235; and *"Pro patria mori,"* passim.

of patriotism on its own behalf, no room existed for infidels. Such trends in the political and religious thought of the thirteenth century certainly made the climate ripe for the exclusion of the Jews, the infidels most deeply imbedded in the society, from Christendom.[31] Still other developments, however, may have predisposed agents of the Church such as the friars to scrutinize the substance of contemporary Judaism and develop the theory of Jewish heresy which justified breaking with the Augustinian precedent of toleration. The power and unity of the *romana ecclesia* reached their peak during the first half of the thirteenth century; by the end of the century and throughout the following one, they proceeded along a course of rather steady decline. Sensing, as most empires do at their point of greatest expansion, the impending threat of centrifugal forces which would lead to contraction and decline, the Church attempted to protect the gains it had achieved.[32] It strove to entrench itself at the summit of its power and exhibited in three significant ways the extreme sort of defensiveness characteristic of declining empires.

First, whereas the drive toward realizing the perfect unity of Christendom included the scholastic effort to produce intellectual syntheses which themselves mirrored that unity, the defensiveness of the thirteenth-century Church manifested itself in an attempt to rule and regulate human thought. Ideas or beliefs that did not accord strictly with those of the establishment were seen not only as undermining the Church's authority but as threatening to destroy the Christian unity that the Church struggled to maintain. And the ideal of an essentially totalistic society toward which the Church strove inevitably stimulated the rise of opposing intellectual and theological currents, which in turn only served to make the ecclesiastical reaction harsher.[33] We have already considered the papacy's definition of heresy during this period as a crime of treason

31. Cf. the comments of N. Daniel, *Islam*, pp. 251–52, on the ideational threat to thirteenth-century Christendom posed by Islam.

32. On the beginnings of decline in the thirteenth-century Church, see Ullmann, *A Short History*, pp. 251–78; and Barraclough, *The Medieval Papacy*, pp. 118–40; and on the general effects of this decline on Europe of the fourteenth century, cf. Joseph R. Strayer, "The Promise of the Fourteenth Century," in *Medieval Statecraft and the Perspectives of History* (Princeton, 1971), p. 315; and Gordon Leff, *The Dissolution of the Medieval Outlook: An Essay on Intellectual and Spiritual Change in the Fourteenth Century* (New York, 1976). On the life-cycles of empires, see Robert G. Wesson, *The Imperial Order* (Berkeley, 1967), pp. 40–52, 190ff.; S. N. Eisenstadt, *The Political Systems of Empires* (London, 1963), pp. 62–64, 140–43.

33. Cf. Wesson, *The Imperial Order*, pp. 167–86, 235–41.

against Christendom and the subsequent founding of the Inquisition to combat it. As we have seen, heresy in general, and contemporary heresies in particular, opposed many of the basic pillars of medieval Christian society. We then need here only emphasize the underlying connection between the Inquisition and the earthly head of Christ's mystical body. As Walter Ullmann has observed,

> The papal Inquisition must be understood from the contemporary medieval standpoint which knew no freedom of expression or thought in regard to matters touching the substance of faith. Hence aberration from faith as papally fixed was not only (as it was said) a sign of intellectual arrogance, but also, and more so, an act of rebellion against constituted authority which claimed a monopoly in all matters relating to the religious foundations of society.[34]

Nor did the papacy limit its expression of such monopolistic claims to the establishment of the Inquisition. The thirteenth century also saw a steady rise in the intervention of the papacy in the affairs of the University of Paris, an attempt to control the pursuits of the finest philosophical and theological minds in Europe; in the eyes of the Church, as F. M. Powicke has remarked, "the university was a function of Christian society, not a separate order."[35] If ideas that did not conform to the established order of things had to be eradicated, one can appreciate the fervor with which the Church pursued the attack on the Talmud and the Judaism it maintained: Living according to the teachings of the Talmud, the Jews did not fulfill their proper function in Christian society; they and their doctrines accordingly detracted from the unity of Christ. And owing to the alleged hostility of rabbinic Judaism toward the proponents and fundamental beliefs of Christianity, the medieval Jew may well have presented an even greater threat to Latin Christendom than the typical heretic. It is perhaps appropriate that Pope Gregory IX issued his famous regulatory bull *Parens scientiarum* to the University of Paris, prohibited the study of unexpurgated texts of Aristotle, ordered that his *Decretales* be adopted at Paris and Bologna as the sole standard legal textbook,[36] and founded the

34. Ullmann, *A Short History*, pp. 253–54. Especially helpful here are the analysis of Bévenot, "The Inquisition," 7:384–93; and the comments of Beck et al., *From the High Middle Ages*, pp. 136–37.
35. F. M. Powicke, "The Medieval University in Church and Society," in *Ways of Medieval Life and Thought: Essays and Addresses* (New York, 1971), p. 201. See also Rashdall, *The Universities*, 1:300–70, passim; and Leff, *Paris and Oxford*, ch. 1.
36. Denifle, *Chartularium*, 1:136–39, 143–44; Ripoll, *Bullarium*, 169.

first permanent tribunals of the Inquisition, all only a few years before he received Nicholas Donin at the papal curia.

A second manifestation of defensiveness in the clerical establishment of the thirteenth century, and perhaps a corollary of the first, was a tendency to fear and to attack innovation in theology. Theoretically, the authentic teachings of Christianity all derived from Scripture, as it had been interpreted by the Church fathers, popes, and councils. What did not ultimately accord with the Bible and the teachings of the early Church had no proper place in the unifying religious synthesis of the period; the very fact of its novelty disqualified any claims to legitimacy and constituted prima facie evidence of heresy. The importance of this outlook in the friars' attack on contemporary Judaism should be evident. The Jews of medieval Europe espoused a new system of belief; they had lost the right to exist in Christendom previously accorded them because of their adherence to ancient, biblical Judaism. The appearance of such argumentation, however, was not limited to the exchanges between mendicants and Jews. One finds it in another controversy, which, like the first attacks on the Talmud, was centered at the University of Paris, but in which the friars themselves were depicted as guilty of *innovatio*. During the conflict between secular and mendicant clergy at the University of Paris, the secular masters expressed particular resentment at the mendicant doctrine of absolute poverty, portrayed by the friars as a necessary prerequisite for achieving the highest level of evangelical piety. The secular masters responded that the Bible did not portray Jesus and the apostles as living in absolute poverty, and that the friars, by maintaining the doctrine, cast aspersions on the piety of popes and prelates since the time of the earliest Church.[37]

William of St. Amour, the first major spokesman for the secular masters, writes in one of his anti-mendicant works that a man is a false rather than a true preacher not only if he preaches against Scripture but even if he teaches what simply does not appear in or derive from the Bible.[38] Turning to the friars, he then explains:

37. The best account of the issues and events of the controversy is M.-M. Dufeil, *Guillaume de Saint-Amour et la polémique universitaire parisienne, 1250–1259* (Paris, 1972). For briefer, more limited discussions, see D. L. Douie, *The Conflict between the Seculars and the Mendicants at the University of Paris in the Thirteenth Century* (London, 1954); Rashdall, *The Universities*, 1:370–97; Peter R. McKeon, "The Status of the University of Paris as *Parens Scientiarum*: An Episode in the Development of Its Autonomy," *Speculum* 39 (1964), 651–75; and James D. Dawson, "William of Saint-Amour and the Apostolic Tradition," *Medieval Studies* 40 (1978), 223–38.

38. William of St. Amour, *Collectiones catholicae et canonicae scripturae ad defensionem ecclesiasticae hierarchiae, et ad instructionem, et praeparationem simplicium fidelium Christi,*

Certain preachers, desiring to convert the people to their new way of life, introduce certain superstitious novelties not within the tradition of the Church but which bear the appearance of sanctity. It appears that they are seeking vain glory. . . . Of this sort seem to be those preachers who [perform] various new and unheard of, simulated works of penitence, in order that it be believed by the multitude. They also practice certain new, unheard of, and superstitious traditions, and they display [them] and teach [that they should] be displayed publicly, contrary to divine Scripture, canonical institutes, and the custom of the Church.[39]

William proceeds to charge that contravening the advice of Seneca against innovation, the friars have invented these new traditions to make themselves appear more perfect, humble, and pious than anyone else. Yet these traditions, dubbed *religiones* by the mendicants, are in fact the creations of men and not of God; one ought more suitably to call them superstition and sacrilege, since they actually violate the word of the divine author of the true religion.[40] For instance, although these preachers conceal money like all other regular clergy and will accept a gift when offered one, they have invented the tradition of evangelical poverty to feign greater perfection, despite its opposition to the rules and teachings of the Church. They teach that one truly pious should not even engage in manual labor but should live entirely from alms, even though canonical tradition explicitly forbids unnecessary begging. Or they falsely state that they have the power of hearing confessions in parishes not specifically their own. In their departure from Scripture, William concludes, "those who under the guise of piety or *religio* contrive such or similar traditions opposed to divine and

---

in *Opera omnia* (Constance, 1632), p. 336: "Si praedicet quis falsa Divinae Scripturae contraria; vel, si quis, ut sic favorem popularem acquirat, praedicet quaedam falsa populo placentia, nec in Scripturis contenta, nec Scripturis contraria. . . ."

39. Ibid., p. 345 (cited and translated in part by Brian Tierney, *Origins of Papal Infallibility, 1150–1350* [Leiden, 1972], p. 72).

40. Ibid., pp. 384–92; see esp. pp. 384–85: "Duodecimum Signum potest esse, Quod Pseudo quandoque, ut populum in se vite novitate convertant, contra illud Senecae . . . , 'Non conturbabit Sapiens publicos mores . . . ,' novas, et insuetas, ac superstitiosas traditiones sibi faciunt, per quas se humiles esse, voluptates contemnere, de humanis honoribus non curare, et omnino perfectiores et Religiosiores esse supra modum aliorum Religiosorum simulant et ostentant; et tales traditiones 'Religionem' appellant. Quae, cum sint praecepta et doctrinae hominum, et non Dei; verius Superstitiones, vel Sacrilegium, quam vera Religio dici possunt; ut pote contra Authorem verae Religionis (id est contra Deum, et eius doctrinam) sacrilega mente inventae."

apostolic documents and the statutes of the holy fathers are similar to the hypocritical Pharisees, who, at the time of the teaching of Christ, on account of their own traditions which bore the appearance of piety, transgressed and caused the transgression of the precepts of God."[41] Just as the traditions of the Pharisees, the first of the rabbis of the Talmud, departed from the authentic traditions of Judaism, so mendicant doctrines may, William wrote, be fairly labeled "superstition" because "they were not handed down to us by the Lord Jesus Christ nor by his apostles nor by the holy councils nor by the canonical writings of the holy doctors but were introduced by certain newcomers of their own will."[42] So deviant were the friars' teachings that William finally dubs them *sectae* or sectarian; they have no place in the true faith and prove the falseness of the mendicant preachers.[43] Gerard d'Abbeville, the next major propagandist for the secular masters, similarly accuses the friars of obscuring the divine teachings of Scripture with their own human traditions. According to Gerard, the mendicant doctrine of poverty challenges the legitimacy of various papal rights and powers, thereby causing the friars to detract from the unity of the body that is the Roman Church and to fall into the sin of heresy.[44]

Admittedly, William and Gerard both wrote years after the first attack on the Talmud at the University of Paris; one could not argue that their campaign against the doctrinal innovation of the friars overflowed into a confrontation between the latter and the Jews. Nevertheless, the similarity between the accusations leveled during the two controversies appears marked, too much so to re-

41. Ibid., p. 388.
42. Ibid., pp. 389–90 (cited and translated by Tierney, *Origins*, p. 72).
43. Ibid., p. 390: "Quod etiam tales traditiones 'Secta,' vel 'Sectae' valeant appellari, ex eo videtur; quoniam illas tradentes, ex habitu animorum suorum, in Religionis cultu longe aliter quam caeteri, opinantur, ut ostensum est supra."
44. Gerard d'Abbeville, "*Contra adversarium perfectionis christianae*," ed. Sophronius Clasen, *Archivum franciscanum historicum* 32 (1939), 129: "Sed mirum est, quod isti volunt, quod traditiones hominum praedicentur et vita Christi et Apostolorum ceterorumque Sanctorum sub silentio occultetur." Gerard, "Sermo factus apud Fratres Minores," in *Bettelorden und Weltgeistlichkeit an der Universität Paris*, ed. Max Bierbaum (Münster, 1920), pp. 210–11: "Vide ergo, quia non decet menbra (!) a capite discedere, sed iuxta scripture testimonium omnia membra caput sequantur. . . . Ergo ecclesie Romane debent sequi caput suum et non se preferre capiti vel conferre in excellentissimi status perfectionem, hoc est a capite membra discedere. Qui enim prerogativam vel privilegium perfectionis excellentissime propter abdicationem proprietatis vel communis possessionis suo statui contendit ascribere, privilegium ecclesie Romane contendit auferre, quando excellentiam sui status ipsius ecclesie Romane intendit preferre; talis dicendus est hereticus."

flect mere coincidence. If the charges of one controversy did not directly lead to those of another—and the possibility does remain that the attack on the Talmud influenced that against the friars—they still manifest the same prevalent intellectual tendency among many clergy of the thirteenth century. All theological ideas required careful scrutiny to insure their conformity with the teachings of Scripture as interpreted in the tradition of the Church. Nonscriptural beliefs detracted from the unity of Christendom and could not be tolerated; they were novel and thus warranted eradication as sectarian or heretical. Given such a context, one can well appreciate the vehemence of the Church's attack on the hitherto unknown Talmud of the Jews.

Finally, a third by-product of the defensiveness of thirteenth-century Christendom emerged in the conversion of quasi-nationalistic sentiments of patriotism on behalf of the universal Church into expressions of nativism. The term "nativism" presently appears most often in the writings of American historians, but this should not impose any necessary limitation on the extent of its usefulness and applicability. Nativism denotes an outlook of a society in which anyone whose basic concerns, allegiances, and ideals lie outside those of the society cannot be a citizen in good standing and threatens the welfare of all other citizens. "Nativism is a state of mind, conscious or unconscious, intimately connected with nationalism. Its roots, like those of nationalism, spring from a sense of common associations, common history, common speech, common customs, common religion, etc."[45] Many in the thirteenth century also seem to have taken this short leap from a sort of aggressive Christian nationalism or patriotism to a defensive nativism. If Europe comprised a wholly Christian unity, every non-Christian not only was alien to Christian society but very quickly became an enemy as well.[46] The Spanish Council of Valladolid in 1322 reflected this mindset when it decreed that "the Church of God, in which the divine offices are celebrated and the sacrament of the Eucharist is consecrated, ought to be purged, in order that it might not be profaned by contact between infidels and the faithful."[47] Foreigners in a homogenous society detracted from the so-

45. W. Darrell Overdyke, *The Know-Nothing Party in the South* (Baton Rouge, 1950), p. 2.

46. David Knowles and Dimitri Obolensky, *The Middle Ages*, The Christian Centuries: A New History of the Catholic Church 2 (New York, 1968), p. 376; E. R. Daniel, *The Franciscan Concept*, pp. 2–3.

47. Mansi, *Sacrorum conciliorum . . . collectio*, 25:717–18: "Ecclesia Dei, in qua celebrantur Divina officia et sacramentum Eucharistiae consecratur, purgari debet, ne

ciety's unity and were therefore prone to antagonism from all good patriotic citizens. And as John Boswell has recently noted in the case of homosexuals, the purging of alien elements did not in itself suffice; even those Christians whose personal values openly differed from those of the majority faced persecution and social ostracism in thirteenth-century Europe.[48] Like the extreme German nationalism of the late ninteenth century, which gave rise to anti-Semitic indictments of the satanic, talmudic culture of contemporary Jews and demanded their exclusion from the fatherland, or the great American reform movement earlier in the century, which denounced Catholics for deserting the truth of Christianity, opposing American ideals, and perpetrating grossly unethical and hostile crimes against society, the Church's scrutinizing and condemnation of medieval Judaism made perfect sense in the context of nativism.[49] For the *romana ecclesia* was also a society which strove to achieve functional unity and root out foreign influences. It too attacked a religious group which detracted from that unity, charging it with the same basic crimes: heretical deviation from

communicatione infidelium cum fidelibus profanetur." Cf. also the comment of Langmuir, "L'absence," p. 246, that the ritual murder accusations leveled at Jews during the thirteenth century were propagated "by those who were most devoted to the ideal of a unified Christian society."

48. John Boswell, *Christianity, Social Tolerance, and Homosexuality: Gay People in Western Europe from the Beginning of the Christian Era to the Fourteenth Century* (Chicago, 1980), esp. pt. 4, demonstrates that whereas homosexuals were rarely the objects of persecution in Christendom until the twelfth century, thereafter their plight worsened drastically, owing to the increasing concern for order and uniformity and to the concomitant decline in tolerance for all minority groups. Boswell illustrates not only the extent of the persecution but also the new, "unnatural" perception of the homosexual which developed in the thirteenth century. See in particular pp. 269–76, where he compares the treatment of homosexuals to that of usurers and Jews, and cf. his concluding remarks on p. 334.

49. On the "Volkish" ideology in nineteenth-century Germany, its nativist orientation, and anti-Judaism, see George L. Mosse, *The Crisis of German Ideology: Intellectual Origins of the Third Reich* (New York, 1964), and *Germans and Jews: The Right, the Left, and the Search for a "Third Force" in Pre-Nazi Germany* (New York, 1970), esp. chs. 1–2; Fritz Stern, *The Politics of Cultural Despair: A Study in the Rise of the Germanic Ideology* (1961; repr., Garden City, N.Y., 1965), esp. pp. 3, 16ff., 85–94; Uriel Tal, *Christians and Jews in Germany: Religion, Politics, and Ideology in the Second Reich, 1870–1914*, trans. N. J. Jacobs (Ithaca, 1975), ch. 2; Jacob Katz, *From Prejudice to Destruction: Anti-Semitism, 1700–1933* (Cambridge, Mass., 1980), esp. pp. 197–200, 219–20; and Norman Cohn, *Warrant for Genocide: The Myth of the Jewish World-Conspiracy and the Protocols of the Elders of Zion* (New York, 1966), pp. 32–40. On American reform and nativism, see above all Ray Allen Billington, *The Protestant Crusade 1800–1860* (1938; repr., New York, 1952), pp. 345–79; and cf. Henry Steele Commager, *The Era of Reform, 1830–1860* (Princeton, 1960), p. 10. Kenneth T. Jackson, *The Ku Klux Klan in the City, 1915–1930* (New York, 1967), pp. 200–201, discusses the similar charges against Catholics in the early twentieth-century movement of One Hundred Percent Americanism.

Scripture, blaspheming the ideals of the society, and immoral and unnatural hostility toward its citizens. Nativism may well have served as at least one catalyst in the development of the view that the Jews had no rightful place in Christendom. If so, one might further appreciate the fact that increased popular persecutions of medieval European Jewry, as well as the expulsion of Jews *en masse* from European countries at the end of the Middle Ages, characteristically accompanied the growth of nationalism and national representative governments.[50]

The intellectual and spiritual climate of thirteenth-century Europe, ingrained with the notion of Christian unity, made the time ripe for a new exclusionist attitude toward the Jews. The monarchic papacy assumed the right of intervention in the internal doctrinal affairs of the Jewish community. Canonists began to claim direct ecclesiastical jurisdiction over the Jews. And as R. W. Southern has noted, the general religious enthusiasm of the time gave "specious justification" for the people of Europe to inflict violence upon the Jews.[51] As we have seen, however, the major work of developing, refining, and justifying the new attitude was performed by the Dominicans and Franciscans. The friars' importance in this regard ought not to be deemed accidental, since the creation and character of the two mendicant orders derived from and responded to the same needs and the same climate of the European religious community of which we have spoken. Modern scholars have called the thirteenth century "the golden age of the friars,"[52] because, in the words of David Knowles,

> St Francis and St Dominic, in different but complementary ways, gave to the Church a new form of religious life, which had an immense and permanent appeal, and one which both attracted a new type of recruit and in its turn inspired an apostolate to the laity, to the heretic and to the heathen. Not only did the appearance of the friars rescue the western church from its drift toward heresy and schism, but the new warmth of devotional life, the preaching, the confessing and the daily counsel of the friars gave a new strength to the lower level of Christian society and indirectly acted as a powerful agent of spiritual growth and social union, thus inevitably compensating for the growing power of legalism and political motives at the higher levels of church life. In addition, the friars had a major share in the wonderful flowering

50. Karl W. Deutsch, "Anti-Semitic Ideas in the Middle Ages," *Journal of the History of Ideas* 6 (1945), 251.

51. Pakter, "De his qui foris sunt," pp. 23–26; Richard W. Southern, *The Making of the Middle Ages* (New Haven, 1953), p. 257.

52. Richard W. Emery, *The Friars in Medieval France* (New York, 1962), p. 5.

of theological genius in the schools. They had a twofold influence in the realm of the spirit. They . . . brought back to the Christian consciousness the earthly life of Christ in its love, its poverty and its suffering as an ideal to be followed to the end, while at the same time they presented the theological expression of Christ's message in the lecture-room and pulpit throughout Christendom.[53]

The friars thus made a decisive impression on Christian society of the period, and in so doing, they contributed much to achieving and maintaining the unity of Christendom of which we have spoken. Established by the Church to teach and preach against heresy, the two mendicant orders actively combatted the centrifugal forces that threatened Christian unity. Pledged to rules which prescribed lives of evangelical piety, the friars exemplified the macrocosm of Christian universality in their own individual behavior. Owing to their own social origins, they added an entirely new dimension to Christian unity, by directing their own spiritual and religious life to meet the needs of the worldliest of middle-class types, the merchant and the financier. The mendicants thereby bridged some of the gap between the *religiosus* and the layman, enabling them to participate together in the same spiritual pursuits. And in disputing with and endeavoring to convert the infidel, the friars tried to expand and perfect the unity of the Christian society, both within and outside the physical domains of European Christendom. In the mystical body of Christ, the friars represented those cells charged with fighting off external enemies and combatting internal infection; or, in the image of Gregory IX's bull *Descendentes*, the friars were meant to set the ship of the Church aright and steer it from darkness into light, successfully catching the fish of the sea in its nets.[54]

A significant number of the friars considered in this book themselves expressed the prevalent conception of an ideally ordered and united Christian society. While serving as Gregory IX's chaplain during the 1230s, Raymond de Peñaforte compiled the *Decretales*, which Gregory proceeded to promulgate as the sole recognized code of canon law, to be studied and implemented universally—clearly a means of promoting Christian unity.[55] Like the Franciscan

53. Knowles and Obolensky, *The Middle Ages*, p. 345; see also Beck et al., *From the High Middle Ages*, pp. 182–83; and Mandonnet, *St. Dominic*, pp. 5ff.
54. Ripoll, *Bullarium*, 1:19.
55. See Gregory's bull *Rex pacificus*, ibid., 1:69: "Volentes igitur, ut hac tantum compilatione universi utantur in judiciis, et in scholis, districtius prohibemus, ne quis presumat aliam facere absque auctoritate Sedis Apostolice speciali."

author of the Bavarian *Schwabenspiegel*, Berthold von Regensburg consistently supported papal attempts to rule and unify Christendom. His two sermons in which he denied Jews access to the "field" of Christendom dealt specifically with the theme of Christian unity. In one of them, Berthold describes the three walls surrounding the field—the papacy, the temporal powers, and the angels—each of which must do its proper duty to protect Christendom or else suffer the punishment of damnation. In the other sermon, Berthold divides the population of Christendom into ten classes, corresponding to the ten orders of angels in heaven. The first three classes, comprising the pope and the secular clergy, the religious orders, and the temporal princes, again have the responsibility for protecting and administering the field, all under the direction of the papacy. Among the next six classes of laymen, every individual must strive to fulfill his own particular function for the sake of the entire society. Only in this way can Christendom preserve its unity. If one should not function properly and thus detract from Christian unity, he will fall into the tenth class of people, the apostates who have allied with the devil.[56] Raymond Lull eagerly awaited the establishment of a universal and united Catholic world order, in the realization of which the conversion of the infidels constituted but one, albeit crucial, step.[57] Bernard Gui's *Practica* was by its very nature committed to preserving and enforcing the unity of Christian faith. And recent research has shown how even Nicholas of Lyra concerned himself with the proper government of Christian society and ecclesiology of the Church; he too enunciated a belief in the unity of Christendom as comprising that of a single body.[58] The attack of these friars on the Jews might well be understood, therefore, as deriving from the overriding concern for Christian unity during the thirteenth and early fourteenth centuries and from their active roles in trying to realize it—whether as inquisitor, missionary, Semitist, poet, or itinerant preacher.

56. Berthold von Regensburg, *Vollständige Ausgabe*, 1:140–56, 357–72; and see G. Kisch, *The Jews in Medieval Germany*, p. 164.

57. See Sugranyes de Franch, *Ramon Lulle*, pp. 51–52: "The conversion of the infidels—of all the infidels—will figure as an indispensable step in a very vast plan of social, political, moral, and religious reform aiming to bring back all the peoples and races of the earth to the unity of the faith and to the unity of the Christian polity." Cf. the conclusion of Wieruszowski, "Ramon Lull," pp. 90–91.

58. Wood, "Nicholas of Lyre," pp. 68ff.

APPENDIX

Textual Parallels in Nicholas of Lyra's *Quodlibetum* and Raymond Martini's *Pugio fidei*

page in *Quodlibetum*	Source	page in *Pugio*
275D	Jeremiah 23:5–6	650
	Haggai 2:8	
276A	Genesis 1:1	485
	Joshua 24:19	485–86
	Jeremiah 23:36	486
	2 Samuel 7:23	486
	Ecclesiastes 2:12	486
276B	Hebrew gloss on Ecclesiastes 2:12	486
	Hebrew gloss on Psalm 50:1	
276C	1 Samuel 28:13	611
276E	Psalm 110:1ff.	337–38, 705
	Isaiah 48:16	492
276F	gloss on Exodus 19 and 20	492–93
276G	Zachariah 12:1 and gloss	493
276H	Rashi on Isaiah 48:16	492
	Ecclesiastes 4:12 and gloss	495
	Psalm 33:6 and gloss	494
	Jeremiah 23:5–6	650
	Genesis 22:14	383, 655–56
	Judges 6:24	655
	Exodus 17:15	655, 656
277A	Maimonides on names of God	648–49
277C	Isaiah 9:5–6	743
277E	Targum on Isaiah 9:6	743

Bibliography

Primary Sources

Abraham ben Azriel. *Sefer 'Arugat ha-Bosem.* Ed. Ephraim E. Urbach. 4 vols. Jerusalem, 1939–63.

Abraham ben Moses Maimonides. *Milḥamot ha-Shem.* Ed. Reuben Margalioth. Jerusalem, 1958.

Abraham ibn Daud. *Sefer ha-Qabbalah.* Ed. Gerson D. Cohen. Philadelphia, 1967.

Alberigo, Joseph, et al., eds. *Conciliorum oecumenicorum decreta.* Alt. ed. Basel, 1962.

Alexander of Hales. *ST.* 5 vols. Florence (Quaracchi), 1924–48.

Alfonso X of Castile (el Sabio). *Opusculos legales.* 2 vols. Madrid, 1836.

Altercatio Aecclesiae contra Synagogam: Texte inédit du X siècle. Ed. Bernhard Blumenkranz. Strasbourg, 1954.

Ashkenazi, Eliezer, ed. *Ṭa'am Zeqeinim.* Frankfurt, 1854.

Augustine. *De civitate Dei.* Ed. and trans. George E. McCracken et al. 7 vols. London, 1957–72.

Baer, Seligman, ed. *Seder 'Avodat Yisra'el.* Rev. ed. Berlin, 1936.

Balme, Franciscus, and Ceslaus Paben, eds. *Raymundiana.* Monumenta Ordinis Fratrum Praedicatorum historica 6. 2 fascs. Rome, 1900.

Baronius, Cesare, and Odericus Raynaldus, eds. *Annales ecclesiastici.* 34 vols. Lucca, 1738–56.

Bernard Gui. *Manuel de l'inquisiteur.* Ed. G. Mollat. 2 vols. Paris, 1926–27.

——. *Practica inquisitionis heretice pravitatis.* Ed. Celestin Douais. Paris, 1886.

Berthold von Regensburg. *Vollständige Ausgabe seiner Predigten.* Ed. Franz Pfeiffer. 2 vols. 1862–80; repr., Berlin, 1965.

——. *Das Wirken . . . gegen die Ketzer.* Ed. Anton E. Schönbach. Studien zur Geschichte der altdeutschen Predigt 3. Vienna, 1904.

Biblia sacra cum glossis, interlineari, et ordinaria, Nicolai Lyrani postilla, ac moralitatibus, Burgensis additionibus, et Thoringi replicis, etc. 6 vols. Venice, 1588.

Bonaventure. *Opera omnia.* 11 vols. Florence (Quaracchi), 1882–1902.

The Book of Tobit. Ed. Adolph Neubauer. Oxford, 1878.

Chazan, Robert, ed. *Church, State, and Jew in the Middle Ages.* New York, 1980.

Collell, Alberto, ed. "Raymundiana: Appéndice a un diplomaterio." *Analecta sacra tarraconensia* 30 (1957), 63–95.

Corpus iuris canonici. Ed. Aemilius Friedberg. 2 vols. 1879; repr., Graz, 1959.

Corpus iuris civilis. Ed. Paul Krueger et al. 3 vols. Berlin, 1900–1905.

De Laurière, Eusèbe, et al., eds. *Ordonnances des roys de France de la troisième race.* 21 vols. Paris, 1723–1848.

Del Giudice, Giuseppe, ed. *Codice diplomatico del regno di Carlo I° e II° d'Angiò.* 3 vols. Naples, 1863–1902.

Delorme, Ferdinand-M., ed. *En marge du bullaire franciscain.* La France franciscaine: Documents de théologie, philosophie, histoire 3. Paris, 1938.

Denifle, Heinrich, ed. *Chartularium universitatis parisiensis.* 4 vols. Paris, 1889–97.

Duplès-Agier, Henri, ed. *Chroniques de Saint-Martial de Limoges.* Paris, 1874.

Duvernoy, Jean, ed. *Le registre de l'inquisition de Jacques Fournier, évêque de Pamiers (1318–1325).* 2 vols. Toulouse, 1965.

Eisenstein, J. D., ed. *Oẓar Wikuḥim: A Collection of Polemics and Disputations* [Hebrew]. New York, 1928.

Finke, Heinrich, ed. *Acta aragonensia.* 3 vols. 1908–22; repr., Aalen, 1966–68.

Florence of Worcester. *Chronicon ex chronicis.* Ed. Benjamin Thorpe. 2 vols. London, 1848–49.

Francis of Assisi. *Opuscula Sancti patris . . . .* 3d ed. Florence (Quaracchi), 1949.

Gerard d'Abbeville. "Contra adversarium perfectionis christianae." Ed. Sophronius Clasen. *Archivum franciscanum historicum* 31 (1938), 276–329; 32 (1939), 89–200.

———. "Sermo factus apud Fratres Minores." In *Betaelorden und Weltgeistlichkeit an der Universität Paris,* pp. 208–19. Ed. Max Bierbaum. Franziskanische Studien 2. Beiheft. Münster, 1920.

Gilbert Crispin. *Disputatio Iudei et Christiani.* Ed. Bernhard Blumenkranz. Utrecht, 1956.

Gilbert of Tournai. *Disputatio Ecclesiae et Synagogae.* In *Thesaurus novus anecdotorum* 5:1497–1506. Ed. Edmund Martène and Ursinus Durand. 5 vols. 1717; repr., New York, 1968.

Giordano da Rivalto. *Prediche.* 2 vols. Florence, 1831.

Gratian. *Decretum.* 2 vols. Venice, 1600.

Haberman, A. M., ed. *Sefer Gezeirot 'Ashkenaz we-Ṣarefat.* Jerusalem, 1945.

Habig, Marion A., ed. *St. Francis of Assisi: Writings and Early Biographies.* Chicago, 1973.

Hayyim ibn Musa. *Magen wa-Romaḥ.* Ed. A. Posnanski. Jerusalem, 1970.

Innocent IV. *Commentaria . . . super libros quinque decretalium.* 2 vols. Frankfurt, 1570.

Jacob ben Elijah Lattès (of Venice). " 'Iggeret (Wikkuaḥ)." Ed. Joseph Kobak. *Jeschurun* 6 (1868), 1–34.

Jacob ben Meir Tam. *Sefer ha-Yashar: Ḥeleq ha-She'eilot weha-Techuvot.* Ed. Ferdinand Rosenthal. 1898; repr., Jerusalem, 1965.

Jacob ben Reuben. *Milḥamot ha-Shem.* Ed. Judah M. Rosenthal. Jerusalem, 1963.

Jean de Joinville. *Histoire de Saint Louis.* Ed. M. Natalis de Wailly. 2d ed. Paris, 1874.

Jennings, A. C., and W. H. Loewe, eds. *The Psalms with Introductions and Critical Notes.* 2d ed. 2 vols. London, 1884–85.

The Jewish-Christian Debate in the High Middle Ages: A Critical Edition of the Nizzaḥon Vetus. Ed. David Berger. Philadelphia, 1979.

Joachim of Flora. *Adversus Iudeos.* Ed. Arsenio Frugoni. Rome, 1957.

Joseph ben Isaac Qimḥi, *The Book of the Covenant.* Trans. Frank Ephraim Talmage. Toronto, 1972.

——. *The Book of the Covenant and Other Writings* [Hebrew]. Ed. Frank Ephraim Talmage. Jerusalem, 1974.

Joseph ben Joshua ha-Kohen. *'Emeq ha-Bakha.* Ed. M. Letteris. 1885; repr., Jerusalem, 1967.

Joseph ben Nathan Official. *Sepher Joseph ha-Mekane* [Hebrew]. Ed. Judah M. Rosenthal. Jerusalem, 1970.

Judah ben Samuel (the Pious). *Das Buch der Frommen* [Hebrew]. Ed. Jehuda Wistinetzki. 2d ed. 1924; repr., Jerusalem, 1969.

Kaufmann, David, ed. "Mikhtav ha-Rav Ḥayyim ibn Musa li-Vno R. Yehudah, Hu"l 'im He'arot u-Fetiḥah 'al Toledot ha-Meḥabber." *Bet Talmud* 2 (1882), 110–25.

Kisch, Guido, ed. *Jewry-Law in Medieval Germany: Laws and Court Decisions Concerning Jews.* New York, 1949.

Kupfer, Ephraim, ed. "The Concluding Portion of Nachmanides' Discourse *Torat Ha-Shem Temima* [Hebrew]." *Tarbiz* 40 (1970), 64–83.

A Life of Ramon Lull. Ed. E. Allison Peers. London, 1927.

Litterae apostolicae diversorum romanorum pontificum pro officio sanctissimae Inquisitionis. Rome, 1579.

Loeb, Isidore, ed. "Bulls inédites des papes." *REJ* 1 (1880), 114–18, 293–98.

Mabillon, Jean, and Michael Germain, eds. *Museum italicum.* 2 vols. Paris, 1724.

McGiffert, Arthur Cushman, ed. *Dialogue between a Christian and a Jew.* New York, 1889.

Mansi, J. D., et al., eds. *Sacrorum conciliorum nova et amplissima collectio.* 53 vols. Florence and Rome, 1757–1927.

Marongiu, A., ed. "Gli Ebrei di Salerno nei documenti dei secoli X-XIII." *Archivio storico per le province napoletane* 62 (1937), 238–66.

Matfre Ermengaud. *Breviari d'amor.* Ed. Gabriel Azaïs. 2 vols. Beziers, 1862.

Moses ben Maimon. *Qoveṣ Teshuvot*. Ed. Abraham Lichtenberg. Leipzig, 1859; pts. 2–3 repr., Jerusalem, 1970.

——. *Treatise on Poisons and Their Antidotes*. Ed. Suessman Munter. The Medical Writings of Moses Maimonides 2. Philadelphia, 1966.

Moses ben Naḥman. *Kitvei ha-Ramban*. Ed. Charles B. Chavel. 2 vols. Jerusalem, 1963.

——. *Writings and Discourses*. Trans. Charles B. Chavel. 2 vols. New York, 1978.

Moses ha-Darshan. *Commentaire de la Genèse* . . . . Ed. Jean Joseph Brierre-Narbonne. Paris, 1939.

——. *Midras Beresit Rabbati ex libro R. Mois Haddarsan* [Hebrew]. Ed. Ch. Albeck. Jerusalem, 1940.

Neubauer, Adolph, and S. R. Driver, eds. *The Fifty-third Chapter of Isaiah According to Jewish Interpreters*. 2 vols. Oxford, 1876–77.

Nicholas Eymeric. *Directorium inquisitorum*. Rome, 1578.

Patrizi, Agostino. *Caeremoniale romanum*. Ed. Jean Mabillon. 1689; repr., Ridgewood, N.J.,1965.

Paulus de Santa Maria (of Burgos). *Scrutinarium scripturarum*. Mantua, 1475.

Peter the Venerable. *Letters*. Ed. Giles Constable. 2 vols. Cambridge, Mass., 1967.

Pfeiffer, Franz, ed. *Deutsche Mystiker des vierzehnten Jahrhunderts*. 2 vols. Leipzig, 1845–57.

Potthast, Augustus, ed. *Regesta pontificum romanorum inde ab. a. post Christum natum MCXCVIII ad a. MCCCIV*. 2 vols. Berlin, 1874–75.

Powicke, Frederick Maurice, and C. R. Cheney, eds. *Councils & Synods with Other Documents Relating to the English Church II: A.D. 1205–1313*. 2 vols. Oxford, 1964.

Profiat (Isaac ben Moes ha-Levi) Duran. "Kelimat ha-Goyim." Ed. Adolf Posnanski. *Ha-Ṣofeh me-'Ereṣ ha-Ger* 3 (1913), 99–113, 143–180; 4 (1914), 37–48, 81–96, 115–32.

Qalonymos ben Qalonymos ben Meir. *Even Boḥan*. Ed. A. M. Haberman. Tel Aviv, 1956.

Rankin, Oliver Shaw, ed. *Jewish Religious Polemic*. Edinburgh, 1956.

Raymond de Peñaforte. *Summa*. Verona, 1744.

Raymond Lull. "Disputatio Petri clerici et Raymundi phantastici." Ed. Marianus Müller. *Wissenschaft und Weisheit* 2 (1935), 311–24.

——. "Le *Liber de acquisitione Terrae Sanctae*." Ed. Ephrem Longpré. *Criterion* 3 (1927), 265–78.

——. El "*Liber predicationis contra Judeos*." Ed. J. M. Millás Vallicrosa. Madrid, 1957.

——. *Libre de Blanquerna*. Obres de Ramon Lull 9. Palma, 1914.

——. *Obras rimadas*. Ed. Gerónimo Rosselló. Palma, 1859.

——. *Obres doctrinales*. Obres de Ramon Lull 1. Ciutat de Mallorca, 1906.

——. *Obres essencials*. 2 vols. Barcelona, 1957.

——. *Opera*. Ed. I. Salzinger. 10 vols. 1721–42; repr., Frankfurt, 1965.

——. *Opera latina*. Ed. S. Galmés et al. 3 vols. Palma, 1952–54.

——. *Opera latina*. Ed. Fridericus Stegmüller. 5 vols. Palma, 1959–67.

Raymond Martini. *Pugio fidei adversus Mauros et Judaeos*. 1687; repr., Farnborough, Eng., 1967.

Régné, Jean. *History of the Jews in Aragon: Regesta and Documents, 1213–1327*. Ed. Yom Tov Assis and Adam Gruzman. Jerusalem, 1978.

Reichert, Benedictus Maria, ed. *Acta capitulorum generalium Ordinis Praedicatorum*, 1. Monumenta Ordinis Fratrum Praedicatorum historica 3. Rome, 1898.

——, ed. *Litterae encyclicae magistrorum generalium Ordinis Praedicatorum ab anno 1233 usque ad annum 1376*. Monumenta Ordinis Fratrum Praedicatorum historica 5. Rome, 1900.

Ripoll, Thomas, ed. *Bullarium Ordinis Fratrum Praedicatorum*. 8 vols. Rome, 1729–40.

Roger Bacon. *The Greek Grammar . . . and a Fragment of His Hebrew Grammar*. Ed. Edmond Nolan and Samuel Abraham Hirsch. Cambridge, Eng., 1902.

——. *Opera quaedam hactenus inedita*. Ed. J. S. Brewer, 1859; repr., n.p., 1965.

——. *The "Opus Majus."* Ed. John Henry Bridges. 3 vols. Oxford, 1897–1900.

Rosenthal, Judah M., ed. "A Religious Disputation between a Jew Called Menahem and the Convert Pablo Christiani [Hebrew]." *Hagut Ivrit ba'Amerika. Studies in Jewish Themes by Contemporary American Scholars*, 3:61–74. Ed. Menahem Zohori et al. Tel Aviv, 1974.

Rubió y Lluch, Antonio, ed. *Documents per l'historia de la cultura catalana mig-eval*. 2 vols. Barcelona, 1908–21.

Rymer, Thomas, and Robert Sanderson, eds. *Foedera, conventiones, litterae, et cujuscunque generis acta publica inter reges Angliae et alios quosvis imperatores, reges, pontifices, principes, vel communitates*. Re-ed. Adam Clarke and Frederick Holbrook. 4 vols. London, 1816–69.

Sbaralea, Joannes, et al., eds. *Bullarium franciscanum romanorum pontificum: Constitutiones, epistolae, ac diplomata*. 7 vols. Rome, 1759–1904.

Sefer Da'at Zeqeinim. Ed. Isaac Joseph Nunez-Vaez. Leghorn, 1783.

Solomon ben Abraham ibn Adret. *Sefer She'eilot u-Teshuvot ha-Rashba*, 4. 1883; repr., Jerusalem, 1970.

Solomon ibn Verga. *Shevet Yehudah*. Ed. Azriel Shohat. Jerusalem, 1946.

Steinschneider, Moritz, et al., eds. "Milhemet ha-Dat: Qevusat Mikhtavim be-'Inyenei ha-Mahloqet 'al Sefer ha-Moreh weha-Mada' 'im He'arot." *Jeschurun* 8 (1871), 17–56, 89–160.

Thomas Aquinas. *Liber de veritate catholice fidei contra errores infidelium*. Ed. Peter Marc et al. 3 vols. Tours, 1961–67.

——. *On the Truth of the Catholic Faith*, 1. Trans. Anton C. Pegis. Garden City, N.Y., 1955.

——. *ST*. 60 vols. Cambridge, Eng., 1964–76.

Bibliography

Thomas of Cantimpré. *Bonum universale de apibus*. Ed. Georgius Colvenerius. Douay, 1627.

Thomas of Celano. *Vita secunda S. Francisci*. In *Analecta franciscana* 10 (1926– 41), 127–268.

Toppi, Nicolo, ed. *Biblioteca napoletana*. Naples, 1678.

Tractatus de haeresi pauperum de Lugduno. In *Thesaurus novus anecdotorum* 5:1777–94. Ed. Edmund Martène and Ursinus Durand. 5 vols. 1717; repr., New York, 1968.

Usque, Samuel. *Consolaçam as tribulaçoens de Israel*. Coimbra, 1906–8.

Wagenseil, Johann Christoph, ed. *Tela ignea Satanae*. Altdorf, 1681.

Waltz, Angelus, ed. *Acta canonizationis S. Dominici*. Monumenta Ordinis Fratrum Praedicatorum historica 16:91–194. Rome, 1935.

William of St. Amour. *Opera omnia*. Constance, 1632.

Yehiel ben Joseph of Paris. *Wikkuah*. Ed. Samuel Grünbaum. Thorn, 1873.

Zedekiah ben Abraham 'Anaw. *Sefer Shibbolei ha-Leqeṭ ha-Shalem*. Ed. Solomon Buber. Vilna, 1886.

Secondary Sources

Albert, Bath Sheva. *The Case of Baruch: The Earliest Report of the Trial of a Jew by the Inquisition* (1320) [Hebrew]. Ramat Gan, 1974.

Altaner, Berthold. *Die Dominikanermissionen des 13. Jahrhunderts*. Schleswig (Habelschwerdt), 1924.

——. "Die fremdsprachliche Ausbildung der Dominikanermissionare während des 13. und 14. Jahrhunderts." *Zeitschrift für Missionswissenschaft und Religionswissenschaft* 23 (1933), 233–41.

——. "Glaubenszwang und Glaubensfreiheit in der Missionstheorie des Raymundus Lullus: Ein Beitrag zur Geschichte des Toleranzgedankens." *Historisches Jahrbuch* 48 (1928), 586–610.

——. "Raymundus Lullus und der Sprachenkanon (can. 11) des Konzils von Vienne (1312)." *Historisches Jahrbuch* 53 (1933), 190–219.

——. "Sprachstudien und Sprachkentnisse im Dienste der Mission des 13. und 14. Jahrhunderts." *Zeitschrift für Missionswissenschaft und Religionswissenschaft* 21 (1931), 113–36.

——. "Zur Kenntnis des Hebräischen im Mittelalter." *Biblische Zeitschrift* 21 (1938), 288–308.

Alvarez, Jesús. *Teología del pueblo judío*. Madrid, 1970.

Ames, Ruth M. "The Source and Significance of 'The Jew and the Pagan.'" *Medieval Studies* 19 (1957), 37–47.

Anchel, Robert. *Les Juifs de France*. Paris, 1946.

Armstrong, Edward A. *Saint Francis: Nature Mystic*. Berkeley, 1973.

Auerbach, Erich. *Literary Language and Its Public in Late Latin Antiquity and the Middle Ages*. Trans. Ralph Manheim. Bollingen Series 74. Princeton, 1965.

Bachrach, Bernard S. *Early Medieval Jewish Policy in Western Europe*. Minneapolis, 1977.

Baer, Yitzhak. "The Disputations of R. Yechiel of Paris and of Nachmanides [Hebrew]." *Tarbiz* 2 (1931), 172–87.

——. "The Historical Background of the 'Raya Mehemna' (A Chapter in the History of Religious-Social Movements in Castile during the 13th Century) [Hebrew]." *Zion*, n.s. 5 (1939), 1–44.

——. *A History of the Jews in Christian Spain*. Trans. Louis Schoffman et al. 2 vols. Philadelphia, 1961–66.

——. *Die Juden im christlichen Spanien. Erster Teil: Urkunden und Regesten*. 2 vols. 1929–36; repr., Farnborough, Eng., 1970.

——. "Ha-Midrashim ha-Mezuyafim shel Raymundus Martini u-Meqomam be-Milḥemet ha-Dat shel Yemei ha-Beinayim." In *Studies in Memory of Asher Gulak and Samuel Klein*, pp. 28–49. Jerusalem, 1942.

——. "Rashi and the Historical Reality of His Times [Hebrew]." *Tarbiz* 20 (1949), 320–32.

——. "The Religious-Social Tendency of 'Sefer Ḥassidim' [Hebrew]." *Zion*, n.s. 3 (1937), 1–50.

Baldwin, John W. "The Medieval Theories of the Just Price: Romanists, Canonists, and Theologians in the Twelfth and Thirteenth Centuries." *Transactions of the American Philosophical Society*, n.s. 49 (1959), no. 4.

Bardinet, Léon. "Condition civile des Juifs du Comtat Venaissin pendant la séjour des papes à Avignon, 1309–76." *Revue historique* 12 (1880), 1–47.

Barnes, W. Emery. "Ancient Corrections in the Text of the Old Testament." *Journal of Theological Studies*, o.s. 1 (1900), 387–414.

Baron, Salo Wittmayer. "'Plenitude of Apostolic Power' and Medieval 'Jewish Serfdom.'" In *Ancient and Medieval Jewish History: Essays*, pp. 284–307, 525–33. Ed. Leon A. Feldman. New Brunswick, N.J., 1972.

——. *A Social and Religious History of the Jews*. 2d ed. 17 vols. New York, 1952–80.

Barraclough, Geoffrey. *The Medieval Papacy*. New York, 1968.

Baumgarten, Albert I. "Justinian and the Jews." In *Rabbi Joseph H. Lookstein Memorial Volume*, pp. 37–44. Ed. Leo Landman. New York, 1980.

Beck, Hans-Georg, et al. *From the High Middle Ages to the Eve of the Reformation*. Handbook of Church History 4. Ed. Herbert Jedin and John Dolan. Trans. Anselm Biggs. New York, 1970.

Bennett, R. F. *The Early Dominicans*. Cambridge, Eng., 1937.

Ben-Sasson, Haim Hillel. "Rabbi Moshe ben Naḥman, 'Ish be-Sivkhei Tequfato." *Molad*, n.s. 1 (1967), 360–66.

Berger, David. "The Attitude of St. Bernard of Clairveaux toward the Jews." *PAAJR* 40 (1972), 89–108.

——. "Christian Heresy and Jewish Polemic in the Twelfth and Thirteenth Centuries." *HTR* 68 (1975), 287–303.

——. "Gilbert Crispin, Alan of Lille, and Jacob ben Reuben: A Study in the Transmission of Medieval Polemic." *Speculum* 49 (1974), 34–47.

Berger, Samuel. *Quam notitiam linguae hebraicae habuerint Christiani Medii Aevi temporibus in Gallia.* Paris, 1893.

Berthier, André. "Les écoles de langues orientales fondées au XIIIe siècle par les Dominicains en Espagne et en Afrique." *Revue africaine* 73 (1932), 84–102.

——. "Un maître orientaliste du XIIIe siècle: Raymond Martin O.P." *AFP* 6 (1936), 267–311.

Bévenot, Maurice. "The Inquisition and Its Antecedents." *Heythrop Journal* 7 (1966), 257–68, 381–93; 8 (1967), 52–69, 152–68.

Billington, Ray Allen. *The Protestant Crusade, 1800–1860.* 1938; repr., New York, 1952.

Bischoff, Bernard. "The Study of Foreign Languages in the Middle Ages." *Speculum* 36 (1961), 209–24.

Blau, Joseph Leon. *The Christian Interpretation of the Cabala in the Renaissance.* New York, 1944.

Bloomfield, Morton W. "Joachim of Flora: A Critical Survey of His Canon, Teachings, Sources, Biography, and Influences." *Traditio* 13 (1957), 249–311.

Blumenkranz, Bernhard. "Anti-Jewish Polemics and Legislation in the Middle Ages: Literary Fiction or Reality." *JJS* 15 (1964), 125–40.

——. "Augustin et les Juifs; Augustin et le Judaisme." *Recherches augustiniennes* 1 (1958), 225–41.

——. *Les auteurs chrétiens latins du Moyen Age sur les Juifs et le Judaisme.* Paris, 1963.

——. "Ecriture et image dans la polémique antijuive de Matfre Ermengaud." In *JJL*, pp. 295–317.

——. *Die Judenpredigt Augustins: Ein Beitrag zur Geschichte der jüdisch-christlichen Beziehungen in den ersten Jahrhunderten.* 1946; repr., Paris, 1973.

——. "Jüdische und christliche Konvertiten im jüdisch-christlichen Religionsgespräch des Mittelalters." In *JIM*, pp. 264–82.

——. "Die jüdischen Beweisgründe im Religionsgespräch mit den Christen in den christlich-lateinischen Sonderschriften des 5. bis 11. Jahrhunderts." *Theologische Zeitschrift* 4 (1948), 119–47.

——. *Le Juif médiéval au miroir de l'art chrétien.* Paris, 1966.

——. *Juifs et Chrétiens dans le monde occidental, 430–1096.* Paris, 1960.

——. "Nicolas de Lyre et Jacob ben Reuben." *JJS* 16 (1965), 47–51.

——. "Une survie médiévale de la polémique antijuive de Saint Augustin." *Revue du Moyen Age latin* 5 (1949), 193–96.

Bonfil, R. "The Nature of Judaism in Raymundus Martini's *Pugio fidei* [Hebrew]." *Tarbiz* 40 (1971), 360–75.

Boswell, John. *Christianity, Social Tolerance and Homosexuality: Gay People in Europe from the Beginning of the Christian Era to the Fourteenth Century.* Chicago, 1980.

Braude, Morris. *Conscience on Trial.* New York, 1952.

Brooke, Christopher. *The Twelfth Century Renaissance.* New York, 1970.

Browe, Peter. "Die Hostienschändungen der Juden im Mittelalter." *Römische Quartalschrift für christliche Altertumskunde und für Kirchenge-schichte* 34 (1926), 167–97.

———. "Die Judenbekämpfung im Mittelalter." *Zeitschrift für katholisches Theologie* 62 (1938), 197–231, 349–84.

———. *Die Judenmission im Mittelalter und die Päpste.* Miscellanea historiae pontificiae 6. Rome, 1942.

———. "Die religiöse Duldung der Juden im Mittelalter." *Archiv für katholisches Kirchenrecht* 118 (1938), 1–76.

Brummer, Rudolf. "Un poeme latin de controverse religieuse." *Estudios lulíanos* 6 (1962), 275–81.

Burns, Robert I. "Christian-Islamic Confrontation in the West: The Thir-teenth-Century Dream of Conversion." *AHR* 76 (1971), 1386–1434.

Carmilly-Weinberger, Moshe. *Censorship and Freedom of Expression in Jewish History.* New York, 1977.

Carreras y Artau, Joaquín. Minutes of 5/24/56 meeting. *Boletin de la Real academia de buenas letras de Barcelona* 26 (1954–56), 316–17.

Carreras y Artau, Tomas and Joaquín Carreras y Artau. *Historia de la filosofia española: Filosofia cristiana de los siglos XIII al XV.* 2 vols. Madrid, 1939–43.

Cassuto, Umberto. *Gli Ebrei a Firenze nell-età del Rinascimento* [Hebrew]. Trans. Menahem Hartom. Jerusalem, 1967.

———. "Hurban ha-Yeshivot be-'Italyah ha-Deromit ba-Me'ah ha-13." In *Studies in Memory of Asher Gulak and Samuel Klein*, pp. 139–52. Jeru-salem, 1942.

———. "Un ignoto capitolo di storia ebraica." In *Judaica: Festschrift zu Hermann Cohens siebzigsten Geburtstage*, pp. 389–404. Berlin, 1912.

Cavallera, F. "L'Explanatio symboli apostolorum de Raymond Martin, O.P." In *Studia mediaevalia in honorem admodum reverendi patris Raymundi Josephi Martin*, pp. 201–220. Bruges, 1948.

Chazan, Robert. "Anti-Usury Efforts in Thirteenth-Century Narbonne and the Jewish Response." *PAAJR* 41–42 (1973–74), 45–67.

———. "Archbishop Guy Fulcodi and His Jews." *REJ* 132 (1971), 587–94.

———. "The Barcelona 'Disputation' of 1263: Christian Missionizing and Jewish Response." *Speculum* 52 (1977), 824–42.

———. "Confrontation in the Synagogue of Narbonne: A Christian Sermon and a Jewish Reply." *HTR* 67 (1974), 433–57.

———. "A Jewish Plaint to Saint Louis." *HUCA* 45 (1974), 287–305.

———. *Medieval Jewry in Northern France: A Political and Social History.* Balti-more, 1973.

Chenu, M.-D. "Moines, clercs, laïcs au carrefour de la vie évangélique (XIIe siècle)." *Revue d'histoire ecclésiastique* 49 (1954), 59–89.

———. *Toward Understanding Saint Thomas.* Trans. A. M. Landry and D. Hugh. Chicago, 1964.

Chroust, Anton-Hermann. "The Corporate Idea and the Body Politic in the Middle Ages." *Review of Politics* 9 (1947), 423–52.

Cohen, Gerson D. "Messianic Postures of Ashkenazim and Sephardim." In *Studies of the Leo Baeck Institute*, pp. 117–56. Ed. Max Kreutzberger. New York, 1967.

Cohen, Jeremy. "The Polemical Adversary of Solomon ibn Adret." *JQR*, n.s. 71 (1980), 48–55.

——. Review of *Catholic Thought and Papal Jewry Policy, 1555–1593*, by Kenneth R. Stow. *Association for Jewish Studies Newsletter* 21 (1977), 12.

Cohen, Martin A. "Reflections on the Text and Context of the Disputation of Barcelona." *HUCA* 35 (1964), 157–92.

Cohen, Yehuda Arye. "Une polémique judéo-chrétienne en Moyen Age et ses rapports avec l'analyse pascalienne de la religion juive." In *Bar Ilan Decennial Volume II (1955–1965)*, pp. XLVII–LX. Ed. Menahem Zvi Kaddari. Ramat Gan, 1969.

Cohn, Norman. *The Pursuit of the Millennium: Revolutionary Millenarians and Mystical Anarchists of the Middle Ages*. Rev. ed. London, 1970.

——. *Warrant for Genocide: The Myth of the Jewish World-Conspiracy and the Protocols of the Elders of Zion*. New York, 1966.

Coll, J. M. "Las disputas teológicas en la Edad Media." *Analecta sacra tarraconensia* 20 (1947), 77–101.

——. "Escuelas de languas orientales an los siglos XIII y XIV." *Analecta sacra tarraconensia* 18 (1945), 59–89; 19 (1946), 217–40.

——. "San Raymundo de Peñafort y las Misiones del Norte Africano en la Edad Media." *Missionalia hispanica* 5 (1948), 417–57.

Colomer, Eusebio. "Die Beziehung des Ramon Llull zum Judentum im Rahmen des spanischen Mittelalters." In *JIM*, pp. 183–227.

Commager, Henry Steele. *The Era of Reform, 1830–1860*. Princeton, 1960.

Coulton, G. G. *Inquisition and Liberty*. 1938; repr., Gloucester, Mass., 1969.

Cruel, R. *Geschichte der deutschen Predigt im Mittelalter*. Detmold, 1879.

Cutler, Allan. "Innocent III and the Distinctive Clothing of Jews and Muslims." In *Studies in Medieval Culture*, 3:92–116. Ed. John R. Sommerfeldt. Kalamazoo, 1970.

Dan, Joseph. "An Ashkenazic Story on the Conversion to Judaism of an Arab King [Hebrew]." *Zion*, n.s. 26 (1961), 132–37.

Daniel, E. Randolph. *The Franciscan Concept of Mission in the High Middle Ages*. Lexington, Ky., 1975.

Daniel, Norman. *Islam and the West: The Making of an Image*. Edinburgh, 1960.

Darmesteter, Arsène. "L'autodafé de Troyes (24 avril 1288)." *REJ* 2 (1881), 199–247.

Dasberg, Lena. *Untersuchungen über die Entwertung des Judenstatus im 11. Jahrhundert*. Paris, 1965.

David, Abraham. "Pogroms against French Jewry during the Shepherds' Crusade of 1251 [Hebrew]." *Tarbiz* 46 (1977), 251–57.

Davidsohn, Robert. *Geschichte von Florence.* 4 vols. Berlin, 1896–1927.

Dawson, James D. "William of Saint-Amour and the Apostolic Tradition." *Medieval Studies* 40 (1978), 223–38.

Deaux, George. *The Black Death, 1347.* New York, 1969.

De Lange, N. R. M. *Origen and the Jews: Studies in Jewish-Christian Relations in Third-Century Palestine.* Cambridge, Eng., 1976.

Delcorno, Carlo. *Giordano da Pisa e l'antica predicazione volgare.* Florence, 1975.

Delisle, Léopold. "Notes sur quelques manuscrits du Musée britannique." *Mémoires de la Société de l'histoire de Paris et de l'Ile-de-France* 4 (1887), 183–238.

——. "Notice sur les manuscrits de Bernard Gui." *Notices et extraits des manuscrits de la Bibliothèque Nationale et autres bibliothèques* 27, 2 (1879), 169–455.

De Lubac, Henri. *Corpus mysticum: L'Euchariste et l'Eglise au Moyen Age.* 2d ed. Paris 1949.

Denifle, Heinrich. "Quellen zur Disputation Pablo Christiani mit Mose Nahmani zu Barcelona 1263." *Historisches Jahrbuch* 8 (1887), 225–44.

De Roover, Raymond. "The Concept of the Just Price: Theory and Economic Policy." *Journal of Economic History* 18 (1958), 418–34.

Deutsch, Karl W. "Anti-Semitic Ideas in the Middle Ages." *Journal of the History of Ideas* 6 (1945), 239–54.

Diez Macho, A. "Acarca de los midrašim falsificados de Raimundo Marti." *Sefarad* 9 (1949), 165–96.

Dinur, Benzion. *Israel in the Diaspora* [Hebrew]. 2d ed. 10 pts. Tel Aviv, 1958–72.

Dondaine, Antoine. "Le Manuel de l'inquisiteur." *AFP* 17 (1947), 85–194.

Dossat, Yves. *Les crises de l'Inquisition toulousaine au XIII* siècle (1233 73).* Bordeaux, 1959.

——. "Inquisiteurs ou enqueteurs? A propos d'un texte d'Humbert de Romans." *Bulletin philologique et historique (jusqu'à 1715) du Comité des travaux historiques et scientifiques,* 1957, pp. 105–13.

Douais, Celestin. *L'Inquisition: Ses origines—sa procedure.* Paris, 1906.

——. "Saint Raymond de Peñafort et les hérétiques: Directoire à l'usage des inquisiteurs aragonais, 1242." *Le Moyen Age* 12 (1889), 305–25.

Douie, D. L. *The Conflict between the Seculars and the Mendicants at the University of Paris in the Thirteenth Century.* London, 1954.

Dronke, Peter. *Poetic Individuality in the Middle Ages: New Departures in Poetry, 1000–1150.* Oxford, 1970.

Dubnow, Simon. *Weltgeschichte des jüdischen Volkes.* 10 vols. Berlin, 1925–30.

Dufeil, M.-M. *Guillaume de Saint-Amour et la polémique universitaire parisienne, 1250–1259.* Paris, 1972.

Easton, Stewart C. *Roger Bacon and His Search for a Universal Science.* New York, 1952.

Eckert, Willehad Paul. "Hoch- und Spätmittelalter—katholischer Humanismus." In *Kirche und Synagoge: Handbuch zur Geschichte von Christen und Juden,* 1:210–306. Ed. Karl Heinrich Rengstorf and Siegfried von Kurtz-fleisch. 2 vols. Stuttgart, 1968–70.

Ehrisman, Gustav. *Geschichte der deutschen Literatur bis zum Ausgang des Mittelalters.* 4 vols. Munich, 1918–35.

Eisenstadt, S. N. *The Political Systems of Empires.* London, 1963.

Emery, Richard Wilder. *The Friars in Medieval France.* New York, 1962.

———. *Heresy and Inquisition in Narbonne.* 1941; repr., New York, 1967.

Enciclopedia universal ilustrada europaeo-americana. 70 vols. Barcelona, 1907–30.

Engelbert, Omar. *Saint Francis of Assisi.* Trans. Eve Marie Cooper. 2d ed. Chicago, 1966.

Epstein, Abraham. *"Bereschit-rabbati.* (Handschrift der prager jüdische Gemeinde.) Dessen Verhältniss zu Rabba-rabbati, Moses ha-Darschan, und *Pugio Fidei."* *Magazin für die Wissenschaft des Judenthums* 15 (1888), 65–99.

———. *Moses ha-Darschan aus Narbonne: Fragmente seiner literarischen Erzeugnisse.* Vienna, 1891.

Erler, L. "Die Juden des Mittelalters. Die Päpste und die Juden." *Archiv für katholisches Kirchenrecht* 48 (1882), 369–416; 50 (1884), 3–64; 53 (1885), 1–70.

Ettinger, Sh. "Jewish Influence on the Religious Ferment in Eastern Europe at the End of the Fifteenth Century [Hebrew]." In *Yitzhak F. Baer Jubilee Volume,* pp. 228–47. Ed. Salo Wittmayer Baron et al. Jerusalem, 1960.

Federbusch, Simon. *Ha-Lashon ha-ʿIvrit be-Yisraʾel uva-ʿAmim.* Jerusalem, 1967.

Foreville, Raymonde. *Latran I, II, III et Latran IV.* Histoire des conciles oecuméniques 6. Paris, 1965.

Freed, John B. *The Friars and German Society in the Thirteenth Century.* Cambridge, Mass., 1977.

Friedman, Yvonne. "An Anatomy of Anti-Semitism: Peter the Venerable's Letter to Louis VII, King of France (1146)." In *Bar-Ilan Studies in History,* pp. 87–102. Ed. Pinhas Artzi. Ramat Gan, 1978.

Funkenstein, Amos. "Basic Types of Christian Anti-Jewish Polemics in the Later Middle Ages." *Viator* 2 (1971), 373–82.

———. "Changes in the Patterns of Christian Anti-Jewish Polemic in the Twelfth Century [Hebrew]." *Zion,* n.s. 33 (1968), 125–44.

———. "Gesetz und Geschichte: Zur historisierenden Hermeneutik bei Moses Maimonides und Thomas von Aquin." *Viator* 1 (1970), 147–78.

———. "Nachmanides' Typological Reading of History [Hebrew]." *Zion,* n.s. 45 (1980), 35–59.

Gierke, Otto. *Political Theories of the Middle Age.* Trans. F. W. Maitland. 1900; repr., Boston, 1958.

Gilson, Etienne, *History of Christian Philosophy in the Middle Ages.* New York, 1955.

Giménez y Martínez de Carvajal, José. "San Raimundo de Peñafort y las Partidas de Alfonso X el Sabio." *Anthologica annua: Publicaciones del Instituto español de estudios eclesiasticos* 3 (1955), 201–338.

Glorieux, Palemon. *Répertoire des maîtres en théologie de Paris au XIIIe siècle.* 2 vols. Paris, 1933–34.

Gottlieb, Efraim. *Studies in the Kabbala Literature* [Hebrew]. Ed. Joseph Hacker. Tel Aviv, 1976.

Gottron, Adam. *Ramon Lulls Kreuzzugsideen.* Abhandlungen zur mittleren und neuren Geschichte 39. Berlin, 1912.

Grabmann, Martin. *Introduction to the Theological Summa of St. Thomas.* Trans. John S. Zybura. St. Louis, 1930.

Grabois, Aryeh. "The Hebraica Veritas and Jewish-Christian Intellectual Relations in the Twelfth Century." *Speculum* 50 (1975), 613–34.

Graetz, Heinrich. "Burning the Talmud in 1322." *JQR*, n.s. 2 (1890), 104–106.

———. "Die Disputation des Bonastruc mit Frai Pablo in Barcelona." *MGWJ* 14 (1865), 428–33.

———. *Geschichte der Juden.* 3d and 4th eds. 11 vols. Leipzig, 1873–1911.

———. "Die Schicksale des Talmud im Verlaufe der Geschichte." *MGWJ* 34 (1885), 529–41.

Gratien, Badin. *Histoire de la fondation et de l'evolution de l'Ordre des Frères Mineurs au XIIIe siècle.* Paris, 1928.

Grayzel, Solomon. "The Avignon Popes and the Jews." *HJ* 2 (1940), 1–12.

———. "Bishop to Bishop I." In *Gratz College Anniversary Volume,* pp. 131–45. Ed. Isidore David Passow and Samuel David Lachs. Philadelphia, 1971.

———. *The Church and the Jews in the XIIIth Century.* Rev. ed. New York, 1966.

———. "The Confession of a Medieval Jewish Convert." *HJ* 17 (1955), 89–120.

———. "Jews and the Ecumenical Councils." In *The Seventy-Fifth Anniversary Volume of the Jewish Quarterly Review,* pp. 283–311. Ed. Abraham A. Neuman and Solomon Zeitlin. Philadelphia, 1967.

———. "The Papal Bull *Sicut Judaeis.*" In *Studies and Essays in Honor of Abraham A. Neuman,* pp. 243–80. Ed. Meir Ben-Horin et al. Leiden, 1962.

———. "Pope Alexander III and the Jews." In *Salo Wittmayer Baron Jubilee Volume,* 2:555–72. Ed. Saul Lieberman and Arthur Hyman. 3 vols. Jerusalem, 1974.

———. "Popes, Jews, and the Inquisition from 'Sicut' to 'Turbato.'" In *Essays on the Occasion of the Seventieth Anniversary of Dropsie University,* pp. 151–88. Ed. Abraham I. Katsch and Leon Nemoy. Philadelphia, 1979.

———. "References to the Jews in the Correspondence of John XXII." *HUCA* 23, 2 (1950–51), 37–80.

———. "The Talmud and the Medieval Papacy." In *Essays in Honor of Solomon B. Freehof,* pp. 220–45. Ed. Walter Jacob et al. Pittsburgh, 1964.

Gross, Henri. *Gallia judaica.* Trans. Moise Bloch. Ed. Simon Schwarzfuchs. Amsterdam, 1969.

———. "Meir b. Simon und seine Schrift Milchemeth Miswa: Analekten." *MGWJ* 30 (1881), 295–305, 444–52, 554–69.

Grossinger, Hermine. "Die Disputation des Nachmanides mit Fra Pablo Christiani, Barcelona 1263." *Kairos*, n.s. 19 (1977), 257–85, 20 (1978), 1–15, 161–81.

Gudde, Erwin Gustav. "Social Conflicts in Medieval German Poetry." *University of California Publications in Modern Philology* 18 (1934–36), 1–139.

Güdemann, Moritz. *Geschichte des Erziehungswesens und der Cultur der abendländischen Juden während des Mittelalters und der neueren Zeit*. 3 vols. 1880–88; repr., Amsterdam, 1966.

Guiraud, Jean. *Histoire de l'Inquisition au Moyen Age*. 2 vols. Paris, 1935–38.

Guttmann, Jacob. *Die Scholastik des dreizehnten Jahrhunderts in ihren Beziehungen zum Judenthum*. 1902; repr., Hildesheim, 1970.

Hailperin, Herman. *Rashi and the Christian Scholars*. Pittsburgh, 1963.

Haskins, Charles Homer. *The Renaissance of the Twelfth Century*. 1927; repr., Cleveland, 1957.

———. "Robert le Bourge and the Beginnings of the Inquisition in Northern France." In *Studies in Medieval Culture*, pp. 193–244. 1923; repr., New York, 1965.

Hayward, Fernand. *The Inquisition*. Trans. Malachy Carrol. New York, 1966.

Heer, Friedrich. *The Medieval World: Europe, 1100–1350*. Trans. Janet Sondheimer. Cleveland, 1962.

Hillgarth, J. N. *Ramon Lull and Lullism in Fourteenth Century France*. Oxford, 1971.

———. *The Spanish Kingdoms, 1250–1516*. 2 vols. Oxford, 1976–78.

Hinnebusch, William A. *The Early English Friars Preachers*. Rome, 1951.

———. *A History of the Dominican Order*. 2 vols. New York, 1966–73.

Hirsch, Samuel Abraham. "Early English Hebraists: Roger Bacon and His Predecessors." *JQR*, o.s. 12 (1900,) 34–98; repr. as book, London, 1905.

Hirsch-Reich, Beatrice. "Joachim von Fiore und das Judentum." In *JIM*, pp. 228–63.

Holmes, Urban T., Jr. "The Idea of a Twelfth-Century Renaissance." *Speculum* 26 (1951), 643–51.

Huerga, Alvaro. "Hipótesis sobre la génesis de la 'Summa contra gentiles' y del 'Pugio fidei.'" *Angelicum* 51 (1974), 533–57.

Hunt, R. W. "The Disputation of Peter of Cornwall against Symon the Jew." In *Studies in Medieval History Presented to Frederick Maurice Powicke*, pp. 143–56. Ed. R. W. Hunt et al. Oxford, 1948.

Jackson, Kenneth T. *The Ku Klux Klan in the City, 1915–1930*. New York, 1967.

Jacobs, Joseph. *An Inquiry into the Sources of the History of the Jews in Spain*. New York, 1894.

Jordan, William C. *Saint Louis and the Challenge of the Crusade*. Princeton, 1979.

Juster, Jean. "La condition légale des Juifs sous les rois visigoths." In *Etudes d'histoire juridique offertes à Paul Frédéric Girard*, 2:275–335. 2 vols. Paris, 1913.

Kaeppeli, Thomas. *Scriptores Ordinis Praedicatorum Medii Aevi*, 1. Rome, 1970.

Kantorowicz, Ernst H. *The King's Two Bodies: A Study in Medieval Political Theology*. Princeton, 1957.

——. "Pro patria mori in Medieval Political Thought." *AHR* 56 (1951), 472–92.

Katz, Jacob. *Exclusiveness and Tolerance: Studies in Jewish-Gentile Relations in Medieval and Modern Times*. 1961; repr., New York, 1962.

——. *From Prejudice to Destruction: Anti-Semitism, 1700–1933*. Cambridge, Mass., 1980.

Kayserling, Meyer. "Die Disputation des Bonastruc mit Frai Pablo in Barcelona." *MGWJ* 14 (1865), 308–13.

Keyes, G. L. *Christian Faith and the Interpretation of History*. Lincoln, Neb., 1966.

Kiekhefer, Richard. *Repression of Heresy in Medieval Germany*. Philadelphia, 1979.

Kisch, Alexander. "Die Anklageartikel gegen den Talmud und ihre Vertheidigung durch Rabbi Jechiel ben Joseph vor Ludwig dem Heiligen in Paris." *MGWJ* 23 (1874), 10–18, 62–75, 123–30, 155–63, 204–12.

Kisch, Guido. *The Jews in Medieval Germany. A Study of Their Legal and Social Status*. 2d ed. New York, 1970.

Klapper, Joseph. "Ein Florilegium talmudicum des 13. Jahrhunderts." *Literaturwissenschaftliches Jahrbuch der Görres-Gesellschaft* 1 (1926), 3–23.

Klibansky, Erich. "Beziehungen des christlichen Mittelalters zum Judentum." *MGWJ* 77 (1933), 456–73.

Kniewasser, Manfred. "Die antijüdische Polemik des Petrus Alphonsi (getauft 1106) und des Abtes Petrus Venerabilis von Cluny († 1156)." *Kairos*, n.s. 22 (1980), 34–76.

——. "Bischof Agobard von Lyon und der Platz der Juden in einer sakral verfassten Einheitsgesellschaft." *Kairos*, n.s. 19 (1977), 203–27.

Knowles, David. *The Religious Orders in England*. 3 vols. Cambridge, Eng., 1948–59.

Knowles, David, and Dimitri Obolensky. *The Middle Ages*. The Christian Centuries: A New History of the Catholic Church 2. New York, 1968.

Koht, Halvan. "The Dawn of Nationalism in Europe." *AHR* 52 (1947), 265–80.

Kook, S. Ch. "The Date of the Burning of the Talmud in France [Hebrew]." *KS* 29 (1953), 281.

Krauss, S. "The Jews in the Works of the Church Fathers." *JQR*, o.s. 5 (1892), 122–57; 6 (1894), 82–99, 225–61.

Kritzeck, James. *Peter the Venerable and Islam*. Princeton, 1964.

Labrosse, Henri. "Biographie de Nicolas de Lyre." *Etudes franciscaines* 17 (1907), 489–505, 593–608.

——. "Ouevres de Nicolas de Lyre." *Etudes franciscaines* 19 (1908), 41–52, 153–75, 368–79.

Ladner, Gerhart B. "Aspects of Medieval Thought on Church and State." *Review of Politics* 9 (1947), 403–22.

——. "The Concepts of 'Ecclesia' and 'Christianitas' and Their Relationship to the Idea of Papal 'Plenitudo Potestatis' from Gregory VII to Boniface VIII." In *Sacerdozio e regno da Gregorio VII a Bonifacio VIII*, pp. 49–77. Miscellanea historiae pontificiae 18. Rome, 1954.

——. "Medieval and Modern Understanding of Symbolism: A Comparison." *Speculum* 54 (1979), 223–56.

Langlois, Charles-Victor. "Nicolas de Lyre, Frère Mineur." *HLF* 36 (1972), 355–400.

Langmuir, Gavin I. "L'absence d'accusation de meurtre rituel à l'ouest du Rhone." In *JJL*, pp. 235–49.

Lapide, Pinchas E. *Hebräisch in den Kirchen*. Forschungen zum jüdisch-christlichen Dialog 1. Neukirchen-Vluyn, 1976.

Laske-Fix, Katja. *Der Bildzyklus des Breviari d'amor*. Münchner kunsthistorische Abhandlungen 5. Munich, 1973.

Lasker, Daniel J. *Jewish Philosophical Polemics against Christianity in the Middle Ages*. New York, 1977.

Lea, Henry Charles. *A History of the Inquisition in the Middle Ages*. 3 vols. New York, 1888.

——. *The Inquisition of the Middle Ages: Its Organization and Procedure*. Ed. Walter Ullman. London, 1963.

Leff, Gordon. *The Dissolution of the Medieval Outlook: An Essay on Intellectual and Spiritual Change in the Fourteenth Century*. New York, 1976.

——. *Heresy in the Later Middle Ages: The Relation of Heterodoxy to Dissent*. 2 vols. Manchester, 1967.

——. *Paris and Oxford Universities in the Thirteenth and Fourteenth Centuries: An Institutional and Intellectual History*. New York, 1968.

Le Goff, Jacques. "Apostolat mendiant et fait urbain dans la France médiévale: L'implantation des ordres mendiants." *Annales* 23 (1968), 335–52.

——. "Ordres mendiants et urbanisation dans la France médiévale." *Annales* 25 (1970), 924–46.

Le Roy Ladurie, Emmanuel. *Montaillou, village occitan de 1294 à 1324*. Paris, 1975.

Lévi, Israel. "Manuscrits du Hadar Zekènim: Recueil de commentaires éxégetiques de rabbins de la France septentrionale." *REJ* 49 (1904), 33–50.

Levy, Ludwig. "Rabbi Rachmon im Pugio fidei." *Zeitschrift für hebraeische Bibliographie* 6 (1902), 30–31.

Lewin, A. "Die Religionsdisputation des R. Jechiel von Paris 1240 am Hofe Ludwigs des Heiligen, ihre Veranlassung und ihre Folgen." *MGWJ* 18 (1869), 97–110, 145–56, 193–210.

Lieberman, Saul. *Hellenism in Jewish Palestine.* 2d ed. New York, 1962.
———. "Raymund Martini and His Alleged Forgeries." *HJ* 5 (1943), 87–102.
———. *Shkiin: A Few Words on Some Jewish Legends, Customs, and Literary Sources Found in Karaite and Christian Works* [Hebrew]. 2d ed. Jerusalem, 1970.
Liebeschütz, Hans. "Relations between Jews and Christians in the Middle Ages." *JJS* 16 (1965), 35–46.
———. "The Significance of Judaism in Peter Abelard's Dialogus." *JJS* 12 (1961), 1–18.
Limborch, Philip van. *Historia inquisitionis.* 2 vols. Amsterdam, 1692.
Little, A. G. "Friar Henry of Wadstone and the Jews." In *Collectanea franciscana* 2:150–57. Ed. C. L. Kingsford et al. British Society of Franciscan Studies 10. Manchester, 1922.
———. "The Mendicant Orders." In *Cambridge Medieval History,* 6:727–62. 8 vols. Cambridge, Eng., 1911–36.
Little, Lester K. *Religious Poverty and the Profit Economy in Medieval Europe.* Ithaca, 1978.
———. "Saint Louis' Involvement with the Friars." *Church History* 33 (1964), 125–48.
Llinares, Armand. *Raymond Lulle: Philosophe de l'action.* Grenoble, 1963.
Loeb, Isidore. "La controverse de 1240 sur le Talmud." *REJ* 1 (1880), 247–61; 2 (1881), 248–70; 3 (1881), 39–57.
——— "La controverse de 1263 à Barcelona entre Paulus Christiani et Moise ben Nahman." *REJ* 15 (1887), 1–18.
———. "La controverse religieuse entre les Chrétiens et les Juifs au Moyen Age en France et en Espagne." *Revue de l'histoire des religions* 17 (1888), 311–337, 18 (1888), 133–56.
———. "Josef Haccohen et les chroniqueurs juifs." *REJ* 16 (1888), 28–56, 211–35; 17 (1888), 74–95, 247–71.
———. "Polémistes chrétiens et juifs en France et en Espagne." *REJ* 18 (1889), 43–70, 219–42.
Loewe, Raphael. "Alexander Neckham's Knowledge of Hebrew." *Medieval and Renaissance Studies* 4 (1958), 17–34.
———. "The Medieval Christian Hebraists of England: Herbert of Bosham and Earlier Scholars." *Transactions of the Jewish Historical Society of England* 17 (1953), 225–49.
———. "The Medieval Christian Hebraists of England: The *Superscriptio Lincolniensis.*" *HUCA* 28 (1957), 205–52.
———. "The Medieval History of the Latin Vulgate." In *The Cambridge History of the Bible,* 2:102–54. Ed. P. R. Ackroyd et al. 3 vols. Cambridge, Eng., 1963–70.
Longpré, Ephrem. "Le B. Raymond Lulle et Raymond Marti., O.P." *Bolletí de la Societat arqueologica luliana* 44 (1933), 269–71.
López, Atanasio. *Obispos en el Africa septentrional desde el siglo XIII.* Instituto General Franco para la investigación hispanio-arabe 3,6. Tangiers, 1941.

Luneau, August. *L'histoire du salut chez les pères de l'Eglise*. Paris, 1964.

McCurry, Charles. "Religious Careers and Religious Devotion in Thirteenth-Century Metz." *Viator* 9 (1978), 325–33.

McGovern, John F. "The Rise of the New Economic Attitudes—Economic Humanism, Economic Nationalism—during the Later Middle Ages and the Renaissance, A.D. 1200–1500." *Traditio* 26 (1970), 217–53.

McKeon, Peter R. "The Status of the University of Paris as *Parens Scientiarum*: An Episode in the Development of Its Autonomy." *Speculum* 39 (1964), 651–75.

Maisonneuve, Henri. "Le droit romain et la doctrine inquisitoriale." In *Etudes d'histoire du droit canonique dédiées à Gabriel le Bras*, 2:931–42. 2 vols. Paris, 1965.

——. *Etude sur les origines de l'Inquisition*. 2d ed. Paris, 1960.

Mandonnet, Pierre. *St. Dominic and His Work*. Trans. Mary Benedicta Larkin. St. Louis, 1944.

Manitius, Max. *Geschichte der lateinischen Literatur des Mittelalters*. 3 vols. Munich, 1911–31.

Mann, Jacob. "Über Jacob b. Elia, Verfasser des polemischen Briefes gegen den Apostaten Pablo [Hebrew]." 'Alim 1 (1934), 75–77.

——. "Une source de l'histoire juive au XIIIe siècle: La lettre polémique de Jacob b. Elie à Pablo Christiani." *REJ* 82 (1926), 363–77.

Manselli, Raoul. "La polémique contre les Juifs dans la polémique anti-hérétique." In *JJL*, pp. 252–67.

March, Joseph M. "En Ramón Marti y la seva 'Explanatio simboli apostolorum.' " *Institut d'estudis catalans—Anuari*, 1908, pp. 443–96.

Marcus, Ivan G. "Penitential Theory and Practice among the Pious of Germany: 1150–1250." Ph.D. diss., Jewish Theological Seminary of America, 1974.

Markus, R. A. *Saeculum: History and Society in the Theology of St. Augustine*. Cambridge, Eng., 1970.

Marsmann, Monika. *Die Epistel des Rabbi Isaak: Untersuchung und Edition*. Siegen, 1971.

Martínez Ferrando, J. E. *Catálogo de la documentación relativa al ántiguo reino de Valencia*. 2 vols. Madrid, 1934.

Maycock, A. L. *The Inquisition from Its Establishment to the Great Schism: An Introductory Study*. London, 1926.

Meersseman, G. "La chronologie des voyages et des oeuvres de Frère Alphonse Buenhombre O.P." *AFP* 10 (1940), 77–108.

Menéndez y Pelayo, Marcelino. *Historia de los heterodoxos españoles*. 2d ed. 7 vols. Madrid, 1911–32.

Merchavya, Ch. "Additional Information Concerning the Rashi Commentary to Ḥelek [Hebrew]." *Tarbiz* 35 (1966), 278–94.

——. "An Anti-Talmudic Pamphlet from the Period of the Burning of the Talmud in Italy [Hebrew]." *Tarbiz* 37 (1967–68), 78–96, 191–207.

——. "The Caustic Poetic Rebuke (*Shamta*) in Medieval Christian Polemical Literature [Hebrew]." *Tarbiz* 41 (1971), 95–115.

——. *The Church versus Talmudic and Midrashic Literature, 500–1248* [Hebrew]. Jerusalem, 1970.

——. "Concerning the Date of R. Meir ben Simeon's *Milḥemet Mizva* [Hebrew]." *Tarbiz* 45 (1976), 296–302.

——. "The Hebrew Versions of 'Pugio fidei' in the Saint Geneviève Manuscript [Hebrew]." *KS* 51 (1976), 283–88.

——. "Regarding the Rashi Commentary to '*Helek*' [Hebrew]." *Tarbiz* 33 (1964), 259–86.

——. "A Spanish-Latin Manuscript Concerning the Opposition to the Talmud in the Beginning of the 15th Century [Hebrew]." *KS* 45 (1970), 271–86, 590–606.

——. "The Talmud in the *Additiones* of Paul of Burgos." *JJS* 16 (1965), 115–34.

Meyer, Paul. "Matfré Ermengau de Béziers, troubador." *HLF* 32 (1898), 16–56.

Michalski, Abraham J. "Raschis Einfluss auf Nicholas von Lyra in der Auslegung der Bücher Leviticus, Numerei und Deuteronomium." *Zeitschrift für die alttestamentliche Wissenschaft* 35 (1915), 218–45; 36 (1916), 29–63.

Millás Vallicrosa, J. M. "Algunas relaciones entre la doctrina luliana y la Cabala." *Sefarad* 18 (1958), 241–53

——. "The Doctrine of the 'Lullian Dignities' and the Sefiroth [Hebrew]." *Yitzhak F. Baer Jubilee Volume*, pp. 186–90. Ed. Salo Wittmayer Baron et al. Jerusalem, 1960.

——. "Extractos del Talmud y alusiones polemicas en un manuscrito de la Biblioteca Catedral de Gerona." *Sefarad* 20 (1960), 17–49.

——. Review of "La chronologie des voyages et des oeuvres de Frère Alphonse Buenhombre O.P.," by G. Meersseman. *Sefarad* 2 (1942), 205–8.

——. "Sobre las fuentes documentales de la controversia de Barcelona en el año 1263." *Anales de la Universidad de Barcelona: Memorias y comunicaciones* (1940), 25–44.

Molinier, August. "Enquête sur un meurtre imputé aux Juifs de Valréas (1247)." *Cabinet historique* 29 (1883), 121–33.

Monti, Gennaro Maria. "Da Carlo I a Roberto di Angiò: Ricerche e documenti." *Archivio storico per le province napoletane* 56 (1931), 199–232; 57 (1932), 31–155; 58 (1933), 67–98; 59 (1934), 137–223; 60 (1935), 154–94.

Moore, George Foot. "Christian Writers on Judaism." *HTR* 14 (1921), 197–254.

Moorman, John. *A History of the Franciscan Order from Its Origins to the Year 1517.* Oxford, 1968.

Morghen, R. "Problèmes sur l'origine de l'hérésie au Moyen Age." *Revue historique* 236 (1966), 1–16.

Mortier, Daniel Antonin. *Histoire des maîtres généraux de l'Ordre des Frères Prêcheurs.* 8 vols. Paris, 1903–14.

Mosse, George L. *The Crisis of German Ideology: Intellectual Origins of the Third Reich.* New York, 1964.

——. *Germans and Jews: The Right, and Left, and the Search for a "Third Force" in Pre-Nazi Germany.* New York, 1970.

Muldoon, James. *Popes, Lawyers, and Infidels: The Church and the Non-Christian World, 1250–1550.* Philadelphia, 1979.

Müller, Ewald. *Das Konzil von Vienne 1311–1312: Seine Quellen und seine Geschichte.* Münster, 1934.

Murphy, Thomas. "The Date and Purpose of the *Contra Gentiles.*" *Heythrop Journal* 10 (1969), 405–15.

Netanyahu, Benzion. *The Marranos of Spain.* 2d ed. Millwood, N.Y., 1973.

Neubauer, Adolph. "Another Convert Named Paulus." *JQR,* o.s. 5 (1893), 713–14.

——. "Jewish Controversy and the 'Pugio Fidei.'" *The Expositor* 7 (1888), 81–105, 179–97.

——. "Raymundus Martini and the Rev. Dr. Schiller-Szinessy." *The Academy,* 17 September 1887, pp. 188–89.

Neuman, Abraham A. *The Jews in Spain: Their Social, Political, and Cultural Life.* 2 vols. Philadelphia, 1942.

Neumann, W. "Influence de Raschi et d'autres commentateurs juifs sur les Postillae perpetuae de Nicolas de Lyre." *REJ* 26 (1893), 172–82; 27 (1893), 250–62.

Newman, Louis Israel. *Jewish Influence on Christian Reform Movements.* 1925; repr., New York, 1966.

Nickerson, Hoffman. *The Inquisition: A Political and Military History of Its Establishment.* 2d ed. Port Washington, N.Y., 1968.

Nicks, J. "La polémique contre les Juifs et le Pugio fidei de Raymond Martin." In *Mélanges d'histoire offerts à Charles Moeller,* 1:519–26. 2 vols. Louvain, 1914.

Nohl, Johannes. *The Black Death: A Chronicle of the Plague.* Trans. C. H. Clarke. New York, 1969.

O'Brien, John A. *The Inquisition.* New York, 1973.

O'Callaghan, Joseph F. *A History of Medieval Spain.* Ithaca, 1975.

Oelsner, Toni. "Wilhelm Roscher's Theory of the Economic and Social Position of the Jews in the Middle Ages: A Critical Examination." *Yivo Annual of Jewish Social Science* 12 (1958–59), 176–95.

Orlinsky, Harry M. "The Origin of the Kethib-Qere System: A New Approach." *Supplements to Vetus Testamentum* 7 (1959), 407–15.

Overdyke, W. Darrell. *The Know-Nothing Party in the South.* Baton Rouge, La., 1950.

Pacios Lopez, Antonio. *La Disputa de Tortosa.* 2 vols. Madrid, 1957.

Packard, Sidney R. *Twelfth Century Europe: An Interpretive Essay.* Amherst, Mass., 1973.

Pakter, Walter J. "De his qui foris sunt: The Teachings of the Medieval Canon and Civil Lawyers Concerning the Jews." Ph.D. dissertation, Johns Hopkins University, 1974.

Pales-Gobilliard, Annette. "L'Inquisition et les Juifs: Le cas de Jacques Fournier." In *JJL,* pp. 97–114.

Panofsky, Erwin. *Gothic Architecture and Scholasticism.* 1951; repr., New York, 1957.

——. *Renaissance and Renascences in Western Art.* Stockholm, 1960.

Parkes, James. *The Conflict of the Church and the Synagogue: A Study in the Origins of Antisemitism.* London, 1934.

——. *The Jew in the Medieval Community.* 2d ed. New York, 1976.

Pasqual, Antonio-Raymundo. *Vindiciae lullianae.* 4 vols. Avignon, 1778.

Peers, E. Allison. *Ramon Lull: A Biography.* 1929; repr., New York, 1969.

Pelizaeus, Theodor. *Beiträge zur Geschichte der Legende vom Judenknaben.* Halle, 1914.

Perles, Joseph. *R. Salomo b. Abraham b. Adreth: Sein Leben und seine Schriften.* Breslau, 1863.

Pflaum, Heinz. "Der allegorische Streit zwichsen Synagoge und Kirche in der europäischen Dichtung des Mittelalters." *Archivum romanum* 18 (1934), 243–340.

——. "Ein französicher Dichter des 14. Jahrhunderts über Raschi." *MGWJ* 76 (1932), 577–86.

——. "Poems of Religious Disputations in the Middle Ages [Hebrew]." *Tarbiz* 2 (1931), 443–76.

Piffl, Rudolph. "Einiges uber Berthold von Regensburg." In *Programm des K.K. deutschen Obergymnasiums der Kleinseite in Prag,* pp. 3–33. Prague, 1890.

Platzeck, Erhard Wolfram. *Raimund Lull.* 2 vols. Berlin, 1962–64.

Post, Gaines. "Two Notes on Nationalism in the Middle Ages." *Traditio* 9 (1953), 281–320.

Powicke, F. M. "The Medieval University in Church and Society." In *Ways of Medieval Life and Thought: Essays and Addresses,* pp. 198–212. New York, 1971.

Prudhomme, Auguste. "Notes et documents sur les Juifs du Dauphiné." *REJ* 9 (1884), 231–39.

Quétif, Jacques, and Jacques Echard. *Scriptores Ordinis Praedicatorum.* 2 vols. 1719–21; repr., New York, 1959.

Rashdall, Hastings. *The Universities of Europe in the Middle Ages.* 2d ed. Ed. F. M. Powicke and A. B. Emden. 3 vols. Oxford, 1936.

Reeves, Marjorie. *The Influence of Prophecy in the Later Middle Ages: A Study in Joachimism.* Oxford, 1969.

Rembaum, Joel E. "A Reevaluation of a Medieval Polemical Manuscript." *Association for Jewish Studies Review* 5 (1980), 81–99.

Renan, Ernst, and Adolph Neubauer. "Les rabbins français du commencement du quartorzième siècle." *HLF* 27 (1877), 431–776 [repr. in separate volume, Farnborough, Eng., 1969].

Ricard, Robert. "Sur Alfonso Bonhome: Notes bibliographiques." *Bulletin hispanique* 60 (1958), 500–504.

Ricketts, Peter T. "The Hispanic Tradition of the *Breviari d'amor* by Matfre Ermengaud of Béziers." In *Hispanic Studies in Honor of Joseph Manson*, pp. 227–53. Ed. Dorothy M. Atkinson and Anthony H. Clarke. Oxford, 1972.

Rieder, Karl. *Das Leben Bertholds von Regensburg.* Freiburg i. Br., 1901.

Robert, Ulysse. "Catalogue des actes relatifs aux Juifs (1183–1300)." *REJ* 3 (1881), 211–24.

Rockinger, Ludwig von. "Berthold von Regensburg und Raimund von Peniafort im sogennanten Schwabenspiegel." *Abhandlungen der historischen Classe der königlich bayerischen Akademie der Wissenschaften* 13,3 (1877), 165–253.

——. "Deutschenspiegel, sogennanter Schwabenspiegel, Bertholds von Regensburg deutsche Predigten in ihrem Verhältnisse zu einander." *Abhandlungen der historischen Classe der königlich bayerischen Akademie der Wissenschaften* 23 (1906), 211–300, 473–536.

Rosenau, Helen. "The Architecture of Nicolaus de Lyra's Temple Illustrations and the Jewish Tradition." *JJS* 25 (1974), 294–304.

Rosenthal, Erwin I. J. "Anti-Christian Polemics in Medieval Bible Commentaries." *JJS* 11 (1960), 115–36.

Rosenthal, Judah M. "The Anti-Christian Dispute [Hebrew]." In *Rashi: His Teachings and Personality*, pp. 45–59. Ed. Simon Federbush. New York, 1958.

——. "Anti-Christian Polemic from Its Beginnings to the End of the 18th Century [Hebrew]." *Aresheth* 2 (1960), 130–79.

——. *Studies and Texts in Jewish History, Literature and Religion* [Hebrew]. 2 vols. Jerusalem, 1967.

——. "The Talmud on Trial." *JQR*, n.s. 47 (1956), 58–76, 145–69.

Rosenwein, Barbara H., and Lester K. Little. "Social Meaning in the Monastic and Mendicant Spiritualities." *Past and Present* 63 (1974), 4–32.

Roth, Cecil. "The Disputation of Barcelona (1263)." *HTR* 43 (1950), 117–44.

——. *The Jews of Medieval Oxford.* Oxford, 1951.

——. "The Medieval Conception of the Jew." In *Essays and Studies in Memory of Linda R. Miller*, pp. 171–90. Ed. Israel Davidson. New York, 1938.

——. "The Popes and the Jews." *Church Quarterly Review* 123 (1936–37), 75–82.

Ruether, Rosemary R. *Faith and Fratricide: The Theological Roots of Anti-Semitism.* New York, 1974.

Saige, Gustav. *Les Juifs de Languedoc antérieurement au XIVe siècle.* 1881; repr., Farnborough, Eng., 1971.

Saperstein, Marc. *Decoding the Rabbis: A Thirteenth-Century Commentary on the Aggadah.* Harvard Judaic Monographs 3. Cambridge, Mass., 1980.

———. "R. Isaac b. Yeda'ya: A Forgotten Commentator on the *Aggada.*" *REJ* 138 (1979), 17–45.

Sarachek, Joseph. *Faith and Reason: The Conflict over the Rationalism of Maimonides,* 1. Williamsport, Pa., 1935.

Schechter, Solomon. "Genizah Specimens: Liturgy." *JQR,* o.s. 10 (1898), 654–59.

———. *Studies in Judaism.* New York, 1896.

Scheich, Rudolf. "Der Humor in den Predigten Bertholds von Regensburg." *Jahresbericht des K.K. Staatgymnasiums in Mähr-Weiskirchen für das Schuljahr 1890–91,* 1891, pp. 5–26.

Scheinert, Max. *Der Franziskaner Berthold von Regensburg als Lehrer und Erzieher des Volkes.* Dresden, 1896.

Schiller-Szinessy, S. M. "The *Pugio Fidei.*" *Journal of Philology* 16 (1888), 131–52.

Schlatter, Richard. *Private Property: The History of an Idea.* London, 1951.

Schlauch, Margaret. "The Allegory of the Church and the Synagogue." *Speculum* 14 (1939), 448–64.

Schmidt, G. "Berthold von Regensburg: Ein christlicher Volksprediger des dreizehnten Jahrhunderts." *Theologische Studien und Kritiken* 37 (1864), 7–82.

Schmidt, Roderich. "Aetates mundi: Die Weltalter als Gliederungsprinzip der Geschichte." *Zeitschrift für Kirchengeschichte* 67 (1955–56), 288–317.

Scholem, Gershom G. *Les origines de la Kabbale.* Trans. Jean Loewenson. Paris, 1966.

Schubert, Kurt. "Das christlich-jüdische Religionsgespräch im 12. und 13. Jahrhundert." *Kairos,* n.s. 19 (1977), 161–86.

Schwarzchild, Steven S., and Saul Berman. "Noachide Laws." In *Encyclopedia Judaica,* 12:1189–91. Ed. Cecil Roth et al. 16 vols. Jerusalem, 1972.

Secret, François. "Notes pour une histoire du Pugio fidei à la Renaissance." *Sefarad* 20 (1960), 401–7.

Seiferth, Wolfgang S. *Synagogue and Church in the Middle Ages: Two Symbols in Art and Literature.* Trans. Lee Chadeayne and Paul Gottwald. New York, 1970.

Selmer, Carl. "Ramon Lull and the Problem of Persuasion." *Thought* 23 (1948), 215–22.

Serper, Arié. "Le debat entre Synagogue et Eglise au XIIIe siècle." *REJ* 123 (1964), 307–23.

Serrano, Luciano. *Los conversos D. Pablo de Santa Maria y D. Alfonso de Cartagena*. Madrid, 1942.

Shachar, Isaiah. *The Judensau: A Medieval Anti-Jewish Motif and Its History*. London, 1974.

Shaḥar, Shulamit. "Catharism and the Beginnings of the Kabbalah in Languedoc [Hebrew]." *Tarbiz* 40 (1971), 483–507.

——. "Dialogus inter Judeum et clericum [Hebrew]." *Michael* 4 (1976), 32–60.

——. "Ecrits cathares et commentaires d'Abraham Abulafia sur le 'Livre de la creation': Images et idées communes." In *JJL*, pp. 345–62.

Shannon, Albert Clement. *The Popes and Heresy in the Thirteenth Century*. Villanova, Pa., 1949.

Shatzmiller, Joseph. "L'Inquisition et les Juifs de Provence au XIIIᵉ siècle." *Provence historique* 93–94 (1973), 327–38.

——. "A Letter from Rabbi Asher ben Gershom to the Rabbis of France at the Time of the Controversy about the Works of Maimonides [Hebrew]." In *Studies in the History of the Jewish People and the Land of Israel in Memory of Zvi Avneri*, pp. 129–40. Ed. A. Gilboa et al. Haifa, 1970.

——. "Paulus Christiani: Un aspect de son activité anti-juive." In *Hommage à Georges Vajda: Etudes d'histoire et de pensée juives*, pp. 203–17. Ed. Gérard Nahon and Charles Touati. Louvain, 1980.

——. "Towards a Picture of the First Maimonidean Controversy [Hebrew]." *Zion*, n.s. 34 (1969), 126–44.

Shneidman, J. Lee. "Protection of Aragon Jewry in the Thirteenth Century." *REJ* 121 (1962), 49–58.

——. *The Rise of the Aragonese-Catalan Empire, 1200–1350*. 2 vols. New York, 1970.

Shoḥat, Azriel. "Concerning the First Controversy on the Writings of Maimonides [Hebrew]." *Zion*, n.s. 36 (1971), 27–60.

Silver, Daniel J. *Maimonidean Criticism and the Maimonidean Controversy, 1180–1240*. Leiden, 1965.

Simon, Marcel. *Verus Israel: Etude sur les relations entre Chrétiens et Juifs dans l'empire romain, 135–425*. Paris, 1948.

Simon, Stanislaus. *Mose ben Salomo von Salerno und seine philosophischen Auseinandersetzungen mit den Lehren des Christentums*. Ohlau i. Schl., 1931.

Simson, Otto G. von. "The Gothic Cathedral: Design and Meaning." In *Change in Medieval Society: Europe North of the Alps, 1050–1500*, pp. 168–87. Ed. Sylvia L. Thrupp. New York, 1964.

Singer, Charles. "Hebrew Scholarship in the Middle Ages among Latin Christians." In *The Legacy of Israel*, pp. 283–314. Ed. Edwyn R. Bevan and Charles Singer. Oxford, 1928.

Singer, Charles, and Dorothea Singer. "The Origin of the Medical School at Salerno, the First University: An Attempted Reconstruction." In *Essays on the History of Medicine Presented to Karl Sudhoff,* pp. 121–38. Ed. Charles Singer and Henry E. Sigerist. London, 1924.

Smalley, Beryl. "Robert Holcot O.P." *AFP* 26 (1956), 5–97.

———. *The Study of the Bible in the Middle Ages.* 2d ed. 1952; repr., Notre Dame, Ind., 1964.

Sommer-Seckendorf, Ellen M. F. *Studies in the Life of Robert Kilwardby, O.P.* Rome, 1937.

Southern, Richard W. *The Making of the Middle Ages.* New Haven, 1953.

———. "St. Anselm and Gilbert Crispin, Abbot of Westminster." *Medieval and Renaissance Studies* 3 (1954), 78–115.

———. *Saint Anselm and His Biographer: A Study of Monastic Life and Thought, 1059–c.1130.* Cambridge, Eng., 1963.

Starr, Joshua. "The Mass Conversion of Jews in Southern Italy, 1290–1293." *Speculum* 21 (1946), 203–11.

Stein, Siegfried. *Jewish-Christian Disputations in Thirteenth-Century Narbonne.* London, 1969.

Steinschneider, Moritz. *Catalogus librorum hebraeorum in Bibliotheca bodleiana.* 3 vols. Berlin, 1852–60.

———. "Christliche Hebräisten." *Zeitschrift für hebräische Bibliographie* 1 (1896–97), 50–54.

———. *Jewish Literature from the Eighth to the Eighteenth Century.* London, 1857.

Stern, Fritz. *The Politics of Cultural Despair: A Study in the Rise of the Germanic Ideology.* 1961; repr., Garden City, N.Y., 1965.

Stern, Moritz. *Urkundliche Beiträge über die Stellung der Päpste zu den Juden.* 2 vols. 1893–95; repr., Farnborough, Eng., 1970.

Stow, Kenneth R. "The Burning of the Talmud in 1553, in the Light of Sixteenth Century Catholic Attitudes toward the Talmud." *Bibliothèque d'Humanisme et Renaissance* 34 (1972), 435–59.

———. *Catholic Thought and Papal Jewry Policy, 1555–1593.* New York, 1976.

———. "Sin'at Yisra'el 'o 'Ahavat Yisra'el: Gishat ha-'Appifyorim la-Yehudim." In *Anti-Semitism Through the Ages* [Hebrew], pp. 91–111. Ed. Shmuel Almog. Jerusalem, 1980.

Strayer, Joseph R. *Medieval Statecraft and the Perspectives of History.* Princeton, 1971.

Sugranyes de Franch, Ramon. "Le 'Livre du Gentil et des trois sages' de Raymond Lulle." In *JJL,* pp. 319–35.

———. *Ramon Lulle: Docteur des missions.* Schöneck-Beckenried, Switzerland, 1954.

Swift, F. Darwin. *The Life and Times of James the First.* Oxford, 1894.

Synan, Edward A. *The Popes and the Jews in the Middle Ages.* New York, 1965.

Tal, Uriel. *Christians and Jews in Germany: Religion, Politics and Ideology in the Second Reich, 1870–1914.* Trans. N. J. Jacobs. Ithaca, 1975.

Talmage, Frank Ephraim. *David Kimhi: The Man and the Commentaries.* Harvard Judaic Monographs 1. Cambridge, Mass., 1975.

———. "An Hebrew Polemical Treatise, Anti-Cathar and Anti-Orthodox." *HTR* 60 (1967), 323–48.

Tamar, D. "More on the Date of the Burning of the Talmud in France [Hebrew]." *KS* 29 (1953), 430–31.

Teetaert, A. "Raymond de Penyafort (Saint)." In *Dictionnaire de théologie catholique*, 13,2:1806–23. Ed. A. Vacant et al. 15 vols. Paris, 1908–50.

Teicher, J. L. "Christian Theology and the Jewish Opposition to Maimonides." *Journal of Theological Studies*, o.s. 43 (1943), 68–76.

Tellenbach, Gerd. *Church, State and Christian Society at the Time of the Investiture Contest.* Trans. R. F. Bennett. 1959; repr., New York, 1970.

Thiel, Matthias. *Grundlagen und Gestalt der Hebräischkentnisse des früheren Mittelalters.* Spoleto, 1973.

Thomas, Antoine. "Bernard Gui, Frère Prêcheur." *HLF* 35 (1921), 139–232.

Thompson, James Westfall. *The Literacy of the Laity in the Middle Ages.* 1915; repr., New York, 1963.

Thomson, Williel R. *Friars in the Cathedral: The First Franciscan Bishops, 1226–61.* Toronto, 1975.

Thorndike, Lynn. *University Records and Life in the Middle Ages.* New York, 1944.

Tierney, Brian. *The Crisis of Church and State, 1050–1300.* Englewood Cliffs, N.J., 1964.

———. *Foundations of the Conciliar Theory.* 1955; repr., Cambridge, Eng., 1968.

———. *Origins of Papal Infallibility, 1150–1350.* Leiden, 1972.

———. "*Tria quippe distinguit iudicia.* Innocent III's Decretal *Per Venerabilem.*" *Speculum* 37 (1962), 48–59.

Touati, Charles. "Les deux conflits autour de Maimonide et des études philosophiques." In *JJL*, pp. 173–84.

Trachtenberg, Joshua. *The Devil and the Jews.* New Haven, 1943.

Troeltsch, Ernst. *The Social Teaching of the Christian Churches.* Trans. Olive Wyon. 2 vols. Glencoe, Ill., 1931.

Turberville, A. S. "Heresies and the Inquisition in the Middle Ages, c. 1000–1305." In *Cambridge Medieval History*, 6:699–726. 8 vols. New York, 1911–36.

———. *Medieval Heresy and the Inquisition.* London, 1920.

Ullmann, Walter. "Die Bulle Unam Sanctam: Rückblick und Ausblick." *Römische historische Mitteilungen* 16 (1974), 45–77.

———. *The Growth of Papal Government in the Middle Ages.* 2d ed. New York, 1962.

———. *A History of Political Thought: The Middle Ages.* Rev. ed. Baltimore, 1970.

———. *A Short History of the Papacy in the Middle Ages.* London, 1972.

———. "The Significance of Innocent III's Decretal 'Vergentis.'" In *Etudes d'histoire du droit canonqiue dédiées à Gabriel le Bras*, 1:729–41. 2 vols. Paris, 1965.

Urbach, Ephraim E. "Etudes sur la littérature polémique au Moyen Age." *REJ* 100 (1935), 49–77.

——. "The Participation of German and French Scholars in the Controversy about Maimonides and His Works [Hebrew]." *Zion*, n.s. 12 (1947), 149–59.

——. *The Tosaphists: Their History, Writing and Methods* [Hebrew]. 4th ed. 2 vols. Jerusalem, 1980.

Valls-Taberner, Fernando. *San Ramon de Penyaforte*. Obras selectas, 1,2. 1936; repr., Madrid, 1953.

Valois, Noël. *Guillaume d'Auvergne, évêque de Paris (1228–1249): Sa vie et ses ouvrages*. Paris, 1880.

Van den Oudenrijn, M. A. "De opusculis arabicis quae Latine vertit Fr. Alphonsus Buenhombre, O.P." *Analecta sacri Ordinis Fratrum Praedicatorum* 28 (1920), 32–44, 35–93, 163–68.

Vattasso, Marco. *Le due Biblie di Bovino ora codice vaticani latini 10510–10511 e le loro note storiche*. Rome, 1900.

Vicaire, Marie-Humbert. "'Contra Judaeos' méridionaux au début du XIIIᵉ siècle: Alain de Lille, Evrard de Béthune, Guillaume de Bourges." In *JJL*, pp. 269–93.

——. "Une nouvelle forme de vie religieuse: Les ordres mendiants." In *Le siècle de Saint Louis*, pp. 245–51. Paris, 1970.

——. *Saint Dominic and His Times*. Trans. Kathleen Pond. London, 1964.

——. "Saint Dominique et les inquisiteurs." *Annales du Midi* 79 (1967), 173–94.

Vidal, J. M. "L'émeute des Pastoureaux en 1320." *Annales de Saint-Louis des Français* 3 (1898–99), 121–74.

Voss, Bernd Reiner. *Der Dialog in der frühchristlichen Literatur*. Munich, 1970.

Wakefield, Walter L. *Heresy, Crusade, and Inquisition in Southern France, 1100–1250*. Berkeley, 1974.

Walther, Hans. *Das Streitgedicht in der lateinischen Literatur des Mittelalters*. Munich, 1920.

Wasner, Franz. "The Popes' Veneration of the Torah." *The Bridge* 4 (1962), 274–93.

Watt, J. A. "The Theory of Papal Monarchy in the Thirteenth Century: The Contribution of the Canonists." *Traditio* 20 (1964), 179–317.

Werblowsky, R. J. Z. "Crispin's Disputation." *JJS* 11 (1960), 69–79.

——. Review of *El "Liber predicationis contra Judeos,"* by Raymond Lull, ed. J. M. Millás Vallicrosa [Hebrew]. *Tarbiz* 32 (1963), 207–11.

Wesson, Robert G. *The Imperial Order*. Berkeley, 1967.

Wieruszowski, H. "Ramon Lull et l'idée de la Cité de Dieu." *Estudis franciscans* 47 (1935), 87–110.

Willi-Plein, Ina, and Thomas Willi. *Glaubensdolch und Messiasbeweis: Die Begegnung von Judentum, Christentum und Islam im 13. Jahrhundert in Spanien.* Neukirchen-Vluyn, 1980.

Williams, A. Lukyn. *Adversus Judaeos: A Bird's-Eye View of Christian Apologiae until the Renaissance.* Cambridge, Eng., 1935.

Wolf, Johann Christoph. *Bibliotheca hebraea.* 4 vols. Hamburg, 1727.

Wolter, Eugen. *Der Judenknabe.* Halle, 1879.

Wood, Rega. "Nicholas of Lyre on the Church." M.A. thesis, Cornell University, 1971.

Yaari, A. *Sereifat ha-Talmud be-'Italyah bi-Mle'ot 'Arba' Mei'ot Shanim la-Gezeirah.* Tel Aviv, 1953.

Yerushalmi, Yosef Hayim. "The Inquisition and the Jews of France in the Time of Bernard Gui." *HTR* 63 (1970), 317–76.

Zunz, Leopold. *Die gottesdienstlichen Vorträge der Juden, historisch entwickelt* [Hebrew]. Ed. Ch. Albeck. Jerusalem, 1947.

Index

In the interest of consistency, ancient and medieval personages appear listed in the alphabetical order of their forenames.

Index

Index

Nicholas of Lyra (*cont.*)
  Responsio ad quemdam Iudeum, 185–87,
    189, 190, 191

Odo of Cambray, 25
Oral law. *See* Rabbinic postbiblical
    Judaism
Ordo romanus, 167

Pablo Christiani, 81, 106, 108, 134, 163,
    168, 188, 221, 225
  and disputation of Barcelona, 108–
    27, 130n2, 136, 145n30, 152n50,
    153–54, 156, 163, 164, 165, 167, 193
Parens scientiarum, 256
Paris: disputation of, *see* Disputation(s)
    University of, *see* University(ies)
Paul of Burgos, 130n2, 176n12
Paulus Alvarus, 148n37
Peter III, king of Aragon, 84
Peter IV, king of Aragon, 84
Peter Abelard, 25, 207n17
Peter Alfonsi, 24, 27–28, 29–30, 31, 75
  Dialogus, 27, 29
Peter Lombard: *Sentences,* 174, 238
Peter of Blois, 148n37
Peter of Genoa, 123
Peter Olivi, 247
Peter Olligoyen, 44
Peter the Venerable of Cluny, 24, 31,
    62n20, 75, 76
  *Tractatus adversus Iudaeorum inveteram
    duritiem,* 28–30
Petrus de Pennis, 79
Pharetra fidei, 78
Philip III, king of France, 80
Philip IV, king of France, 80, 84, 93
Polemic, Jewish-Christian, 44, 59, 115,
    129, 223
  by converts, 27, 122, 130n2, 192,
    199–200
  in early Middle Ages, 19–32, 145,
    174n8, 186, 190
  influence on doctrine, 164–69, 171,
    200
  literary, 66–76, 226–28, 246
  See also Disputation(s); Liturgy;
    Nicholas of Lyra; Raymond Lull;
    Raymond Martini
Pope(s):
  coronation of, 166–67
  disputes over dominion of, 34
  plenitudo potestatis of, 252–53, 254
  See also entries for individual popes

Portugal, 14, 62
Profiat Duran: *Kelimat ha-Goyim,* 191

Qalonymos ben Qalonymos ben Meir,
    81n15

Rabbinic postbiblical Judaism:
  Christian knowledge/ignorance of,
    22–32 *passim,* 75–76, 79, 124, 134,
    138, 145n30, 162, 173, 175, 181–87
  in early medieval polemic, 16, 22–32
    passim, 167, 171
  literature attacked, 51–76, 78–81, 84–
    85, 96, 124–25, 142, 154, 164–65,
    180, 193, 194, 212 (*see also* Talmud,
    the)
  oral law/tradition attacked, 76, 181
Rashi (Solomon ben Isaac of Troyes),
    95, 96n61, 152, 175, 176–77, 178,
    182, 189
Rationalism, 52, 107n10
  as basis for conflict in Jewish com-
    munity, 61
  Jewish deficiency in, 24, 27, 28–29,
    62n20, 119–20, 147
  in polemic, 24, 25, 27, 119
Raymond de Miedas, 81
Raymond de Peñaforte, 104–5, 189,
    237n39, 263
  influence and teachings/disciples of,
    106, 107–8, 123–30 *passim,* 137,
    139, 154, 157, 163–69, 170, 190,
    200, 223, 242
Raymond Lull, 130n2, 162, 224–27 *pas-
    sim,* 232, 241, 243, 264
  early life and works of, 199–205
  Liber predicationis contra Iudeos, 205,
    209, 214–23
  Libre del Gentil e los tres savis, 205–14
Raymond Martini, 106, 129–30, 163–64,
    168, 181, 205, 211, 221, 225, 227
  corpus of polemic of, 131–36
  Pugio fidei, 96n61, 129, 131–35, 164,
    165, 166, 170–71, 183, 188–91 *pas-
    sim,* 243, 265–66; arguments of,
    136–53, 154; conclusions of, 153–
    56; and forgeries of Jewish
    sources, 135; Jewish response to,
    156–63
Relapsi, 43, 48, 86–94 *passim,* 127
  children of, 49
  and rejudaizing process, 93–94, 95
  See also Conversion (to Christianity);
    Heresy; Inquisition

300

The Friars and the Jews

Designed by Richard E. Rosenbaum.
Composed by Eastern Graphics
in 10 point Linotron 202 Palatino, 2 points leaded,
with display lines in Palatino.
Printed offset by Thomson/Shore, Inc. on
Warren's Number 66 Antique Offset, 50 pound basis.
Bound by John H. Dekker & Sons, Inc.
in Holliston book cloth
and stamped in Kurz-Hastings foils

Library of Congress Cataloging in Publication Data

Cohen, Jeremy, 1953–
  The friars and the Jews.

  Bibliography: p.
  Includes index.
    1. Antisemitism—Europe—History. 2. Christianity and antisemitism. 3. Friars.
  4. Jews—Europe—History. I. Title.
  DS145.C573   305.8'924'094   81-15210
  ISBN 0-8014-1406-7   AACR2